Communications
in Computer and Information Science 1892

Rationale
The CCIS series is devoted to the publication of proceedings of computer science conferences. Its aim is to efficiently disseminate original research results in informatics in printed and electronic form. While the focus is on publication of peer-reviewed full papers presenting mature work, inclusion of reviewed short papers reporting on work in progress is welcome, too. Besides globally relevant meetings with internationally representative program committees guaranteeing a strict peer-reviewing and paper selection process, conferences run by societies or of high regional or national relevance are also considered for publication.

Topics
The topical scope of CCIS spans the entire spectrum of informatics ranging from foundational topics in the theory of computing to information and communications science and technology and a broad variety of interdisciplinary application fields.

Information for Volume Editors and Authors
Publication in CCIS is free of charge. No royalties are paid, however, we offer registered conference participants temporary free access to the online version of the conference proceedings on SpringerLink (http://link.springer.com) by means of an http referrer from the conference website and/or a number of complimentary printed copies, as specified in the official acceptance email of the event.

CCIS proceedings can be published in time for distribution at conferences or as post-proceedings, and delivered in the form of printed books and/or electronically as USBs and/or e-content licenses for accessing proceedings at SpringerLink. Furthermore, CCIS proceedings are included in the CCIS electronic book series hosted in the SpringerLink digital library at http://link.springer.com/bookseries/7899. Conferences publishing in CCIS are allowed to use Online Conference Service (OCS) for managing the whole proceedings lifecycle (from submission and reviewing to preparing for publication) free of charge.

Publication process
The language of publication is exclusively English. Authors publishing in CCIS have to sign the Springer CCIS copyright transfer form, however, they are free to use their material published in CCIS for substantially changed, more elaborate subsequent publications elsewhere. For the preparation of the camera-ready papers/files, authors have to strictly adhere to the Springer CCIS Authors' Instructions and are strongly encouraged to use the CCIS LaTeX style files or templates.

Abstracting/Indexing
CCIS is abstracted/indexed in DBLP, Google Scholar, EI-Compendex, Mathematical Reviews, SCImago, Scopus. CCIS volumes are also submitted for the inclusion in ISI Proceedings.

How to start
To start the evaluation of your proposal for inclusion in the CCIS series, please send an e-mail to ccis@springer.com.

Sanjaya Kumar Panda · Rashmi Ranjan Rout ·
Manjubala Bisi · Ravi Chandra Sadam ·
Kuan-Ching Li · Vincenzo Piuri
Editors

Computing, Communication and Learning

Second International Conference, CoCoLe 2023
Warangal, India, August 29–31, 2023
Proceedings

 Springer

Editors
Sanjaya Kumar Panda ⓘ
National Institute of Technology
Warangal, India

Rashmi Ranjan Rout ⓘ
National Institute of Technology
Warangal, India

Manjubala Bisi ⓘ
National Institute of Technology
Warangal, India

Ravi Chandra Sadam ⓘ
National Institute of Technology
Warangal, India

Kuan-Ching Li ⓘ
Providence University
Taichung City, Taiwan

Vincenzo Piuri ⓘ
University of Milan
Milan, Italy

ISSN 1865-0929   ISSN 1865-0937 (electronic)
Communications in Computer and Information Science
ISBN 978-3-031-56997-5   ISBN 978-3-031-56998-2 (eBook)
https://doi.org/10.1007/978-3-031-56998-2

This Springer imprint is published by the registered company Springer Nature Switzerland AG
The registered company address is: Gewerbestrasse 11, 6330 Cham, Switzerland

Paper in this product is recyclable.

Preface

The Second International Conference on Computing, Communication, and Learning (CoCoLe 2023) took place in Warangal, India, during August 29–31, 2023, and was hosted by the National Institute of Technology (NIT) Warangal, Warangal – 506004, Telangana, India and sponsored by the Science and Engineering Science Board, Department of Science and Technology, Government of India.

The CoCoLe conference focuses on three areas of computer science and other allied branches, namely computing, communication, and learning. However, CoCoLe 2023 primarily focused on well-defined areas, namely the application of supervised and unsupervised learning in computing and computing in communication networks. It provided a unique platform for academicians, researchers, scientists, engineers, practitioners, industry personnel, developers, and students to exchange state-of-the-art knowledge, present and publish their research findings, and also deliberate on contemporary topics in the area of computing, communication, and learning. The main aim of CoCoLe is to provide quality publications to the research community and to provide a direction to carry out further research.

CoCoLe 2023 received 120 full paper submissions. Each submission considered for publication was reviewed by three to four technical program committee members and reviewers of national and international repute. Based on the reviews, the conference chairs decided to accept 25 papers for presentation at the conference, with an acceptance rate of 21%. We would like to express our sincere gratitude to all the authors and co-authors who submitted their work to this conference. Our special thanks to all technical program committee members and reviewers, who generously offered their expertise and time, which helped the conference chairs to select the papers and prepare the conference program.

We were fortunate to have eight esteemed academicians as our advisory committee members: Rajkumar Buyya from the University of Melbourne and Manjrasoft Pvt. Ltd., Australia, Mohammad S. Obaidat from the University of Texas Permian Basin, USA, King Abdullah II School of Information Technology and the University of Jordan, Jordan, Sajal K. Das from the Missouri University of Science and Technology, USA, D. V. L. N. Somayajulu from the IIITDM Kurnool and IIIT Sri City, India, Manoj Singh Gaur, IIT Jammu, India, Narasimha Sarma N. V. S. from the IIIT Trichy, India, Shyam Sundar Pattnaik from NITTTR Chandigarh, India, and C. R. Tripathy from the BPUT Rourkela, India. Their constant support and guidance helped us to plan this conference successfully.

We were also fortunate to have three esteemed academicians as our general chairs: Kuan-Ching Li from Providence University, Taiwan, Rajkumar Buyya from the University of Melbourne and Manjrasoft Pvt. Ltd., Australia and Prof. R. B. V. Subramanyam from NIT Warangal, India. Their constant suggestions and guidance enabled us to conduct this conference without hindrance.

We were also fortunate to have seven invited keynote speakers: Sudip Misra, IEEE Fellow, from Indian Institute of Technology Kharagpur, India, Prasanta K. Jana, from

IIT (Indian School of Mines (ISM)) Dhanbad, India, Katarzyna Wasielewska, from Systems Research Institute, Polish Academy of Sciences, Warsaw, Poland, Pawel Szmeja, from Systems Research Institute, Polish Academy of Sciences, Warsaw, Poland, Siba K. Udgata, from University of Hyderabad, India, Saroj Kumar Meher, from Indian Statistical Institute Bangalore, India, and Tanmoy Chakraborty, from IIT Delhi, India. Their talks gave us a unique opportunity to listen the leaders of their field.

A number of people including colleagues have worked very hard to make this conference a huge success. First, we wish to express our thanks to the steering committee members who planned the second edition of the conference at NIT Warangal, India. Further, we wish to extend our thanks to the registration chairs, session management chairs, publicity chairs, publication chairs, website management chairs, and student volunteers for their valuable suggestions and coordination. Lastly, we thank the faculty members of the Department of Computer Science and Engineering (CSE), NIT Warangal, Telangana, India, for their timely support.

The Department of CSE, NIT Warangal, Telangana, India, the host of the conference, provided various support and facilities for organizing the conference. In particular, we express our sincere gratitude to Bidyadhar Subudhi, the Chief Patron of this conference and the Director, NIT Warangal, and R. Padmavathy, the Patron of this conference and the Head of the Department of CSE, for their continuous support.

The conference program was prepared with the help of EasyChair and Microsoft Conference Management Toolkit (CMT) for efficient and smooth handling of all activities starting from paper submissions to the preparation of the proceedings. We thank Communications in Computer and Information Science (CCIS), Springer for publishing the conference proceedings, International Journal of Computational Science and Engineering (IJCSE), Inderscience, International Journal of Embedded Systems (IJES), Inderscience, and Connection Science, Taylor & Francis, for publishing the extended version of the selected papers. We sincerely thank the staff of Springer for their cooperation and constant support throughout the publication process of this CCIS volume.

We hope you will find the papers in this collection helpful in carrying out further research.

August 2023

Sanjaya Kumar Panda
Rashmi Ranjan Rout
Manjubala Bisi
Ravi Chandra Sadam
Kuan-Ching Li
Vincenzo Piuri

Organization

Steering Committee

Sanjaya Kumar Panda	NIT Warangal, India
Rashmi Ranjan Rout	NIT Warangal, India
Ravi Chandra Sadam	NIT Warangal, India
Bala Venkata Subramanyam Rayanoothala	NIT Warangal, India

Advisory Committee

Rajkumar Buyya	University of Melbourne and Manjrasoft, Australia
Mohammad S. Obaidat	University of Texas Permian Basin, USA, and University of Jordan, Jordan
Sajal K. Das	Missouri University of Science and Technology, USA
D. V. L. N. Somayajulu	IIITDM Kurnool and IIITDM Sri City, India
Manoj Singh Gaur	IIT Jammu, India
Narasimha Sarma N. V. S.	IIIT Trichy, India
Shyam Sundar Pattnaik	NITTTR Chandigarh, India
C. R. Tripathy	BPUT Rourkela, India

General Chairs

Kuan-Ching Li	Providence University, Taiwan
Rajkumar Buyya	University of Melbourne and Manjrasoft, Australia
Bala Venkata Subramanyam Rayanoothala	NIT Warangal, India

Technical Program Committee

A. Sudarshan Chakravarthy	NIT Calicut, India
Aakanksha Sharaff	NIT Raipur, India

Abhimanyu Kumar	NIT Uttarakhand, India
Abhinav Tomar	NSUT New Delhi, India
Achyuth Sarkar	NIT Arunachal Pradesh, India
Adepu Sridhar	University of Bristol, UK
Ajay Kumar Yadav	Banasthali Vidyapith, India
Alekha Kumar Mishra	NIT Jamshedpur, India
Alina Dash	VSSUT Burla, India
Alina Mishra	VSSUT Burla, India
Amit Garg	IIIT Kota, India
Amit Joshi	MNIT Jaipur, India
Amiya Kumar Rath	BPUT Rourkela, India
Anand Bihari	VIT Vellore, India
Anshul Agarwal	VNIT Nagpur, India
Anshul Verma	BHU Varanasi, India
Ansuman Mahapatra	NIT Puducherry, India
Anurag Singh	NIT Delhi, India
Arijit Karati	National Sun Yat-sen University, Taiwan
Arka Prokash Mazumdar	MNIT Jaipur, India
Arti Jain	JIIT Noida, India
Arun Agarwal	SOA Deemed to be University, Bhubaneswar, India
Arun Kishor Johar	Chandigarh University, India
Ashok Kumar Das	IIIT Hyderabad, India
Ashok Kumar Turuk	NIT Rourkela, India
Asis Tripathy	VIT Vellore, India
Atul Vikas Lakra	VSSUT Burla, India
B. Acharya	NIT Raipur, India
B. B. Gupta	Asia University, Taiwan
B. Satya Sekhar	IIT Jammu, India
Balaprakasa Rao Killi	NIT Warangal, India
Balu L. Parne	SVNIT Surat, India
Benazir Neha	KIIT University, India
Bhabendu Kumar Mohanta	K L Deemed to be University, India
Bharat Gupta	NIT Patna, India
Bikramaditya Das	VSSUT Burla, India
Binayak Kar	National Taiwan University of Science and Technology, Taiwan
Biswajit R. Bhowmik	NITK Surathkal, India
Bunil Kumar Balabantaray	NIT Meghalaya, India
Ch. Sudhakar	NIT Warangal, India
Chouhan Kumar Rath	NIT Durgapur, India
D. Chandrasekhar Rao	VSSUT Burla, India

Damodar Reddy Edla	NIT Goa, India
Debasis Gountia	OUTR Bhubaneswar, India
Debasis Mohapatra	PMEC Berhampur, India
Deepak Ranjan Nayak	MNIT Jaipur, India
Deepak Singh	NIT Raipur, India
Deepak Singh Tomar	MANIT Bhopal, India
Deepsubhra Guha Roy	VIT Vellore, India
Devashree Tripathy	IIT Bhubaneswar, India
Devesh C. Jinwala	SVNIT Surat, India
Diptendu Sinha Roy	NIT Meghalaya, India
Durga Prasad Mohapatra	NIT Rourkela, India
Felix Harer	University of Fribourg, Switzerland
Gargi Bhattacharjee	IIT Jodhpur, India
Gopal Behera	GCEK Bhawanipatna, India
Greeshma Lingam	NIT Warangal, India
Hemraj Lamkuche	SIU Pune, India
Himansu Shekhar Pradhan	NIT Warangal, India
Ila Sharma	MNIT Jaipur, India
Indrajeet Gupta	Bennett University, India
Jagadeesh Kakarla	IIITDM Kancheepuram, India
Jai Prakash Verma	Nirma University, India
Jitendra Kumar Rout	NIT Raipur, India
Jyoti Prakash Singh	NIT Patna, India
K. Ramesh	NIT Warangal, India
K. V. Kadambari	NIT Warangal, India
Kalyan Kumar Jena	PMEC Berhampur, India
Khumanthem Manglem Singh	NIT Manipur, India
Kshira Sagar Sahoo	Umeå University, Sweden
Kshiramani Naik	VSSUT Burla, India
Kumar Abhishek	NIT Patna, India
Lalatendu Behera	NIT Jalandhar, India
Lalatendu Muduli	Utkal University, India
Lov Kumar	NIT Kurukshetra, India
M. Sandhya	NIT Warangal, India
Madhukrishna Priyadarsini	NIT Tiruchirappalli, India
Mahasweta Sarkar	San Diego State University, USA
Marcin Paprzycki	Polish Academy of Sciences, Poland
Maria Ganzha	Warsaw University of Technology, Poland
Masilamani V.	IIITDM Kancheepuram, India
Md. Asif Thanedar	NIT Warangal, India
Mrutyunjaya Panda	Utkal University, India
Mukesh Kumar	NIT Patna, India

Munesh Singh	IIITDM Jabalpur, India
N. Renugadevi	IIIT Tirchy, India
Nabajyoti Mazumdar	IIIT Allahabad, India
Nagesh Bhattu Sristy	NIT Andhra Pradesh, India
Neelamadhab Padhy	GIET University, India
Nevine Makram Labib	Institute of National Planning, Egypt
Niladri Bihari Puhan	IIT Bhubaneswar, India
Niranjan Panigrahi	PMEC Berhampur, India
Nitin Singh Singha	NIT Delhi, India
P. Radha Krishna	NIT Warangal, India
P. Rangababu	NIT Meghalaya, India
P. Renjith	NIT Calicut, India
P. Santhi Thilagam	NITK Surathkal, India
Pabitra Mohan Khilar	NIT Rourkela, India
Padmalochan Bera	IIT Bhubaneswar, India
Pawel Szmeja	Polish Academy of Sciences, Poland
Pradeep Kumar Roy	IIIT Surat, India
Pranesh Das	NIT Calicut, India
Prasan Kumar Sahoo	Chang Gung University, South Korea
Prasant Kumar Sahu	IIT Bhubaneswar, India
Pratyay Kuila	NIT Sikkim, India
Pravati Swain	NIT Goa, India
Preeti Chandrakar	NIT Raipur, India
Preeti Ranjan Sahu	NIST Berhampur, India
Priya Ranjan Muduli	IIT (BHU) Varanasi, India
Priyanka Chawla	NIT Warangal, India
Priyanka Parimi	NIT Warangal, India
Priyanka Singh	SRM University, Andhra Pradesh, India
R. Padmavathy	NIT Warangal, India
Rajeev Kanth	Savonia University of Applied Science, Finland
Rakesh Ranjan Kumar	CVRGU Bhubaneswar, India
Rakesh Ranjan Swain	IIT Kanpur, India
Ramalingaswamy Cheruku	NIT Warangal, India
Ranjita Das	NIT Mizoram, India
Rashmi Panda	IIIT Ranchi, India
Ravi Maddila	MNIT Jaipur, India
Roshni Pradhan	KIIT University, India
S. Gopal Krishna Patro	GLA University, India
S. Karthick	NIT Andhra Pradesh, India
Sai Krishna Mothku	NIT Tiruchirappalli, India
Sambit Praharaj	Ruhr University Bochum, Germany
Sampa Sahoo	CVRGU Bhubaneswar, India

Sandeep Kumar Dash	NIT Mizoram, India
Sandeep Singh Sengar	Cardiff Metropolitan University, UK
Sangharatna Godboley	NIT Warangal, India
Sangram Ray	NIT Sikkim, India
Sanjeet Kumar Nayak	IIITDM Kancheepuram, India
Sanjib Kumar Nayak	VSSUT Burla, India
Sanjib Kumar Raul	NIT Warangal, India
Santi Kumari Behera	VSSUT Burla, India
Santosh Kumar Sahu	ONGC Dehradun, India
Sarat Chandra Nayak	Yonsei University, South Korea
Saroj Kumar Meher	ISI Bangalore, India
Satya Prakash Sahu	NIT Raipur, India
Satyasai Nanda	MNIT Jaipur, India
Satyendra Singh Yadav	NIT Meghalaya, India
Sharmila Subudhi	SOA Deemed to be University, India
Shelly Sachdeva	NIT Delhi, India
Siba K. Udgata	University of Hyderabad, India
Siba Mishra	Zoho Corporation, India
Sibarama Panigrahi	NIT Rourkela, India
Situ Rani Patre	NIT Rourkela, India
Slokashree Padhi	NIT Warangal, India
Smita Naval	MNIT Jaipur, India
Sohan Kumar Pande	SIT Sambalpur, India
Somesula Manoj Kumar	NIT Jalandhar, India
Sourav Kanti Addya	NITK Surathkal, India
Sourav Kumar Bhoi	PMEC Berhampur, India
Srinivas Naik N.	IIITDM Kurnool, India
Srinivas Sethi	IGIT Sarang, India
Sriram Kailasam	NIT Warangal, India
Subasish Mohapatra	OUTR Bhubaneswar, India
Subhransu Padhee	SUIIT Burla, India
Suchismita Chinara	NIT Rourkela, India
Sudhansu Bala Das	NIT Rourkela, India
Sugyan Mishra	NIT Durgapur, India
Sujata Pal	IIT Ropar, India
Sujit Das	NIT Warangal, India
Suneet Gupta	Bennett University, India
Sunil Gautam	Nirma University, India
Suraj Sharma	GGV Bilaspur, India
Surendra Singh	NIT Uttarakhand, India
Sushree B. B. Priyadarshini	SOA Deemed to be University, India
Suvendu Chandan Nayak	SIT Bhubaneswar, India

Tapas Kumar Mishra	SRM University, Andhra Pradesh, India
Tanmoy Chakraborty	IIT Delhi, India
U. S. N. Raju	NIT Warangal, India
Umakanta Majhi	NIT Silchar, India
Uma Shankar Ghugar	GITAM University, India
Valentina Emilia Balas	Aurel Vlaicu University of Arad, Romania
Vasundhara	NIT Warangal, India
Venkateswara Rao Kagita	NIT Warangal, India
Vinay Raj	NIT Tiruchirappalli, India

Contents

Application of Supervised Learning in Computing

Recursive Feature Selection and Intrusion Classification in NSL-KDD Dataset Using Multiple Machine Learning Methods

Subrat Mohanty⬤ and Mayank Agarwal$^{(⊠)}$⬤

Indian Institute of Technology, Patna 801106, India
{subrat_2111mc12,mayank265}@iitp.ac.in

Abstract. IDS are critical components of modern computer networks, designed to detect and alert administrators of malicious activity. In order to detect network irregularities and keep data secure, it is critical to build an effective IDS that prevents unauthorized access to network resources. In this study, several machine learning classifiers were used to detect attacks in the NSL-KDD dataset. These classifiers included SVM, Naive Bayes, Random Forest, Decision Tree, and XGBoost. We have chosen 13 feature subsets using the recursive feature selection technique from the NSL-KDD dataset and used them to assess the model's performance. Because the dimension of the data influences how well this IDS performs, the data was pre-processed, and superfluous attributes were deleted. The experimental results demonstrate that for all attack classes utilizing distinctive feature subsets, the accuracy of Decision Tree (DT), Nave Bayes (NB), Random Forest (RF), Linear Regression, XGBoost, AdaBoost, and Support Vector Machine (SVM) was over 95%. Overall, the performance of XGBoost in conjunction with recursive feature selection was the best.

Keywords: IDS · Recursive feature selection · Machine Learning · NSL-KDD dataset

1 Introduction

The IDS is a system that monitors networks for possibly harmful activities and eliminates false alerts. Security concerns are a major barrier in this digital era because they compromise the user's privacy and lead to data losses. Additionally, a massive amount of data is now present on the internet due to the widespread use of IoT devices and applications, which are often vulnerable. The same IDS must be utilized to quickly identify these weaknesses in order to protect the privacy of the user. Even while many security measures, including firewalls and encryption methods, have already been implemented over time, cyberattacks are still becoming more sophisticated.

Security has now become a primary issue in computer networks, and it is difficult to avoid the increasing number of security threats. Additionally, a security attack might lead to significant losses and negatively impact critical IT

© The Author(s), under exclusive license to Springer Nature Switzerland AG 2024
S. K. Panda et al. (Eds.): CoCoLe 2023, CCIS 1892, pp. 3–14, 2024.
https://doi.org/10.1007/978-3-031-56998-2_1

infrastructure, which would create data inadequacies during cyberwarfare. Firewalls and other forms of encryption have been implemented to protect against intrusions, yet many attackers still find ways to breach them. Therefore, early detection is essential for minimizing risk to essential resources.

The IDS monitors network data for malicious behavior that might jeopardize the system or network, making it an important line of defense for network controllers. Signature-based IDS and anomaly detection systems are the two main IDS varieties. In signature-based IDS, data from the network is matched to a predetermined attack signature in the database to establish the attack class. Signature-based IDS have a high detection rate but cannot detect new attacks to a certain extent.

However, with anomaly detection, every deviation from normal behavior has been deemed an assault, and it is incapable of distinguishing new types of attacks. But it may result in numerous false positives as well. Machine learning algorithms are often used to find intrusions because they can learn from data and change as attack patterns change. Various ML algorithms like Decision Tree (DT), Nave Bayes (NB), Random Forest (RF), XGBoost, and Support Vector Machine (SVM) are widely used in various fields and have proven to be efficient and effective in intrusion classification tasks. [2,3,5].

The contributions of this paper are: 1) We use the recursive feature selection approach in conjunction with various machine learning algorithms for intrusion classification in the NSL-KDD dataset. 2) We compare and contrast various machine learning methods and show how the feature selection approach can help in achieving high accuracy with less number of features. The algorithms that will be used in this research are: Decision Tree (DT), Nave Bayes (NB), Random Forest (RF), Linear Regression, XGBoost, AdaBoost, and Support Vector Machine (SVM).

The goal of this research is to compare the performance of these algorithms and identify the best-performing algorithm for intrusion detection on the NSL-KDD dataset.

2   Related Work

Various machine learning techniques are used to create strong IDS since they can handle and analyze massive volumes of data. The work presented here marks a considerable improvement in the state of the art of IDS, which are used to detect many types of network attacks. In this scenario, IDSs are created by using ML algorithms in order to process the massive amount of data and enable network administrators to halt the attack. The dataset was made accessible and contains a variety of simulated invasions into a network environment. Various ML based approaches are used in literature along with discrete event system based approach [1,3,4].

The precision and accuracy of the model were enhanced by gradient descent optimization. On the NSL-KDD dataset [9] with 13 features, it worked 99.9% of the time. Similarly, Random Forest (RF) was implemented with the NSL-KDD dataset, and performance was analyzed with selected features with 99.76%

accuracy. For the Support Vector Machine (SVM), accuracy with the selected feature was 99.492%. And for AdaBoost, it has been observed 99.785% accuracy, and finally, Nave Bayes has 91.426% accuracy.

The proposed method uses a knowledge-based technique to browse target classes, choose the optimal model, and provide accurate predictions. DT, SVM, and Naive Bayes were the three classifiers used to essentially analyze the different feature sets included in this dataset. The best outcomes were achieved by using the wrapper technique, which makes use of 11 features for U2R and 41 attributes for DoS and probing attacks.

The PCA [10] method was used to implement dimensionality reduction and data [9] classification. The accuracy of models such as SVM, NB, DT, XGBoost, and AdaBoost was 99.37%, 99.01%, 99.63%, 99.81%, and 99.58%, respectively. Fuzzy logic and temporal concepts were used in a DT classifier that was trained and tested on a dataset using recursive feature selection. The results showed accuracy rates of 99.8%, 99.57%, 96.80%, and 99.68% for DoS, Probe, R2L, and U2R, respectively. When compared to previous research, this work has a higher level of accuracy. Although it achieves high detection accuracy, it still needs improvement. Therefore, the simple network framework proposed here can improve a solution or a new attempt in the current research domain.

3   Dataset Description

Previously, the KDD Cup 99, [14,15] dataset was introduced in 1999 and was one of the most used datasets for cyber security research using data mining techniques. This dataset was mostly used for training the models and anomaly detection. Several researchers who examined this dataset for IDS [16] reported poor execution results for the anomaly detection technique. Due to the duplicate data, the learning algorithm favors frequent records and is unable to learn from fewer records that are more detrimental to networks, such as U2R and R2L attacks. The researcher created the NSL-KDD dataset, which only comprises chosen elements from the whole NSL-KDD dataset, to address this issue in the KDD Cup 99 [14] datasets. There are several advantages to using the NSL-KDD dataset, as listed.

1. This dataset is the largest and most comprehensive one available for intrusion detection.
2. The NSL-KDD dataset is derived from real-world network traffic data and includes a variety of different types of intrusions and attack patterns.
3. The NSL-KDD dataset has already undergone a significant amount of pre-processing, including the removal of redundant and irrelevant data and the labeling of normal and intrusive connections.

We chose the NSL-KDD dataset in this study since it is a better dataset for assessing all ML models than the KDD Cup 99 dataset, which had numerous faults. This dataset contains 41 features, but some of the features cannot be represented during the training of the model. So for that, we normalize the dataset to the range of [0, 1] with a min-max operation (Table 1).

Table 1. Training and Testing Distribution for the NSL-KDD Dataset

Attacks	Train data	Percentage	Test data	Percentage
DoS	45,927	36.45%	7,457	33.08%
R2L	995	0.79%	2,754	12.21%
Probe	11,656	9.25%	2,421	10.74%
U2R	52	0.04%	200	0.88%
Normal	67,342	53.45%	9,710	43.07%

In the training dataset, 21 of the 37 attacks from the test dataset are also present. The training datasets only contain the known attack types, but the test dataset also contains unique attacks that aren't present in the training datasets. Here we found 4 types of attacks such as DoS, Probe, U2R, and R2L, and the most significant attacks in the training and test datasets are given below.

- **DoS** : Neptune, Udpstorm, Back, Worm, Smurf, Processtable, Land, Mailbomb, Teardrop, Apache2, Pod.
- **Probe** : Saint, Satan, Nmap, IPsweep Portsweep, Mscan.
- **R2L** : Snmpgetattack, Sendmail, Multihop, Httptunnel, Xlock, Phf, Xsnoop, Guess_password, Snmpguess, Warezmaster, Ftp_write, Named, Imap.
- **U2R** : Xterm, Ps, Rootkit, Perl, Buffer_overflow, Sqlattack, Loadmodule.

The selected records from the entire KDD data set consist of a (125,973) training dataset and a (22,544) testing dataset comprising 41 attributes that are either attacks or normal. The several attack methods in this collection include R2L, U2R, DOS, and probe attacks, to name just a few. The section below provides the justifications for these different attack types.

- **DoS** : This kind of attack limits the resources' processing time in order to deny access to the targeted user.
- **Probe** : The next time, the attacker would do some penetrations after looking at the network to learn more about it.
- **Remote to user** : The attacker is not authorized to access as a local user. R2L attacks fall under the categories of host-based or network-based IDS [11].
- **User to Root** : An attacker tries to figure out a user's password so that they can take the user's place and get to the user's data.

Preprocessing is the process of replacing or deleting symbolic or non-numeric features. Data Pre-processing is necessary for dimensional reduction, which shortens the time the data must be processed.

4 The Proposed Model

(See Fig. 9) The use of normalization ensures that all feature values fall within the range of 0 and 1 after preparing the raw dataset. The model was trained using a training set, and its performance was then assessed using a testing set. Key features from the training set were selected using the recursive feature elimination method [13], and these key features were then combined with the testing set during the prediction phase. In order to evaluate the model, predictions are made concerning a test set (Fig. 1).

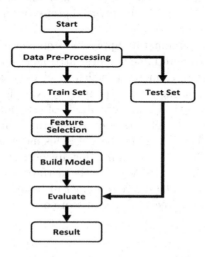

Fig. 1. Proposed model diagram

4.1 Data Pre-processing

Data pre-processing is a crucial step in the development of any machine learning model, as it helps prepare the data for analysis and model training. In the context of intrusion detection using the NSL-KDD [7] Dataset and machine learning, data pre-processing involved several steps to clean and transform the data in order to improve the performance of our models.

- Numbers are assigned to the nominal attributes in the dataset. Protocols are classified into three types: protocol_type, service, and flag, which have features 2, 3, and 4.
- The dataset's attacks are converted into their numerical categories at the end.

4.2 Data Normalization

The NSL-KDD dataset [12] contains characteristics that have continuous or discrete values. Because the values' ranges varied, it was impossible to compare them.

Test features were normalized using the mean and standard deviation of each feature from the training datasets. In our research, we employed the Min-Max normalization technique in order to improve the performance of our models. This technique scales the data to a range between 0 and 1 by subtracting the minimum value from each feature and dividing by the range.

4.3   Features Selection

The feature selection stage of data pre-processing for IDS is one of the most crucial ones [8]. Reducing the number of features allows for the separation of unnecessary data and the acquisition of crucial properties influencing input identification.

The recursive feature elimination approach is employed as the feature selection methodology [6]. To determine the best attribute subset, recursive feature elimination uses the wrapper method, which involves selecting a single model (Random Forests), eliminating all but the most relevant features, and doing the same operation on progressively smaller subsets of attributes.

We created a weighted model using recursive feature elimination with random forest [17] to rank the features in the dataset. This method recursively removes features by building a model and evaluating its performance, then removing the feature that contributes the least to the performance of the model, and repeating the process until the desired number of features are selected. In this feature selection method, it received a high score of more than 99 percent with 13 selected features.

5   Description of Classification Methods

In the current work, we used SVM, DT, LR, NB, RF, XGBoost, and AdaBoost for intrusion detection to classify the data as normal or an attack. The input vector is first mapped, and then the ideal hyperplane is constructed, which splits the information based on the greatest distance between the support vectors. Since the hyperplane is calculated based only on the support vectors and not the whole training set, SVM is not affected by outliers.

In this research, we used the radial basis kernel function to train our models since previous work has shown that this method yields encouraging results when applied to non-linear data. To calculate the likelihood of a target variable, logistic regression, a supervised learning method, is utilized. It describes the link between dependent and independent variables and is predictive in nature (Fig. 2).

Naive Bayes is a classifier collection that employs the Bayes theorem, which states that each record may be classified separately. The GNB was used in this research work since it performs well with numerical data. Here, 100 neurons from a single hidden layer were used in the model during training and testing using a rectified linear unit function.

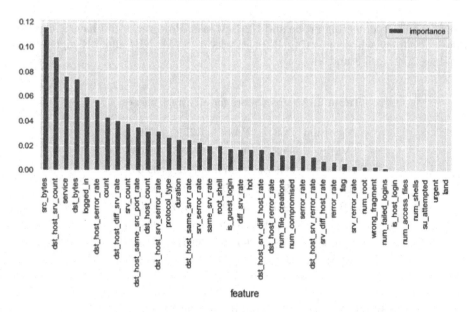

Fig. 2. Feature selected by applying Recursive Feature Elimination.

A tree-like structure is created in a decision tree to address the classification issue. The qualities are represented by the tree's nodes, and their potential values are shown by the nodes' paths. The recursive process of the decision tree ends once all the data has been classified because its depth was set to zero.

To categorize the data into the proper classes, the random forest considers the results of various decision trees. When using RF, significant qualities are chosen at random from a list of attributes, which improves the classification model. The main difference between RF and the extra-tree classifier is how the trees are built. It is helpful for network intrusion detection because it efficiently categorizes the data by combining the findings of several de-correlated decision trees in a forest.

6 Results

The results of our network IDS, trained on the NSL-KDD dataset, are presented in this section. Using a combination of 13 selected features from the dataset, which were used to train and evaluate the system for better results, classifiers such as Support Vector Machine, K-Nearest Neighbor, Naive Bayes, XGBoost, Logistic Regression, AdaBoost, and Decision Tree were trained and evaluated on 125973 and 22544 instances of NSL-KDD, respectively.

A number of parameters were used to evaluate the model's performance. Table 2 shows the accuracy of different types of attacks using seven algorithms. The model performed particularly well in detecting denial-of-service attacks, with more than 99% accuracy for all seven algorithms. It also had a strong performance in detecting probe and U2R attacks. However, it did have a slightly lower accuracy while detecting R2L attacks in SVM, NB, and LR algorithms (Tables 3, 4, 5, 6, 8 and 9).

Table 2. Accuracy score for all attack classes

Algorithm	DoS	Probe	R2L	U2R
SVM	99.37%	98.45%	96.79%	99.63%
DT	99.63%	99.57%	97.92%	99.65%
RF	99.76%	99.36%	97.94%	99.71%
NB	99.01%	98.89%	96.73%	99.03%
LR	99.39%	98.44%	96.56%	99.68%
XGBoost	99.81%	99.43%	99.04%	99.31%
AdaBoost	99.58%	99.42%	99.62%	99.74%

Table 3. Accuracy, Precision, Recall, and F1-Score for SVM

Attack Class	Accuracy	Precision	Recall	F1-Score
DoS	99.37%	99.10%	99.45%	99.27%
Probe	98.45%	96.90%	98.36%	97.61%
R2L	96.79%	94.85%	96.26%	95.52%
U2R	99.63%	91.05%	82.90%	84.86%

Table 4. Accuracy, Precision, Recall, and F1-Score for DT

Attack Class	Accuracy	Precision	Recall	F1-Score
DoS	99.62%	99.49%	99.65%	99.57%
Probe	99.59%	96.40%	99.31%	99.35%
R2L	96.65%	95.74%	98.35%	96.42%
U2R	99.69%	86.77%	91.01%	87.84%

The results of our network intrusion detection study using the NSL-KDD dataset are encouraging. We trained and tested seven different machine learning models-SVM, DT, RF, NB, LR, and AdaBoost-on the dataset and found that all of them were able to achieve high levels of accuracy, precision, recall, and F1 score (Figs. 3, 4, 5, 6, 7 and 8).

The DoS attack class showed the most promising findings among the attack classes because the NSL-KDD dataset contains a good number of entries for this attack class, while the U2L attack showed less promising results. From Table 7, we learned that the highest overall accuracy was achieved by the XGBoost model,

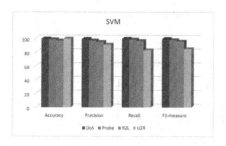

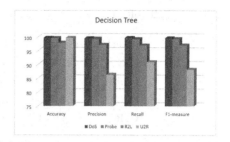

Fig. 3. Performance of Support Vector Machine mode

Fig. 4. Performance of Decision Tree model

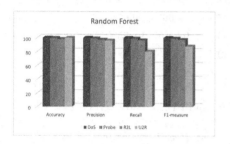

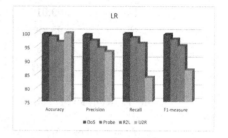

Fig. 5. Performance of Random Forest model

Fig. 6. Performance of Logistic Regression model

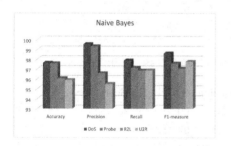

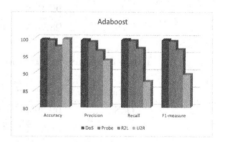

Fig. 7. Performance of Naive Bayes model

Fig. 8. Performance of AdaBoost model

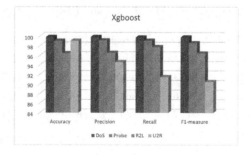

Fig. 9. Performance of XGBoost model

Table 5. Accuracy, Precision, Recall, and F1-Score for RF

Attack Class	Accuracy	Precision	Recall	F1-Score
DoS	99.76%	99.78%	99.69%	99.74%
Probe	99.36%	98.96%	98.82%	98.91%
R2L	97.94%	97.15%	96.40%	96.92%
U2R	99.71%	95.92%	80.09%	87.58%

Table 6. Accuracy, Precision, Recall, and F1-Score for NB

Attack Class	Accuracy	Precision	Recall	F1-Score
DoS	99.01%	99.67%	99.66%	99.67%
Probe	98.89%	98.60%	98.50%	98.55%
R2L	96.73%	95.30%	95.48%	95.38%
U2R	99.03%	93.14%	85.07%	87.83%

Table 7. Accuracy, Precision, Recall, and F1-Score for XGBoost

Attack Class	Accuracy	Precision	Recall	F1-Score
DoS	99.81%	99.83%	99.73%	99.78%
Probe	98.77%	99.23%	99.01%	99.25%
R2L	99.13%	99.10%	99.76%	99.36%
U2R	98.24%	93.14%	88.29%	88.45%

Table 8. Accuracy, Precision, Recall, and F1-Score for LR

Attack Class	Accuracy	Precision	Recall	F1-Score
DoS	99.39%	99.09%	99.51%	99.30%
Probe	98.44%	97.10%	99.01%	98.09%
R2L	96.56%	94.46%	96.05%	95.22%
U2R	99.68%	93.06%	83.76%	86.48%

Table 9. Accuracy, Precision, Recall, and F1-Score for AdaBoost

Attack Class	Accuracy	Precision	Recall	F1-Score
DoS	99.58%	99.47%	99.57%	99.52%
Probe	99.42%	98.96%	99.23%	99.10%
R2L	97.62%	96.33%	97.01%	96.66%
U2R	99.74%	93.61%	87.45%	89.47%

with an accuracy of 99.81% for DoS attacks. It also had the highest precision and recall scores, at 99.83% and 99.73%, respectively. This provides a comprehensive comparison among ML algorithms. We have used standalone probability ensemble-based algorithms for prediction. The F1-score for the XGBoost model was also the highest, at 99.78%. The RF model had the second-highest overall accuracy, at 99.76%. It also had a high precision score of 99.78% and a recall score of 99.69%. Its F1 score was 99.74%.

The SVM, DT, RF, NB, and AdaBoost models all performed well, with overall accuracies ranging from 95.56% to 99.76%. All five models had precision scores above 90% and recall scores above 80%. Their F1 scores ranged from 84.86% to 99.67%. Overall, our results show that all seven models are effective in detecting network intrusions using the NSL-KDD dataset. Further research could be done to optimize the models and potentially improve their performance even further.

7   Conclusion and Future Scope

Security has become a significant issue as a result of an increase in the availability of attacks on resources. Machine learning algorithms are now often used in IDS because of their versatility, generalization potential, and robustness.

The results of the comprehensive empirical investigation conducted as part of the current study employing machine learning algorithms such as SVM, Decision Tree, Logistic Regression, Naive Bayes, Random Forest, XGBoost, and AdaBoost to detect network intrusion were assessed using the NSL-KDD dataset. After preprocessing the dataset using recursive feature selection, the model was trained and tested using some important attributes.

According to the results, all classifiers produce positive results for DoS attacks, with U2R having the least amount of data and thus producing the least accurate result. Future studies could concentrate on the possibility of using optimization approaches to provide improved IDS performance. As a result, ensemble-based methods, which integrate the output of many algorithms to anticipate the outcomes, can be investigated. Additionally, several feature selection techniques can be examined to reduce the system's computational complexity. Overall, XGBoost provided us with the best results when combined with the proposed feature selection technique.

References

1. Agarwal, M.: Detecting flooding, impersonation and injection attacks on AWID dataset using ml based methods. In: 2022 IEEE 4th International Conference on Cybernetics, Cognition and Machine Learning Applications (ICCCMLA), pp. 221–226. IEEE (2022)
2. Agarwal, M., Biswas, S., Nandi, S.: Detection of de-authentication dos attacks in Wi-Fi networks: a machine learning approach. In: 2015 IEEE International Conference on Systems, Man, and Cybernetics, pp. 246–251 (2015). https://doi.org/10.1109/SMC.2015.55

3. Agarwal, M., Pasumarthi, D., Biswas, S., Nandi, S.: Machine learning approach for detection of flooding dos attacks in 802.11 networks and attacker localization. Int. J. Mach. Learn. Cybern. **7**, 1035–1051 (2016)
4. Agarwal, M., Purwar, S., Biswas, S., Nandi, S.: Intrusion detection system for PS-Poll DoS attack in 802.11 networks using real time discrete event system. IEEE/CAA J. Autom. Sinica **4**(4), 792–808 (2016)
5. Agarwal, M., Purwar, S., Biswas, S., Nandi, S.: Intrusion detection system for PS-Poll DoS attack in 802.11 networks using real time discrete event system. IEEE/CAA J. Autom. Sinica **4**(4), 792–808 (2017). https://doi.org/10.1109/JAS. 2016.7510178
6. Aghdam, M.H., Kabiri, P., et al.: Feature selection for intrusion detection system using ant colony optimization. Int. J. Netw. Secur. **18**(3), 420–432 (2016)
7. Ahmad, T., Aziz, M.N.: Data preprocessing and feature selection for machine learning intrusion detection systems. ICIC Express Lett. **13**(2), 93–101 (2019)
8. Ambusaidi, M.A., He, X., Nanda, P., Tan, Z.: Building an intrusion detection system using a filter-based feature selection algorithm. IEEE Trans. Comput. **65**(10), 2986–2998 (2016)
9. Benaddi, H., Ibrahimi, K., Benslimane, A.: Improving the intrusion detection system for NSL-KDD dataset based on PCA-fuzzy clustering-KNN. In: 2018 6th International Conference on Wireless Networks and Mobile Communications (WIN-COM), pp. 1–6. IEEE (2018)
10. Gurung, S., Ghose, M.K., Subedi, A.: Deep learning approach on network intrusion detection system using NSL-KDD dataset. Int. J. Comput. Netw. Inf. Security **11**(3), 8–14 (2019)
11. Jiang, K., Wang, W., Wang, A., Wu, H.: Network intrusion detection combined hybrid sampling with deep hierarchical network. IEEE Access **8**, 32464–32476 (2020)
12. Liu, Z., et al.: A method of SVM with normalization in intrusion detection. Procedia Environ. Sci. **11**, 256–262 (2011)
13. Mohammed, B., Gbashi, E.K.: Intrusion detection system for NSL-KDD dataset based on deep learning and recursive feature elimination. Eng. Technol. J. **39**(7), 1069–1079 (2021)
14. Ravipati, R.D., Abualkibash, M.: Intrusion detection system classification using different machine learning algorithms on KDD-99 and NSL-KDD datasets-a review paper. Int. J. Comput. Sci. Inf. Technol. (IJCSIT), 11 (2019)
15. Sapre, S., Ahmadi, P., Islam, K.: A robust comparison of the KDDCup99 and NSL-KDD IoT network intrusion detection datasets through various machine learning algorithms. arXiv preprint arXiv:1912.13204 (2019)
16. Su, T., Sun, H., Zhu, J., Wang, S., Li, Y.: BAT: deep learning methods on network intrusion detection using NSL-KDD dataset. IEEE Access **8**, 29575–29585 (2020)
17. Zhou, Y., Cheng, G., Jiang, S., Dai, M.: Building an efficient intrusion detection system based on feature selection and ensemble classifier. Comput. Netw. **174**, 107247 (2020)

Forecasting Crude Oil Prices: A Machine Learning Perspective

Sourav Kumar Purohit[1] and Sibarama Panigrahi[2](✉)

[1] Department of Computer Science Engineering and Applications, Sambalpur University Institute of Information Technology, Jyoti Vihar, Burla, Odisha 768019, India
[2] Department of Computer Science and Engineering, National Institute of Technology, Rourkela, Odisha 769008, India
panigrahi.sibarama@gmail.com

Abstract. The crude oil price (COP) has substantial implications on world economy, as it impacts industries ranging from transportation to manufacturing. Given the volatile nature of COP, accurate forecasting is very much crucial for businesses and policymakers alike. Forecasting crude oil prices is a challenging task for the complex and volatile nature of the global oil market. As a result, estimating the price of crude oil has been a challenging and crucial component of forecasting research. In this study, we employ fourteen machine learning (ML) models for predicting the weekly and daily crude oil price. To evaluate the effectiveness of ML models, four performance measure metrics are utilized, including "mean absolute scaled error (MASE), symmetric mean absolute percentage error (SMAPE), root mean square error (RMSE), and mean absolute error (MAE)". Detailed statistical analyses of data obtained using the Wilcoxon Signed-Rank test demonstrate that the linear support vector regression (SVR) model for weekly COP data, and linear regression for daily COP data are statistically more effective in predicting COPs than other models considered. The linear regression model acquires the statistically best rank across three accuracy metrics (SMAPE, MAE, MASE) and Gradient Boosting acquires the best rank based on RMSE accuracy metrics considering both weekly and daily COP data according to the Friedman and Nemenyi hypothesis test.

Keywords: Machine Learning · Crude Oil Price Forecasting · Time Series Forecasting

1 Introduction

Crude oil, often called 'black gold', plays often a significant role in the world's economy and other macroeconomic factors. Currently, one of the most significant sources of energy on earth is crude oil. With about a third of the world's energy usage, it continues to be the most popular fuel. Moreover, refined crude oil is used to make petroleum products, fossil fuels. Also, to address the climate catastrophe, deliberate efforts are being conducted worldwide to phase out fossil fuels. Petroleum is crucial to industry and civilization as it supplies a sizeable portion of the world's energy needs and plays a crucial role in world

S. K. Panda et al. (Eds.): CoCoLe 2023, CCIS 1892, pp. 15–26, 2024.
https://doi.org/10.1007/978-3-031-56998-2_2

politics and international relations [1]. Rise of oil prices lead to a surge in inflation and hence impair the financial state of oil-importing nations while fall in the price of oil may induce economic crises and political unrest in nations that export oil. Further, the price fluctuation may result in financial losses as a slight increase in crude oil price (COP) can decrease the purchasing value of money.

In the past few decades, significant fluctuations have been observed in crude oil prices. It has risen and fallen substantially at various points. Since oil is a strategic commodity, it has a major impact on the country's economy and macroeconomic indicators such as inflation, GDP, interest rates, recession, exchange rates and so on. As a result, one of the most popular topics among energy specialists and economists has been the predictors of oil prices and their variations. India is the third-largest importer of crude oil worldwide. In spite of a 15% rise in total import volume to 116.6 million tons, India's cost of importing crude oil increased by 76% to $90.3 billion in the first half of 2022–23 [2]. As India is an importer nation; a rise in crude oil price will result in inflation and eventually triggering a recession. So, precise prediction of the COP has been drawing significant attention from the Indian government since it helps decision-makers to formulate suitable policies and strategies for managing energy resources [3]. For this reason, it would be crucial for policymakers to develop an exact and dependable forecasting system and find solutions to the complicated issues surrounding crude oil pricing. It has been attempted to predict the movements, swings or volatility of COP using a variety of approaches.

Extensive studies have been carried out on forecasting COP; still, it is drawing tremendous research attention owing to its importance in the global economy. Despite several studies used ML models to predict COP, no systematic comparative study employing statistical analysis is performed to predict COP using machine learning models with bagging, boosting and stacking. Motivated from this, in this paper extensive studies are made to predict the COP using promising machine learning based forecasting techniques employing bagging, boosting and stacking. More on these methods is found below in literature review section. The procedure used to produce forecasts is described in Methodology section. Results and discussion section contains the dataset description, performance measures and comparison of each individual model. The final section contains conclusion and future scope.

2 Literature Review

According to the documented data in [4], ML techniques outperform traditional statistical procedures in most situations while forecasting complex financial time series. However, there exists a few exceptions. Nevertheless, these traditional techniques are still applicable in predicting COP.

Conventional statistical and econometric approaches are initially used for COP predictions. There are several diversified studies that utilized time series as well as econometric concepts in forecasting oil prices. Among these studies, [5] credited to conduct the first study on COP forecasting using a small-scale econometric model to estimate the commodity's price. The ability to forecast actual COP using time-varying parameter-Value-at-Risk (TVP-VAR) models discussed in [6]. In [7], the West Texas Intermediate

(WTI) COP was predicted by using co-integration analysis. A probabilistic approach for forecasting oil prices was proposed in [8]. The relationship between COP and product prices is discussed in [9]. To calculate oil price Value-at-Risk forecasts, in [10] authors designed the historical simulation using autoregressive moving average (ARMA). In [11], authors studied whether generalized autoregressive conditional heteroskedasticity (GARCH) models are more practical for predicting short-term oil prices. To investigate the advantages of leveraging the forward-looking information incorporated in the pricing of derivative contracts, [12] employed autoregressive conditional heteroskedasticity models (ARCH). Conventional econometric models, however, assume the characteristic of oil price series to be linear or nearly linear. In reality, the price of crude oil has been called a complicated and chaotic phenomenon. Although statistical time series forecasting (TSF) models are highly effective in modelling linear patterns, they are ineffective in modelling the complicated nonlinear patterns found in the COP time series.

Alternatively, due to the accessibility of a vast quantity of data related to crude oil, increased computational capability, the ability to utilize universal estimations, and the capability to deal with nonlinear patterns, in recent years, ML models have been used in predicting the COP. In [13], authors proposed a hierarchical conceptual model where they emphasized the design of a quantitative model for long-term prediction employing artificial neural network (ANN) based qualitative techniques. The capacity of abductive networks and neural networks to estimate monthly energy consumption for a year using univariate modelling of demand time series from the previous six years is compared in [14]. To improve the neural network's forecasting efficiency in [15], where each historical datum is given a random weight that varies depending on when it appears in the model, and also uses probability density functions to categorize distinct variables from training samples. A wrapper-based feature selection technique with multi-objective optimization and a forecasting model based on support vector regression (SVR) was developed in [16]. The use of an ANN for predicting COP is presented in [17] as an innovative and distinctive method.

Even though ML models have been applied in predicting COP, a systematic study is still necessary to evaluate the statistical comparative forecasting performance analysis of promising ML models ("Linear Regression, Ridge Regression, Huber Regression, Stochastic Gradient Descent (SGD) Regressor, Adaboost, Random Forest, Gradient Boosting, Linear Support Vector Regression (Linear SVR), Multilayer Perceptron (MLP), Support Vector Regression (SVR), Extra Tree Regression, Bagging Regression, Decision Tree, eXtreme Gradient Boosting (XGB)") in predicting the COP. Moreover, none of the research included weekly and daily COP data for statistically assessing the effectiveness of ML models.

3 Methodology

In this study, we employed fourteen ML models to forecast the weekly and daily COP. The study's approach is laid forth in Algorithm 1. No values are missing from the weekly and daily COP. As a result, the dataset is split into 80% and 20% ratios to form the train and test datasets, respectively. The first 80% of the original data is used for training, while the following 20% of the original data is considered for testing. The test set is used to evaluate the model's effectiveness and the training set is used to create the model.

We have considered eighteen promising ML models for forecasting COP, but four models have been excluded as the performance measure of the model is highly inferior from other models such as: "Linear Regression, Ridge Regression, Huber Regression, SGD Regressor, Adaboost, Random Forest, Gradient Boosting, Linear SVR, MLP, SVR, Extra Tree Regression, Bagging Regression, Decision Tree, XGB". First, the sliding window technique is utilized to convert the COP time series data into a supervised learning problem. The number of previous time steps data are known as size of the lag. The value of the lag (k) is set to 7 and 24 for weekly and daily COP dataset. The sliding window technique is used to transform the time series $y = [y_1, y_2, \ldots\ldots\ldots, y_n]^T$ to a pattern set of size (n-k). The min-max normalization approach is used to transform the data onto a similar scale. The ML model parameters are then computed using the train set before being applied to the test set to get normalized predictions. The normalized forecasts are then de-normalized to get the actual forecasts y'. Considering the original time series y and forecasts y', the prediction accuracy is measured.

Algorithm 1: Methodology

1: Input the COP time series $y = [y_1, y_2, \ldots\ldots\ldots\ldots, y_n]^T$

2: Specify the value of lag (k) for ML models. The COP time series is turned into a pattern set of size $n - k$ using the sliding window technique based on the number of inputs (k).

3: Employ the min-max normalization approach to normalize the patterns.

4: Split the original dataset into Train and Test set.

5: To develop the ML model, use training set. Get the forecasts on the test set using the model that was obtained and the test patterns.

6: De-normalize the forecasts to obtain the actual forecasts y'.

7: Using the original COP time series (y) and COP forecasts (y'), determine the model's forecasting performance measure.

---

4 Result and Discussion

4.1 Data Description

In this paper, we have taken WTI Crude Oil Price (COP) data which is a major worldwide oil benchmark dataset. We obtained the two different subsets of WTI COP data i.e., weekly, daily from the website (investing.com) [18]. The selection and division process of the data set into train and test set is shown in Table 1.

Table 1. Data set selection and division.

Data set	Training	Test	Start Date	End Date
WTI Weekly	7357	1839	03/01/1986	01/07/2022
WTI Daily	1524	381	02/01/1986	30/06/2022

4.2 Performance Measure

This section describes the simulation outcomes using the RMSE (Eq. 1), SMAPE (Eq. 2), MAE (Eq. 3) and MASE (Eq. 4) measures encompassing two separate subsets (train and test) of the original WTI COP data. All models are evaluated on a daily and weekly COP data [18]. Smaller RMSE, SMAPE, MAE, and MASE values are preferred for a better forecasting model. The ML Models are implemented using Python. We performed the simulations 50 separate times because some ML models are stochastic in nature, and we only used the best 20 simulations based on the RMSE value for comparison. The best 20 simulation's means and standard deviations (std. Dev.) are presented.

$$RMSE = \sqrt{\frac{1}{n}\sum_{i=1}^{n}\left(y_i - y_i'\right)^2} \tag{1}$$

$$SMAPE = \frac{1}{n}\sum_{i=1}^{n}\frac{\left|y_i - y_i'\right|}{\left(|y_i| - |y_i'|\right)/2} \tag{2}$$

$$MAE = \frac{1}{n}\sum_{i=1}^{n}\left|y_i - y_i'\right| \tag{3}$$

$$MASE = \frac{1}{n}\sum_{i=1}^{n}\frac{\left|y_i - y_i'\right|}{\frac{1}{n-1}\sum_{j=2}^{n}|y_i - y_{i-1}|} \tag{4}$$

We have considered fourteen ML models in predicting the daily and weekly COP, namely, Linear Regression, Ridge Regression, Huber Regression, SGD Regressor, Adaboost, Random Forest, Gradient Boosting, Linear SVR, MLP, SVR, Extra Tree Regression, Bagging Regression, Decision Tree and, XGB. In addition to these fourteen models, we have implemented additional four ML models for predicting the daily and weekly COP, namely Lasso regression, Elastic net regression, Stacked regression and Tweedie regression. These models, however, are excluded from the comparison due to significantly lower performance than the other fourteen models. We have evaluated the performance of fourteen ML models in predicting weekly COP and the results are summarized in Table 2. From Table 2, it is observed that Linear SVR has the least mean RMSE and SMAPE value among the fourteen ML models in predicting weekly COP time series. It is also noted that computationally simpler models like linear regression provide better accuracy than other models in MAE and MASE measures. Further, "Wilcoxon Signed-Rank test" is being applied for a pairwise comparison of Linear SVR with other ML models and the Table 3 represents the test results. It is clear from Table 3 that all the ML models considered in this study are statistically inferior to Linear SVR in the prediction of weekly COP data in RMSE and SMAPE measure. We have also analyzed the performance of ML models for daily COP forecasting. Table 4 presents the test results of ML models on daily COP data. It is observed from Table 4 that Gradient Boosting provides the smallest mean RMSE value and linear regression provides the lowest mean SMAPE, MAE and MASE value. Here also "Wilcoxon Signed-Rank test" is applied and the test results are represented in Table 5 which indicates that Gradient Boosting is statistically better than other models in the prediction of daily COP in RMSE measure, while linear regression is the best model considering SMAPE, MAE and MASE measure. As linear regression outperforms in three performance measures, linear regression is considered as the best model for predicting daily COP.

Table 2. Mean RMSE, SMAPE, MAE and MASE of Statistical and Machine Learning models on Weekly COP.

MODEL	RMSE	SMAPE	MAE	MASE
Linear Regression	$2.936 \pm 9.113E{-}16$	$4.266 \pm 1.8225E{-}15$	**$1.901 \pm 6.83E{-}16$**	**$0.964 \pm 1.139E{-}16$**
Ridge	$3.504 \pm 4.556E{-}16$	$5.202 \pm 9.113E{-}16$	$2.515 \pm 4.56E{-}16$	$1.276 \pm 2.278E{-}16$
Huber Regressor	$2.947 \pm 4.556E{-}16$	4.266 ± 0	$1.903 \pm 0.00E+00$	0.965 ± 0
SGD Regressor	$5.492 \pm 4.762E{-}03$	8.044 ± 0.015	$3.979 \pm 8.02E{-}03$	2.018 ± 0.004
AdaBoost	$3.277 \pm 3.287E{-}02$	4.823 ± 0.101	$2.352 \pm 4.44E{-}02$	1.193 ± 0.022
Random Forest	$3.242 \pm 1.384E{-}02$	4.584 ± 0.031	$2.257 \pm 1.35E{-}02$	1.145 ± 0.006
Gradient Boosting	$3.215 \pm 3.058E{-}03$	4.479 ± 0.006	$2.193 \pm 2.08E{-}03$	1.112 ± 0.001
Linear SVR	**$2.925 \pm 8.397E{-}04$**	**4.223 ± 0.010**	$1.910 \pm 4.17E{-}03$	0.969 ± 0.002
MLP	$4.557 \pm 3.487E{-}01$	6.802 ± 0.505	$3.311 \pm 2.55E{-}01$	1.679 ± 0.129
SVR	$5.450 \pm 0.00E+00$	8.781 ± 0	$4.361 \pm 0.00E+00$	$2.212 \pm 4.556E{-}16$
ExtraTrees Regressor	$3.256 \pm 2.027E{-}02$	4.593 ± 0.032	$2.197 \pm 1.38E{-}02$	1.115 ± 0.006
Bagging Regressor	$3.270 \pm 1.985E{-}02$	4.701 ± 0.056	$2.317 \pm 2.42E{-}02$	1.175 ± 0.012
Decision Tree Regressor	$4.372 \pm 2.480E{-}02$	6.184 ± 0.079	$3.155 \pm 3.37E{-}02$	1.600 ± 0.017
XGB	$3.372 \pm 0.00E+00$	$4.753 \pm 1.823E{-}15$	$2.361 \pm 4.56E{-}16$	$1.198 \pm 2.278E{-}16$

4.3 Ranking ML Models Using Weekly and Daily COP Data

In this subsection, the ML models are ranked based on different performance measures for predicting the weekly, and daily COP as a whole. Using the Friedman and Nemenyi

Table 3. Results from the Wilcoxon Signed-Rank Test indicating the machine learning model better (+), worse (-) and equivalent (≈) at predicting weekly COP data than Linear SVR.

MODEL	RMSE	SMAPE	MAE	MASE
Linear Regression	–	–	+	+
Ridge	–	–	–	–
Huber Regressor	–	–	–	–
SGD Regressor	–	–	–	–
AdaBoost	–	–	–	–
Random Forest	–	–	–	–
Gradient Boosting	–	–	–	–
MLP	–	–	–	–
SVR	–	–	–	–
ExtraTrees Regressor	–	–	–	–
Bagging Regressor	–	–	–	–
Decision Tree Regressor	–	–	–	–
XGB	–	–	–	–

Table 4. Mean RMSE, SMAPE, MAE and MASE of Statistical and Machine Learning models on daily COP.

MODEL	RMSE	SMAPE	MAE	MASE
Linear Regression	$2.260 \pm 4.556E{-}16$	**$2.273 \pm 9.113E{-}16$**	**$1.102 \pm 0.00E + 00$**	**1.008 ± 0**
Ridge	$2.271 \pm 0.000E + 00$	2.702 ± 0	$1.266 \pm 2.28E{-}16$	$1.159 \pm 4.556E{-}16$
Huber Regressor	$2.255 \pm 4.556E{-}16$	$2.399 \pm 9.113E{-}16$	$1.133 \pm 0.00E + 00$	$1.038 \pm 4.556E{-}16$
SGD Regressor	$4.190 \pm 7.487E{-}03$	5.815 ± 0.025	$2.944 \pm 1.44E{-}02$	2.695 ± 0.013
AdaBoost	$2.495 \pm 1.770E{-}02$	3.148 ± 0.056	$1.613 \pm 2.77E{-}02$	1.477 ± 0.025
Random Forest	$2.120 \pm 3.845E{-}03$	2.374 ± 0.008	$1.199 \pm 4.02E{-}03$	1.097 ± 0.003
Gradient Boosting	**$2.106 \pm 1.886E{-}03$**	2.296 ± 0.002	$1.161 \pm 1.06E{-}03$	1.063 ± 0.0009
Linear SVR	$2.258 \pm 3.578E{-}03$	2.286 ± 0.015	$1.107 \pm 8.63E{-}03$	1.013 ± 0.007
MLP	$2.731 \pm 1.051E{-}01$	3.463 ± 0.182	$1.639 \pm 7.67E{-}02$	1.500 ± 0.070
SVR	$4.709 \pm 9.113E{-}16$	$6.793 \pm 1.823E{-}15$	$3.457 \pm 4.56E{-}16$	$3.165 \pm 9.113E{-}16$

(*continued*)

Table 4. (*continued*)

MODEL	RMSE	SMAPE	MAE	MASE
ExtraTrees Regressor	2.165 ± 6.019E–03	2.436 ± 0.011	1.213 ± 4.00E–03	1.110 ± 0.003
Bagging Regressor	2.162 ± 9.456E–03	2.473 ± 0.025	1.252 ± 1.18E–02	1.146 ± 0.010
Decision Tree Regressor	2.720 ± 3.550E–02	3.375 ± 0.025	1.725 ± 1.16E–02	1.579 ± 0.010
XGB	2.215 ± 4.556E–16	2.504 ± 4.556E–16	1.263 ± 0.00E + 00	1.156 ± 2.278E–16

Table 5. Results from the Wilcoxon Signed-Rank Test indicating the machine learning model better (+), worse (-) and equivalent (≈) at predicting daily COP data than Gradient Boosting.

MODEL	RMSE	SMAPE	MAE	MASE
Linear Regression	−	+	+	+
Ridge	−	−	−	−
Huber Regressor	−	−	−	−
SGD Regressor	−	−	−	−
AdaBoost	−	−	−	−
Random Forest	−	−	−	−
Linear SVR	−	+	−	−
MLP	−	−	−	−
SVR	−	−	−	−
ExtraTrees Regressor	−	−	−	−
Bagging Regressor	−	−	−	−
Decision Tree Regressor	−	−	−	−
XGB	−	−	−	−

Hypothesis test, the best 20 independent simulations for each of the interval weekly and daily COP separately for each performance measure are taken into account when rating the models. Figure 1 displays the test results based on RMSE, SMAPE, MAE, and MASE. Figure 1 shows that, when RMSE measure is taken into account, the Gradient Boosting model has the lowest mean rank (means best rank) among all the models. Although, Linear SVR model provides the best mean rank for SMAPE measure, the Linear regression model is statistically equivalent to the Linear SVR model (the mean rank difference falls short of the critical distance of 14.0). In both MAE and MASE measure, again linear regression model possesses the least mean rank. Therefore, the linear regression model is the overall statistically superior model for forecasting COP irrespective of forecasting interval i.e., weekly or daily.

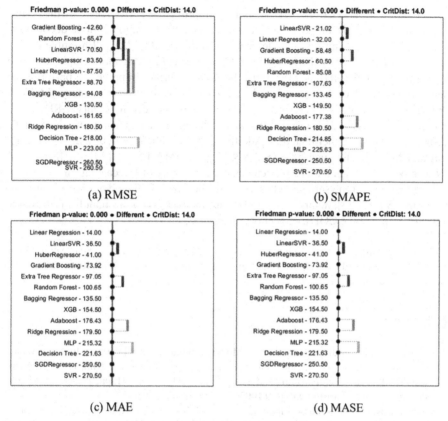

(a) RMSE   (b) SMAPE

(c) MAE   (d) MASE

Fig. 1. Ranking of ML Models using Friedman and Nemenyi Hypothesis test (a) RMSE, (b) SMAPE, (c) MAE and (d) MASE measure.

5   Conclusion and Future Scope

In this paper, a study has been conducted for statistical analysis of the performance of fourteen ML models in predicting the daily and weekly COP. The results show that Linear SVR, and linear regression, respectively, perform statistically well in weekly COP, and daily COP. Irrespective of interval of COP data, if one wants to employ a model then linear regression model is best suited for predicting weekly and daily COP time series based on Friedman Nemenyi Hypothesis test using RMSE, SMAPE, MAE and MASE accuracy measure.

This research uses state-of-the-art ML models to predict the COP time series as a preliminary investigation. Many enhancements can be made to improve forecasting accuracy. First, to determine the ML model parameters and apply them to COP time series, one can use evolutionary and swarm algorithms such as "Differential Evolution (DE)" [19, 20], "Particle Swarm Optimization (PSO)" and "Teaching Learning based Optimization (TLBO)" [21]. This may improve the performance of the resulting model. Second, decomposition techniques, such as "Variational mode decomposition (VMD)" [22], "Empirical mode decomposition (EMD)" [23], "Ensemble empirical mode decomposition (EEMD)" [24], "Complementary ensemble empirical mode decomposition (CEEMD)" [25] can also be used to further improve the performance measures. Third, deep learning models such as "Long short-term memory (LSTM)" [26], "Convolutional neural network (CNN)" [27], "Gated recurrent units (GRU)" [23], "Bidirectional LSTM (Bi-LSTM)" [28] can also be implemented to improve the model's predicting accuracy. Other than that, Additive and Multiplicative hybrid models (statistical and ML models) such as ETS-ANN [29], ARIMA-LSTM [29], ARIMA-SVM [29] can be used which may further enhance the accuracy of forecasting. In contrast to conventional crisp time series models, one can use fuzzy TSF models [30–35] that use traditional [30, 32, 33], neutrosophic [34], intuitionistic [31] or hesitant [35] fuzzy sets to further improve the COP forecasting performance.

Acknowledgements. This research paper is catalyzed and supported by the Science and Engineering Research Board (SERB), DST, Government of India with Grant No. CRG/2021/006122.

References

1. Nigam, S.: Single Multiplicative Neuron Model in Reinforcement Learning. In: Neha Yadav, Anupam Yadav, Jagdish Chand Bansal, Kusum Deep, Joong Hoon Kim, (ed.) Harmony Search and Nature Inspired Optimization Algorithms. AISC, vol. 741, pp. 889–895. Springer, Singapore (2019). https://doi.org/10.1007/978-981-13-0761-4_84
2. Jayaswal, R.: India's crude oil import bill soars 76% to $90.3 billion in April-September. Hindustan Times (2022). https://www.hindustantimes.com/india-news/indias-crude-oil-import-bill-soars-76-to-90-3-billion-in-aprilseptember-101666983745873.html
3. Cavalcanti, T., Jalles, J.T.: Macroeconomic effects of oil price shocks in Brazil and in the United States. Appl. Energy **104**, 475–486 (2013)
4. Bahrammirzaee, A.: A comparative survey of artificial intelligence applications in finance: artificial neural networks, expert system and hybrid intelligent systems. Neural Comput. Appl. **19**(8), 1165–1195 (2010)
5. Amano, A.: A small forecasting model of the world oil market. J. Policy Model. **9**(4), 615–635 (1987)
6. Drachal, K.: Forecasting crude oil real prices with averaging time-varying VAR models. Resour. Policy **74**, 102244 (2021)
7. Gulen, S.G.: Efficiency in the crude oil futures market. J. Energy Finance Dev. Elsevier **3**(1), 13–21 (1998)
8. Abramson, B., Finizza, A.: Probabilistic forecasts from probabilistic models: a case study in the oil market. Int. J. Forecast. **11**(1), 63–72 (1995)
9. Lanza, A., Manera, M., Giovannini, M.: Modeling and forecasting cointegrated relationships among heavy oil and product prices. Energy Econ. **27**, 831–848 (2005)
10. Cabedo, J.D., Moya, I.: Estimating oil price 'Value at Risk' using the historical simulation approach. Energy Econ. **25**, 239–253 (2003)
11. Morana, C.: A semiparametric approach to short-term oil price forecasting. Energy Econ. **23**, 325–338 (2001)

12. Høg, E., Tsiaras, L.: Density forecasts of crude-oil prices using option-implied and ARCH-type models. J. Futur. Mark. **31**(8), 727–754 (2011)

13. Abdullah, S.N., Zeng, X.: Machine learning approach for crude oil price prediction with artificial neural networks-quantitative (ANN-Q) model. In: The 2010 International Joint Conference on Neural Networks (IJCNN), pp. 1–8. IEEE (2010)

14. Abdel-Aal, R.E.: Univariate modeling and forecasting of monthly energy demand time series using abductive and neural networks. Comput. Ind. Eng. **54**, 903–917 (2008)

15. Xu, W., Wang, J., Zhang, X., Zhang, W., Wang, S.: A new hybrid approach for analysis of factors affecting crude oil price. In: Shi, Y., van Albada, G.D., Dongarra, J., Sloot, P.M.A. (eds.) ICCS 2007. LNCS, vol. 4489, pp. 964–971. Springer, Heidelberg (2007). https://doi.org/10.1007/978-3-540-72588-6_154

16. Karasu, S., Altan, A., Bekiros, S., Ahmad, W.: A new forecasting model with wrapper-based feature selection approach using multi-objective optimization technique for chaotic crude oil time series. Energy **212**, 118750 (2020)

17. Gupta, N., Nigam, S.: Crude oil price prediction using artificial neural network. Procedia Comput. Sci. **170**, 642–647 (2020)

18. Crude Oil WTI Futures Historical Prices. (n.d.). Investing.com India. https://in.investing.com/commodities/crude-oil-historical-data?interval_sec=daily

19. Karali, Y., Panigrahi, S., Behera, H.S.: A novel differential evolution based algorithm for higher order neural network training. J. Theor. Appl. Inf. Technol. **56**, 355–361 (2013)

20. Panigrahi, S., Behera, H.S.: Time series forecasting using differential evolution-based ANN modelling scheme. Arab. J. Sci. Eng. **45**, 11129–11146 (2020)

21. Panigrahi, S., Behera, H.S.: Nonlinear time series forecasting using a novel self-adaptive TLBO-MFLANN model. Int. J. Comput. Intell. Stud. **8**, 4–26 (2019)

22. Huang, Y., Deng, Y.: A new crude oil price forecasting model based on variational mode decomposition. Knowl.-Based Syst. **213**, 106669 (2021)

23. Wang, B., Wang, J.: Energy futures and spots prices forecasting by hybrid SW-GRU with EMD and error evaluation. Energy Econ. **90**, 104827 (2020)

24. Srivastava, M., Rao, A., Parihar, J.S., Chavriya, S., Singh, S.: What do the AI methods tell us about predicting price volatility of key natural resources: evidence from hyperparameter tuning. Resour. Policy **80**, 103249 (2023)

25. Abdollahi, H.: A novel hybrid model for forecasting crude oil price based on time series decomposition. Appl. Energy **267**, 115035 (2020)

26. Karasu, S., Altan, A.: Crude oil time series prediction model based on LSTM network with chaotic Henry gas solubility optimisation. Energy **242**, 122964 (2022)

27. Zou, Y., Yu, L., Tso, G.K., He, K.: Risk forecasting in the crude oil market: a multiscale convolutional neural network approach. Physica A **541**, 123360 (2020)

28. Zhang, C., Ma, H., Hua, L., Sun, W., Nazir, M.S., Peng, T.: An evolutionary deep learning model based on TVFEMD, improved sine cosine algorithm, CNN and BiLSTM for wind speed prediction, Energy, 124250 (2022)

29. Purohit, S.K., Panigrahi, S. Sethy, P.K., Behera. S. K.: Time series forecasting of price of agricultural products using hybrid methods. Appl. Artif. Intell. **35**(15) 1–19 (2021)

30. Panigrahi, S., Behera, H.S.: A study on leading machine learning techniques for high order fuzzy time series forecasting. Eng. Appl. Artif. Intell. **87**, 103245 (2020)

31. Pattanayak, R.M., Behera, H.S., Panigrahi, S.: A novel probabilistic intuitionistic fuzzy set based model for high order fuzzy time series forecasting. Eng. Appl. Artif. Intell. **99**, 104136 (2021)

32. Pattanayak, R.M., Panigrahi, S., Behera, H.S.: High-order fuzzy time series forecasting by using membership values along with Data and Support Vector Machine. Arab. J. Sci. Eng. **45**, 10311–10325 (2020)

33. Panigrahi, S., Behera, H.S.: A computationally efficient method for high order fuzzy time series forecasting. J. Theor. Appl. Inf. Technol. **96**, 7215–7226 (2018)
34. Pattanayak, R.M., Behera, H.S., Panigrahi. S.: A non-probabilistic neutrosophic entropy-based method for high-order fuzzy time-series forecasting. Arabian J. Sci. Eng. **47**(2), 1–23 (2021)
35. Pattanayak, R.M., Behera, H.S., Panigrahi, S.: A novel high order hesitant fuzzy time series forecasting by using mean aggregated membership value with support vector machine. Inf. Sci. **626**, 494–523 (2023)

Yolo and RetinaNet Ensemble Transfer Learning Detector: Application in Pavement Distress

Ravi Khatri[1(✉)] and Kuldeep Kumar[2]

[1] Dr B R Ambedkar National Institute of Technology Jalandhar, Barnala, Punjab, India
ravik.cs.21@nitj.ac.in
[2] National Institute of Technology Kurukshetra, Thanesar, India
kuldeepkumar@nitkkr.ac.in

Abstract. The significance of using roads for transportation has always been important and it plays a major role in the economy of a country. However, with the increase in population and urbanization, the number of vehicles on the roads as well as the length of roads have significantly increased. This has led to issues such as cracks and potholes caused by heavy rainfall and road construction materials which pose a serious risk to road users. Therefore, it is crucial to detect and maintain these defects. To address this issue, we developed a new method that uses ensemble transfer learning to identify road damages automatically. To improve the dataset, we increased the number of images and balanced the classes by augmenting the dataset resulting in 263,360 images across eight different categories. In addition, we improved the picture quality using various image processing techniques such as sharpening, histogram equalization, grey scaling, and smoothening. We trained and validated two pre-trained deep learning models over the dataset and combined them using an ensemble approach to create a final model. Our proposed model achieved an F1 score of 0.927, which suggests that it could serve as a benchmark for road damage detection.

Keywords: Pavement Distress · Deep Learning · Object detection · YoLo · Transfer Learning

1 Introduction

India, unfortunately, tops the list with 11% of the world's fatalities caused by road accidents [1]. These deaths predominantly occur between the ages of 18 and 60 [1], the most productive age group in the country, resulting in a significant loss of the country's most precious asset, its human resources. Road accidents stand at the eighth position among the major causes of death in the world, according to the World Health Organization [38]. The fatalities caused by road accidents not only incur treatment costs but also hinder the productivity of the deceased, impaired, and their family members. Multiple causes lead to such accidents, including over speeding, driver's negligence, bad road conditions, presence of cracks and potholes, weak vehicle standards, etc. [2]. However, the poor condition of roads with multiple defects is one of the major reasons for the high number of fatalities, which are caused by heavy rainfall, rising numbers of vehicles, the use of low-quality construction materials, and unstable soil.

© The Author(s), under exclusive license to Springer Nature Switzerland AG 2024
S. K. Panda et al. (Eds.): CoCoLe 2023, CCIS 1892, pp. 27–38, 2024.
https://doi.org/10.1007/978-3-031-56998-2_3

Efficient road maintenance and ensuring people's safety on the roads require the assessment of the extent of road damage. The extent of road damage may be assessed manually, semi-automatically, or fully automatically. Manual assessment involves assessors traveling slowly along the road, visually assessing the extent of defects, which is a time-consuming process and requires extensive human involvement. Semi-automated assessment involves automated systems collecting images of the road while moving rapidly, which are sent for manual defect detection, requiring human intervention. In fully automated road damage assessment, sophisticated sensors are installed on moving vehicles to gather images of the roads, which are sent for automated defect detection. However, fully automated systems are costly, and many countries lack the necessary funds to implement such systems. In contrast, mobile phone devices with impressive computation power and cameras provide an economical and efficient solution to this problem.

Roads and infrastructure are critical to national growth, driving economic growth. Natural disasters, environmental causes, human interference, inexpensive building materials, and normal wear and tear degrade roads, causing cracks, potholes, and other deformations that lead to accidents, human and animal deaths, and economic slowdowns. Identifying and repairing these issues is critical. After deep learning's excellent performance in image processing tasks, researchers have analyzed its ability to recognize road damage automatically. This paper presents all the significant and state-of-the-art methodologies implemented in this domain in the past decade (2012–2022), along with their advantages, limitations, and performance over key evaluation measures. Moreover, this study includes a proposed methodology for the problem domain. The study aims to help future scholars obtain a benchmark solution in this field.

Moreover, we discuss the multifold contribution of our study related to automated road damage assessment. The study comprises various techniques and methodologies, leading to the development of a cost-effective, efficient, and reliable system for automated road damage assessment.

1) The study processed an open dataset consisting of images of different road damages using standard image processing techniques and augmented the dataset to evade overfitting. This helped in developing a more robust dataset for the classification task.
2) The study proposed a transfer learning-based approach to handle the classification of such images and utilized sophisticated models like Yolov7 and RetinaNet to solve the task. These models helped in achieving better accuracy and precision in identifying damages from the input images.
3) The study created an ensemble model, which combined the outputs of different models, leading to a more effective and robust classification system.
4) The study compared the performance of models over key evaluation metrics like accuracy, precision, recall, F1-score, and time complexity, to determine the best approach. This helped in selecting the most suitable method for automated road damage assessment.

5) The study conducted an extensive analysis of the state-of-the-art techniques and methodologies employed in the field of automated road damage assessment, highlighting their strengths and limitations. This helped in identifying the gaps in the current research and potential future directions for development.
6) The study provided a comprehensive literature review of the research conducted in this domain over the past decade, aiding future researchers in gaining a deeper understanding of the current state-of-the-art.
7) The proposed methodology achieved competitive results, with the ensemble model exhibiting the highest accuracy, precision, recall, and F1-score, demonstrating the effectiveness of the approach.
8) Finally, the study contributes towards the development of a cost-effective, efficient, and reliable system for automated road damage assessment, which can aid in the timely maintenance of roads, reduce the occurrence of accidents, and ensure the safety of commuters. This has significant practical implications for the transportation industry and can improve the overall road infrastructure.

The rest of the paper is structured as follows: Sect. 2, discusses some of the key terms associated with this study. In Sect. 3, we thoroughly reviewed research articles related to the problem domain. Section 4 includes the proposed methodology and experimental setup. Section 5 contains the results. Finally, in Sect. 6, we concluded the paper and discussed the future scope.

2 Basic Concepts and Terminologies

This section summarizes basic concepts and terminologies such as Transfer Learning (TL) and image processing.

2.1 Transfer Learning

Due to the massive quantity of data and processing power needed, building a deep learning model from scratch is impracticable in many applications. Transfer learning deploys and fine-tunes public CNN models pretrained on natural images. Transfer learning lets you apply what you learned in one activity to a related one. A human detection model can be used to train a female identification model. Medicine, natural language processing, optical character recognition, recommendation systems, and others use this technology [3, 4]. It is of utmost importance to have a large dataset for deep learning algorithms to achieve high accuracy. However, in situations where the dataset is limited, transfer learning can be utilized to train neural networks with minimal data. In this study, the researchers explored transfer learning strategies and achieved promising results in the problem domain.

2.2 Image Processing

The goal of image processing is to create a high-quality output image that can be used as input to a machine learning model with minimal information loss while also reducing the amount of background noise in the original. Image processing techniques include spatial domain smoothing, frequency domain image sharpening, histogram equalization, thresholding, edge detection techniques such as Sobel operator, Roberts cross operator, canny edge detection, morphological image processing such as erosion and dilation, image restoration, image segmentation, and so on [5]. Because each approach is designed to perform a specific activity over an image, it is not necessary to use all of them. If the image quality was already good, performing image processing operations would be an unnecessary burden and waste of computing resources. These methods can be used only when the image quality is insufficient, and a specific result is required [6]. This study has utilized various image processing techniques to enhance the quality of images, filtering noise, resulting in better classification performance.

3 Literature Review

Pavement distress detection research is extensive. This section summarizes research methods. Table 1 lists all domain datasets. We investigated advanced detection algorithm machine learning methods for the above problem domain.

Du et al. [7] assessed road damage using a vast dataset of 45,788 photos from a camera placed on a dedicated vehicle traversing over 200 km at fewer than 80 km/h. The YOLO algorithm projected the fault position and category in each input image. They have not collected images utilizing mobile phones cost-effectively. They employed modern high-resolution cameras instead. The high-accuracy YOLO-based model detects without operator intervention.

Majidifard et al. [8] suggested utilizing a labelled collection of top-down and wide-view pictures for classification. They manually labelled street-view photographs using the Google API into nine road damage types. They also found that the YOLO-based model outperforms the Faster R-CNN model. They only have 7,237 photos. Google street-view photographs make their approach easier.

Patra et al. [9] employ a CNN-based model to detect potholes using Google API pictures. Six conventional models were compared to theirs. Their framework achieves 97.6% accuracy. AUC is also higher than the other models.

Goodfellow et al. [10] recommend using at least 5,000 photos per category for image classification. The following authors' picture gathering methods using the Google API have the advantage of easily accessible, free photographs, but they need time-consuming manual tagging of each image.

Maeda et al. [11] employed smartphones to capture pavement distress photographs. This study was groundbreaking and sparked future research. It divided Japan's road flaws into eight kinds. The Road Damage Dataset-2018 was made open-source for simple access. They created a mobile app to assess road damage instantly. Japanese townships adopted this application. At the US's 2018 IEEE Big Data Conference, numerous teams presented road damage type identification algorithms for the Big Data Cup. While providing unique and more accurate solutions than Maeda et al. [11], these teams used the same dataset.

Alfarrarjeh et al. [12] utilize Deep Learning to discover the entity of interest in an input image. They employed YOLO object detection. Japan Road Association damage categories were used to train the model.

Kluger et al. [13] modified the model presented by [11] by tweaking hyperparameters in their 2018 IEEE Big Data Cup solution. They showed how to improve the dataset. The 9,053-image dataset [10] was also modified.

Wang et al. [14] submitted their model again to the IEEE Big Data Cup challenge 2018. Object recognition utilized Faster R-CNN and SSD methods. These object detection models used VGG-16 and ImageNet pre-trained ResNet-101. Ensemble methods improve accuracy. Wang et al. [15] trained Faster R- CNN using [10]'s dataset to classify road damage. The aspect ratio and damage area were used to modify the settings. Before training, some data augmentation was done.

Angulo et al. [16] added Mexican and Italian photos to [11]. They collected 1, 803, 454 cell phone photographs. This massive dataset comes from public datasets and crowdsourced photos. Each image was individually labelled with location, damage type, and extent. This dataset trained conventional and DL-based models, which were compared. The LBP-Cascaded Classifier and RetinaNet and MobileNet DL models were employed.

Roberts et al. [17] used [11]'s mobile app to collect more Italian photos. They classified road damage kind and intensity. Biçici and Zeybek [18] employed UAV photogrammetry to construct point clouds for road distress detection, a high-accuracy, efficient, automated approach. SFM generated a high-density 3D model using UAV pictures. After that, a vertically based algorithm removed irrelevant environmental features from a 3D point cloud.

Zhang et al. [19] developed CrackNet, a CNN-based pavement crack detection technique. It contains over five layers and learns over one million parameters. It was trained on many three-dimensional road photos under different settings and tested satisfactorily. The major goal is cost-effective training using a gradient-based optimization algorithm. They studied Mini-batch Gradient Descent. Their model found pixel-level cracks. CrackNet is slow and has trouble detecting hairline cracks.

Another study [20] categorizes 500 photos using supervised deep CNN to train. Phones took the photos. With a threshold of 0.5, the Drop out methodology reduces overfitting of their suggested model. Silva and Lucena [21] used a machine learning model to detect concrete defects and automate with UAVs (unmanned aerial vehicles). This model was developed using VGG16, an open-source model.

Anand et al. [22] used Deep Neural Networks to detect potholes and fissures using texture and spatial information. They classify damaged roads using image texture. They integrated two datasets: grayscale mobile phone images and sensor images. They outperform other models.

Fan et al. [23] created a method for understanding crack structure without changing unprocessed pictures to analyze pavement conditions. The model used two cell phone picture datasets. Their model was compared to others. Their pavement texture handling is better. Unprocessed photos can teach the network.

Zhu et al. [24] used Faster R-CNN, YOLOv3, and YOLOv4 to locate road potholes. UAV data trained these. YOLOv3 predicted with 56.62% accuracy, outperforming the other approaches.

Zhang et al. [25] used CNN to detect pavement deterioration with cost-effective video data collecting. This work groups detectors. When two cracks were merged, the F1-score increased.

Guerrieri et al. [26] built a stone pavement damage dataset from numerous available sources. They trained a pavement damage model with DL and YOLOv3. Loss, precision, recall, and RSME measure performance. Several faults were found between 91.0% and 97.3%.

Wen et al. [27] trained a decent DL model on 2D and 3D pictures. The model's detection accuracy was 83.7% based on "interaction over union."

Table 1. Datasets available for road damage detection.

Dataset Name	Collected From (Location)	Size of the Dataset
CrackIT [28]	NK	< 1000
CrackTree200 [29]	NK	< 1000
SDNET2018 [30]	USA	< 1000
Crack500 [31]	USA	< 1000
GAPs v1 [32]	Germany	Between 1000–5000
GAPs v2 [33]	Germany	Between 1000–5000
Majidifard et al. [8]	USA	> 5000
Maeda et al. [11]	Japan	> 5000
Angulo et al. [16]	Italy, Japan, Mexico	> 5000
RDD-2020 [34]	India, Japan, Czech Republic	> 5000
Du et al. [7]	China	> 5000

4   Materials and Methods

This section will address dataset description, image processing and annotations utilized, data augmentation, model training, and building an ensemble of highest-ranking classifiers.

4.1   Selection and Description of the Dataset

We made use of the freely available RDD 2020 dataset [34]. There are 26336 images of roads from India, Japan, and the Czech Republic in the dataset. More than 31,000 instances of road damages are depicted in these photographs. The dataset contains labels for four types of damage: longitudinal cracks (D00), transverse cracks (D10), alligator cracks (D20), and potholes (D40), which were further subdivided to yield a total of eight classes, as shown in Fig. 1. Images of RDD2020 were captured by smartphones mounted in moving cars. This gives municipalities and transportation agencies a resource for developing low-cost methods of monitoring road pavement quality. Images are composed of three channels encoded in RGB color space and can be of various resolutions and dimensions. These images were saved in JPEG format at various sizes.

Damage type			Detail	Class name
Crack	Linear Crack	Longitudinal	Wheel-marked part	D00
			Construction joint part	D01
		Lateral	Equal interval	D10
			Construction joint part	D11
	Alligator Crack		Partial pavement, overall pavement	D20
Other Damage			Pothole	D40
			Cross walk blur	D43
			White line blur	D44

Fig. 1. Description of the RDD 2020 dataset

4.2 Image Preprocessing, Augmentation and Annotation

Because some of the images retrieved in the previous phase were of poor quality, some processing was required to improve the quality of the acquired images, resulting in better classification performance. We preprocessed and resized all the images to the same size to enhance the image quality and reduce noise in the dataset. Only files with a resolution greater than 450 * 450 pixels were chosen for the classification task and used a variety of techniques such as frequency domain sharpening, grayscaling of the input images, and histogram equalization. All these processes produced higher-quality images, which were then supplemented with additional training data to keep the model from overfitting. Used techniques such as horizontal and vertical image flipping, random zoom in and zoom out, affine transform and warping, gamma contrasting, random rotation in 45, 90, 270 degrees, image shearing, and grayscaling for augmentation. After augmentation, the total number of images in the eight classes increased to 2, 63, 360, assisting in avoiding the class imbalance that existed in the source dataset.

Further, a third-party web-based software RoboFlow [35] is used to manually annotate the images with a polygon box and assign it a class among our 8 classes, then exported the annotated dataset into various formats compatible with YoLo, TensorFlow, VOC, and RetinaNet.

4.3 Developing and Training the Deep Transfer Learning Networks

We deployed YoloV7 [36] and RetinaNet [37] and evaluated their performance based on accuracy and F1 score, before combining them to create the final structure. The YoLov7 model was trained by creating a custom yaml file that included the paths to the training and validation datasets as well as the number and names of the classes. The batch size was set to four with an image size of 416, and the training lasted 500 epochs. Other than the YoLo model, results from the RetinaNet pre-trained network were fed into a Fully Connected (FC) layer with 1024 neurons and the ReLU function, then through a dropout layer to the next FC layer with 512 neurons and the ReLU function, and finally to an FC layer with 8 output neurons and the SoftMax activation function. Replaced the final FC layer with a fresh FC layer with 8 output nodes, followed by a SoftMax activation layer, while transferring layers from existing models to our implementation. For all networks, used max-pooling, 30% dropout, and the ReLU function. Used the Adam optimizer to compile the networks, used categorical cross entropy loss, but only allowed learning of the upper layers of the neural networks, effectively suspending learning of the pretrained networks. The validation set contained 26, 336 original files, while the training set contained 2, 63, 360 augmented and annotated files. The transfer learning technique was developed in Python with 150 epochs and the Keras DL framework. The proposed approach is depicted in Fig. 2.

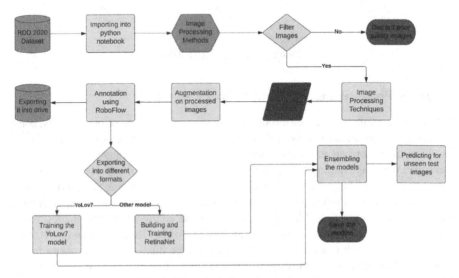

Fig. 2. Flow depiction of our approach

5   Results and Discussion

This study achieved the findings based on the evaluation methods mentioned in the previous section, which was accuracy and F1 score of the fitted models, after completing training and validation steps. Since the Harmonic Mean reduces the impact of outliers, we employ it. True positives and negatives are prioritized by using accuracy, while false positives and negatives are prioritized by using F1-score. At last, we developed an ensemble of YoLov7 and RetinaNet. Table 2 displays the ensemble model's classification results. It also represents the comparison of our proposed approach on some other state-of-the-art approaches.

It is of utmost importance to have a large dataset for deep learning algorithms to achieve high accuracy. However, in situations where the dataset is limited, transfer learning can be utilized to train neural networks with minimal data. In this study, the researchers explored transfer learning strategies and achieved promising results on the problem domain.

The classification of road damages is limited by the number of classes we selected for this study which was originally incorporated in the selected dataset. More types of damages can be incorporated for a robust study. This study utilized a publicly available dataset for this study which itself is a dependency upon the data acquisition methods. They collected images from various countries which pose different quality related challenges. We averted them by using several image processing and augmentation methods as the feature extraction is ultimately dependent over the quality of the images in an image-based classification task.

In summary, this study helps in understanding the role of transfer learning and the impact of the number of parameters on the accuracy of deep learning models. The study concludes that transfer learning is a better approach in situations where computational resources are limited, and the proposed ensemble model is a promising solution for road damage classification.

Table 2. Comparing the classification performance of the selected models on the validation dataset

Name of model	Achieved Accuracy	F1 score
RetinaNet	0.8527	0.7727
YoLov7	0.89	0.84
Ensemble Model	0.954	0.927
Wen et al. [27], 2022	0.83	–
Mei et al. [39], 2020	–	0.90
Stricker et al. [33], 2019	–	0.90

6 Conclusion and Future Scope

This work shows that a deep learning model for detecting pavement damage can achieve a high level of classification accuracy. There needs to be a large dataset so that a wide range of DL algorithms can be used to reduce errors and get a very high level of accuracy. But because initially did not have a lot of data, we switched to looking at a TL strategy [3, 4] that lets neural networks be trained with very little data. Also, we used image processing techniques along with our models, which helped us get the best results. In the future, the work could be expanded to include more types of damage, predict how bad the damage will be, work better in different types of lightning, and even be used on a moving vehicle. The suggested future steps will help make our system easier to understand and more resilient in general. A fully automated application for the public can also be made from our proposed framework.

References

1. Road Accidents in India, Ministry of Road Transport and Highways, Transport Research Wing, Govt. of India. https://morth.nic.in/sites/default/files/Road_Accidednt.pdf (2018)

2. Hatmoko, J., Setiadji, B., Wibowo, M.: Investigating causal factors of road damage: a case study. MATEC Web Conf. **258**, 02007 (2019). https://doi.org/10.1051/matecconf/201925 802007

3. Shin, H., Roth, H.R., Gao, M., Lu, L., Xu, Z., Nogues, I., et al.: Deep convolutional neural networks for computer-aided detection: CNN architectures, dataset characteristics and transfer learning. IEEE Trans. Med. Imaging **35**, 1285–1289 (2016)

4. Kermany, D.S., et al.: Identifying medical diagnoses and treatable diseases by image-based deep learning. Cell **172**(5), 1122–1131.e9 (2018)

5. Hegadi, R.: Image Processing: Research Opportunities and Challenges (2010)

6. Gonzalez, Rafael Digital image processing. New York, NY: Pearson. ISBN 978–0–13–335672–4. OCLC 966609831(2018)

7. Yuchuan, D., Pan, N., Zihao, X., Fuwen Deng, Y., Shen, H.K.: Pavement distress detection and classification based on YOLO network. Int. J. Pavement Eng. **22**(13), 1659–1672 (2020). https://doi.org/10.1080/10298436.2020.1714047

8. Majidifard, H., Jin, P., Adu-Gyamfi, Y., Buttlar, W.G.: Pavement image datasets: a new benchmark dataset to classify and densify pavement distresses. Transp. Res. Rec. **2674**, 328–339 (2020). https://doi.org/10.1177/0361198120907283

9. Patra, S., Middya, A.I., Roy, S.: PotSpot: participatory sensing based monitoring system for pothole detection using deep learning. Multimedia Tools Appl. **80**(16), 25171–25195 (2021). https://doi.org/10.1007/s11042-021-10874-4

10. Goodfellow, I., Bengio, Y., Courville, A.: Deep Learning, MIT press (2016). http://www.dee plearningbook.org

11. Maeda, H., Sekimoto, Y., Seto, T., Kashiyama, T., Omata, H.: Road damage detection and classification using deep neural networks with smartphone images. Comput. Aided Civ. Infrastruct. Eng. **33**, 1127–1141 (2018). https://doi.org/10.1111/mice.12387

12. Alfarrarjeh, A., Trivedi, D., Kim, S.H., Shahabi, C.: A deep learning approach for road damage detection from smartphone images, In: 2018 IEEE International Conference on Big Data (Big Data), IEEE, pp. 5201–5204 (2018). https://doi.org/10.1109/BigData.2018.8621899

13. Kluger, F., et al.: Region-based cycle-consistent data augmentation for object detection, In: 2018 IEEE International Conference on Big Data (Big Data), IEEE, pp. 5205–5211 (2018). https://doi.org/10.1109/BigData.2018.8622318

14. Wang, Y.J., Ding, M., Kan, S., Zhang, S., Lu, C.: Deep proposal and detection networks for road damage detection and classification. In: 2018 IEEE International Conference on Big Data (Big Data), IEEE, pp. 5224–5227 (2018). https://doi.org/10.1109/BigData.2018.8622599

15. Wang, W., Wu, B., Yang, S., Wang, Z.: Road damage detection and classification with faster R-CNN. In: 2018 IEEE International Conference on Big Data (Big Data), IEEE, pp. 5220–5223 (2018). https://doi.org/10.1109/BigData.2018.8622354

16. Angulo, A., Vega-Fernández, J.A., Aguilar-Lobo, L.M., Natraj, S., Ochoa-Ruiz, G.: Road damage detection acquisition system based on deep neural networks for physical asset management. In: Martínez-Villaseñor, L., Batyrshin, I., Marín-Hernández, A. (eds.) MICAI 2019. LNCS (LNAI), vol. 11835, pp. 3–14. Springer, Cham (2019). https://doi.org/10.1007/978-3-030-33749-0_1

17. Roberts, R., Giancontieri, G., Inzerillo, L., Di Mino, G.: Towards low-cost pavement condition health monitoring and analysis using deep learning. Appl. Sci. **10**, 319 (2020). https://doi.org/10.3390/app10010319

18. Biçici, S., Zeybek, M.: An approach for the automated extraction of road surface distress from a UAV-derived point cloud. Autom. Constr. **122**, 103475 (2021). https://doi.org/10.1016/j.aut con.2020.103475

19. Zhang, A., et al.: Automated pixel-level pavement crack detection on 3D asphalt surfaces using a deep-learning network. Comput. Aided Civ. Infrastruct. Eng. **32**, 805–819 (2017). https://doi.org/10.1111/mice.12297

20. Zhang, L., Yang, F., Zhang, Y.D., Zhu, Y.J.: Road crack detection using deep convolutional neural network. In: 2016 IEEE International Conference on Image Processing (ICIP). IEEE, pp. 3708–3712 (2016). https://doi.org/10.1109/ICIP.2016.7533052

21. Silva, W.R.L.d., Lucena, D.S.d.: Concrete cracks detection based on deep learning image classification. In: Multidisciplinary Digital Publishing Institute Proceedings, vol. 2, p. 489 (2018). https://doi.org/10.3390/ICEM18-05387

22. Anand, S., Gupta, S., Darbari, V., Kohli, S.: Crack-pot: autonomous road crack and pothole detection. In: 2018 Digital Image Computing: Techniques and Applications (DICTA), IEEE, pp. 1–6 (2018).https://doi.org/10.1109/DICTA.2018.8615819

23. Fan, Z., Wu, Y., Lu, J., Li, W.: Automatic pavement crack detection based on structured prediction with the convolutional neural network, arXiv preprint arXiv:1802.02208 (2018)

24. Zhu, J., Zhong, J., Ma, T, Huang, X., Zhang, W., Zhou, Y.: Pavement distress detection using convolutional neural networks with images captured via UAV, Autom. Constr. **133**, 103991 (2022). https://doi.org/10.1016/j.autcon.2021.103991

25. Zhang, C., Nateghinia, E., Miranda-Moreno, L.F., Sun, L.: Pavement distress detection using convolutional neural network : a case study in Montreal, Canada, Int. J. Transportation Sci. Technol. **11**(2), 298–309 (2022)https://doi.org/10.1016/j.ijtst.2021.04.008

26. Guerrieri, M., Parla, G.: Flexible and stone pavements distress detection and measurement by deep learning and low-cost detection devices. Eng. Fail. Anal. **141**, 106714 (2022). https://doi.org/10.1016/j.engfailanal.2022.106714

27. Wen, T., et al.: Automated pavement distress segmentation on asphalt surfaces using a deep learning network. Int. J. Pavement Eng. **24**(2), 2027414 (2022). https://doi.org/10.1080/10298436.2022.2027414

28. Oliveira, H., Correia, P.L.: CrackIT—an image processing toolbox for crack detection and characterization. In: 2014 IEEE International Conference on Image Processing (ICIP), IEEE, pp. 798–802 (2014). https://doi.org/10.1109/ICIP.2014.7025160

29. Zou, Q., Cao, Y., Li, Q., Mao, Q., Wang, S.: CrackTree: automatic crack detection from pavement images. Pattern Recog. Lett. **33**(3), 227–238 (2012). https://doi.org/10.1016/j.patrec.2011.11.004

30. Dorafshan, S., Thomas, R.J., Maguire, M.: SDNET2018: an annotated image dataset for non-contact concrete crack detection using deep convolutional neural networks. Data Brief **21**, 1664–1668 (2018). https://doi.org/10.1016/j.dib.2018.11.015

31. Yang, F., Zhang, L., Yu, S., Prokhorov, D., Mei, X., Ling, H.: Feature pyramid and hierarchical boosting network for pavement crack detection. IEEE Trans. Intell. Transp. Syst. **21**, 1525–1535 (2020). https://doi.org/10.1109/TITS.2019.2910595

32. Eisenbach, M., et al.: How to get pavement distress detection ready for deep learning? a systematic approach. In: International Joint Conference on Neural Networks (IJCNN), pp. 2039–2047 (2017). https://doi.org/10.1109/IJCNN.2017.7966101

33. Stricker, R., Eisenbach, M., Sesselmann, M., Debes, K., Gross, H.M.: Improving visual road condition assessment by extensive experiments on the extended gaps dataset. In: International Joint Conference on Neural Networks (IJCNN), pp. 1–8 (2019). https://doi.org/10.1109/IJCNN.2019.8852257

34. Arya, D. Maeda, H., Ghosh, S.K., Toshniwal, D., Mraz, A., Sekimoto, Y.: Deep learning-based road damage detection and classification for multiple countries, Autom. Construct. **132**, 103935 (2021). ISSN 0926–5805.https://doi.org/10.1016/j.autcon.2021.103935

35. Roboflow: Give Your Software the Power to See Objects in Images and Video. https://roboflow.com

36. Wang, C.Y., Bochkovskiy, A., Liao, H.Y.: YOLOv7: trainable bag-of-freebies sets new state-of-the-art for real-time object detectors. https://doi.org/10.48550/arXiv.2207.02696 (2022)

37. Lin, T.Y., Goyal, P., Girshick, R., He, K., Dollár, P.: Focal Loss for Dense Object Detection. In: IEEE Transactions on Pattern Analysis and Machine Intelligence, vol. 42, 2, pp. 318–327 (2020). https://doi.org/10.1109/TPAMI.2018.2858826
38. https://www.who.int/data/gho/data/themes/topics/topic-details/GHO/road-traffic-mortal ity#:~:text=Road%20traffic%20injuries%20are%20currently,safety%20in%20a%20holi stic%20manner
39. Mei, Q., Gül, M.: A cost effective solution for pavement crack inspection using cameras and deep neural networks. Constr. Build. Mater. **256**, 119397 (2020). https://doi.org/10.1016/j. conbuildmat.2020.119397

Stock Market Prediction Performance Analysis by Using Machine Learning Regressor Techniques

Neelamadhab Padhy[1]([✉]), Srinivasarao Dharmireddi[2],
Dushmanta Kumar Padhy[1], R. Saikrishna[3], and K. Srujan Raju[4]

[1] Department of Computer Science and Engineering, GIET University, Gunupur,
Odisha, India
dr.neelamadhab@giet.edu
[2] MasterCard Cybersecurity Department, st.Louis, MO, USA
srini.Dharmireddi@mastercard.com
[3] Department of CSE, CMR Technical Campus, Hyderabad, Telangana, India
[4] Training and Placement, CMR Technical Campus, Secunderabad, Telangana, India

Abstract. Stock market prediction is a highly popular topic among investors, traders, and financial analysts. It involves predicting the future direction of stock prices, which can help investors make decisions about buying or selling stocks. One method of predicting stock prices is through sentiment analysis. Sentiment analysis has become an increasingly popular method for predicting stock prices in the stock market. Stock market forecasting is vital nowadays. In this study, machine learning techniques are used to predict the stock market and are proven effective. The main objective of this study is to enhance the accuracy of machine learning regressor algorithms. This article uses the state of the art of five different machine learning regressors. These are namely Bagging Regressor, XGB Regressor, LGBM Regressor, Hist Gradient Boosting Regressor, and AdaBoost Regressor. Of these five algorithms, Bagging Regressor outperforms the other four, obtaining better R-square and RMSE values. This study shows that the experimental results obtained are reliable. Bagging Regressor produced the R-square value of 99.9774 and RMSE value of 8.305, taking a time of 0.185652733 ms. It summarizes the findings from the experiments conducted and suggests that the Bagging regressor performed well in terms of accuracy.

Keywords: Bussiness Forecasting · Stock Market · Machine Learning Techniques · Regression

1 Introduction

The stock market is the domain in which company shares are traded. Due to the nonlinear nature of the stock market, it is a tedious job to predict the stock market. Machine learning techniques made it possible to predict the stock market.

© The Author(s), under exclusive license to Springer Nature Switzerland AG 2024
S. K. Panda et al. (Eds.): CoCoLe 2023, CCIS 1892, pp. 39–50, 2024.
https://doi.org/10.1007/978-3-031-56998-2_4

Machine learning regression algorithms are very powerful in forecasting the stock market [12]. It is a process of predicting future stock prices based on past prices. This kind of prediction is very useful for investors to gain maximum profit. This prediction can be done using two approaches: Technical and Fundamental analysis. The technical analysis concentrates on historical data, and the fundamental analysis concentrates on the company's financial conditions [11].

Bagging is an ensemble algorithm that conclaves predictions from different decision trees. It is a meta-estimator. It can be used to avoid variance of decision trees, and it applies randomization to do so.

XGBoost provides a powerful way for introducing supervised regression models. This method concentrates on the difference between actual values and predicted values. This method calculates how predicted values are close to actual values. It is an ensemble learning method. LGBM is an extension of the gradient boosting algorithm as it provides a way for automatic feature selection. LGBM increases the speed even for large data sets also. LGBM regressor is a very effective machine learning algorithm for predicting the stock market. The research [1] provides a fusion framework for predicting financial market direction using ensemble models and technical indicators. While individual models and indicators may have shortcomings, the authors contend that combining them can increase predicting accuracy. The proposed framework combines four different ensemble models (Random Forest, Gradient Boosting, AdaBoost, and XGBoost) with six technical indicators (MACD, Relative Strength Index (RSI), Stochastic Oscillator (SO), Commodity Channel Index (CCI), Average Directional Index (ADX), and Bollinger Bands (BB). The writers use these models and indicators to forecast the direction of the S&P-500 Index. The framework is tested on data from 2000 to 2019, and its performance is compared to that of individual models and metrics. They discover that the fusion framework surpasses individual models and indicators in terms of accuracy, precision, recall, and F1 score. The study [14] provides a feature enhancement-based stock prediction technique to increase stock market prediction accuracy by improving the features employed in the prediction process. The proposed technique can help investors and traders make better judgments by offering more accurate stock price predictions. The suggested solution employs a combination of feature engineering techniques and machine learning algorithms to improve the predictive potential of the features employed in the prediction process. The authors also offer a novel feature selection method that considers stock price data's non-linear and temporal nature. Hist gradient boosting regressor is a powerful algorithm for predicting the stock market. The research in [15] proposes a novel intelligent fusion model for stock market prediction that combines portfolio selection and machine learning techniques. The model intends to solve the difficulties of stock market forecasting, such as volatility, uncertainty, and complexity. To forecast stock values, the proposed model employs a combination of feature selection approaches, machine learning algorithms, and portfolio optimization methods. According to the authors, the model exceeds previous methods in terms of accuracy and efficiency. Adaboost regressor can also be used in predicting the stock market. The studies in [1,4], and the current study proved that the Adaboost regressor is an effective algorithm for predicting the stock market. All five algorithms mentioned above are effective in predicting the stock market. The current study proves it with accurate results discussed in Sect. 4.

Major Contributions

- We have applied the Yahoo data set from May 2000 to June 2019 to five different regression algorithms.
- Experimental results revealed that the Bagging regressor is very accurate.

In this article, there are totally five sections. In section two literature of recent papers has been reviewed, and the Literature outcome has been analyzed. Literature gap and Research questions have been added to section two. Section three discusses the proposed model and the data set used. In section four, Experimental results are discussed, and solutions to research questions are discussed. In section five, we concluded our work and mentioned about future work.

2   Literature Review

In this section literature of previous articles has been analyzed. The implementation results of various algorithms in the past articles have been analyzed. We found that there are not much literature available that predicts the stock market using a huge data set. The drawback found in the previous articles is the volatility of the market and noise in the data. There is a need to implement regression algorithms for huge data set and nullify the noise present in the data set.

Krollner et al. [5] have verified work related to machine learning and artificial intelligence techniques in predicting the stock market. The author [6] has noted that neural networks can also be used in stock market forecasting. The author has also found that various publications are trying to forecast stock within one day by using data that are available. Authors have noticed that there is a lack of literature to depend on. Yue et al. [7] used regression to find out the frequency of stock market changes and thereby tried to improve the forecasting of the stock market. The author has found a 6.33 unit difference in stock price change. The R-square value obtained is 0.09243. Kim et al. [8] use SVM to forecast stock prices. The study showed that result accuracy depends on parameters provided to the SVM model. The author has compared the outputs of the SVM model with the outputs of the Neural Network model and found that SVM produced better results.

Ballings et al. [9] have compared the outputs of AdaBoost, Random Forest algorithms with SVM, KNN Logistic regression, and ANN. The authors have used a European company's price as a data set. The final results showed that the Random forest produced better results than the remaining. Kadiyala et al. [3] have implemented Bagging, Random forest, and Extremely randomized trees. The bagging regressor produced an R-square value of 0.595, the Random forest produced an R-square value of 0.597, and Extremely randomized trees produced an R-square value of 0.589. Out of three algorithms, Random forest proved better than the other two algorithms. Pathak et al. [10] have implemented Random forest, SVM, KNN, and Logistic regression algorithms. The author proved that Random forest has more accuracy in predicting the stock market. Padhi et al. [13] have described stock market prediction techniques utilizing an ensemble-based conglomerate model with technical indicators.

2.1   Literature Outcome

Table 1 shows the literature outcome. In the literature outcome, the authors have analyzed the results obtained for various algorithms and compared them with the R-square and RMSE (Root Mean Square Error) values obtained in this study. The results show the R-square and RMSE values obtained in the study are better compared to previous studies. The parameters used are R-square and RMSE. The source used are [1–3], and [4].

In the proposed model, the authors have used five algorithms that have produced accurate results even when the data is noisy and volatile. The authors used 20 years of data, and the Bagging regressor produced better results compared to the other four algorithms.

Table 1. Literature outcome

Algorithms	R-Square	RMSE	Source
LR	0.93	5.8523	Padhy et al. [1]
DT Regressor	0.92	6.4070	Padhy et al. [1]
RF Regressor	0.9179	6.5505	Padhy et al. [1]
Catboost Regressor	0.9852	2.7784	Padhy et al. [1]
XGB Regressor	0.9427	5.5745	Padhy et al. [1]
AdaBoosst Regressor	0.9511	5.0555	Padhy et al. [1]
RF	0.9537	0.0058	Dhupia and Bhawna [2]
LR	0.9335	0.0067	Dhupia and Bhawna [2]
RNN	0.9433	0.0365	Dhupia and Bhawna [2]
Bagging	0.595	8.030	Kadiyala et al. [3]
Random forest	0.597	7.963	Kadiyala et al. [3]
Gradient Boosting	0.561	9.586	Kadiyala et al. [3]
Light Gradient Boosting	0.541	10.171	Kadiyala et al. [4]
Extreme Gradient Boosting	0.567	8.480	Kadiyala et al. [4]
Adaptive Boosting	0.433	11.209	Kadiyala et al. [4]

2.2   Literature Gap

1. Literature available in stock market prediction confirms that live testing in stock price prediction is tedious.

Table 2. Proposed Model

Algorithms	R-Square	RMSE
Bagging Regressor	99.9774	8.305
XGB Regressor	99.9713	9.374
LGBM Regressor	99.9696	9.644
Hist Gradient Boosting Regressor	99.9671	10.035
AdaBoost Regressor	99.7668	26.729

2. Literature gap in this scenario is finding various algorithms and methodologies suitable for real-time.
3. Most of the literature talks about prediction based on previous prices in the stock market.
4. Most literature reviews discuss prediction based on the available data set. There is no guarantee of accuracy if these data sets are noisy and volatile. This is the major literature gap found by the authors of this study.

2.3 Research Questions

- **Research Question 1**: Is Bagging Regressor producing better results with accurate R-square and RMSE values?
- **Research Question 2**: Can the algorithms used in the study produce accurate predictions for the stock market, and can these be used for live testing in stock market prediction?
- **Research question 3**: If the data set is large, like 50 years data set, then there is a possibility of data imbalance, and how these data imbalance, underfit and over-fit problems have been resolved in the current study?

3 Proposed Model

The proposed system is highly flexible when compared to the existing system. Not all existing systems support huge volumes of data; as we know, stock analysis needs huge data, and hence proposed system easily tackles these situations by handling large volumes of data without hesitation. This system's other main goal is to analyze and accurately predict the data, which cannot be found in other systems. Not only with large data sets, it works well with small and medium data sets. In the proposed model, the Data sources have been explored and considered a huge data set. Once the data set is ready, the authors processed the data and extracted features to apply machine learning techniques like Bagging Regressor, XGB Regressor, LGBM Regressor, Hist Gradient Boosting Regressor, and AdaBoost Regressor. The three research questions have been applied to the machine learning techniques, and the authors have used R-Square and RMSE for performance evaluation. The authors analyzed the experimental results and found that Bagging Regressor has outperformed all remaining four algorithms. The authors have rigorously examined the stock market data while implementing five algorithms.

Authors have applied data pre-processing in an effective way to the data set, and features have been selected from the data set. The authors have applied five algorithms to the data set of 20 years, and from the data set, the authors successfully produced accurate results for the five algorithms. The results have been compared with the previous studies mentioned in the literature outcome in Sect. 2.1, and it has been proved that the proposed model produces very accurate results for the prediction of the stock market. Figure 1 shows our proposed model.

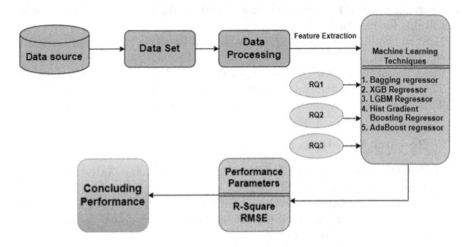

Fig. 1. Proposed Model

3.1   Data Set

For our primary experiment, we have downloaded the S & P-500 data set of each transaction day from the Yahoo/Finance portal. The period of data set available for the experiment is from May 2000 to June 2019, with 4816 records with preexisting features like Open, High, Low, Close, and Volume.

4   Experimental Results and Discussion

4.1   XGB Regressor

In the XGB Regressor algorithm, We have calculated similarity scores first. The data set has been converted to a data structure, namely Dmatrix. Next is to calculate the gain, and we found the difference between gain and gamma. Finally, the output value has been calculated using the following formula. where y_i is the observed value and p_i is the predicted value.

4.2   Bagging Regressor

In Bagging Regressor, We have considered multiple observations and features in 20 years stock data set. Then selected random sample without replacement. We have chosen a subset of selected features and created a model. While creating a model, observations are taken into consideration. Now the features offering the best results are filtered. These steps are repeated until the best prediction is obtained. Samples are drawn from the original distribution P; the following equation holds if P is discrete.

4.3   LGBM Regressor

The optimization of the features selected is carried out in LGBM Regressor. We have incorporated automatic feature selection, focusing on considering large gradient values.

For LGBM Regression, we use the following equation to make a prediction

4.4   HistGradient Boosting Regressor

We have prepared a feature histogram while analyzing the data set, thereby attaining more speed and accuracy in prediction.

4.5   AdaBoost Regressor

We have initialized the data point having the same weight as the data points. Then use these data points as input to our model created. Finally, after several iterations, we get accurate results. The following equation is used to predict using AdaBoost Regressor.

4.6   Discussion on Results

The results obtained prove that out of five algorithms, Bagging Regressor has outperformed other algorithms with an R-square value of 99.9774, an RMSE value of 8.305, and by taking the time of 0.185652733 ms. The parameters used in the implementation are R-Square and RMSE. The authors have used 20 years data set in the implementation.

In this study, We obtained experimental results for R-square as shown in Fig. 2. RMSE values are shown in Fig. 3, and the time taken by each algorithm is shown in Fig. 4. In Bagging Regressor, we have taken random subsets from the data set samples. These samples and features extracted are taken into consideration during estimation. Research question 1 was also answered through these results.

Quartiles divide a data set into four equal parts. The first quartile (Q1) is the value below which 25%

Using the quartile values we calculated, the box plot for the given data set would look like the following Fig. 5.

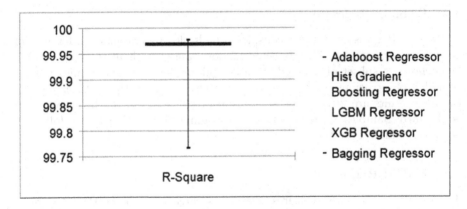

Fig. 2. R Square

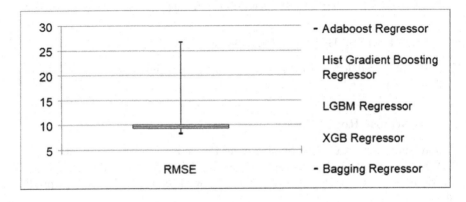

Fig. 3. RMSE

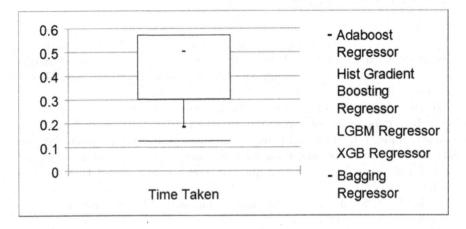

Fig. 4. Time Taken

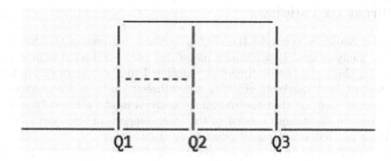

Fig. 5. Box plot

The whiskers would extend from Q1 to the minimum value (99.7668) and from Q3 to the maximum value (99.9774). Since there are no outliers in this data set, no points would be plotted beyond the whiskers.

4.7   Solutions to Research Questions

Solution to the Research Question 1
In this study, we have implemented five algorithms, and Bagging Regressor has produced extremely accurate results. Table 3 shows experimental results obtained in the implementation.

Table 3. Experimental Results

Algorithms	R-Square	RMSE	Time Taken
Bagging Regressor	99.9774	8.305	0.185652733
XGB Regressor	99.9713	9.374	0.302654982
LGBM Regressor	99.9696	9.644	0.126618862
Hist Gradient Boosting Regressor	99.9671	10.035	0.573096275
AdaBoost Regressor	99.7668	26.729	0.5036273

Solution to Research Question 2
This study's experimental results prove that the bagging regressor is a good machine-learning algorithm for predicting the stock market. The experimental results accuracy in the current study recommends that these five algorithms can be used in live testing for stock market prediction.

Solution to Research Question 3
In this study, we overcome the data imbalance factor by using 20 years of data set. Initially, attempts were made to use 50 years of the data set and found some under-fit and over-fit situations in the results. Then, the authors decided to use 20 years of data set and finally got accurate results. Care has also been taken to avoid volatility and noise in the data should not affect the result's accuracy.

5   Threat to Validity

Construct validity refers to the degree to which a measure (in this case, a sentiment analysis model) is actually measuring the construct it is intended to measure (in this case, the sentiment or emotional tone of the stock market).In the context of stock market prediction for sentiment analysis, construct validity would involve ensuring that the sentiment analysis model accurately measures and analyzes the sentiment related to the stock market and not just sentiment related to a particular company, industry, or news event.

Here are a few ways to enhance construct validity in stock market prediction for sentiment analysis: Use a diverse set of data sources: By using a variety of news sources, social media platforms, and other sources of data, you can ensure that the sentiment analysis model is not biased toward a particular type of data. Train the model using a representative data set. The training data set used to develop the sentiment analysis model should be diverse and representative of the entire stock market. This will help ensure that the model can accurately capture the range of sentiment related to the stock market. Validate the model using independent data: Once the sentiment analysis model has been trained, it's important to validate its accuracy using independent data. This can help ensure that the model is actually measuring the intended construct. Use expert knowledge to validate results: It's also important to validate the results of the sentiment analysis model using expert knowledge. This can involve comparing the model's predictions to expert opinions and insights related to the stock market. By taking these steps, you can enhance the construct validity of the sentiment analysis model and improve the accuracy and reliability of stock market predictions. There are several threats to validity that could impact the accuracy and reliability of stock market prediction using sentiment analysis. Here are a few:

1. **Sampling Bias:** The sentiment analysis model may not be representative of the entire population or may have a biased sample. For example, it may be trained on data from specific sources or time periods, which may not be representative of the current market conditions.
2. **Text Processing Issues:** The model may not accurately interpret and analyze the text used in stock market prediction. This can happen when the language used in financial news or social media is complex, sarcastic, or uses jargon.
3. **Contextual Limitations:** Sentiment analysis may not be able to consider the context of the market, such as news events or changes in economic indicators. The sentiment analysis model may also be unable to account for the impact of multiple factors affecting the stock market.
4. **Limited Data:** The sentiment analysis model may not have enough data to make accurate predictions. This can happen when there are limited sources of data or when the data used to train the model is too small or too narrow in scope.
5. **Model Selection Bias:** The choice of sentiment analysis model may also impact the validity of the stock market prediction. Different models have

different strengths and weaknesses; selecting the wrong model can lead to inaccurate predictions.

6   Conclusion and Future Work

In this study, we implemented five stock market prediction algorithms: Bagging Regressor, XGB Regressor, LGBM Regressor, Hist Gradient Boosting Regressor, and AdaBoost Regressor. The experimental results produced accurate results for all five algorithms, and the Bagging regressor produced very accurate results. The parameters used are R-square and RMSE. The authors have used 20 years of data sets; most are volatile and noisy. Even then, the results obtained are very accurate. The authors have successfully answered all three research questions framed. Authors are looking to achieve the same with classification algorithms in the future. We conclude that Bagging Regressor is achieving better results in comparison to the other four algorithms, namely XGB Regressor, LGBM Regressor, Hist Gradient Boosting Regressor, and AdaBoost Regressor. The bagging regressor has an R-square value of 99.9774, an RMSE value of 8.305, and the time taken is 0.185652733 ms. Our model's prediction results have been shown in Table 2.

Future Work: Future scope of this study is to incorporate more parameters in the implementation. In the near future, we will implement the classification algorithms to achieve the same accuracy. Once more parameters are incorporated, better estimation of stock prices can be expected. The future scope of this study also includes the incorporation of sentiment analysis in this scenario. Once sentiment analysis is incorporated, the understanding and confidence of investors will increase.

References

1. Padhi, D.K., Padhy, N., Bhoi, A.K., Shafi, J., Ijaz, M.F.: A fusion framework for forecasting financial market direction using enhanced ensemble models and technical indicators. Mathematics **9**(21), 2646 (2021)
2. Dhupia, B.: Ensemble machine learning modelling for medium to long term energy consumption forecasting. Turk. J. Comput. Math. Educ. (TURCOMAT) **12**, 459–463 (2021)
3. Kadiyala, A., Kumar, A.: Applications of python to evaluate the performance of bagging methods. Environmental Progress & Sustainable Energy, Wiley Online Library (2018)
4. Kadiyala, A., Kumar, A.: Applications of Python to evaluate the performance of decision tree-based boosting algorithms. Environ. Prog. Sustain. Energy **37**, 618–623 (2017)
5. Krollner, B., Vanstone, B., Finnie, G.: Financial time series forecasting with machine learning techniques: a survey. In: Proceedings of the 18th European Symposium on Artificial Neural Networks (ESANN 2010) (2010)

6. Lam, M.: Neural network techniques for financial performance prediction: integrating fundamental and technical analysis. Decis. Support Syst. **37**(4), 567–581 (2004)
7. Xu, S.Y., Berkely, C.U.: Stock price forecasting using information from Yahoo finance and Google trend. UC Brekley (2014)
8. Kim, K.: Financial time series forecasting using support vector machines. Dongguk University, Department of Information Systems (2003)
9. Ballings, M., Van den Poel, D., Hespeels, N., Gryp, R.: Evaluating multiple classifiers for stock price direction prediction. Expert Syst. Appl. **42**(20), 7046–7056 (2015)
10. Pathak, A., Pathak, S.: Study of machine learning algorithms for stock market prediction. Int. J. Eng. Res. Technol. **9**, 295–300 (2020)
11. Niranjan, L., Priyatham, M.M.: Lifetime ratio improvement technique using special fixed sensing points in wireless sensor network. Int. J. Pervasive Comput. Commun. **17**(5), 483–508 (2021). https://doi.org/10.1108/IJPCC-10-2020-0165
12. Niranjan, L., Manoj Priyatham, M.: An energy efficient and lifetime ratio improvement methods based on energy balancing. Int. J. Eng. Adv. Technol. (IJEAT) 9(1S6) (2019). ISSN: 2249–8958
13. Padhi, D.K., Padhy, N.: Prognosticate of the financial market utilizing ensemble-based conglomerate model with technical indicators. Evol. Intell. **14**, 1035–1051 (2021)
14. Padhi, D.K., Padhy, N., Bhoi, A.K.: Feature enhancement-based stock prediction strategy to forecast the fiscal market. In: Reddy, K.A., Devi, B.R., George, B., Raju, K.S., Sellathurai, M. (eds.) Proceedings of Fourth International Conference on Computer and Communication Technologies. LNNS, vol. 606, pp. 551–559. Springer, Singapore (2023). https://doi.org/10.1007/978-981-19-8563-8_53
15. Padhi, D.K., Padhy, N., Bhoi, A.K., Shafi, J., Yesuf, S.H.: An intelligent fusion model with portfolio selection and machine learning for stock market prediction. Comput. Intell. Neurosci. **2022** (2022)

Nearest Neighbor and Decision Tree Based Cloud Service QoS Classification

Soumya Snigdha Mohapatra[1(✉)], Rakesh Ranjan Kumar[1], and Sujit Bebortta[2]

[1] Department of Computer Science and Engineering, C.V. Raman Global University, Mahura, Bhubaneswar 752045, India
soumyasnigdha.praharaj@gmail.com, rakeshranjan@cgu-odisha.ac.in
[2] Department of Computer Science, Ravenshaw University, Cuttack 753003, Odisha, India

Abstract. Cloud services can be categorized based on their Quality of Service (QoS) parameters. Service recommendations can help users to select the best services among other alternatives. Mostly the recommendations are done either manually or rule-based. However, such recommendations also can be done using Machine Learning (ML) based approaches based on past collected data and user experience. In this work, we have performed classification to categorize cloud services based on the QoS parameters using a public data set. A comparison between widely accepted classifiers such as 1) Decision Tree (DT) and K Nearest Neighborhood (KNN) is carried out with standard performance measures such as Overall Accuracy (OA), Average Accuracy (AA), and Kappa coefficient. The preliminary result suggests that the KNN classifier is strongly suggested as compared to the DT approach for the cloud service QoS classification problem.

Keywords: Cloud Service · QoS · Classifier · KNN · Decision Tree · clustering · K Means

1 Introduction

With the exponential expansion of service computing, cloud computing has emerged as a new paradigm that has transformed the delivery of computing and service solutions. A method of providing IT-enabled capabilities to users in the form of elastic and scalable "services," cloud computing lets users access resources, platforms, and applications without having to own and maintain the technology [30]. Several of the Services perform functions that are analogous to one another or even the same. Users will be presented with a large selection of available services that are suitable to meet their requirements if they select services according to the purpose they serve. People choose their needs according to the non-functional quality of the services that they receive (QoS). QoS is not only an important indicator for interactions between customers and service providers, but it is also important when choosing a cloud service. There is a

S. K. Panda et al. (Eds.): CoCoLe 2023, CCIS 1892, pp. 51–64, 2024.
https://doi.org/10.1007/978-3-031-56998-2_5

complex challenge that has to be solved regarding how to choose the best suitable service from a huge number of services that satisfy functional requirements and the QoS value of cloud services. It is important to explore how to effectively and rapidly find cloud services that fulfill the requirements, and improving the performance of cloud service classification is an emerging area of interest in the current research [2].

These days, a huge number of businesses, like Amazon, IBM, Microsoft, and Google, offer multiple cloud computing services to their customers. These services garner increased interest because they offer inexpensive to access, dependable high-performance hardware and software resources, avoidance of security problems and maintenance costs, and scalability. Additionally, the pay-as-you-go element of cloud computing technology gives service providers the ability to offer their services in a variety of configurations in accordance with the service level agreements that their customers have made (SLA) [18]. How to choose the most appropriate service from a multitude of services that satisfy functional requirements based on the QoS value of cloud services is a challenge that must be resolved. Although the ranking of cloud services was performed mostly, their classification can give more clues to the user for service selection. Cloud service classification can be carried out using their QoS attributes. Several such methods have been proposed in the last decade including machine learning algorithms that proved to be efficient to address the QoS classification problem. From the existing research, it has been observed that there is a scope for exploration of different ML approaches like KNN, DT, Random Forest, Naive Bayes, etc. [16,17,19,21]. that can increase the accuracy of cloud service QoS classification problems. We have experimented with KNN and DT. The algorithms like decision trees and K-nearest neighbors (KNN) are often used for cloud computing service selection because they efficiently handle complex decision-making processes. Decision trees are basic models that may assess many factors and their relationships to help you make smart decisions. Decision trees may analyze performance, reliability, cost, and security to choose the best cloud service based on defined criteria. The non-parametric KNN approach categorizes occurrences based on their proximity to recognized data points. KNN can detect comparable cloud services based on their attributes to pick them. This enables customers to choose services with traits that are similar to ones they have previously used or preferred. Decision tree and KNN algorithms assist users choose a cloud computing service by considering their requirements and preferences. However, for the considered dataset KNN outperformed the DT algorithm in terms of its prediction efficacy. This research includes the following steps to find the best classifier for QoS aware cloud service classification problem.

– Preparation of data by K-means clustered annotation using QoS attributes to assign synthetic class labels for each cloud service.
– Implementation of state-of-art classifiers such as KNN, and Decision Tree for QoS classification problem.

– Comparison of cutting-edge classifiers utilizing robust performance metrics like Overall Accuracy, Average Accuracy, and Kappa coefficient.

The remaining sections of this work are structured as follows. Section 2 contains the context related to relevant research. Section 3 provides a thorough description and preparation of the dataset. Section 4 describes the proposed QoS classification mechanism. Section 5 discusses the experimental specifics. Section 6 provides a summary of the results and discussion. Section 7 finally discusses concluding remarks.

2   Background and Related Works

QoS is a crucial indication for nonfunctional quality requirements for online services, and it may be used to distinguish across cloud services with the same purpose [1,13]. Menasce provides a summary of the current QoS-based research environment [15]. In order to measure each QoS category and the models that are associated with it for its representation, Ran creates a set of metrics [22]. Cloud services are grouped by Perryea and Chung into several communities to aid users in addressing non-functional concerns [20]. Global and local QoS restrictions are differentiated by Ardagna and Pernici [3]. A QoS-aware middleware for Cloud service composition is proposed by Zeng et. al. [29]. In terms of linearly stated QoS, their modeling technique may be employed as a generic strategy for global optimization criteria. Each of the techniques listed above is based on the notion of precise measurement and incisive analysis of QoS standards. A challenge involving multiple criteria decision-making also known as MCDM is one in which a Cloud service is chosen from a collection of service options based on two or more QoS variables [23]. However, the conventional multiple criteria programming is too rigid when creating the system assessment model. Two of these come to mind. a) The values for the qualitative QoS requirements are frequently acquired or specified inexactly under numerous circumstances. The dynamic heterogeneous environment in which a Cloud service operates causes the run-time quality to vary along with changes in the configuration of the Cloud service's linked components and/or hardware resources and the state of its network connection. b) Because human assessments are sometimes imprecise, Moreover, it is challenging to define the precise weight of each QoS criterion. This issue was resolved by the introduction of a broker-based strategy [6]. However, using fuzzy numbers or linguistic variables is probably the best method to address the issues raised above.

In contrast to the majority of earlier traffic classification work, which focused on identifying individual applications, Wang et.al. developed a method that sorts network traffic into several different groups according to the requirements of QoS, which provides the essential data to enable fine-grained and QoS-aware traffic engineering [24] for software-defined networks. Cloud services discovery has become exceedingly difficult due to the Internet's explosive rise in Cloud services. A useful technique for service discovery and administration is classifying Cloud services with comparable functionalities [26]. Unfortunately, the functional description papers for Cloud services are often brief in length, have few characteristics, and include little information. As a result, most topic models are unable to accurately describe the brief language, which has an impact on the categorization of Cloud services. Hongfan Ye et al. proposed a Bi-LSTM model to solve such a problem [28]. A machine learning-based traffic categorization of QoS types using IP queries and deep packet inspection [9] helped to identify the hidden encrypted traffic. A similar approach for network encrypted traffic behavior is proposed [10] which is strongly in favor of the use of machine learning algorithms for QoS classification. Since QoS prediction is crucial and must be of high accuracy, recently a hidden-state-aware network [25] is proposed which suggests the use of ML approaches [27] for high-accuracy QoS predictions. A hybrid traffic classification problem is well addressed [10] with the help of ML by using IP and port-based deep packet inspection to handle encrypted traffic. Recommendation of service composition is another requirement that also uses the QoS parameters. Hussain et.al. solved such a problem [5] by using Recurrent Neural Network and Naive Bayes. They also extended their research on QoS predictions [11] using artificial neural networks. Recently, deep neural networks have gained traction and have seen widespread use. One such network also helped to manage resources for cloud computing [12]. Hence from the several works of literature, it can be observed that some of the literature related to single service selection only focuses on the ranking which could not be applied to the broad prospect and optimization approach that has been used in composite service selection is a heuristic approach, where there may be a chance to lose good service provider based on user requirement However, we have restricted our survey which is limited to classifying cloud services based on QoS attributes where user can easily classify the service provider based upon the requirement and decision can be made based on the class label.

3   Dataset Description and Preparation

An essential difficulty for service-centric software engineering is the necessity to facilitate the categorization and semantic annotation of services [4]. This paper incorporates such data preparation by annotating the collected QoS attributes. For the experiment, we used the public WS-DREAM data set [31]. This data set contains information of 5825 Cloud services which were accessed by 339 service users. For each combination of Cloud service and service user, their response time and throughput are collected [32]. A summary of such data is presented in the Table 1. Also, the histogram of throughput and response time are presented in Fig. 1.

The dataset has two matrices 1) rtMatrix is of size 339 × 5825 containing response time information, and 2) tpMatrix is also of size 339 × 5825 containing throughput information. Since our aim is to classify Cloud services, response time and throughput information have been merged for 339 service users. This resulted in a table of size 5825 × 678. Where 5825 samples represent the number of Cloud services and 678 samples represent a combination of response time (339

Table 1. Statistical details of experimented dataset

	Response Time	Throughput
Min	−1	−1
Max	19.99	1000
Median	0.29	12.11
Mean	0.81	44.03

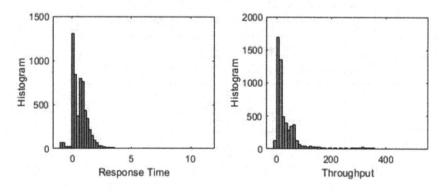

Fig. 1. Histogram of experimented data set: Response Time and Throughput

users) and throughput (339 users). The dataset is divided into four clusters, assuming that there are four categories of Cloud services such as 1) best, 2) good, 3) average, and 4) poor. Classification labels are created using a K-means clustering algorithm [8].

4   Proposed QoS Classification Framework

Cloud services are the URL resources that users can find and invoke through a network. The number of cloud services is increasing at a rate that is comparable to exponential growth over time. It is true that there exist several cloud services which are composed of similar functionalities, creating a large pool of solutions for a user. This imposes difficulties on the user to choose an appropriate commodity that can satisfy the user's requirements. QoS is a major indicator of transactions among users and cloud services and also a basic requirement that can help in the ranking and classification of cloud services. In the literature, there are several methods for single-service and composite-service ranking using QoS attributes. However, the classification of services is limited in the literature. This paper uses the framework in Fig. 2 for QoS classification for cloud service selection problems.

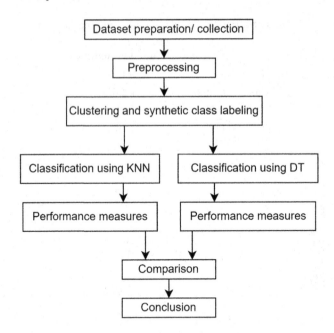

Fig. 2. Flow diagram of proposed QoS classification framework

4.1 K-Nearest Neighbor

The supervised classification learning algorithm k-nearest neighbor (KNN) is used to categorize samples. This algorithm is intended to classify the new sample based on its characteristics and labeled training samples. The approach is memory-based and requires no model fitting. With given a query point x0, the k training points closest in Euclidean distance to x0 are identified. The new query is classified to its cluster based on the majority of neighbors detected. Any ties in voting are resolved at random.

A dataset is required for the nearest neighbor classifier to accurately identify and forecast a class label indicating the kind of input pattern. The term "training data" describes these examples. The notation serves as a representation of the training vector as x_{tp} where x_{tp} is the pth training vector having N dimensions. Indicative of the overall number of training patterns included in the data set is represented by N_v. The representation of the input test vector is x_p here.x_p is the pth test vector with N-dimensions. The number of classes as a whole is depicted by N_c. The identifiers or the class labels are symbolized by i.

In order to determine the right class of the classifier, the input test vector is evaluated, when compared with the training data also known as example vectors, using the nearest neighbor classifier. Exemplary vectors are illustrated by m_{ik} where m_{ik} is the kth example vector of the ith class. m_{ik} be all of the training data. This is how the standard nearest neighbor algorithm works.

$$m_{ik} = x_p \tag{1}$$

We are assuming to have a set of points in a metric space Ω, with a label assigned for each point 0 or 1. Let (X1, Y1),(X2, Y2), . . . ,(Xn, Yn) be a labeled sample, and let (X, Y) be the query. Based on which class is most prevalent among the k closest points to X in the labeled sample, the k-nearest neighbor classifier forecasts the query's label. Figure 3 provides an illustration of this in practice.

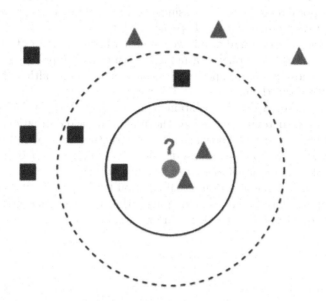

Fig. 3. An instance of k-NN. When k = 3, we classify the query as a triangle, and for k = 5, classify it as a square

To prevent ties, we chose an odd value for k in our example. In our technique, ties can happen in one of two situations: it is conceivable for different classes to occur equally frequently among the k-nearest neighbors of the query, and it is also possible for multiple points to have distance ties at the same distance from the query. To avoid the scenario of distance ties, several writers discuss consistency for distributions with a density; however, we will demonstrate universal consistency here and will not make such assumptions. The literature discusses various methods for breaking ties. One common method for breaking ties is by random selection, so that if there is a voting tie, we pick a random label from the most common labels, and if there is a distance tie, we pick a random point at that distance.

4.2   Decision Tree

For classification and regression, Decision Trees (DT) could be used as a non-parametric supervised learning method. Every internal node of the DT stands for a different "test" property, every branch symbolizes the outcome of a test, and every leaf node is a feature that may be investigated. A decision tree has three different sorts of nodes: decision nodes, chance nodes, and end nodes. The contents of the leaf node are the outcome, and the criteria that are encountered along the path produce a conjunction inside the if clause of the decision tree. If-then rules are used to apply to DT in general. Developing association rules with the target variable on the right can be used to create decision rules indicating casual or temporal relationships. Classification or regression rules are represented by the pathways from root to leaf. Being a white box model DT is simple to understand and interpret and also it works with a little amount of training data. When predicting the accuracy of a model, decision tree approaches are among the best and most popular supervised learning algorithms, although ensemble methods outperform them.

When a structured decision contains complex branching, a decision tree is used as a graphical representation of the unique decision situations. Decision trees are utilized to derive knowledge by constructing decision rules from the immense quantity of available data. A decision tree classifier has a basic, compact storage structure and classifies new data efficiently. In this study, we analyze various decision tree classification and prediction techniques. Figure 4 illustrates a sample application of a decision tree algorithm that classifies cloud services based on the quality of service(QoS) parameters.

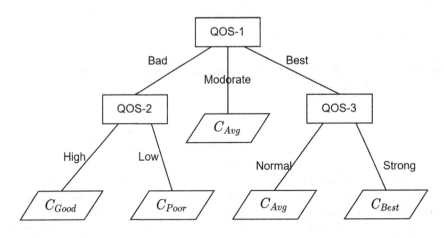

Fig. 4. Example of DT classifier

5   Experimental Setup

All experiments were implemented in MATLAB 2018b and executed on Windows 7 with Intel (R) Core (TM) 2 Duo T6570 CPU@2.10 GHz.

The experiment is carried on three steps by dividing the data set into three subsets of training and testing sets such as 1) 30% training - 70% testing, 2) 40% training - 60% testing, and 3) 50% training and 50% testing. Their results are depicted in the form of tables and figures as confusion matrices.

5.1   Performance Metrices

The confusion matrix for binary classification has been presented to facilitate comprehension of our classification measures in Fig. 5. Each column in the figure corresponds to the original class designations as *true* and *false* which are the information provided in the data, likewise, each row represents the classification result of the classifier.

Ground Truth

		True	False
	True	TP	FN
Obtained	**False**	FP	TN

Fig. 5. Confusion matrix for binary classification.

True positive (TP) and true negative (TN) refers to instances wherein both the original (ground truth) and resultant (classified) class labels are true and false respectively. While contradictions are depicted as off-diagonal false positives (FP) and false negatives (FN) in the confusion matrix. Let N number of samples be tested, i.e., $N = \sum (TP + TN + FP + FN)$. Therefore, improved accuracy is associated with larger TP and TN values; but decreased accuracy is shown with larger FP and FN values that reject the classifier.

Overall Accuracy (OA)

The OA is expressed as a percentage of all samples N that were examined out of those that were correctly classified and can be expressed as Eq. 2.

$$OA = \frac{TP + TN}{N} \tag{2}$$

Average Accuracy (AA)

Let us say, out of N tested samples let there are N_1 and N_2 samples labeled as *True* and *False* respectively for binary classification, (where $N = N_1 + N_2$). The Average Accuracy is the mean accuracy obtained for each class, represented as in Eq. 3 (binary classification).

$$AA = \frac{1}{2} \left(\frac{TP}{N1} + \frac{TN}{N2} \right) \tag{3}$$

Kappa Coefficient (κ)

The Overall Accuracy (OA) and the Expected Accuracy (EA) are both measures of accuracy that are used in the calculation of the Kappa (κ) statistic. While the EA is calculated by adding up the Expected Accuracy scores of each individual class. For the *True* class the EA denoted as EA_t can be termed as in Eq. 4.

$$EA_t = \frac{(TP + FP) \times (TP + FN)}{N} \tag{4}$$

Similarly, for *False* class the Expected Accuracy EA_f can be represented as in Eq. 5.

$$EA_f = \frac{(FN + TN) \times (FP + TN)}{N} \tag{5}$$

The overall Expected Accuracy (EA) of classification can be demonstrated as in Eq. 6.

$$EA = EA_t + EA_f \tag{6}$$

Finally, the formula for determining the value of the statistical coefficient Kappa (K) can be evaluated as in Eq.

$$\kappa = \frac{(OA - EA)}{1 - EA} \tag{7}$$

According to Cohen [7] and McHugh [14] Kappa result be interpreted as:

1 $\kappa \leq 0$: no agreement
2 $0.01 < \kappa < 0.20$: none to slight
3 $0.21 < \kappa < 0.40$: fair
4 $0.41 < \kappa < 0.60$: moderate
5 $0.61 < \kappa < 0.80$: substantial
6 $0.81 < \kappa < 1.00$: almost perfect agreement

6   Results and Discussion

The confusion matrix for 30% training and 70% testing classification results of KNN and DT classifiers are presented in Fig. 6. From Fig. 6 It is possible to draw the conclusion that the KNN classifier is able to correctly categorize a greater number of samples than the DT classifier is able to do.

Classification results of DT and KNN classifiers over three subsets as 1) 30% training - 70% testing, 2) 40% training - 60% testing, and 3) 50% training and 50% testing are presented in the Table 2. We have observed the classification

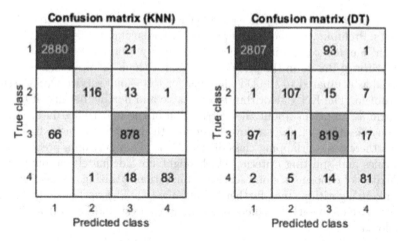

Fig. 6. Confusion matrix (training 30% and testing 70% of classification results for KNN classifier and DT classifier

accuracy difference between these two methods. Better performances are highlighted for each experiment. From this table, it is clear that the KNN classifier resulted better as compared to the DT algorithm and the OA of DT is 93.5% while for KNN is 97% claiming approx 4% improvement for 30–70 training-testing subsets. Similar results can be observed for AA and Kappa. Also, for other subsets of experiments, KNN outperformed the DT approach.

Table 2. Classification results of DT and KNN classifier over various training-testing subsets

	Training-Testing (30–70)		Training-Testing (40–60)		Training-Testing (50–50)	
	DT	KNN	DT	KNN	DT	KNN
Class-1	96.76	**99.28**	97.31	**99.36**	96.86	**99.08**
Class-2	82.31	**89.23**	70.27	**99.11**	89.25	**90.32**
Class-3	86.76	**93.01**	86.42	**94.68**	90.22	**92.14**
Class-4	79.41	**81.37**	77.01	**86.36**	68.06	**83.33**
OA	93.55	**97.06**	93.42	**97.94**	94.37	**96.81**
AA	86.31	**90.72**	82.75	**94.88**	86.10	**91.22**
Kappa	0.8526	**0.9318**	0.8478	**0.9526**	0.8720	**0.9260**

7   Conclusion

Cloud service categorization is crucial due to the rise of service providers. Such classification can be carried out based on relevant QoS parameters. In this study, WS-DREAM real-world data set has been experimented with, which contains the throughput and response time of 5825 Cloud services collected across 339 service users. Preliminary annotations were performed using the K-Means clustering approach. Further comparison of classification is performed between KNN and DT algorithms. Based on the preliminary results, the KNN approach is strongly suggested as compared to the DT classifier for the Cloud service QoS classification problem. The KNN algorithm is adaptable and flexible because it does not make firm assumptions about the distribution of the underlying data. Decision trees, on the other hand, can have trouble with data that is very dimensional or when there are overlapping class distributions. They rely on a predetermined set of rules and splitting criteria, which might not adequately account for the complexities of choosing a cloud service. Annotations utilizing different grouping and ranking algorithms may further be investigated. The worldwide importance of other state-of-the-art classifiers like Random Forest and Deep Learning may be explored.

References

1. Adacal, M., Bener, A.B.: Mobile web services: a new agent-based framework. IEEE Internet Comput. **10**(3), 58–65 (2006)
2. Alrifai, M., Risse, T., Dolog, P., Nejdl, W.: A scalable approach for QoS-based web service selection. In: Feuerlicht, G., Lamersdorf, W. (eds.) ICSOC 2008. LNCS, vol. 5472, pp. 190–199. Springer, Heidelberg (2008). https://doi.org/10.1007/978-3-642-01247-1_20
3. Ardagna, D., Pernici, B.: Global and local QoS constraints guarantee in web service selection. In: IEEE International Conference on Web Services (ICWS 2005). IEEE (2005)
4. Bruno, M., Canfora, G., Di Penta, M., Scognamiglio, R.: An approach to support web service classification and annotation. In: 2005 IEEE International Conference on e-Technology, e-Commerce and e-Service, pp. 138–143. IEEE (2005)
5. Chen, M., Cheng, J., Ma, G., Tian, L., Li, X., Shi, Q.: Service composition recommendation method based on recurrent neural network and Naive Bayes. Sci. Program. **2021**, 1–9 (2021)
6. D'Mello, D.A., Ananthanarayana, V., Thilagam, S.: A Qos broker based architecture for dynamic web service selection. In: 2008 Second Asia International Conference on Modelling & Simulation (AMS), pp. 101–106. IEEE (2008)
7. Econometrics, M.G.S., York, N.: This Week's Citation Classic Ⓡ. This week's citation classic (49), 1990 (1990)
8. Feng, Y., Gao, M., Zhang, Z.: Web service QoS classification based on optimized convolutional neural network. In: 2019 IEEE 14th International Conference on Intelligent Systems and Knowledge Engineering (ISKE), pp. 584–590. IEEE (2019)
9. Huang, Y.F., Chung, C.M., Lin, C.B., Peng, Y.B., Liu, S.H., Chen, H.: Traffic classification of QoS types based on machine learning combined with ip query and deep packet inspection. In: 2020 14th International Conference on Signal Processing and Communication Systems (ICSPCS), pp. 1–4. IEEE (2020)
10. Huang, Y.F., Lin, C.B., Chung, C.M., Chen, C.M.: Research on QoS classification of network encrypted traffic behavior based on machine learning. Electronics **10**(12), 1376 (2021)

11. Hussain, W., Gao, H., Raza, M.R., Rabhi, F.A., Merigo, J.M.: Assessing cloud QoS predictions using OWA in neural network methods. Neural Comput. Appl. **34**(17), 14895–14912 (2022)
12. Jeong, B., Baek, S., Park, S., Jeon, J., Jeong, Y.S.: Stable and efficient resource management using deep neural network on cloud computing. Neurocomputing **521**, 99–112 (2023)
13. Liu, Y., Ngu, A.H., Zeng, L.Z.: QoS computation and policing in dynamic web service selection. In: Proceedings of the 13th International World Wide Web Conference on Alternate Track Papers & Posters, pp. 66–73 (2004)
14. McHugh, M.L.: Interrater reliability: the kappa statistic. Biochemia Medica **22**(3), 276–282 (2012)
15. Menasce, D.A.: Qos issues in web services. IEEE Internet Comput. **6**(6), 72–75 (2002)
16. Nayak, S.K., Panda, S.K.: A user-oriented collaborative filtering algorithm for recommender systems. In: 2018 fifth International Conference on Parallel, Distributed and Grid Computing (PDGC), pp. 374–380. IEEE (2018)
17. Panda, S., Senapati, M., Sahu, P.: An item-oriented collaborative filtering algorithm for recommender systems. In: 60th Annual Technical Session, the Institute of Engineers. India, pp. 228–236 (2019)
18. Panda, S.K., Jana, P.K.: Sla-based task scheduling algorithms for heterogeneous multi-cloud environment. J. Supercomput. **73**, 2730–2762 (2017)
19. Patro, S.G.K., et al.: A hybrid action-related k-nearest neighbour (HAR-KNN) approach for recommendation systems. IEEE Access **8**, 90978–90991 (2020)
20. Perryea, C.A., Chung, S.: Community-based service discovery. In: 2006 IEEE International Conference on Web Services (ICWS 2006), pp. 903–906. IEEE (2006)
21. Pradhan, R., Panda, S.K., Sathua, S.K.: K-means min-min scheduling algorithm for heterogeneous grids or clouds. Int. J. Inf. Process. **9**(4), 89–99 (2015)
22. Ran, S.: A model for web services discovery with QoS. ACM Sigecom Exchanges **4**(1), 1–10 (2003)
23. Steuer, R., Qi, Y., Hirschberger, M.: Multiple Criteria Decision Making. Whiley, Hoboken (1986)
24. Wang, P., Lin, S.C., Luo, M.: A framework for QoS-aware traffic classification using semi-supervised machine learning in SDNs. In: 2016 IEEE International Conference on Services Computing (SCC), pp. 760–765. IEEE (2016)
25. Wang, Z., Zhang, X., Yan, M., Xu, L., Yang, D.: HSA-Net: hidden-state-aware networks for high-precision QoS prediction. IEEE Trans. Parallel Distrib. Syst. **33**(6), 1421–1435 (2021)
26. Xiao, Y., Liu, J., Kang, G., Cao, B.: LDNM: a general web service classification framework via deep fusion of structured and unstructured features. IEEE Trans. Netw. Serv. Manage. **18**(3), 3858–3872 (2021). https://doi.org/10.1109/TNSM. 2021.3084739
27. Yang, Y., et al.: Servenet: a deep neural network for web services classification. In: 2020 IEEE International Conference on Web Services (ICWS), pp. 168–175 (2020). https://doi.org/10.1109/ICWS49710.2020.00029
28. Ye, H., Cao, B., Peng, Z., Chen, T., Wen, Y., Liu, J.: Web services classification based on wide & Bi-LSTM model. IEEE Access **7**, 43697–43706 (2019)
29. Zeng, L., Benatallah, B., Ngu, A.H., Dumas, M., Kalagnanam, J., Chang, H.: QoS-aware middleware for web services composition. IEEE Trans. Software Eng. **30**(5), 311–327 (2004)
30. Zheng, X., Da Xu, L., Chai, S.: QoS recommendation in cloud services. IEEE Access **5**, 5171–5177 (2017)

31. Zheng, Z., Zhang, Y., Lyu, M.R.: Distributed QoS evaluation for real-world web services. In: 2010 IEEE International Conference on Web Services, pp. 83–90. IEEE (2010)
32. Zheng, Z., Zhang, Y., Lyu, M.R.: Investigating QoS of real-world web services. IEEE Trans. Serv. Comput. 7(1), 32–39 (2012)

Object Recognition Through Content Based Feature Extraction and Classification of Sounds in IoT Environment

Srinivas Sethi[1], Manisa Rath[2], Sanjaya Kumar Kuanar[2],
and Ramesh Kumar Sahoo[1(✉)]

[1] Computer Science Engineering and Applications, IGIT Sarang, Dhenkanal, India
ramesh0986@gmail.com
[2] Computer Science Engineering, GIET, Gunupur, India
{manisa.rath,sanjay.kuanar}@giet.edu

Abstract. The content-based order of urban sound classes is an important aspect of several emerging techniques and applications as a result, the research issue has gotten a lot of attention recently. The goal of this work is to develop an effective Machine Learning(ML) based approach for urban sound categorization in cities for intelligent object detection and recognition through sound for environmental study. Audio samples from urban space has been classified through various ML algorithms based on Mel spectrogram technique. Where, mel spectrogram techniques is a frequency based approach for extraction of features from audio samples for classification. The Urban Sound dataset, which contains a total of 8732 number od sound samples belongs to ten different classes, has been used in this work. This may be used for smart object detection through sound coming from objects in different applications, such as Traffic Management, Agriculture, Smart city, etc.

Keywords: Audio Classification · Machine Learning(ML) · Urban Sound categorization · environmental study · Mel spectrogram · smart object detection

1 Introduction

The emerging Internet of Things technology-based applications with sensing and multimedia technology boost multimedia information, which enhance the production of ultra-large-scale multimedia information databases [1, 2, 10]. It is very difficult to make the description and retrieve multimedia information, which needs a kind of effective retrieval method for multimedia. Content based information retrieval [4] is used quickly and accurately to find the needed multimedia information. Audio and video are the essential ingredients of multimedia information. Audio signals conatins lots of information it may about the source or the environment or the context. It is essential to analyse this to get the required

S. K. Panda et al. (Eds.): CoCoLe 2023, CCIS 1892, pp. 65–73, 2024.
https://doi.org/10.1007/978-3-031-56998-2_6

information. Human perception can also be observed through proper analysis of audio signals. Audio files need to be organised as per the semantic information due to vast enhancement of multimedia formats. Due to the complexity of audio retrieval, it is more difficult than image and video retrieval.

As the original audio data is made up of non-semantic and non-structured binary streams, it lacks semantic description and structured organization. Moreover, the audio data has the characteristics of complex structure, massive data, and high requirements for data processing. Therefore, it brings great difficulties to deeply process and analyze audio information, and the audio retrieval and content filtering applications are hard to design. It is of great importance to extract structured information and semantic contents from audio data.

Audio classification emerges as an essential and important aspect of pattern recognition and artificial intelligence. Frame, clip, shot, and semantic values are the layers of the hierarchical structure of the audio sample and their features can be estimated based on mel frequency, zero crossing rate, and short time energy [7]. Mel frequency represents the short-term power spectrum of a sound used to estimate the pitch's subjective extent. The rate of transition of signal from +ive to zero to -ive or from -ive to zero to +ive is known as the zero crossing rate. Classification of silenced, voice and unvoiced speech classification can be estimated using short time energy.

The rest of paper is has been described as follows. Section 2 has been discussed the review for related work. Section 3 explains the proposed methods and its used in detail. Result analyses with Comparison has been discussed in Sect. 4, followed by conclusion and future scope has been mentioned in Sect. 5.

2   Background

An audio signal has three-dimensional architecture that contains three major components time, frequency, and amplitude. Generally, time and frequency have been used as sources of features in audio signals. Mel Spectrogram is an emerging approach based on the frequency of audio samples to extract various features from audio samples that can be used for classification. Audio classification is an approach to detect objects from sounds through machine learning. Zero shot learning technique [13] has been considered for audio classification that is purely based on textual information of class labels and it provides 26% more across than traditional random guess. It can also be used with semantic embedding for better results [14]. Audio samples may contain important information. It can be analyzed through proper analysis of its multiple features and that can be extracted using chroma, wavelet analysis, centroid based approach [3]. It can be used to analyze the behavior of a person through emotional classification. Music and lyrics of an audio sample can be considered for emotional classification to study the behavior of a person [8]. Fuzzy-rough nearest neighbor clustering(FRNNC) has been considered for automatic audio classification based on audio content [15]. It can also be done through feature extraction and analysis on the frame and clip level through smooth pitch ratio, harmonicity ratio, pitch frequency standard deviation, and silence ratio [6]. The nearest feature line approach as well as the supervised machine learning approach Support vector machine(SVM) learning approach has been discussed in [5] for audio classification and its retrieval purely based on content. Audio classification has been done to observe and monitor the environment through sound classification by a collaborative work through a local binary pattern that is based on textual data and audio features [9].

Various work has been done on object detection through classification of audio samples like behavioral analysis, emotional analysis, and environmental study. In the proposed work, it has tried to classify audio signals in our surroundings to detect the source of the sound through the sound extracted using the mel spectrogram method. Standard and well known supervised machine learning algorithms such as Naive Bayes, Decision tree(J48), Support Vector Machine (SVM), and Random Forest algorithm has been considered for audio classification and the performance of all the algorithms have been compared using various evaluation parameters such as F1-score, precision, recall, and accuracy to select the best algorithm for prediction.

3 Methodology

Row sample audio data may not be perfect one for classification, it need to be preprocessed for elimination of noise based on different frequency and amplitude using special filters. Further, it is essential to extract features from audio samples using different signal processing algorithms that will be used for classification through machine learning algorithms. ML algorithms is well known for developing a model through proper training using the valid dataset and further it can be used for prediction. In this work, Various Supervised ML algorithms has been considered for classification instead of one and the best ML algorithm for the work has been selected after proper evaluation of performance of various ML algorithms. It can be used to correctly detect the source of sound for accurate identification of object in environment through their sound.

Data Collection Approach. In the proposed work, data has been obtained from Urban Sound 8K dataset [11]. The dataset consists of audio files and metadata in comma-separated value format with features like filename, class ID, and class label of each audio sample. Audio samples contain sounds of various objects available in urban spaces like animals, humans, vehicles, musical instruments, home appliances, etc. It has been analyzed and classified to detect the source of sounds from audio samples.

Preparing Training Data. The training data contains the features such as the paths of the audio file to access required audio sample and the target labels will be considered as the class/category names and metadata that we can use directly. The dataset has been transformed into a data frame of the panda module of Python for data preprocessing to handle missing and invalid audio signals to have valid audio signals in the dataset.

Audio Pre-processing. Pre-processing of audio samples is essential and unavoidable as it will improve the quality of data as well as transform the data in a format that will be better accepted by the model and give better performance. The pre-processing will be performed dynamically at runtime after the task of reading and loading the audio files. Further, batchwise training of the model has been done.

Generation of Mel Spectrogram. The augmented audio signal is converted to a Mel Spectrogram [12] which captures the required features of the audio. It will be used for audio classification. An audio signal has three major components time, amplitude, and frequency in its architecture. In this work, time and frequency have been used as features through the mel spectrogram that will generate 10 to 20 features for classification. Mel spectrogram approach has been considered in the proposed work to extract the essential features from audio signals for audio classification. It is based on a frequency domain filter bank for feature extraction. All the audio samples have been converted to an augmented Mel Spectrogram for feature extraction required for classification. It has been in four stages. In the first stage, audio signals have been parsed to 2048 windows with the hop size 512 for the next window. In the 2nd stage, Fast Fourier Transform(FFT) has been determined for each window to have a frequency domain from the time domain. In the third stage, mel scale has been generated by using the frequency spectrum to get 128 evenly spaced frequency based mel scales for each window. Evenly spaced distribution of frequency is based on the distances computed as per the sound audible not as per the distance. Finally, in the 4th stage, a spectrogram has been generated by converting the magnitude of the signal linked with the frequency of mel scale into the required components/features for each window.

Machine Learning Algorithms Used for Audio Classification. Well-known and standard supervised ML algorithms such as Naive Bayes, SVM, Random Forest, and Decision Tree(J48) have been considered for audio classification in the proposed work. Recursive, top-down, and divide-and-conquer approaches are considered in J48 to detect appropriate and best attributes to split each node for better accuracy. Scikit-image and scikit-learn module has been used for audio classification in Python environment. Precision, Recall, F1-score, and accuracy have been considered as evaluation parameters to judge the efficiency of the considered machine learning algorithms. It has been used to fetch the best machine learning algorithm for prediction.

Training and Testing the Model. The dataset is used to train the working model in which, The model observe and learns from the data. The working model is then trained in iterative manner and validated on different sets. Cross Validation mode has been considered for classification as it is a robust one and it avoids overfitting. After training the model on the new dataset, the model evaluates the test set to show the label of the input audio.

Dataset. In the proposed work, Urban Sound 8K [11] dataset has been considered for analysis. It is a collection of audio samples from various objects in urban spaces. It has a total of 8732 sound samples from urban spaces. It has been categorized into 10 categories as per the source of sounds in urban spaces. street_music, air_conditioner, dog_bark, gun_shot, siren, car_horn, engine_idling, children_playing, jackhammer, and drilling are the different categories of sounds considered in the proposed work for analysis. The classes are drawn from the urban sound taxonomy. All the Data has been stored locally in the computer for compilation and execution.

4   Result and Discussion

Audio samples have been collected from various sources in the IoT environment. Features have been extracted using the Mel spectrogrammer approach for audio classification. Various well known and standard supervised ML algorithms such as Naive Bayes, SVM, Decision Tree(J48), and Random Forest have been used and their performance has been evaluated to select the best algorithm that can be used for prediction. Further, A comparative analysis has been done.

Table 1. Statistical analysis of actual and predicted Records.

Class	Actual Quantity	Naive Bayes	SVM	Decision Tree(J48)	Random Forest
Air_Conditioner	490	125	439	500	496
Car_Horn	219	164	154	215	201
Children_Playing	500	198	1707	482	498
Dog_Bark	479	99	344	485	479
Drilling	533	264	427	521	531
Engine_Idling	472	1725	284	464	466
Gun_Shot	205	236	109	197	199
JackHammer	526	231	374	518	540
Siren	442	577	250	456	440
Street_Music	500	747	278	528	516

Figure 1 and Table 1 provide a comparative view of total number of actual records and a total no. of predicted records in various categories of sounds. Audio samples have been taken in the dataset for various categories as mention in Table 1. No of Records is reflected in the X axis whereas Y-axis reflects the categories of sound. A total of 490 records have been taken for Air_Conditioner but the after classification, no. of predicted records are 125, 439, 500, and 496 by Naive Bayes, SVM, Decision Tree(j48), and Random Forest algorithm respectively. Similarly, a total of 219 records are taken as actual records for Car_Horn sound category but a total of 164, 154, 215 and 201 records have been predicted

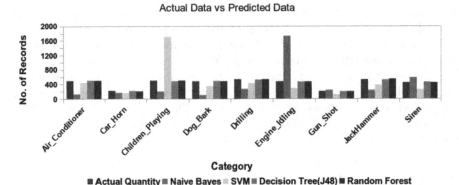

Fig. 1. Comparative analysis of actual and predicted no. of records in various categories

by Naive Bayes, SVM, Decision Tree(j48) and Random Forest algorithm respectively. A total of 500 records have been taken for Children_Playing but the after classification, no. of predicted records are 198, 1707, 482, and 498 by Naive Bayes, SVM, Decision Tree(j48) and Random Forest algorithm respectively. Similarly, a total of 479 records are taken as actual records for Dog_Bark sound category but a total of 99, 344, 485 and 479 records have been predicted by Naive Bayes, SVM, Decision Tree(j48) and Random Forest algorithm respectively. A total of 533 records have been taken for Drilling but the after classification, no. of predicted records are 264, 427, 521 and 531 by Naive Bayes, SVM, Decision Tree(j48), and Random Forest algorithm respectively. Similarly, a total of 472 records are taken as actual records for Engine_Idling sound category but a total of 1725, 284, 464, and 466 records has been predicted by Naive Bayes, SVM, Decision Tree(j48), and Random Forest algorithm respectively. A total of 205 records have been taken for Gun_Shot but the after classification, no. of predicted records are 236, 109, 197, and 199 by Naive Bayes, SVM, Decision Tree(j48), and Random Forest algorithm respectively. Similarly, a total of 526 records are taken as actual records for the JackHammer sound category but a total of 231, 374, 518, and 540 records have been predicted by Naive Bayes, SVM, Decision Tree(j48), and Random Forest algorithm respectively.

A total of 442 records have been taken for Siren but the after classification, no. of predicted records are 577, 250, 456, and 440 by Naive Bayes, SVM, Decision Tree(j48) and Random Forest algorithm respectively. Similarly, a total of 500 records are taken as actual records for the Street_Music sound category but a total of 747, 278, 528 and 516 records have been predicted by Naive Bayes, SVM, Decision Tree(j48) and Random Forest algorithm respectively. It is observed that in all the categories of sounds, no. of predicted records provided by Random Forest and The decision Tree(J48) algorithm is closer to the actual no. of records than that of other considered ML algorithms. Further, the performance of all considered ML algorithms has been compared and evaluated using precision, recall, F1-Score and Accuracy to select the best ML algorithm that can be used for prediction.

Table 2. Comparative analysis of audio classification.

Algorithm	Precision	Recall	F1-Score	Accuracy
Random Forest	0.97	0.97	0.97	0.973
Decision Tree(J48)	0.94	0.94	0.94	0.939
SVM	0.68	0.55	0.57	0.545
Naive Bayes	0.45	0.35	0.34	0.352

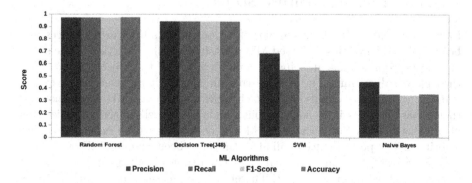

Fig. 2. Audio classification through various ML algorithms

Row dataset based on audio samples has been classified using various machine learning(ML) algorithms like Naive Bayes, Random Forest, SVM, and Decision Tree(J48) Algorithms. A comparative study has been done using Fig. 2 and Table 2. In Fig. 2, X-axis reflect the score, and Y-axis reflect ML algorithms. Precision, Recall, F1-Score, and Accuracy are the various evaluation parameters used to estimates the performance of different ML algorithms. Precision of Random Forest, Decision Tree(J48), SVM, and Naive Bayes Algorithms are 0.97, 0.94, 0.68, are 0.45 respectively. Similarly, 0.97, 0.94, 0.55, and 0.35 are the recall of Random Forest, Decision Tree(J48), SVM, and Naive Bayes Algorithms respectively. F1-Score of Random Forest, Decision Tree(J48), SVM and Naive Bayes Algorithms are 0.97, 0.94, 0.57, are 0.34 respectively. Similarly 0.973, 0.939, 0.545, and 0.352 are the Accuracy level provided by Random Forest, Decision Tree(J48), SVM, and Naive Bayes Algorithms respectively. The precision, recall, and the F1-score of the Random Forest algorithm is more than other considered ML algorithms but it is quite closer to Decision Tree(J48) algorithm. Due to higher Precision and Recall, the accuracy score of the Random Forest algorithm is quite higher than other ML algorithms which makes it a better choice in comparison to others. The performance of Random Forest is best with a 0.973 accuracy score and Naive Bayes is the worst with a 0.352 accuracy score.

From the above analysis, it is observed that the F1-score, precision, recall, and Accuracy of the Random Forest algorithm are better than Decision Tree(J48), SVM, and Naive Bayes algorithms. Due to more precision and Recall, F1-Score, and accuracy is also higher in the Random Forest algorithm. The accuracy score of the Random Forest algorithm is 0.973(97.3%) which is higher than Decision Tree(J48) 0.939(93.9%), SVM 0.545(54.5%) and that of Naive Bayes 0.352(35.2%). Random Forest provides 4% better accuracy than the closest Decision Tree(J48) algorithm. Therefore, it is concluded that the Random Forest algorithm performs better than other ML algorithms and can be considered for prediction to detect the species from audio samples.

5   Conclusion and Future Scope

In the proposed work, audio samples of various objects from urban spaces have been analyzed through supervised ML algorithms for the detection of the source of objects from sounds. It helps to correctly identify the objects from sounds through ML algorithms. The Mel spectrogram approach has been used to extract features from audio samples for audio classification through ML algorithms. Further, it has been classified using various standard and well-known supervised ML algorithms such as Naive Bayes, SVM, Random Forest and Decision Tree(J48) algorithm. The performance of all algorithms has been compared through Accuracy, F1-Score, precision, and recall. Predicted values of all categories of sounds closely match with actual output. Therefore, the precision, recall, and F1-Score of the Random Forest algorithm are better than others. Hence, Random Forest algorithm provides a better accuracy score(0.973) than others. It can be used for prediction. In subsequent research, cost and benefit analysis can be used to enhance the accuracy of the working model for better performance.

References

1. Bhoi, A., et al.: IOT-IIRS: Internet of things based intelligent-irrigation recommendation system using machine learning approach for efficient water usage. PeerJ Comput. Sci. **7**, e578 (2021)
2. Bhoi, S.K., et al.: IoT-EMS: an internet of things based environment monitoring system in volunteer computing environment. Intell. Autom. Soft Comput **32**(3), 1493–1507 (2022)
3. Kumar, K., Chaturvedi, K.: An audio classification approach using feature extraction neural network classification approach. In: 2nd International Conference on Data, Engineering and Applications (IDEA), pp. 1–6. IEEE (2020)
4. Lew, M.S., Sebe, N., Djeraba, C., Jain, R.: Content-based multimedia information retrieval: state of the art and challenges. ACM Trans. Multimedia Comput. Commun. Appl. (TOMM) **2**(1), 1–19 (2006)
5. Li, S.Z.: Content-based audio classification and retrieval using the nearest feature line method. IEEE Trans. Speech Audio Process. **8**(5), 619–625 (2000)
6. Liang, B., Yaali, H., Songyang, L., Jianyun, C., Lingda, W.: Feature analysis and extraction for audio automatic classification. In: 2005 IEEE International Conference on Systems, Man and Cybernetics, vol. 1, pp. 767–772. IEEE (2005)
7. Rong, F.: Audio classification method based on machine learning. In: 2016 International Conference on Intelligent Transportation, Big Data & Smart City (ICITBS), pp. 81–84. IEEE (2016)

8. Shi, W., Feng, S.: Research on music emotion classification based on lyrics and audio. In: 2018 IEEE 3rd Advanced Information Technology, Electronic and Automation Control Conference (IAEAC), pp. 1154–1159. IEEE (2018)

9. Toffa, O.K., Mignotte, M.: Environmental sound classification using local binary pattern and audio features collaboration. IEEE Trans. Multimedia **23**, 3978–3985 (2020)

10. Tripathy, B.K., Jena, S.K., Reddy, V., Das, S., Panda, S.K.: A novel communication framework between manet and WSN in IoT based smart environment. Int. J. Inf. Technol. **13**, 921–931 (2021)

11. UrbanSound8K: UrbanSound8K (2008). https://urbansounddataset.weebly.com/ urbansound8k.html. Accessed 29 May 2023

12. Wang, S., Politis, A., Mesaros, A., Virtanen, T.: Self-supervised learning of audio representations from audio-visual data using spatial alignment. IEEE J. Sel. Topics Signal Process. **16**(6), 1467–1479 (2022)

13. Xie, H., Virtanen, T.: Zero-shot audio classification based on class label embeddings. In: 2019 IEEE Workshop on Applications of Signal Processing to Audio and Acoustics (WASPAA), pp. 264–267. IEEE (2019)

14. Xie, H., Virtanen, T.: Zero-shot audio classification via semantic embeddings. IEEE/ACM Trans. Audio Speech Lang. Process. **29**, 1233–1242 (2021)

15. Yang, W., Yu, X., Deng, J., Pan, X., Wang, Y.: Audio classification based on fuzzy-rough nearest neighbour clustering (2011)

Detection of Malicious Activity on Credit Cards Using Machine Learning

Rayudu Satwika[1], Bhabendu Kumar Mohanta[3] (ID), Gurpreet Singh Chahbra[1] (ID),
and Asesh Kumar Tripathy[2(✉)] (ID)

[1] Department of CSE, GITAM (Deemed to be University), Visakhapatnam, India
`121910314002@gitam.in`
[2] Department of CSE, Koneru Lakshmaiah Education Foundation, Vijayawada
522502, Andhra Pradesh, India
`asesh.tripathy@gmail.com`
[3] College of Information Technology, United Arab Emirates University, P.O. Box
15551, Al Ain, United Arab Emirates
`bhabendu@uaeu.ac.ae`

Abstract. In the contemporary digital era, credit card fraud has become a top concern for financial institutions and credit card companies. Machine learning algorithms are routinely used to detect fraudulent transactions in real time by examining enormous amounts of historical transaction data and discovering patterns of fraudulent behavior. The thought drifts, on the other hand, may make this process more challenging because factors may alter over time in unanticipated ways, leading to data imbalances and lowering the precision of fraud detection algorithms. To overcome the issue of notion drift, this research uses a feedback mechanism that adapts to changing circumstances over time. This approach relies on keeping track of crucial transaction data and forecasting fraud using the SVM, random forest, and decision tree algorithms. The research looks for the classifier with the highest rating value in an effort to create a reliable method of detecting fraud in credit card transactions. The challenges caused by idea drift in the detection of card fraud appear to be amenable to being overcome by the suggested technique. This system, which continuously adapts to changing parameters over time, may boost the accuracy and dependability of the finding of cheating models in a real-world situation.

Keywords: Security · Malicious attack · Detection · Machine Learning · Accuracy

1 Introduction

One of the alluring characteristics that draw customers to it-and fraudsters-is the flexibility of purchase. Because unauthorized transactions are so prevalent, both financial institutions and individuals suffer financial loss. We must accurately predict fraud that may take place in the near future in order to mitigate

S. K. Panda et al. (Eds.): CoCoLe 2023, CCIS 1892, pp. 74–86, 2024.
https://doi.org/10.1007/978-3-031-56998-2_7

the problem. This is the reason why many researchers are attracted to this area of study. Alarfaj, Fawaz Khaled, et al. [1] worked on a European data set using CNN with 20 layers which provided 99.72% accuracy in the detection of credit card fraud but its performance decreased significantly with unseen data. Kim, Jinsung, et al. [2] proposed a new malware detection system known as MAPAS that detects malicious applications based on common patterns of their API call graphs. Even though this approach is quite interesting it shows only 91% accuracy as far as unknown malware detection is concerned. Ashfaq, Tehreem, et al. [3] tried to detect fraud in Bitcoin transactions using blockchain and machine learning algorithms. The data set they used contained fewer fraud transactions and hence they used a SMOTE to generate synthetic malicious data points. Even though the proposed method successfully detected fraudulent transactions, it can be affected by adversarial attacks. Alarfaj, Fawaz Khaled, et al. [4] used European data sets to detect fraudulent transactions. The data set had only 0.172% of the total data as fraudulent data. So, they used SMOTE to generate synthetic fraudulent data points. They applied Matthews Correlation Coefficient (MCC) on the unbalanced set and obtained an accuracy of 70% which is quite low. Sailusha, Ruttala, et al. [5] used European data set to detect credit card fraud using mainly two algorithms Random Forest and Adaboost. The data set has given the best result for Random Forest. Detecting fraud in credit card usage on real-time data is carried out by Thennakoon, Anuruddha, et al. [6]. Support Vector Machine (SVM) showed 91% accuracy out of 4 different models tried over the data set. The proposed model lacks detection of location-based fraudulent transactions. The ability of machine learning algorithms was compared by Itoo, Fayaz, Meenakshi, and Satwinder Singh [7] and found that Logistic regression (LR) showed optimal performance (95%) as compared to other models. However, they didn't apply the models to skewed data sets. Caroline Cynthia, P., and S. Thomas George [8] showed that unsupervised machine learning algorithms are better performers as far as fraudulent transaction detectors. However, the model is not applied to skewed data sets. The discussion demonstrates that there is still a need for improved machine learning algorithms that can effectively forecast and detect fraudulent credit card usage. This paper is organized as follows. Section 2 discusses a literature survey related to the detection of fraudulent transactions in credit card usage. The Sect. 3 defines the problem statement and discusses the proposed solution giving theoretical model basics. The proposed theoretical models are implemented in the Sect. 6. It also includes the parameters such as Recall, Precision, Accuracy, and F1 Score of each model including the confusion matrix. Finally the Sect. 7 brings this discussion to an end.

2   Literature Survey

Financial institutions and credit card companies all across the world are very concerned about credit card fraud. Over the years, a number of scholars have looked at how to spot and stop fraudulent transactions using various algorithms. In this overview of the literature, we'll take a look at some of the most recent studies on algorithms and comparisons for credit card fraud detection. The authors in [9] study to identify credit card fraud. They proposed a method using a memory-based Recurrent Neural Network to find the occurrence of fraud in credit card systems. The reduction of false positives in credit card fraud cases is one of the major benefits in terms of cost-effectiveness in the credit card system. In [10] and [11] papers, authors explained that a group of deep neural networks has been put to the test by processing alerts sent by a fraud detection system to determine how well they can identify false positives. A details analysis of credit card fraud using machine learning approaches is also outlined. The paper [12] and [13] authors work on the challenges that exist in datasets in credit card fraud detection. Due to the dataset's extreme imbalance, detecting credit card fraud proves to be a challenging task. In other words, there are considerably more legitimate cases than fraudulent ones. The authors in [14] made a contribution by creating a fraud detection system that makes use of a deep learning architecture and an innovative feature engineering method that utilizes behavior evaluation. The creation of systems to guarantee the integrity and security of credit card transactions is important. The authors in [15] proposed a model to address the security concern in credit card fraud detection. In conclusion, the research examined in this literature review assessed the efficacy of several machine learning algorithms in identifying credit card fraud. According to the findings of these investigations, the most successful algorithms for detecting credit card fraud are RF, SVM [15,16], and Hybrid CNN-LSTM. It is important to note, however, that the efficacy of these methods will vary depending on the amount and complexity of the dataset employed.

3   Problem Identification and Objectives

3.1   The Problem

While making purchases or completing transactions online, credit cards are frequently chosen by customers. Credit cards' ease, meanwhile, also makes them a target for scammers who take benefit of vulnerabilities. Both the credit card business and the user may suffer large financial losses as a result of fraudulent actions including stealing, hacking, and identity theft. Creating efficient fraud detection systems that can quickly recognize and react to suspicious activity is a problem. To examine huge amounts of transaction data and spot patterns of fraudulent conduct, a multi-pronged strategy is needed, one that includes machine learning algorithms. Financial institutions can keep ahead of fraudsters and defend both their clients' money and their companies' reputations by utilizing cutting-edge technologies. Objectives are as follows:

1. Improve performance as a whole
2. Effectively classifies and predicts the Fault
3. Predict or detect Credit card Fault Detection
4. Implements the machine learning algorithm

3.2   The Proposed Solution

The data set is analyzed and the features that are not closely related to the classifier are eliminated from analysis using Principal component Analysis(PCA). The primary goal of our study is to tackle the problem of concept drift to put it into practice in the actual world. The proposed system first collects the fundamental characteristics that are generated when a transaction is made. Then the features are applied to classification models like SVM, random forest, and decision tree algorithms. Finally, the performance Analysis is calculated. The proposed system has advantages which are: (a) It is suitable for a large number of data sets. (b) The performance analysis shows that our proposed algorithm is more effective. (c) The proposed system delivers High performance and provides accurate prediction results including avoiding sparsity problems.

4   System Design

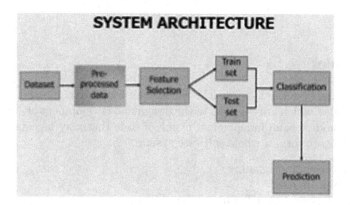

Fig. 1. System Architecture

The process of developing the design, components, modules, interfaces, and data for a system to meet defined criteria is system design. As shown in Fig. 1 it entails describing the boundaries, inputs, outputs, and behavior of the system, as well as determining the technologies, tools, and frameworks that will be utilized to implement the system. The purpose of system design is to construct a scalable and resilient system that can satisfy the demands of its users while being manageable, extendable, and responsive to changing requirements.

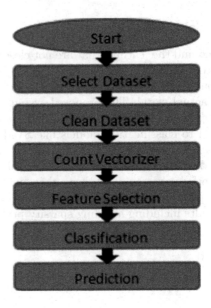

Fig. 2. Flowchart of the system

5   Modules

A modular and systematic approach, as shown in Fig. 2, to coding is made possible by modules, which are essential to the design and development of any software project. A module is an independent chunk of code that may be combined with other modules to form a whole software system.

1. Data Selection and Loading
2. Data pre-processing
3. Splitting Data set into Train and Test Data
4. Classification
5. Prediction
6. Result Generation

5.1   Data Selection and Loading

A dataset repository was used to acquire the input data. The Credit card dataset used in our approach is downloaded from Kaggle. The data set is loaded into memory and preprocessed for further analysis.

a) Dataset: The data contains transactions made by cardholders in September 2013 over 2 days. A total of 284,807 transactions were made, and 492 of those were fraudulent, making about 0.172% of all transactions. The imbalance in this dataset is extreme. The confidentiality of a customer's transaction information is deemed to be at risk if disclosed, therefore, the majority of the dataset's features are changed by Principal Component analysis (PCA). Time, quantity, and class are the features that are not used by PCA, whereas V1, V2, V3,..., and V28 are characteristics that are used. Time - The interval in seconds since the most recent transaction. Amount: Transaction amount, Class: 0 (genuine), 1 (fraud) as shown in Fig. 3. The genuine user spends a reasonable amount of time completing the transaction while a fraudulent user takes very less time to complete the transaction as is seen in Figs. 4 and 5.

5.2   Data Processing

When dealing with irrelevant and missing data, data cleansing is an essential step. Two methods can be used to fill in missing data. Avoiding missing value tuples; is only appropriate for huge datasets with numerous missing values per tuple. Manually filling in blanks or using the characteristic mean or most likely value. With integer encoding, where labels are changed to integers, categorical data with finite label values may be encoded. One-hot encoding, in which each label is represented by a binary vector. Since machine learning algorithms need mathematical inputs as well as outputs, collected variables must first be encoded before being used. Scikit- learn's A feature representation module for text data is called Count Vectorizer. Count Vectorizer converts a set of text documents into a vector of term/token counts. Furthermore, Count Vectorizer does the text process also, and this makes it a more versatile visualization of feature modules for text.

5.3   Splitting Dataset into Train and Test Data

Data splitting is processed by separating available information into 2 halves for cross-validation. One set of data is used to build a predictive model, while the other is used to evaluate the model's efficiency and accuracy. The separation of data into training and testing sets is a step in analyzing data mining algorithms. When a data set is partitioned into a training set and a testing set, the bulk of the data is used for training and just a less amount of portion is utilized for testing. Regardless of the type of dataset used, any machine learning model must be trained using training and testing data.

5.4   Classification

Classification is the problem of detecting which of a variety of classifications a new discovery corresponds to, relying on a trained set of data that contains observations in identified categories. Machine learning is a predictive problem that predicts a class label for a particular sample of the data set. It is a machine learning predictive modeling task that predicts a classifier for a given sample of data input. In our case, the data is classified as either "genuine" or "fraud" data as shown in Fig. 3. In machine learning, it is a supervised learning concept that essentially categorizes a set of data into classes. We should have divided the data into training and testing sets before classifying it. The majority of the data is used for training, with only a tiny portion used for testing. Training data is employed. The model is evaluated using training data, while the model's efficiency is forecasted using testing data. After separating the data, we must build the classification method. A support vector machine must be used in our procedure (SVM).

5.5   Prediction

Predictive analytics algorithms strive for the lowest possible error through "boosting" or "bagging". Classifier accuracy is related to the classifier's abilities. It anticipates the class label and predictive accuracy applies to how well a given prediction forecasts the importance of a predicted feature for data received.

5.6   Result Generation

1) Confusion Matrix: A confusion matrix is a table that is widely utilized to assess the effectiveness of a classifying model by contrasting anticipated and actual labels from test data. The matrix lists the total amount of true positives, true negatives, false positives, and false negatives that the model accurately predicted. A confusion matrix's data may be adapted to evaluate the accuracy, precision, recall, and F1 score, among other performance measures that can be used to assess the success of a classification model.

a) Accuracy: One of the performance measures that may be determined from a confusion matrix is accuracy. It has been referred to as the ratio of the total count of right predictions (including TP and TN) to the total number of predictions generated by the model. It is expressed mathematically as per Eq. 1 :

$$Accuracy = \frac{(TP + TN)}{(TP + TN + FP + FN)} \tag{1}$$

b) Precision: Another performance indicator that may be determined from a confusion matrix is precision. It is expressed as the proportion of true positives to total positive predictions made by the model. In other words, precision counts the number of the model's optimistic predictions that came true. For minimizing false positives that are, when it's crucial to prevent predicting a positive label when the actual label is negative-precision is a valuable statistic. Mathematically, precision is represented as shown in Eq. 2:

$$Precision = \frac{TP}{(TP + FP)} \tag{2}$$

c) Recall: Another performance measure that may be calculated using a confusion matrix is recall. It is derived by dividing the total number of real positive samples by the count of actual positive samples in the test. The percentage of positive data in the test set that the model properly recognized is represented by a recall. A recall is a helpful statistic when the aim is to reduce false negatives, that is, when it is critical to identify all positive samples in the test set, even if some negative samples are labeled as positive. Recall may be expressed mathematically as shown in Eq. 3:

$$Recall = \frac{TP}{(TP + FN)} \tag{3}$$

d) F1- Score: F1- Score: The F1 score is a performance statistic that includes accuracy and recalls into a single value. It gives a fair assessment of the model's effectiveness on both positive and negative samples and is the mean of accuracy and recall. Mathematically, the F1 score may be stated as shown in Eq. 4:

$$F1score = 2 * \frac{(precision * recall)}{(precision + recall)} \tag{4}$$

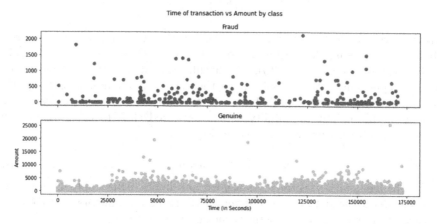

Fig. 3. Time of Transaction vs Amount by class.

6 Methodology

6.1 Naive Bayes

Assumption of independence is frequently false in real-world issues, Naive Bayes gets its name from it. Naive Bayes may be surprisingly effective in many real-world applications, especially when there are a lot of characteristics. This is

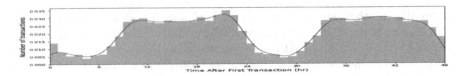

Fig. 4. Transaction time for genuine users.

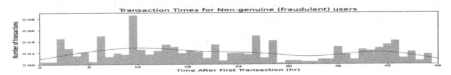

Fig. 5. Transaction time for fraud users.

despite its simplifying assumptions. Spam filtering, text categorization, sentiment analysis, and other applications of machine learning and natural language processing have all made extensive use of naive Bayes. The Bayes theorem and the presumption of feature independence serve as the foundation of the Naive Bayes formula. It comes from the Eq. 5:

$$P(\frac{y}{x}) - P(\frac{y}{x}) * (\frac{P(y)}{P(x)})$$ (5)

where: Given the feature vector x, $P(\frac{y}{x})$ is the posterior probability. The probability of witnessing the feature vector x given the class y is $P(\frac{y}{x})$. The prior probability for the classy is $P(y)$. The likelihood of witnessing the feature vector x independent of the class is called the evidence probability, or $P(x)$ [15]. We compute the posterior probabilities of each potential class y and select the class with the highest probability as the projected class to categorize a new observation with feature vector x as per Eq. 6:

$$P(y - x) = \hat{y} = argmax(y)$$ (6)

In which $argmax(y)$ is the highest y without limits. After applying the Naive Bayes model to our data set the different performance parameters are taken into consideration. One such parameter is shown in Fig. 6(a)

6.2 Decision Tree

A decision tree is a type of machine-learning algorithm. The technique builds a model of decisions and their possible outcomes in a tree-like structure, with each node representing a decision based on a single feature or attribute and each branch representing a possible value of that feature. To forecast the target variable of a new observation, the algorithm iteratively separates the data into subsets depending on the values of the characteristics. After applying the Decision Tree model to our data set the different performance parameters are taken into consideration. One such parameter is shown in Fig. 6(b).

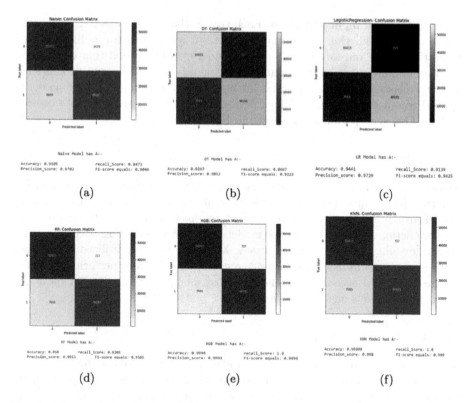

Fig. 6. The confusion Matrix of (a): The Naive Bayes model, (b): The Decision Tree model, (c): The Logistic Regression Model, (d): The Random Forest Model, (e): The XGB Model, and (f): The KNN model

6.3 Logistic Regression

Logistic regression is an ML approach applied for binary classification issues that predicts a binary output that relays on a set of input information or data. It uses a logistic or *sigmoid* function to predict the probability of the binary result as a function of the input characteristics and maximum likelihood estimation to estimate the function's parameters. Based on its input properties, the trained model may then predict the binary result of a new observation. The various performance factors are taken into account once the Logistic Regression model is applied to our data set. In Fig. 6(c), one such parameter is displayed.

6.4 Random Forests

Random forests are a form of training approach used for categorization, regression, and other uses. It is an ensemble learning approach for making more accurate predictions by combining numerous decision trees. Random forests generate a huge number of decision trees, each trained on a randomly selected part of the training data and input attributes. Each tree in the forest guesses a prediction, and the final prediction is the majority vote or average of the individual tree projections. Random forests are a strong and versatile method that can handle noisy and high-dimensional data and are frequently utilized in applications such as image classification, biology, and finance. Once the Random Forest model is applied to our data set, the various performance criteria are taken into consideration. One such parameter is shown in Fig. 6(d).

6.5   XGBoost

XGBoost is a strong and efficient machine learning algorithm that is used for tasks involving supervised learning like classification and regression. It is a supervised learning approach that integrates numerous decision trees to create accurate predictions and optimizes the model via gradient boosting. Because of its speed, flexibility, and excellent accuracy, XGBoost is widely utilized in business and has won several machine-learning contests. The different performance criteria are taken into account once the XGBoost model is applied to our data set. Figure 6(e) displays one such parameter.

6.6   K - Nearest - Neighbour

KNN (K-Nearest-Neighbour) is a basic and widely utilized ML method for classifying and regression models. It works by locating the K nearest training examples (neighbors) to a new data point in the feature space and predicting its title or value based on the overall label or average value of its neighbors. It is a nonparametric approach, which implies that it makes no assumptions about the underlying dispersion of the data. KNN is simple to construct and interpret, but it can be computationally costly and sensitive to distance metrics and K value. After applying the KNN model to our data set the different performance parameters are taken into consideration. One such parameter is shown in Fig. 6(f)).

7   Conclusion

Overall, the data shows that XGBoost is a viable method for a broad variety of machine learning applications, outperforming popular algorithms like k-NN, Naive Bayes, Logistic Regression, and so on in many circumstances. Some of the important elements that contribute to XGBoost's exceptional performance include its ability to handle high-dimensional data and missing features, its regularisation approach, and its ability to handle unbalanced datasets. Its use of decision trees and gradient boosting also enables it to understand complicated relationships between variables and generate accurate predictions. While other algorithms like Logistic Regression k-NN, Naive Bayes, and Decision Trees, Random Forest also has their advantages, XGBoost's unique blend of decision trees and gradient boosting sets it apart as a powerful option.

References

1. Alarfaj, F.K., Malik, I., Khan, H.U., Almusallam, N., Ramzan, M., Ahmed, M.: Credit card fraud detection using state-of-the-art machine learning and deep learning algorithms. IEEE Access **10**, 39700–39715 (2022)
2. Kim, J., Ban, Y., Ko, E., Cho, H., Yi, J.H.: MAPAS: a practical deep learning-based android malware detection system. Int. J. Inf. Secur. **21**(4), 725–738 (2022)
3. Ashfaq, T., et al.: A machine learning and blockchain based efficient fraud detection mechanism. Sensors **22**(19), 7162 (2022)
4. Dornadula, V.N., Geetha, S.: Credit card fraud detection using machine learning algorithms. Procedia Comput. Sci. **165**, 631–641 (2019)
5. Sailusha, R., Gnaneswar, V., Ramesh, R., Rao, G.R.: Credit card fraud detection using machine learning. In: 2020 4th International Conference on Intelligent Computing and Control Systems (ICICCS), pp. 1264–1270. IEEE (2020)
6. Thennakoon, A., Bhagyani, C., Premadasa, S., Mihiranga, S., Kuruwitaarachchi, N.: Real-time credit card fraud detection using machine learning. In: 2019 9th International Conference on Cloud Computing, Data Science & Engineering (Confluence), pp. 488–493. IEEE (2019)
7. Itoo, F., Meenakshi, Singh, S.: Comparison and analysis of logistic regression, Naïve Bayes and KNN machine learning algorithms for credit card fraud detection. Int. J. Inf. Technol. **13**, 1503–1511 (2021)
8. Caroline Cynthia, P., Thomas George, S.: An outlier detection approach on credit card fraud detection using machine learning: a comparative analysis on supervised and unsupervised learning. In: Peter, J.D., Fernandes, S.L., Alavi, A.H. (eds.) Intelligence in Big Data Technologies—Beyond the Hype. AISC, vol. 1167, pp. 125–135. Springer, Singapore (2021). https://doi.org/10.1007/978-981-15-5285-4_12
9. Roseline, J.F., Naidu, G.B.S.R., Pandi, V.S., Alias Rajasree, S.A., Mageswari, N.: Autonomous credit card fraud detection using machine learning approach. Comput. Electr. Eng. **102**, 108132 (2022)
10. Carrasco, R., Sicilia-Urban, M.-A.: Evaluation of deep neural networks for reduction of credit card fraud alerts. IEEE Access **8**, 186421–186432 (2020). https://doi.org/10.1109/ACCESS.2020.302622
11. Madhurya, M.J., Gururaj, H.L., Soundarya, B.C., Vidyashree, K.P., Rajendra, A.B.: Exploratory analysis of credit card fraud detection using machine learning techniques. Global Transit. Proc. **3**(1), 31–37 (2022)
12. Jessica, A., Raj, F. V., Sankaran, J.: Credit card fraud detection using machine learning techniques. In: 2023 2nd International Conference on Vision Towards Emerging Trends in Communication and Networking Technologies (ViTECoN), pp. 1–6. IEEE (2023)
13. Borse, D.D., Patil, S.H., Dhotre, S.: Credit card fraud detection using Naive Bayes and robust scaling techniques. Int. J. **10**(1), 1–5 (2021)
14. Zhang, X., Han, Y., Xu, W., Wang, Q.: HOBA: a novel feature engineering methodology for credit card fraud detection with a deep learning architecture. Inf. Sci. **557**, 302–316 (2021)

15. Ileberi, E., Sun, Y., Wang, Z.: Performance evaluation of machine learning methods for credit card fraud detection using SMOTE and AdaBoost. IEEE Access **9**, 165286–165294 (2021)
16. Sahu, S.K., Mohapatra, D.P., Panda, S.K.: A self-trained support vector machine approach for intrusion detection. In: Tripathy, A.K., Sarkar, M., Sahoo, J.P., Li, K.-C., Chinara, S. (eds.) Advances in Distributed Computing and Machine Learning. LNNS, vol. 127, pp. 391–402. Springer, Singapore (2021). https://doi.org/10.1007/978-981-15-4218-3_38

Agent-Based Modeling for Optimum Location Selection: Enhancing Day-Ahead Market Analysis for Microgrid Integration

K. V. Vrindha Venugopal$^{(\boxtimes)}$ and K. R. M. Vijaya Chandrakala

Department of Electrical and Electronics Engineering, Amrita School of Engineering, Coimbatore, Amrita Vishwa Vidyapeetham, Coimbatore, India
kv_vrindha@cb.students.amrita.edu, krm_vijaya@cb.amrita.edu

Abstract. Integrating a microgrid has both positive and negative effects on the local distribution network. One of the challenging combinatorial optimization problems involves deciding where a microgrid should be situated inside a distribution system. Improper location of a microgrid on the utility side might result in power flowing in the opposite direction, which can have unfavorable effects, particularly during times of peak utility demand. Utility companies may be reluctant to adopt microgrids if they already have issues with excessive power loss and poor voltage profiles. This paper presents an agent-based modeling pathway to find the optimum location of a microgrid using the DC Optimal Power Flow method. A 30-bus system is considered for the analysis and demonstration for optimally locating the Micro Grid (MG) for the efficient day-ahead market operation to maximize the Generating Company (GenCo) profit. This work also interprets the best microgrid placement scenario which prompts the participation of even the highest cost generator.

Keywords: Agent-based Modeling · Microgrid · Renewable Energy Resources · Day-ahead Market · GenCo · Load Serving Entity · Independent System Operator (ISO) · Electricity Market · Day-ahead Real Time Pricing

1 Introduction

The extensive use of sustainable power has been significantly increasing in recent years due to growing worries about pollution and resource depletion in conventional methods of electricity generation. The current changes in the local systems have resulted in the so-called Micro Grid (MG), which are rapidly growing entities that promote the integration of autonomously operating agents into power systems that may have various localized resources and consumption factors [1, 2]. The main goal of MG is to maintain system stability under different network disturbances. Although the notion of AC microgrids is quite simple, the direct equipping of high-penetration DC loads such as Electric Vehicles, home, and office appliances, as Distributed Energy Resources such as fuel cell stack assembly, solar panels, and batteries, have led to increased interest in DC microgrids recently [3].

S. K. Panda et al. (Eds.): CoCoLe 2023, CCIS 1892, pp. 87–98, 2024.
https://doi.org/10.1007/978-3-031-56998-2_8

Private electricity generators may also benefit from microgrid interconnection with the utility at the distribution level, which can improve electricity reliability. MGs must overcome financial, commercial, and administrative obstacles to be integrated into the electric grid [4]. Microgrid energy markets enable a local, dependable, and sustainable balance between production and consumption [5]. So, this gives a practical means of economically integrating distributed RERs into the existing electricity grid. Additionally, this encourages investments in local generations, empowers prosumers and small-scale energy consumers, and promotes the growth of self-sufficient microgrid communities. To effectively manage the electrical grid, locating generating capabilities close to consumers is necessary. Integrating Renewable Energy Resources (RER) more deeply could cause distribution systems to become congested [6–8]. All the above-mentioned concerns require novel or modified approaches for evaluating electricity systems to provide effective decision support [9]. Agent-based simulation (ABS) approaches have been used to investigate electrical systems and markets and have received acclaim for their effectiveness [10, 11]. Agents in an Agent-based simulation model are occasionally permitted to interact with one another, which causes the simulation model to change and maybe show new behavior or patterns. As a result, an understanding of the bottom system's dynamics may be attained.

Based on the analysis of existing works discussed so far, it is seen that no thorough assessment is done on finding an optimum location for microgrid in a deregulated market environment, using ABS modeling. This paper focuses on maximizing the Genco profit by strategic positioning of microgrid using the ABS testbed, thus executing a comprehensive techno-economic assessment to assess the financial sustainability and profitability of various microgrid placement scenarios.

The work is structured in the following sections. Section 1 introduces the work. Section 2 portrays the characterization of the day-ahead market for the IEEE 30 bus network with Micro Grid (MG). Section 3 outlines the Agent-Based Framework of Electricity Market modeling and analysis for Micro Grid. Section 4 exemplifies the outcomes and interpretation, and the paper concludes with Sect. 5.

2   Characterization of the Day-Ahead Market for the IEEE 30 Bus Network with Micro Grid (MG)

For efficient power market operation, the competitive participation of GenCo and Load Serving Entity (LSE) is required, and optimal location-based participation of MG is another challenging task. An Independent System Operator (ISO) uses LMP for market settlement. The method for determining electric power prices depends on when and where it will be pumped into or eliminated from the power system grid. The least expensive option for the system to supply an additional megawatt (MW) of electrical power at any given transmission network bus is a Locational Marginal Price (LMP) for that bus [12].

Therefore, to meet the impact of MG for enhancing GenCo's profit-making potential for day-ahead market analysis is considered, and the modified IEEE 30 bus test system is illustrated in Fig. 1. The test network has 30 buses, 41 branches, 9 GenCos and 21 LSEs. Table 1 shows the GenCo parameters. GenCo 1 is the least expensive generator, while Genco 9 is the highest-cost generator followed by GenCo 8.

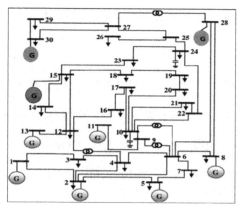

Fig. 1. Modified IEEE- 30 bus test bus system

Table 1. Input GENCO parameters.

GenCo	At bus	F_{cost}($/h)	a($/MWh)	b($/MW^{2}h)	Cap^L(MW)	Cap^U(MW)
Genco 1	1	0	10.694	0.0046	0	100
Genco 2	2	0	18.1	0.0061	0	80
Genco 3	5	0	13.327	0.0087	0	50
Genco 4	8	0	13.353	0.0089	0	50
Genco 5	11	0	37.889	0.0143	0	20
Genco 6	13	0	19.327	0.0103	0	70
Genco 7	15	0	18.3	0.0071	0	60
Genco 8	24	0	39.889	0.0163	0	20
Genco 9	30	0	49.327	0.0243	0	20

A minimization problem is presented for choosing the best location for a microgrid and cost analysis of the overall electrical grid [13]. The target is constructed under a number of constraints [14]. Equation 1 illustrates the expression for the total actual power loss in each bus i.

$$P_{loss} = \sum_{i=1}^{n} I_i^2 R_i \tag{1}$$

In a bus i for each time period t, the total generated power (P_g) plus MG injected power (P_{mg}) should balance the total demand (P_d) plus losses (P_{loss}) as shown in Eq. (2).

$$\sum_{t=0}^{23} P_g(t) + P_{mg}(t) = \sum_{t=0}^{23} P_d(t) + \sum_{t=0}^{23} P_{loss}(t) \tag{2}$$

The microgrid is anticipated to produce the active power (P_{mg}) within the minimum limit P_{mg}(min) and maximum limit P_{mg}(max) as listed in Eq. (3).

$$P_{mg}(min) \leq P_{mg} \leq P_{mg}(max) \tag{3}$$

The cost minimization is formulated as shown in Eq. (4).

$$\min \sum_{j=1}^{m} C_j P_{gj} \tag{4}$$

where C_j is the total cost function of generator j and P_{gj} is the generated power of generator j.

The generator's function of the overall cost ($/MWh) is given as Eq. (5).

$$C_j(P_{gj}) = a_j P_{gj} + b_j P_{gj}^2 + F_{costj}, \forall j \tag{5}$$

where a_j ($/MWh) and b_j ($/MW^{2}h)) are cost coefficients and F_{costj} ($/MWh) is the fixed cost, subject to the constraint given in Eq. (6).

$$P_g(\min) \leq P_g \leq P_g(\max) \tag{6}$$

3 Agent-Based Framework of Electricity Market Modeling and Analysis for Micro Grid

Electricity market modeling entails supply and demand matching w.r.t time using a dynamic price-varying scheme. Li, Tesfatsion, and Mooney of Iowa State University proposed an agent-based conceptual model, namely Agent-based Modeling of Electricity Systems (AMES) [15]. AMES has four main components: ISO, markets, transmission grids, and traders. Both buyers (load-serving entities) and sellers (generators) are included in the trader agent. A day-ahead auction and a real-time market serve as two settlements of market components. In order to estimate the production offers for the day-ahead trade, they disclose to the ISO AMES GenCos employ stochastic reinforcement learning.

The simulation framework for traders' adaptive decision-making incorporates a reinforcement learning module termed JreLM. Each and every day D in the logical chain of occurrences in the AMES market consists of 24 sequential hours H = 00, 01,..., 23. [15–18]. Each LSE's goal is to guarantee energy for its retail clients. LSEs have no learning capabilities. The ISO determines hourly bid/offer-based DC optimal power flow (DC-OPF) problems based on hourly power supply agreements and LMPs for the following day's market. In an agent-based approach, the agents take the role of different entities present in the electricity market with learning capability [19]. The market operates in real-time and on a day-ahead basis using various bids and offers. The LMP approach is utilized to manage the congested transmission lines while meeting supply and demand [20]. The agent-based modeling hierarchy is shown in Fig. 2.

AMES is a Java-based modeling platform applicable to the electricity market, which is wholesale. The ability to learn is the traders' key characteristic in AMES. The AMES participants are shown in Fig. 3.

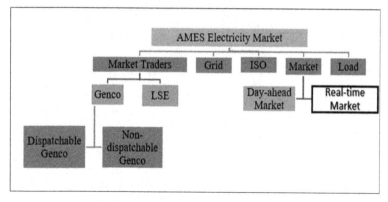

Fig. 2. Hierarchy of Agent-based Modeling

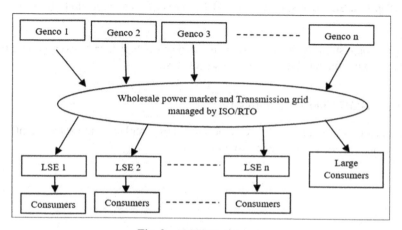

Fig. 3. AMES Participants

4   Outcomes and Interpretation

The simulation is carried out in the open-source test bed Agent based Modeling of Electricity Systems (AMES). Figure 1 displays the test rig with MG, developed using AMES architecture programming under the JAVA platform and modeled agents as respective market entities. An analysis of the optimum location of MG is done by connecting MG to the 30-bus system at various buses replacing the earlier connected GenCos, which is similar to a permutation-combination technique. Each Genco agent is replaced with the MG, and the system is compared. Figure 4(a) and Fig. 4(b) based on GenCo commitments shown in Table 1 without MG are modeled, and the LMP computed using agent-based modeling is highlighted below.

Figure 4(a), the Genco commitment curve portrays that the least cost generator Genco 1 is providing the power to the heaviest demand. The LMP curve in Fig. 4(b) shows that Locational Marginal Pricing remains constant for all buses due to the non-appearance

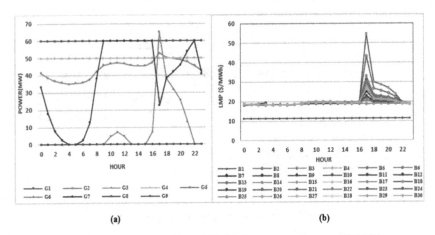

(a)   (b)

Fig. 4. IEEE 30 bus system without MG (a) Genco commitments (b) LMP curve

of branch congestion. At hour 17, since the demand is high LMP also appeared to be highest showing the involvement of congestion cost.

4.1   Case 1-MG Connected to Bus 1

The simulation of the grid with MG attached to bus 1 replacing the actual GenCo 1 is done. Figure 5.a. shows the Genco commitments.

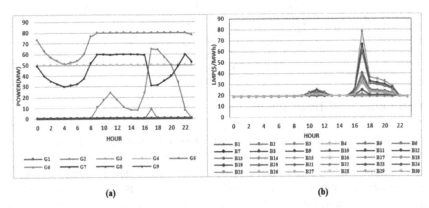

(a)   (b)

Fig. 5. MG connected at bus 1 (a) Genco commitments (b) LMP curve.

It is seen that MG was completely supplying its generated power, which had replaced the position of Genco 1. The nearest generator, Genco 2 supplied the highest power. Genco 8 and Genco 9 had not participated. Figure 5.b. shows the LMP curve, where the congestion appeared to be nil or little throughout and the LMP was high at hour 17, which accounted for congestion at peak demand.

4.2   Case 2-MG Connected to Bus 2

Here the combination is taken as MG connected to bus 2 replacing the conventional Genco 2 supply. Figure 6.a. shows the commitment curve of GenCos with MG in bus 2.

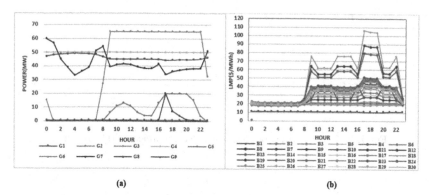

(a)   (b)

Fig. 6. MG connected at bus 2 **(a)** Genco commitments **(b)** LMP curve.

It is seen that GenCos 3 and 4 supplied constant power throughout, while the maximum supply was provided by GenCo 6 during the peak load hours. MG was always providing the minimum production level, s and the high-cost generator Genco 9 was not engaged in the supply. Figure 6.b. shows the LMP of a day. LMP remained constant at nodes 1 and 15. At all other nodes, a slab-wise change of LMP was noticed during the peak hours, exhibiting branch congestion.

4.3   Case 3-MG Connected to Bus 5

Here actual GenCo 3 is replaced with MG at bus 5. Figure 7.a. depicts the GenCo commitment. MG supplied the minimum constant power throughout the day, and Genco 4 supplied the fully produced power of 50 MW. The highest supply was provided by Genco 2, whereas GenCo 9 remained without any involvement. LMP is shown in Fig. 7.b. where all nodes except node 1 and 2 shows congestion during peak hours.

4.4   Case 4-MG Connected to Bus 8

MG is connected, replacing GenCo 4 supply at bus 8. Figure 8.a. shows the commitment. Even though GenCo 1 and GenCo 3 supplied constant power throughout the full capacity they generated, GenCo 6 supplied the highest power during peak hours. Genco 8 produced the minimum power, whereas GenCo 9 did not participate. The MG supplied the highest generated power. Figure 8.b shows the LMP graph. Nodes 1 and 2 had constant LMP showing they were congestion free. All other nodes had branch congestion during high-demand hours accounting for high LMP.

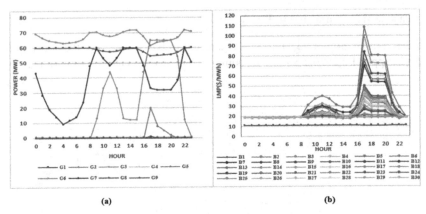

(a)   **(b)**

Fig. 7. MG connected at bus 5 **(a)** GenCo commitments **(b)** LMP curve

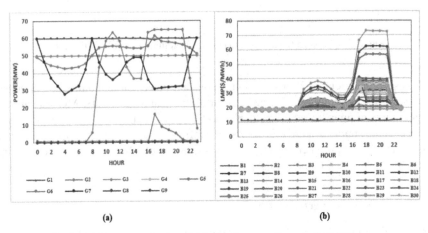

(a)   **(b)**

Fig. 8. MG connected at bus 8 **(a)** GenCo commitments **(b)** LMP curve

4.5   Case 5-MG Connected to Bus 11

Here the MG is connected, replacing the actual GenCo 5 at bus 11. Figure 9.a. and Fig. 9.b show the GenCo commitment and LMP. GenCos 1, 3 and 4 maintained a constant supply throughout with Genco 1 supplying 60% of its maximum production while GenCos 3 and 4 supplied the full generated power. MG supplied the minimum generated power. GenCos 8 and 9 did not involve in the generation.

The LMP profile remained approximately the same when the MG was connected to bus 13, bus 15, bus 24, and bus 30, replacing the original GenCos 6,7, 8, and 9 respectively. In this condition, the LMP values remained stagnant and high-cost Gen-Cos' participation in the market was extremely poor. The profit among the GenCos participation with the locational impact of MG is accounted in USD, shown in Table 2. Table 3 shows the analysis of the Market Clearing Price (MCP) and Market Clearing Volume (MCV) obtained from the simulated supply-demand calculation.

Lecture Notes of the Institute for Computer Sciences, Social Informatics and Telecommunications Engineering 571

The LNICST series publishes ICST's conferences, symposia and workshops.

LNICST reports state-of-the-art results in areas related to the scope of the Institute. The type of material published includes

- Proceedings (published in time for the respective event)
- Other edited monographs (such as project reports or invited volumes)

LNICST topics span the following areas:

- General Computer Science
- E-Economy
- E-Medicine
- Knowledge Management
- Multimedia
- Operations, Management and Policy
- Social Informatics
- Systems

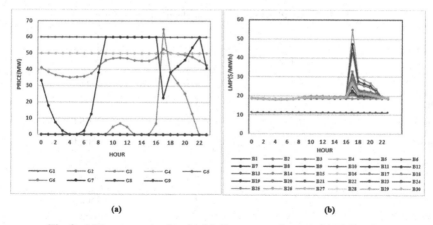

Fig. 9. MG connected at bus 11 **(a)** Genco commitments **(b)** LMP curve

Table 2. GenCo profits at different locations of MG.

Genco ID	Profit per day at different locations of MG ($)								
	Bus 1	Bus 2	Bus 5	Bus 8	Bus 11	Bus 13	Bus 15	Bus 24	Bus 30
1	163.84	235.94	378.11	396.13	397.44	392.87	394.39	397.44	397.44
2	3,613.11	263.55	659.68	398.16	283.82	293.63	311.16	283.9	283.79
3	8,066.15	21,448.80	395.94	9,085.38	6,370.19	6,757.94	7,201.56	6,370.23	6,370.18
4	8,055.00	18,833.59	11,263.05	177.63	6,851.21	7,618.14	8,487.00	6,851.19	6,851.21
5	1.21	587.2	188.43	5.9	−87.04	1.04	2.19	0	0
6	180.29	629.92	273.74	451.89	78.73	17.84	397.54	78.71	78.72
7	521.09	340.66	422.31	346.99	427.22	1,841.30	46.01	427.12	427.17
8	0	7.53	0.02	0	0	0	0	−97.63	0
9	0	0	0	0	0	0	0	0	−143.05

Each cell represents GenCo's daily profit in USD when MG is connected at different locations. It can be seen that the overall profit per day of GenCos is high when MG is connected to bus 2, the second largest is when MG is connected to bus 1, and the profit is least when MG is connected to bus 8. The microgrid, when connected at bus 11, bus 24, and bus 30 in the place of GenCo 5, GenCo 8, and GenCo 9, respectively, yields a loss. Table 3 shows that the highest revenue is generated by the combination of MCP of 26.81$/MWh and MCV of 360.5 MW, which gives a revenue of 9665.00 dollars. Therefore, this combination is the most profitable when MG is at locations bus 5 and bus 8.

The comparison of all case studies and tabular analysis shows that all nodes exhibited approximately constant LMP. Hour 17 exhibited a high LMP, which is consistent with the LSE demand and reflects the addition of congestion costs during that hour in

Table 3. MCP and MCV data for electricity generation

MG location	MCP ($/MWh)	MCV (MW)	Revenue ($)
Bus 1	30.12	310.7	9358.3
Bus 2	29.15	330.5	9634.1
Bus 5	26.81	360.5	9665.0
Bus 8	26.81	360.5	9665.0
Bus 11	18.62	265.5	4943.6
Bus 13	28.00	340.5	9534.0
Bus 15	18.70	249.5	4665.7
Bus 24	18.63	265.5	4946.3
Bus 30	18.62	265.5	4943.6

the day-ahead market operation. Even though cases, where MG is connected to buses 5 and 8, displayed better congestion management, these are the positions where maximum revenue is generated. The participation of high-cost GenCos 9 and 8 was pull down. Therefore, these GenCos need to participate in a bilateral contract to sustain their better involvement in the competitive electricity market. It is also seen that when MG is connected to buses 11, 24 and 30, it is yielding negative profit. So the optimum location of MG in the IEEE 30 bus could be at bus 5 and bus 8 which maximized the GenCo profit and effective competitive electricity market participation could be met.

5 Conclusion

This work focuses on finding the optimum location of MG at the utility grid under day-ahead market analysis using the Agent-based Modeling computational method. The optimum locations are found by analyzing the branch congestion, GenCo profits, and revenue from supply-demand data. In general, it is derived that a well-designed and well-run MG has the potential to boost GenCo's profit by introducing new income streams and lowering operating expenses. Ultimately, a node with an MG generator will be profitable depending on several variables, such as the MG's operational efficiency, the local demand for electricity, the price, and the policy regime. Through agent-based modeling, the highest revenue is generated by the combination of MG integrated into the IEEE 30 bus system with a Market Clearing Price (MCP) of 26.81$/MWh and Market Clearing Volume (MCV) of 360.5 MW, which gives a revenue of 9665.00 dollars based on the optimal location of MG at bus 5 and bus 8. The future work includes developing a methodology to incorporate an effective aggregator model in a networked microgrid structure in a real-time electricity market to increase the overall efficacy and cost-effectiveness of resource utilization.

References

1. Saeed, M.H., Fangzong, W., Kalwar, B.A., Iqbal, S.: A review on Microgrids' challenges & perspectives. IEEE Access, (**9**), 166502–166517 (2021)
2. Ahmed, M., Meegahapola, L., Vahidnia, A., Datta, M.: Stability and control aspects of Microgrid architectures–a comprehensive review. IEEE Access (**8**), 144730–144766 (2020)
3. Bharath, K.R., Krishnan, M., Kanakasabapathy, P.: A review on DC Microgrid control techniques, applications and trends, Int. J. Renew. Energy Res. (**9**), 1328–1338 (2019)
4. Manuel De Villena, M., Aitahar, S., Mathieu, S., Boukas, I., Vermeulen, E., Ernst, D.: Financial optimization of renewable energy communities through optimal allocation of locally generated electricity. IEEE Access (**10**), 77571–77586 (2022)
5. Bandyopadhyay, S., Valsan, V., Kanakasabapathy, P.: Operation analysis of grid integrated solar micro hydro hybrid system for rural community. In: 2021 IEEE 2nd International Conference on Electrical Power and Energy Systems (ICEPES), pp. 1–6. Bhopal, India (2021)
6. Sridhar, A., Ravindra, K., Affijulla, S.A.: Review on architecture of electricity markets. In: 2022 4th International Conference on Energy, Power and Environment (ICEPE), pp. 1–6. Shillong, India (2022)
7. Chaphekar, S.N., Nale, A., Dharme, A.A., Mate, N.: Optimal Location and Sizing of Microgrid for Radial Distribution Systems. In: Kalam, A., Niazi, K., Soni, A., Siddiqui, S., Mundra, A. (eds.) Intelligent Computing Techniques for Smart Energy Systems. Lecture Notes in Electrical Engineering, vol. 607, pp. 105–113. Springer, Singapore (2020)
8. Zheng, S., Liao, K., Yang, J., He, Z.: Optimal scheduling of distribution network with autonomous Microgrids: frequency security constraints and uncertainties. IEEE Trans. Sustain. Energ. **14**(1), 613–629 (2023)
9. Xiang, X., et al.: Management of bilateral contracts for Gencos considering the risk in spot market. Energ. Procedia (159), 298–303 (2019)
10. Philipp, R., Dogan, K., Wolf, F.: Agent-based modelling and simulation of smart electricity grids and markets – a literature review, Renew. Sustain. Energ. Review. (**57**), 205–215 (2016)
11. Ebrahimi, M., Gazafroudi, A.S., Ebrahimi, M., Laaksonen, H., Shafie-Khah, M., Catalão, J.P.N.: Iterative game approach for modeling the behavior of agents in a competitive flexibility trading, IEEE Access (**9**), 165227–165238 (2021)
12. Yusoff, N.I., Zin, A.A.M., Bin Khairuddin, A.: Congestion management in power system: A review. In: 2017 3rd International Conference on Power Generation Systems and Renewable Energy Technologies (PGSRET), pp. 22–27, Johor Bahru, Malaysia (2017)
13. Durvasulu, V., Hansen, T.M.: Market-based generator cost functions for power system test cases. IET Cyber-Phys. Syst. Theor. Appl. 3(4), 194–205 (2018)
14. Kiran, P., Dr. Vijaya Chandrakala, K. R. M., Nambiar, T.N.P.: Agent based locational marginal pricing and its impact on market clearing price in a deregulated electricity market, J. Electr. Syst. (**15**), 405–416 (2019)
15. Somani, A., Tesfatsion, L.: An agent-based test bed study of wholesale power market performance measures. IEEE Comput. Intell. Mag. 3(4), 56–72 (2008)
16. Kiran, P., Chandrakala, K.R.M.V., Nambiar, T.N.P.: Day ahead market operation with agent based modelling. In: 2017 International Conference on Technological Advancements in Power and Energy (TAP Energy), pp. 1–4.Kollam, India (2017)
17. Kiran, P., Vijaya Chandrakala, K.R.M., Balamurugan, S., Nambiar, T.N.P., Rahmani-Andebili, M.: A New Agent-Based Machine Learning Strategic Electricity Market Modelling Approach Towards Efficient Smart Grid Operation. In: Rahmani-Andebili, M. (ed.) Applications of Artificial Intelligence in Planning and Operation of Smart Grids. PS, pp. 1–29. Springer, Cham (2022). https://doi.org/10.1007/978-3-030-94522-0_1

18. Tofighi-Milani, M., Fattaheian-Dehkordi, S., Gholami, M., Fotuhi-Firuzabad, M., Lehtonen, M.: A novel distributed paradigm for energy scheduling of islanded multiagent Microgrids. IEEE Access, (**10**), 83636–83649 (2022)
19. Cherukuri, A., Cortés, J.: Iterative bidding in electricity markets: rationality and robustness, IEEE Trans. Netw. Sci. Eng. **7**(3), 1265–1281 (2020)
20. Vijaya Chandrakala, K.R.M., Balamurugan, S., Sankaranarayanan, K.: Genetic algorithm tuned optimal variable structure system controller for enhanced load frequency control. Int. Rev. Electr. Eng. **7**(2), 4105–4112 (2012)

A Comparative Approach for Skin Cancer Detection Using Artificial Bee Colony

Subasish Mohapatra[1]([✉]) [iD], Subhadarshini Mohanty[1], Santosh Kumar Maharana[1], Arabinda Dash[1], Sankarsan Sahoo[2], and Subham Kumar Sahoo[1]

[1] Odisha University of Technology, Bhubaneswar, India
{smohapatra,sdmohantycse}@outr.ac.in
[2] GITA Autonomous College, Bhubaneswar, India

Abstract. The importance of the Artificial Bee Colony (ABC) algorithm is increasing day by day in various domains. Medical image analysis holds the attention of researchers in this field because these images are important in the field of human health. The occurrence of skin cancer is increasing rapidly, leading to a higher mortality rate. If the cancer is detected in the early stage, then the chances of survival are increased. In this work, ABC is used on available datasets from various sources. This dataset contains images that are impacted by some anomalies. Databases are formed by including images sourced from various sites and vary in type of lighting, and resolution. Morphological filtering was used to remove image noise and the ABC algorithm is used to find the optimal threshold for skin cancer detection. To demonstrate the strength of this work, the comparisons are made with different measures with existing techniques for skin cancer recognition.

Keywords: ABC Algorithm · optimization · medical imaging

1 Introduction

To detect diseases, digital imaging and its analysis are very essential. Usage of radiology equipment has surged in recent years with the increase of technology advancements. It is estimated that there will be almost 19.1 million new cancer cases in 2023–2024, out of which approximately 9.6 million may not be cured. Timely awareness is required for preventing any harmful disease that can be life threatening. The low ratio of number of highly qualified doctors to the total world population, timely diagnosis is difficult.

Skin cancer has proven to be a major health challenge in the medical field [1]. Among skin cancers, melanoma is the most violent. It appears in one area and can spread to other parts of the body. It has a higher ability to proliferate to other organs, and, even with low incidence it has the highest mortality rate [2]. The increased cases of skin cancer occur due to over-exposure to the sun [3], especially in light-skinned people, which can cause pre-malignant and malignant lesions, along with early aging. Out of the different types of skin cancer, melanoma has lowest occurrence but more violent because it can extend to other body parts, when the lesions are still small. The National Cancer Institute

S. K. Panda et al. (Eds.): CoCoLe 2023, CCIS 1892, pp. 99–110, 2024.
https://doi.org/10.1007/978-3-031-56998-2_9

reports that solitary 2% of all skin malignancies are melanoma of various malignant skin growth, melanoma is the deadliest.

The ABC optimization algorithm [4] is favored in almost all areas of artificial intelligence problems. It is a very successful optimization technique used in global optimization. The algorithm is inspired by nature and mimics the movement of a honey bee swarm. The main intention is to explore the outcome of the ABC algorithm on problems of medical images, related to humans. Finally, a detailed review is given, so that people working in the domain can benefit.

2 Literature Survey

Sl. No	Title of paper	Author	Year	Key Finding
1	Identification and classification of melanoma as benign or Malignant [5]	A Gautam et al	2020	Histogram mapping and different descriptors need to be carefully studied for (very close to the truth or true number) identification and classification of melanoma as harmless or harmful
2	Classification of melanoma and dark nevus lesions [6]	MQ Khan et al	2019	They used the medical image processing way of doing things to classify melanoma and dark skin mole skin (damage to body parts)
3	Artificial flora (AF) optimization algorithm. [7]	L cheg et al	2018	A set of computer instructions is used to solve some complex, linear, discrete optimization problems. Plants although immobile, can disperse their seeds to certain range, allowing their progeny to find a good environment. It is beneficial for computer programs in intelligent optimization of instructions of computer
4	Detection and classification of melanoma skin cancer [8]	Hiam Alquran et al	2018	The detection and classification of melanoma skin cancer using the machine called support vector machine dermo copy imaging

(continued)

(*continued*)

Sl. No	Title of paper	Author	Year	Key Finding
5	Malignant melanoma classification: Implementation of automatic ABC rule. [9]	R Kasmi et al	2016	Image processing ways of doing things were used for an automatic ABCD rule putting into use to discriminate harmful melanoma from harmless (damage to body parts). We depend on a pre-processing step based on a middle-point filter to remove interesting (old) objects (bubbles and thin hair)
6	Analysis of skin lesions for melanoma detection [10]	D Gut man et al	2016	Describe the design and (putting into) use of a publicly (easy to get to, use, or understand) (skin-related medicine) image analysis challenge. The objective is to support research and development of sets of computer instructions for the automated (identification of a disease or problem, or its cause) of melanoma
7	Delone Triangulation (DT) method for Melanoma Detection [11]	A Penisi et al	2015	Delone Triangulation is used to extract a binary mask of the (damage to a body part) area without the need for any training training. A (having to do with measuring things with numbers experimental (process of figuring out the worth, amount, or quality of something) has been managed and did/done on a publicly available (computer file full of information), by taking into account six well-known methods for comparison

(*continued*)

(*continued*)

Sl. No	Title of paper	Author	Year	Key Finding
8	PH^2 - a database for research (consisting of dermascopic images) [12]	JS Marques et al	2013	The database has in it a total of 200 thermoscopic images of light hearted and serious, violent skin wounds, and it was designed to help persons making observations undergo growth and test machine helped diagnosis systems forskin cancer
9	Identifying lung cancer using image processing techniques [13]	D. Sharma et al	2011	Proposed an automatic computer-helped (identifying a disease or its cause) system that uses images of CT scan collected various souces. They used (more than two, but not a lot of) methods to decide/figure out the presence of lung cancer
10	Artificial Bee Colony Algorithm [4]	D karaboga	2010	Defined ABC Algorithm based on model proposed by Tereshko and Loengarov for foraging behaviour of bee colonies

3 Materials and Methods

3.1 Artificial Bee Colony

In 2005, Dervis Karaboga proposed ABC algorithm [4] which is a population-based meta-heuristic algorithm. This method is mostly based on the behaviour of bee swarm and has some manipulate parameters that include:

a. Solution number - available food sources
b. Maximum cycle – maximum possible generations
c. Limit – Number of abandoned of food sources

The processes involved in ABC algorithm are:

a. Population process - variational process that find different regions.
b. Selection process - use prior experiences.

Phase of algorithm:

a. Initialization phase - initiate food sources population
b. Employed Bee phase – evaluate fitness using greedy selection
c. Onlooker Bee phase – Food is chosen using fitness information
d. Scout Bee Phase – randomly search for better solution

In ABC, the fitness is given by food location and amount of nectar. The number of employed bee and the number of solutions must be equal because each bee is related to a food source (Fig. 1).

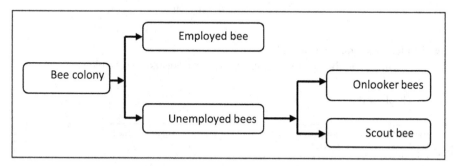

Fig. 1. Representation of Bee Members

The initial population of the worker bees S is generated by the artificial bee colony using the threshold values from the histogram of gray image, where S = total number of bees.

Let $A_a = [A_{a,1}, A_{a,2},..., A_{a,M}]$ represent the ath solution in bees group, and M represent total length. Each worker bee A_i, that create unique solution B_i within area of proximity is given by;

$$B_{a,b} = A_{a,b} + \sigma_{a,b}. (A_{a,b} – A_{c,b})$$

Where,

A_c - randomly selected partner solution ($i \neq c$),
b - random index selected within the group,
$\sigma_{a,b}$ - random number between − 1 and 1.

Greedy selection is used when a new partner solution B_a is generated. If the fitness of B_a is greater than old A_a, then Y_i is replaced with Z_i; else Y_i remains same. Worker bees after completing the search task, they share the food information with onlooker bees by continuously vibrating. Onlooker bee get this information, calculate the nectar present in it. If the position has not changed and the limit has reached, then the food will be discarded. Let the rejected source is C_a, so scout bee search for new food source to replace with C_a by following equation,

$$C_{a,b} = LB_{a,b} + d (U_{a,b} – L_{a,b})$$

Where,

d – arbitrary number in range (0,1),
b – lower limit,
$\sigma_{a,b}$ – upper limit

- Input parameters for ABC Algorithm: -

  - Objective function –sphere function is used
  - Colony size (using threshold values)
  - Number of dimensions
  - Maximum number of iterations
  - Fitness function =

$$\text{Fit} = \begin{cases} 1/(1+f) & \text{if } f >= 0 \\ 1 + |f| & \text{if } f < 0 \end{cases}$$

  - Limits on the number of trials =
      Limit = number of dimensions * number of decision variable
  - Probability =
      $\text{Prob} = 0.9 * \frac{fit}{max(fit)} + 0.1$

---

1. Initialize bees' group (By using threshold values from the histogram of RGB image from dataset)
2. Initial swarm solution is updated
3. For each worker bee: a partner solution is produced
                 Fitness is calculated
                 Greedy selection is applied
4. Onlooker bee calculate Probability
5. Again, produce another new partner solution and compare it with present food (the solution) and the best one is selected
6. Scout bee find the abandoned food source, assuming that food remains and updates it
7. Make iteration +=1
8. **if** number of iterations > maximum iteration, then
9.   Stop and display results
10. **else** jump to step 2 and repeat
11. **end**

3.2 Melanoma Skin Lesions Detection Methodology

Skin lesions are difficult to detect in dermatoscopic imaging (Fig. 2), but pictures taken using a digital camera show shadows that cover lesions of the skin. Artifacts such as bubble type, metachromatic lesion, mirror reflections, hair presence, and rough illumination are also present in dermatologic images. The suggested method aims to extract the lesion from its context without affecting the color, format, or geometry.

   The database includes images collected from various sources that vary from each other. In the first step, morphological filtering was used to remove noise from the image. The method must reject the contiguous structures and reconstruct/reduce them in dermatoscopic images. Threshold values were found using a histogram of magnified images by taking the help of the ABC algorithm. Using this threshold, segmentation & finding the margins of lesions become easier.

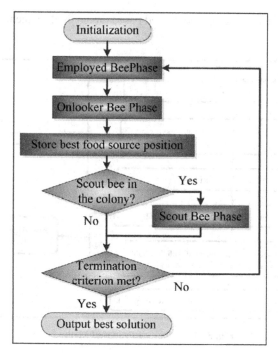

Fig. 2. Flowchart of Bee Colony Algorithm

To evaluate performance, the results obtained (segmented images) are compared to the ground truth image, and at last, the result as well as ground truth images are superimposed on the actual dermatoscopic image.

Steps and explanation: -

- In the first step the RGB image of the dataset image is converted to into gray image.
- Appropriate functions of median filtering and morphological filtering is applied to the gray image.
- The grey image is then used to calculate the histogram of the given dataset image.
- The histogram is used to depict the color pixel of the gray image. Total pixel size is 256 (i.e., range is 0–255).

  - 0- completely Black pixel
  - 255- completely White pixel

- The frequency of each pixel is taken as individual threshold values and is used as input to the Artificial Bee Colony Algorithm and an optimal threshold value is computed using the algorithm.
- Then segmentation of the gray image using this optimal threshold value by highlighting the boundaries which occur at threshold value (image segmentation step).
- The final segmented image is compared with the ground truth image.

• The performance metrices are computed based on the final segmented image.

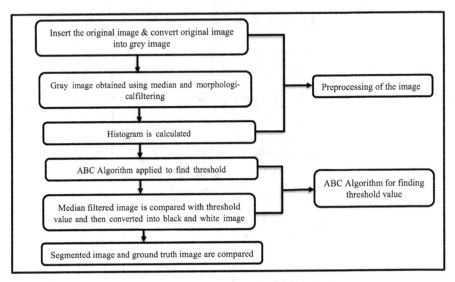

Fig. 3. Flowchart of Proposed Method

4 Implementation and Simulation

Proposed technique was implemented in the MATLAB software by using available datasets (Fig. 3). Simulation environment – MATLAB R2021b

Results (in %):

Table 1. Performance evaluation in different measures by varying Databases

Databases	Accuracy	Sensitivity	Specificity
PH2	97.02	96.5	99.4
ISBI 2016	96.24	94.42	98.31
ISBI 2017	98.61	98.64	98.52
DermIS	96.24	97.25	91.46

5 Results and Discussion

The proposed technique was assessed using four datasets to generate a segmented image and compare it to the corresponding ground truth (GT) images. Some terminologies were computed (Tables 1 and 2), those are:

- Accuracy (ACC) – used to depict the final pixel along with analysis of segmentation
- Sensitivity (SEN) – show number of correctly segmented cancer affected skin lesions
- Specificity (SPE) – ratio of wrongly segmented skin-cancer non-lesions pixels

Table 2. Representation of Various Formulas for Computation

Measure	Formula
ACC	$(P + Q)/(P + Q + R + S)$
SEN	$P/(P + S)$
SPE	$Q/(R + Q)$

Where,

P: true positive values, Q: t rue negative values, R: false positive values
S: false negative values

5.1 Comparison with prevailing models for different databases

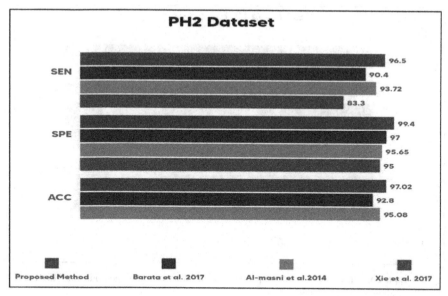

Fig. 4. Graph comparing results of proposed method with existing methods for "PH2 dataset" for given set of parameters.

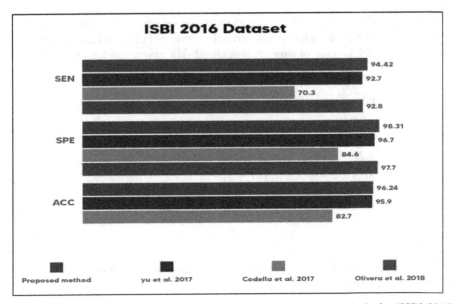

Fig. 5. Graph comparing results of proposed method with existing methods for "ISBI 2016 dataset" for given set of parameters.

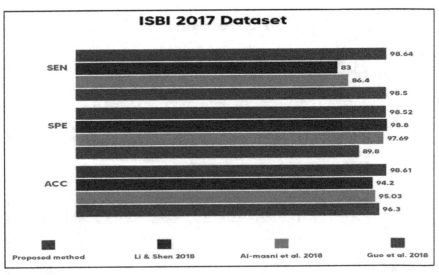

Fig. 6. Graph comparing results of proposed method with existing methods for "ISBI 2017 dataset" for given set of parameters.

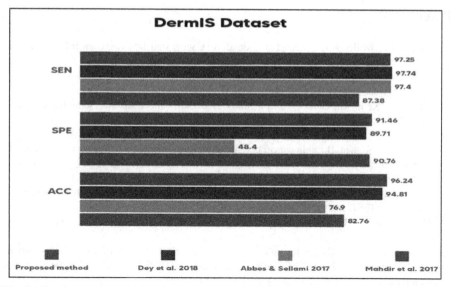

Fig. 7. Graph comparing results of proposed method with existing methods for "DermIS dataset" for given set of parameters

The comparative analysis of proposed approach with some existing approaches with varying dataset PH2, ISBI 2016, ISBI 2017, and Derm IS dataset respectively in Fig. 4, Fig. 5, Fig. 6 and Fig. 7 respectively.

6 Conclusion

The main part of the cancer detection method is the segmentation of the injury area, as the area is close to the actual skin lesion. The proposed method demonstrates a fully automated technique to detect skin lesions, without requiring any learning steps. This method proposes an Artificial bee colony algorithm and applies it to images of skin from the databases, and calculates threshold value based on the histogram of the image. The aim of applying the ABC Algorithm is to detect the edges of the lesion. For detecting cancer, the technique got 97% accurate. The results were better than the existing algorithm test results. The ABC algorithm is very efficient and can improve the accuracy of early detection of skin lesions, thereby reducing mortality.

The time it takes for the method to process is very short, and this method has the best accuracy and sensitivity. The results may reach 100% accuracy and success rate in the future. Hence, this is the best way to detect cancer in the skin.

References

1. Siegel, R.L., Miller, K.D., Fuchs, H.E., Jemal, A.: Cancer statistics, CA: Cancer J. Clin. **72**(1), 7–33 (2022)
2. Celebi, M.E., et al.: A methodological approach to the classification of dermoscopy images. Comput. Med. Imaging Graph. **31**(6), 362–373 (2007)
3. Leiter, U., Keim, U., Garbe, C.: Epidemiology of skin cancer: update, Sunlight, Vitam. D Skin Cancer, 123–139 (2019)
4. Karaboga, D.: Artificial bee colony algorithm, Scholarpedia, **5**(3), 6915 (2010)
5. Gautam, A., Raman, B.: Skin cancer classification from dermoscopic images using feature e xtraction methods. In: 2020 IEEE REGION 10 CONFERENCE (TENCON), pp. 958–963. IEEE (2020)
6. Khan, M.Q., et al.: Classification of melanoma and nevus in digital images for diagnosis of skin cancer. IEEE Access **7**, 90132–90144 (2019)
7. Cheng, L., Wu, X.H., Wang, Y.: Artificial flora (AF) optimization algorithm. Appl. Sci. **8**(3), 329 (2018)
8. Alquran, H., et al.: The melanoma skin cancer detection and classification using support vector machine. In: 2017 IEEE Jordan Conference on Applied Electrical Engineering and Computing Technologies (AEECT), pp. 1–5, IEEE (2017)
9. Kasmi, R., Mokrani, K.: Classification of malignant melanoma and benign skin lesions: implementation of automatic ABCD rule. IET Image Proc. **10**(6), 448–455 (2016)
10. Codella, N.C., et al.: Skin lesion analysis toward melanoma detection: a challenge at the 2017 international symposium on biomedical imaging (ISBI), hosted by the international skin imaging collaboration (ISIC). In: 2018 IEEE 15th International Symposium on Biomedical Imaging (ISBI 2018), pp. 168–172, IEEE (2018)
11. Pennisi, A., Bloisi, D.D., Nardi, D., Giampetruzzi, A.R., Mondino, C., Facchiano, A.: Melanoma detection using delaunay triangulation. In: 2015 IEEE 27th International Conference on Tools with Artificial Intelligence (ICTAI), pp. 791–798. IEEE (2015)
12. Mendonça, T., Ferreira, P.M., Marques, J.S., Marcal, A. R., Rozeira, J.: PH 2-A dermoscopic image database for research and benchmarking. In: 2013 35th annual international conference of the IEEE engineering in medicine and biology society (EMBC), pp. 5437–5440, IEEE (2013)
13. Sharma, D., Jindal, G.: Identifying lung cancer using image processing techniques. In: International Conference on Computational Techniques and Artificial Intelligence (ICCTAI), vol. 17, pp. 872–880 (2011)

Application of Unsupervised Learning in Computing

A Hybrid Approach to Enhance Software Quality by Sentiment Analysis of Developer

Archana Patnaik[✉] and Neelamadhab Padhy

Department of Computer Science and Engineering, GIET University, Odisha, Gunupur, India
{archanapatnaik,dr.neelamadhab}@giet.edu

Abstract. Sentiment analysis evaluates the software developer's emotions during product development. Quality of the real time project can be assured by the detecting the amount of code smell present in the software code snippet. In our work we have collected data from Oryx, Antlr4, Eclipse, Junit project and reduced the dimensionality using PCA and KPCA techniques. Our methodology focuses on the use of Ensemble approach for emotion analysis which is done on weekly basis. It is observed that Random Forest classifier consists of multiple numbers of decision trees which reduces the problem of over fitting and provides highest accuracy of 95%. JUnit open source project provides highest performance as the amount of clean code is more than dirty code that occurs due to positive sentiment of the developer. In our work we have assured the quality of the real time software projects by studying positive and negative emotions from which we can evaluate the type of code smell and in the further steps manual refactoring is performed by restructuring the code and quality is improved.

Keywords: Code Smell · Quality Assurance · Sentiment Analysis and Ensemble Techniques

1 Introduction

Software engineering involves improvement of performance of different real time project by enhancing its quality, reliability and maintainability. Sentiment analysis can be applied for various tasks like software code designing, developing, testing and refactoring the code snippet at different levels. It evaluates the performance of the software projects and improves its quality by reducing complexity. In order to assure the quality three aspects of emotions like negative, neutral and positive are studied based on which amount of dirty code is extracted from the source. Dirty code can be referred as the line of code that results in high space and time complexity. It occurs due to presence of negative sentiment of the software developer that is extracted from emotion score evaluated from source code metrics. These metrics are considered as the statistical measuring parameters of the probable value that lies within the range of 0 to 1. Negative sentiments includes feelings like anger, sadness, depression, anticipation which effects the mental state of the developer as a result of which improper code is design not have any functional issues but often leads to other structural defects. If there is any issue in the internal structure of the code snippet that can be identified during white box testing performed by the software testers.

S. K. Panda et al. (Eds.): CoCoLe 2023, CCIS 1892, pp. 113–125, 2024.
https://doi.org/10.1007/978-3-031-56998-2_10

The major issues that widely effects the quality is due the complexity of the code which is technically termed as code smell that occurs at various steps of high level and low level structural design. Positive sentiment includes feeling like happiness, joy, excitement that results in development of high quality products by increasing the rate of clean code as compared to dirty code. Neutral emotional gives neither good nor bad impact on the maintainability of the product as its produces moderate effect on code development. Based on the types of emotion found software quality is assured and assessed by the research and quantity of code smell is evaluated by using different machine learning and deep learning algorithms. The emotion score can be by using different automated tools like SentiCR, SentiStrength etc. which is further processed and taken as input for different algorithms based on which final sentiment analysis of the developer is done either on daily, weekly or monthly basis. Basically the value of negative, neutral and positive emotions lies within -1, 0 and $+1$ that can be correlated by its sentiment dependent features. The concept of code smell arises from the comparison of dirty code and clean code. Dirty code occurs due presence of more line zof code, multiple class, extra comment line, extra methods, unnecessary variable memory allocation which reduces the usability, maintainability and reliability of the software. It contributes towards delivery of good software product with high performance and more efficiency. Considering the internal organization of code various types of smells like large class, long method, long parameter list, data clumps, switch statements, lazy class, dead code, duplicate code, comments, divergent changes and parallel inheritance hierarchies are identified. The primary cause of code smell is the negative sentiment that widely affects the developer's mind during software code design. Sometime it also occurs due to improper code design, lack of technical knowledge, lack of programming skills and no proper idea of the software engineer. Large class smell occurs due to presence of lengthy code either in base class and derived class which contributes a lot towards time issues. Use of multiple number of nested classes can also be considered as major cause for large class code smell. Long method smell occurs due to more number of lines where LOC is more than 10 as a result of which the execution time is increased. Duplicate codes are the repetition of pieces of code multiple times in a program which may not change the result and leads to increase of number of lines. Lazy class code smell represents the class rarely used in a program but often increases the software code base. Divergent change code smell occurs due to changes made out- side the class multiple times. Dead codes are the unused part that is not required during program execution. In our work the dirty code analysis is done by using ensemble learn ing approach. The emotional score extracted from the probable value of source project is used for analysis of dirty code. Initially the raw data set collected is preprocessed by using data normalization concept. As the dataset contains many irrelevant features so the dimensionality is reduced by using Principal Component Analysis (PCA) and Kernel Principal Component Analysis (KPCA). By using machine learning algorithms accuracy of the proposed model is calculated. Ensemble learning is used to identify the best classifier which can also predict the sentiment which may analysis of the developer on weekly basis. Performance of each real time project used is also compared and plotted in the graph which explained in result analysis part.

In Sect. 1 we have discussed regarding the introduction part of our work which includes the detail about sentiment analysis and impact of code smell on developer emotion is evaluated by using ensemble learning. Section 2 illustrates about the literature survey and explained about the related work based on which the comparative analysis of our work is done.

Section 3 highlights the research background of our work that focuses about the source code metrics and implementation details. Section 4 discussed about the proposed research framework explained in phase wise manner starting from data collection to performance evaluation of different open source projects. Section 5 shows the result part and answers all the framed research questions. In Sect. 6 we have concluded our work by highlighting all the important aspects of emotion based on which our future work is also explained. Based on several experimental study and literature survey our entire workflow is illustrated by framing three research questions:

RQ 1: How ensemble approach is used in sentiment analysis?
In order to conduct sentiment survey extraction of emotion score is done by considering the probable value of source code metrics. By considering these scores ensemble approach is done by using Random Forest classifier and various boosting approach like AdaBoost, XGBoost and Gradient Boost algorithms. It uses voting prediction where random sample emotion scores helps to build multiple models and output of all the models are combined to generate the best sentiment score.

RQ 2: What are the effects of emotion based classification based on which weekly analysis is done?
Basically sentiment study is done based on the different aspects of emotions like positive, negative and neutral emotions on weekly basis starting from Monday to Friday. Based on the mental state of the developer emotion based classification is done and its effects are been identified by our work.

RQ 3: Which real time project is having high quality with low complexity?
The primary aim of our work is to improve the quality of the existing open source real time projects like JUnit, Antlr4 and Eclipse. The efficiency of all the projects are evaluated by the presence of positive and negative emotions based on which the amount of dirty code and clean code is measured. It is observed that JUnit is having highest performance as the proportion of clean code is more.

2   Related Works

Code smell detection [1] can be done by following various deep learning algorithms like Convolution Neural Network (CNN) that is used to detect smells like God class, Brain Class and Brain Method in which the execution is done by using keras library. The hybrid approach [2] of code smell detection uses different algorithms like PCA, Bayesian Network, Autoencoder, Gaussian Model, K means classifier from which accuracy percentage of clustering approach is considered to be highest as compared to other algorithms. Sentiment of developer [3] can also be analyzed by considering commit level message where final score is calculated from positive, negative and neutral emotions. Various real time issues related to the GitHub [4] comments are explored at special level by using various data visualization techniques by the software community. Effects of change on the source code [5] are studied based on the types of commit histories performed by the code framer who continuously updates the existing code. It is observed that sometime the use of automated sentiment tools [6] have a negative effect on software engineering domain by interpreting the original data value. The complex issues arises while studying the GitHub [7] message is been spotted by several commenters and the effect is been compared from the contributor. The impact of code complexity [8] is also studied by using various types of regression approach and accuracy of model is more than 90%. Accuracy prediction [9] of various open source projects like Antlr4, JUnit and Oryx is done by using Naïve Bayes classifiers where class level refactoring is used to restructure the internal behavior of the software system. In order to overview the commit message [10], different libraries like Scikit learn, Theano and Tensorflow are used to assess quality of software code. In field of software engineering [11], 40k labeled sentences are manually operated by using recommender system using JIRA environment. Open source software [12] target different target mining statements by studying the positive behavior of OSS community and helps to complete all the tasks within stipulated time period. Different developers [13] have conducted the study of sentiment polarity based on various functionalities by performing qualitative and quantitative analysis of comments. In this work researchers [14] have compared rudeness with neutral emotions by considering the extracted features and predicted the accuracy as 67% for two sample open source projects. The work rate of various [15] online projects is studied based on number of projects comments on weekly basis which can controlled by decreasing the number of comments used in technical dimensions. The robustness [16] of project is overviewed by using two original dataset where 186 negative, 25 neutral and 130 positive emotion is been evaluated by using some automated sentiment analysis tools. Perception [17] of software developer community is estimated by considering 998 projects where 10,996 commits has been performed by GHTorrent dataset. Commit level [18] analysis is done by using different projects like Eclipse, JEdit, ArgoUML and JUnit projects where 8 classification of emotion are collected based on different task assigned to the develop.

3   Research Background

A. Sample Open Source Projects Dataset

In order to perform the quality assurance test of the existing software system we have used the dataset of different open source real time projects like Antlr, JUnit, Oryx and Eclipse. The experimental analysis is done by considering the probable values that varies within the range of 0 to 1. Antlr language recognition based projects uses java, python, C# and Python languages to develop the code snippets. JUnit open source projects consider the test cases from which we can extract the probable values that can be used for code smell analysis. Eclipse project uses dataset from Git repositories that helps to model different java frameworks. Oryx project can also be used to perform sentiment analysis of software code commits at method and class level.

The dataset related to the open source project are collected from the Tera Promise repository which is further cleaned and preprocessed before the code smell detection based on emotion analysis. The detailed description of the dataset is represented in the table below which consists of different features like project name, code smell details and sentiment scores of the software developers. Table 1 represents the probable values of different projects based on five source code metrics (Table 2.).

Table 1. Dataset For Antlr

Software Metrics	Refactored Class	Non-Refactored Class	P-Value
LOC	180	70	1
KLOC	45	12	1
WMC	95	15	0
NOI	36	8	0
CCL	110	32	1

Table 2. Dataset For JUnit

Software Metrics	Refactored Class	Non-Refactored Class	P-Value
LOC	95	20	0
KLOC	80	14	1
WMC	67	13	1
NOI	58	9	0
CCL	90	22	1

Table 3. Dataset For Eclipse

Software Metrics	Refactored Class	Non-Refactored Class	P-Value
LOC	59	10	1
KLOC	60	12	1
WMC	59	3	0
NOI	70	17	0
CCL	112	32	1

Table 5 represents the type and amount of code smell data present in the source dataset collected from different real time projects. Based on the average survey of four projects percentage of dirty and clean code is evaluated by considering lines and structure of code design. By examining the piece of code snippet developed in Java language six types of code smell are identified with detailed description explained in the table below (Tables 3 and 4).

Table 4. Dataset For Oryx

Software Metrics	Refactored Class	Non-Refactored Class	P-Value
LOC	210	60	1
KLOC	189	24	0
WMC	75	12	1
NOI	40	8	0
CCL	94	12	1

Table 5. Experimental Code Smell Analysis

Types of Code Smell	Percentage of Dirty Cod e(%)	Percentage of Clean Code (%)
Long Method	45.33	54.22
Dead Code	18.67	71.88
Comments	32.33	63.12
Data Class	25.33	74.45
Lazy Class	42.77	58.33

B. Machine Learning Algorithms

In our work we have used various aspects of machine learning approach at different phases. Initially the data cleaning is done in order to remove the null and missing value followed by data balancing using normalization method. As the original dataset contain many extra features which is refined by using dimensionality reduction methods using Principal Component Analysis (PCA) and Kernal Principal Component Analysis (KPCA). In order to study the various aspects of emotions ensemble approach is used by combining different algorithms like Random Forest Classifiers, Adaboost, Gradient Boost and XGradient Boost approach.

$$G = 1 - \sum (Pi)^2 \tag{1}$$

$$H(x) = sign \sum a_t h_t(x) \tag{2}$$

1. Random Forest Classifiers: It is an ensemble approach which combines several decision tree classifiers to give a best hybrid classifier with higher accuracy. The subsets collected from individual projects are combined using voting prediction which is used for code smell detection and emotion score verification.

   The gini index of each tree is calculated by subtracting the relative frequency Pi of each classifier from 1 based on which project based data classification is done.

2. AdaBoost Classifier: Adaptive boosting approach technique uses our real time project based dataset to reassign weight to incorrectly assigned classifiers. In our work we

have segregated multiple weak classifiers which is then combined to form a strong classifier.

where H(x) represent the output of the model, ht(x) is the input for weak classifier and a_t is the weight assigned to the individual classifier.

3. Gradient Boost Classifier: This approach frames the prediction model by using both classification and regression analysis that ensembles the weak classifiers to form a strong classifier. The best results of the previous level can be used as the input for the next level that contributes a lot to minimize the model error.

where α is the learning rate, yp represents the prediction value of input and yt represents the value of target variable.

4. XGradient Boost Classifier: Extreme Gradient Boost algorithm is the extended version of gradient boost approach that accurately combines the input data to predict the final output. It is a parallel tree boosting approach that works on ranking problem using regression and classification approach.

$$yp = yp - a * 2 * \sum yt - yp \tag{3}$$

4 Hybrid Research Framework

The Fig. 1 describes about different steps involved in our entire workflow in phase wise manner. Using this framework we have also identified solution to our framed research questions.

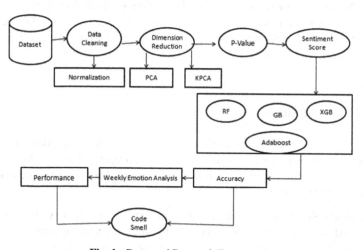

Fig. 1. Proposed Research Framework

Phase 1: Raw Dataset Collection from Various Open Source Real Time Projects
In the first step raw data is collected from different existing source projects like Antlr4, JUnit, Eclipse and Oryx and measured in terms of source code metrics. It is measured in terms of probable value that lies within the range of 0 to 1.

Phase 2: Data Preprocessing and Reduction of Dimensionality of the Dataset
In order to generate accurate value in the result part raw data need to be preprocessed by using normalization method. Then the comparative analysis is done by analyzing the data with and without normalization by using feature selection techniques like PCA and KPCA.

Phase 3: Evaluation of Emotion Score Based on Probable Value
The data collected from project are stored in terms of probable values can be either 0 or 1 that is in binary format. Based on these value sentiment score prediction is done that is –1 for negative, 0 for neutral and + 1 for positive emotions.

Phase 4: Implementation Done by Using Ensemble Learning
The emotional score collected in the above step act as an input parameter for machine learning algorithm used. In order to predict best result ensemble learning algorithms like Random Forest Classifier, Gradient Boost, XGBoost and Adaboost are used and accuracy lies within the range of 85 to 95%.

Phase 5: Result Analysis on Weekly Basis Based on Percentage of Code Smell Detected
Based on the accuracy of the algorithms used rate of code smell is detected and plotted in graph to identify the percentage of clean and dirty code present in the source projects.

Phase 6: Performance Evaluation of the Open Source Real Time Project
In the last step performance of all the four projects are evaluated and JUnit project is considered to have highest performance with good quality and maintainability as the amount of clean code is more than dirty code with positive sentiment of the software developer.

5   Result Discussions

The result discussion reflects our work in different stages. We have identified solution to our research questions by performing several experimental analyses. As the original dataset consist of many impurities and bias value, it needs to be pre processed before any using it for the next step.

Dimensionality Reduction: As we are using kernel function in PCA, the KPCA algorithm is used to reduce the dimensionality by applying feature selection methods. Figures 2 and 3 shows various features of the raw dataset after reducing its dimensions.

RQ 1: Can Developer's Emotional Score Survey Done by Using Hybrid Approach?
By using the concept of ensemble approach we have combined multiple models which can be used for efficient emotion score prediction. In order to improve the performance of the model this approach is used which completely focuses on the voting prediction.

In Fig. 4 we have used Random Forest Classifier to evaluate the efficiency of the hybrid model. In this algorithm we have combined emotional score for three different

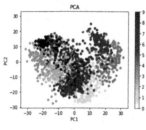

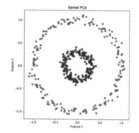

Fig. 2. PCA

Fig. 3. KPCA

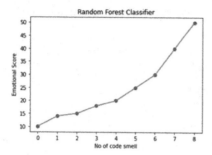

Fig. 4. Random Forest Classifier

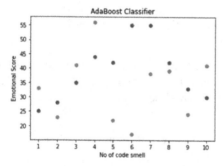

Fig. 5. AdaBoost Classifier

decision tree and evaluated the best score and tested it for many software developer working in this domain. It is observed that accuracy of the model is 95%.

Figure 5 shows the implementation of AdaBoost classifiers for sentiment analysis which is considered as a weak learner. In order to improve the performance of the model boosting approach is used to adjust the dataset as per the requirement of the users.

Figure 6 shows the shows the implementation of gradient boost algorithms that considers all the equal emotional score for computation of data in fast manner. It combines more number of weak learning model to evaluate the best emotion score based on which quality of product is assured.

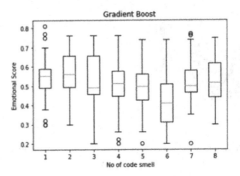

Fig. 6. Gradient Boost Algorithms

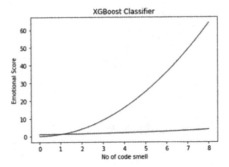

Fig. 7. XGBoost Classifier

In Fig. 7 shows the implementation of Extreme Gradient boost algorithm which overcomes all the drawbacks of gradient boost classifier and produces best result in case of emotion analysis of software code commit.

Table 6. Performance Analysis

Sl No	Algorithm Used	Accuracy
1	AdaBoost Classifier	85%
2	Gradient Boost Classifier	89%
3	Random Forest Classifier	95%
4	Extreme Gradient Boost Classifiers	91%

In the above Fig. 8 accuracy of different ensemble learning algorithm lile Random Forest classifier with 95% and boosting algorithms like AdaBoost, Gradient Boost and XGBoost classifier with accuracy rate of 85%, 89% and 91% respectively (Tables 6 and 7).

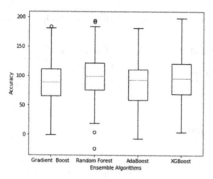

Fig. 8. Comparison of Accuracy

RQ 2: What are the Effects of Emotion Based Classification Based on Which Weekly Analysis is Done?

In our work we have analyzed the emotions of the developer community on daily and weekly basis starting from Monday to Thursday which is shown in Fig. 9 which depends on amount of code smell collected from the existing project.

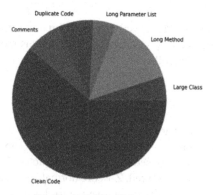

Fig. 9. Code Smell Percentage

RQ 3: Which Real Time Project is Having More Efficiency and High Performance?

We have done the experimental analysis for the projects like Antlr4, JUnit, Eclipse and Oryx based on which the prediction shows JUnit source project is having highest performance.

Figure 10 shows the comparison of performance of all the real time project based on the positive and negative sentiments of the developers. In Antlr, Eclipse and Oryx project rate of positive sentiment is less as compared to negative sentiment. Antlr project developer have negative sentiment as the amount of dirty and clean code are 65.22% and 35.14%. Eclipse project framework contains 55.63% diriy code and 44.23% clean code. Oryx open source project contains 28.55% clean code and 71.24% dirty code resulting in negative sentiment of software developer. JUnit project developer have positive sentiment

Table 7. Comparative Analysis of Different Open Source Projects

Project Name	Sentiment Type	Dirty Code (%)	Clean Code(%)
Antlr	Negative	65.22	35.14
JUnit	Positive	14.77	85.45
Eclipse	Negative	55.63	44.23
Oryx	Negative	71.24	28.55

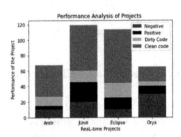

Fig. 10. Comparative Analysis of Different Project

with 14.77% dirty code and 85.45% clean code. So JUnit is considered as the project with highest performance because the proportion of clean code is more resulting in product with high quality and maintainability.

6 Conclusion

Our research work identifies various aspects of emotion by using ensemble machine learning approach which combines multiple models and computes the best sentiment score of the software developer. Based on the score predicted the quality and maintainability of the software project is assured. Z-Score normalization is used as to preprocess the raw original dataset and in order to remove the irrelevant features PCA and KPCA method is used. In order to obtain good end product the amount of code smell should be very less. After using four different ensemble techniques, it is predicted that Random Forest classifier is having highest performance of 95% which suits best to the proposed model. We have identified five different types of code smell that is long method, large class, comments, duplicate code and long parameter list. In order identify the best product we have compared the performance of all the four projects and it is observed that JUnit is a high quality project with less code complexity and high quality.

References

1. Das, A.K., Yadav, S., Dhal, S.: Detecting code smells using deep learning. In: TENCON 2019–2019 IEEE Region 10 Conference (TENCON), pp. 2081–2086. IEEE (2019)
2. Patnaik, A., Padhy, N.: A hybrid approach to identify code smell using machine learning algorithms. Int. J. Open Source Soft. Processes (IJOSSP) **12**(2), 21–35 (2021)

3. Sinha, V., Lazar, A., Sharif, B.: Analyzing developer sentiment in commit logs. In: Proceedings of the 13th International Conference on Mining Software Repositories, pp. 520–523 (2016)
4. Liao, Z., He, D., Chen, Z., Fan, X., Zhang, Y., Liu, S.: Exploring the characteristics of issue-related behaviors in github using visualization techniques. IEEE Access **6**, 24003–24015 (2018)
5. Zanjani, M.B., Swartzendruber, G., Kagdi, H.: Impact analysis of change requests on source code based on interaction and commit histories. In: Proceedings of the 11th Working Conference on Mining Software Repositories, pp. 162–171 (2014)
6. Jongeling, R., Sarkar, P., Datta, S., Serebrenik, A.: On negative results when using sentiment analysis tools for software engineering research. Empir. Softw. Eng. **22**, 2543–2584 (2017)
7. Destefanis, G., Ortu, M., Bowes, D., Marchesi, M., Tonelli, R.: On measuring affects of github issues commenters. In: Proceedings of the 3rd International Workshop on Emotion Awareness in Software Engineering, pp. 14–19 (2018)
8. Patnaik, A., Padhy, N.: Does code complexity affect the quality of real-time projects? detection of code smell on software projects using machine learning algorithms. In: Proceedings of the International Conference on Data Science, Machine Learning and Artificial Intelligence, pp. 178–185 (2021)
9. Patnaik, A., Panigrahi, R., Padhy, N.: Prediction of accuracy on open source java projects using class level refactoring. In: 2020 International Conference on Computer Science, Engineering and Applications (ICCSEA), pp. 1–6, IEEE (2020)
10. Ronchieri, E., Juric, R., Canaparo, M.: Sentiment analysis for software code assessment. In: 2019 IEEE Nuclear Science Symposium and Medical Imaging Conference (NSS/MIC), pp. 1–2. IEEE (2019)
11. Lin, B., Zampetti, F., Bavota, G., Di Penta, M., Lanza, M., Oliveto, R.: Sentiment analysis for software engineering: How far can we go? In: Proceedings of the 40th International Conference on Software Engineering, pp. 94–104 (2018)
12. Ferreira, J., Glynn, M., Hunt, D., Babu, J., Dennehy, D., Conboy, K.: Sentiment analysis of open source communities: an exploratory study. In: Proceedings of the 15th International Symposium on Open Collaboration, pp. 1–5 (2019)
13. Carigé, R.S., de Figueiredo Carneiro, G.: Sentiment polarity of programmers in an open source software project: an exploratory study. In: Proceedings of the XXXIV Brazilian Symposium on Software Engineering, pp. 147–156 (2020)
14. Veenendaal, A., Daly, E., Jones, E., Gang, Z., Vartak, S., Patwardhan, R.S.: Sentiment Analysis in Code Review Comments. Comput. Sci. Emerg. Res. J. **3** (2015)
15. Sarker, F., Vasilescu, B., Blincoe, K., Filkov, V.: Socio-technical work-rate increase associates with changes in work patterns in online projects. In: 2019 IEEE/ACM 41st International Conference on Software Engineering (ICSE), pp. 936–947 IEEE (2019)
16. Lin, B., Zampetti, F., Oliveto, R., Di Penta, M., Lanza, M., Bavota, G.: Two datasets for sentiment analysis in software engineering. In: 2018 IEEE International Conference on Software Maintenance and Evolution (ICSME), p. 712. IEEE (2018)
17. Venigalla, A.S.M., Chimalakonda, S.: Understanding emotions of developer community towards software documentation. In 2021 IEEE/ACM 43rd International Conference on Software Engineering: Software Engineering in Society (ICSE-SEIS), pp. 87–91 IEEE (2021)
18. Patnaik, A., Padhy, N.: Sentiment analysis of software project code commits. In: Kumar, R., Pattnaik, P.K., Tavares, J.M. (eds.) Next Generation of Internet of Things: Proceedings of ICNGIoT 2022, pp. 79–88. Springer, Singapore (2022). https://doi.org/10.1007/978-981-19-1412-6_7

Unsupervised Sentiment Analysis of Amazon Fine Food Reviews Using Fuzzy Logic

Aakanksha Sharaff[✉], Nandini Rajput, and Sai Rohith Papatla

Department of Computer Science and Engineering, National Institute of Technology Raipur,
Raipur, India
asharaff.cs@nitrr.ac.in

Abstract. Sentiment analysis has been increased popularity among the social media. The sentiment classification with machine learning identifies the positive and negative sentiment but the problem is that it doesn't identify the duplication of reviews by the same individual. In this study, the sentiment of food reviews is assessed by employing a set of fuzzy rules and this suggested fuzzy system uses NLP (Natural Language Processing) techniques accompanied by an experimental unsupervised fuzzy rule-based system consisting of nine rules to classify the reviews into positive and negative. Unsupervised fuzzy rule-based systems are particularly advantageous in handling intricate and disorganized data, where the interrelationships among variables may not be precisely defined or readily apparent. This research took the dataset from Amazon fine food reviews and explores the more insight of food reviews. The proposed method considers the unlabeled text that utilizes the VADER tool with Fuzzy based system that outperforms among the other state-of-art algorithms with 86.3% of accuracy.

Keywords: Unstructured Sentiment Analysis · Fuzzy Logic · Positive Review · Negative Review

1 Introduction

User reviews on e-commerce websites such as Amazon or Flipkart provide a good platform for users to provide information about the specifications and experience about the products. Some already-used approaches in sentiment analysis are described in next few lines. Sentiment analysis on reviews serves as a measure for a product's performance and helps in improving customer service. There are three principal categories of well-known approaches that used in sentiment analysis with review system. Hybrid methods like combining fuzzy rules with unsupervised learning and using semantic rules is widely explored and becomes a hot topic in analyzing sentiments of reviews [1]. Statistical approaches considered as when two words appear together regularly, they have more chances of having the same sentiment. Knowledge-based techniques make use of a semantic knowledge base which is created with the help of NLP techniques. Statistical methods grasp elements from machine learning like bag of words, support vector machines, deep learning etc. Usual classification techniques such as Naive Bayes, SVM

S. K. Panda et al. (Eds.): CoCoLe 2023, CCIS 1892, pp. 126–137, 2024.
https://doi.org/10.1007/978-3-031-56998-2_11

and decision trees [2] are commonly used to identify sentiment. Sentiment analysis using unsupervised techniques have the primacy that they can confirm to dynamically changing subjects and viewpoints in social media. Amazon fine food reviews dataset is one of the most popular review datasets consisting of 500, 000 reviews. Some confrontations in analyzing the reviews are removing duplicate reviews (more than one review by the same user), use of abbreviations and short forms. To overcome these issues, this study applied an unsupervised method using fuzzy rules. These techniques label a chunk of text as negative or positive.

In the food chain industry, consumer and owner are directly proportional and in this online era, customer instantly provide their views so it is necessary to know that either this feedback is coming as a genuine concern or applaud and this duplication is a kind of spam in review system that if not removed then it get highly inclined towards one aspect of either positive or negative and that may harm the owner.

The objective is to create a model that accurately identifies the different perspective towards the different subjects by customers and to overcome the above-mentioned issues, by using the unsupervised method using fuzzy rules that determines the reviews which then classified as either positive or negative. The previous work mostly on the labeled dataset and with limited boundaries and here our objective is to analyze each text that is related to food reviews by using the tool called VADER and then apply the fuzzy logic to define 9 different rules. The output of fuzzy logic is a real number between 0 and 1. Since we have usually vague information in real life, most of the conclusions we make in everyday life are not based on precise numbers, this forms the roots for fuzzy logic. The literature of fuzzy logic aims at converting a binary classification problem into a value determination problem. When it comes to set theory, deterministic logic agrees with crisp sets, which propounds that every element wholly belongs to the set. One can correlate fuzzy logic to fuzzy sets, for all the elements in the set only have partial membership in the set or in other words belongingness to a set is only up to a defined level [3]. The degree of a fuzzy membership is computed by various membership functions like triangular membership function, trapezoidal member-ship function, etc. The real world is filled with lots of uncertainties. For example, consider the opinion words, "Very good", "Good" and "Nice", the boundaries among them are indecisive. Such terms can be characterized and classified to different classes with some degree of membership using fuzzy logic. Fuzzy logic was found to be of good use since opinions have usually fuzzy character and there can be different elucidations of their meaning. This research employs nine fuzzy rules to measure the emotions of the reviews in our dataset.

The motivation of this research is that previously much research discussed only positive and negative aspect of reviews, but the existing research doesn't handle the duplication of reviews by the same individual, also different abbreviation and short form that may affect the analysis of reviews and unlabeled text with different rules that precisely identifies each aspect of reviews and give the efficient results.

The paper provides the contribution to determine the most efficient approach for detecting positive and negative sentiment among reviews.

1. Document preprocessing is done on the large dataset of Amazon food reviews.
2. Vader is applied on the unlabeled dataset to define the sentiment polarity.

3. The sentiment score is generated through fuzzy inference system with 9 different rules.
4. The defuzzification is done by converting fuzzy set into a crisp set by using the centroid method.

The novelty of this work is that it can handle the uncertainty by capturing the boundaries through fuzzy rules and determine the positive and negative sentiment for an unlabeled text and by using the VADER tool that directly generates fuzzy rules by discovering patterns and generates 9 rules of sentiment association in Amazon food review data.

VADER (Valence Aware Dictionary and Sentiment Reasoner) is a natural language processing (NLP) technique developed specifically for sentiment analysis. It is designed to analyze the tone of textual data, particularly social media texts such as tweets and product evaluations. The food industry is one of the application areas where each negative and positive review effect the owner of company or chain and its un/success purely based on customer reviews, so it is important that each review analyzed minutely so that no organization get negatively affected.

Section 2 discussed the literatures related to the problem. The methodology has been described in the Sect. 3. Section 4 presents experimental details of proposed work and results and discussions. Section 5 talks about the practical implications of the work. Conclusions and future work have been discussed in Sect. 6.

2 Literature Work

Ebrahimi et al. [4] discovered the sentiment analysis to extract or classify sentiment in sentiment reviews has a vital role in many areas. It can be used for finding out the attitude of people towards politics. Chowdhury et al. [5] handled the twitter post that relates with product-keyword-based searching and generates the statistical report to determine the losing and gaining the customers in the market. Xu et al. [6] addressed the decision-making, and sentiment analysis plays a vital role for e-commerce because consumers also desire low prices for good quality products which cannot be verified directly, here reading product reviews come into the picture and help the consumers. Yang et al., [7] conducted the research on detecting sentiment on e-commerce website with different deep learning models that generates effective and accurate learning technique. Sharaff and Soni, [8] discussed the feature specific outcome in product reviews that helps in deciding whether to purchase a product or not. Also, Sharaff and Soni [9] focused on time-based features that may improve the model accuracy. Sharma and Kalra, [10] studied the fuzzy logic with sentiment and in AI, this is another way to denote human knowledge will be to convert the statements into "IF this THEN that" expression rules and fuzzy logic can help in improving with multiple lexicon-based dataset. Bedi and Khurana, [11] discussed the fuzzy rules are the basis for robust classification systems and well-known tools for pattern recognition and such systems will be able to handle uncertainty, or ambiguity due to the very nature of fuzziness efficiently. Alharbi and Alhalabi, 2020 [12] proposed the method that classifies in five categories to provide the better information using a hybrid approach of dictionary based with fuzzy inferences were implemented to improve the existing model and these emotions can be classified in multiple ways; attributes like term frequency, n-grams etc., drive multiple algorithms in machine learning for emotion classification. Montoro et al. [13] released a new model named ANEW, which stands for "Affective Norms for English Words" with their emotion measures: For each word parameters like arousal, dominance and valence were used in creating a classification model. This model based on fuzzy builds upon Principal Component Analysis (PCA), trapezoidal membership and k-means clustering. Sharma and Sharaff [14] explored genetic based programming approach to detect spam messages that involves the slang, misspelled words and acronyms are effectively identified. Liu and Cocea [15] used the fuzzy rule-based system to interpret the sentiment and interpret the uncertainty of language and fuzzy logic can be useful for converting words into numerical values; hence it is useful in language processing. Jefferson et al., [16] offered a new way of identifying the positive and negative labels based on membership degree of different intensities. Sharaff and Choudhary [17] analyzed the stock market to predict various trends using machine learning approach that helps in improving the efficiency of the model.

The overall observation of the existing work is that various statistical and machine learning approaches are used. Also, various fuzzy rules based model with pre-defined boundaries are there to decide the positive and negative sentiment and all these research of acquiring sentiment is done on different application areas like food industry, tourism industry, brand management, and e-commerce, etc., because these all industries run by consumers and their feedback or reviews that create the trends and may sublime the market; so sentiment plays major role inside this reviews but the major issue is that for unlabeled text the rule generation is quite complex and here in this research this problem has been solved by using the VADER tool that utilizes a lexicon based approach and after analyzing sentiment 9 rules are generated with fuzzy rule system that described in next section.

3 Methodology

The proposed work is explained in this section. An unsupervised fuzzy rule-based system is a form of artificial intelligence system that builds a set of fuzzy rules from input data without the requirement for labelled training examples. Fuzzy logic and unsupervised learning techniques are used in such a system. An unsupervised fuzzy rule-based system is also known as an unsupervised fuzzy rule-based artificial intelligence system. It was developed with the purpose of extracting patterns, correlations, and rules straight from the raw data. A model is trained using examples that have been labelled in the classic supervised learning manner. In these instances, both the inputs and the outputs of the model are known. The learning process, on the other hand, is purely dependent on the input data in an unsupervised fuzzy rule-based system. This means that the system does not have any prior knowledge of the output or target values. As shown in Fig. 1 that explains the fuzzy logic architecture, using membership rules, we convert a crisp value to a fuzzy value, and this is termed as fuzzification.

Generally, the truth value is either 0 or 1, but in fuzzy logic, it varies from 0 to 1. In deterministic logic, we deal with crisp sets where an element either completely belongs to a set or it does not belong to that set. However, we have fuzzy sets in fuzzy logic, where an element can partially belong to a class. In other words, the element's associate

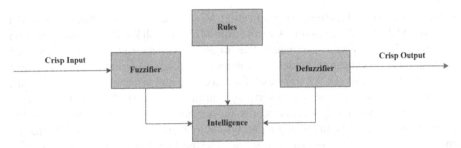

Fig. 1. Fuzzy Architecture

ship with the class is up to a specific degree. This is termed as a fuzzy membership degree. There are various membership functions like triangular, Gaussian, and trapezoid membership functions which can be used.

Fuzzy logic is acceptably effective in handling uncertainties in terms of linguistics. Instead of considering classification problems as *'black and white'* problems, Fuzzy logic considers them to be *'degree of grey'* problems. When fuzzy logic is compared to traditional models in sentiment analysis, rule-based logic is more explainable because they are straightforward when it comes to depicting correspondence between input and output. The fusion of rule-based systems and fuzzy logic can make rules depicted in a form that is profoundly indistinguishable to natural language and can thus make the information drawn out from rules more comprehensible. The triangular-fuzzy membership function is chosen since it can be comprehended in a simple understandable way. Also, it is one of the most confronting in practice. Centroid, bisector, mean of maximum, largest of maximum are some common methods of defuzzification. The approach used in this paper is Centroid defuzzification since it has worked the best. Computed fuzzy membership values are returned by 'trimf' utilizing the below triangular membership function as shown in Eq. 1.

$$f(x; a, b, c) = max(min(x - a/(b - a), c - x/(c - b)), 0)$$

$$\mu S(x) = 0, x <= d$$

$$\mu S(x) = (x - d)/(e - d), d < x <= e \tag{1}$$

$$\mu S(x) = (f - x)/(f - e), e < x <= f$$

$$\mu S(x) = 0, x >= f$$

Fuzzy logic acknowledges that precise numbers cannot be given for numerous uncertainties in life. Information is not always perfect, and errors can exist in data. Fuzzy logic expands choices and considers subjective attributes by considering if/then possibilities instead of binary either/or options. The Fig. 2 shows the flowchart of the proposed work.

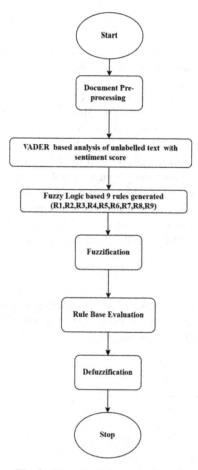

Fig. 2. Flowchart of proposed work

3.1 Document Preprocessing

Amazon food review comments has been considered as dataset for this work. In the Amazon fine food reviews dataset, the first stage is 'document preprocessing'. It is essential to remove noisy data. Hence, first, the data must be cleaned. After gathering dataset, text preprocessing techniques stemming, stop-word removal and Lemmatization has been performed. In the Amazon food reviews, the label has 'scores' from 1 to 5, where a score greater than 3 is counted as a positive review, less than 3 is counted as a negative review and 3 is a neutral review. Only positive and negative reviews were considered for this study since neutral reviews did not amount much to the analysis. Hence, the reviews with a score of 3 were not included. The essential steps include,

  i. Deleting HTML tags
 ii. Deleting punctuation marks and special characters
iii. Deleting alpha-numeric characters

iv. Change the text to lowercase
v. Removal of stop words
vi. Reviews with helpfulness numerator greater than helpfulness denominator and removed them as it is practically not possible.

"VADER (Valence Aware Dictionary for Sentiment Reasoning) is a tool used for analyzing the sentiment for the text". It tells us about the polarity score and the intensity of emotion. It can be applied directly to unlabeled text since it does not demand a whit of training data. VADER has been discovered to be very effective when analyzing social media texts, product reviews, movie reviews etc. VADER sentiment analysis uses a dictionary which is used to map lexical features to sentiment scores. The total sentiment score of a text can be found by adding up the individual intensities of words in the text. One of the main elements of a fuzzy logic system is 'Fuzzy Inference System'. It aids in constructing important decision rules by using the "IF…THEN" rules along with connectors "OR" or "AND".

3.2 Rule Base

In this paper, nine rules were exercised. The combination of positive and negative scores provided us with the above-mentioned rules. The rules were formulated on the premise that the higher score reflects the emotion of a review.

$R1 = \text{low\_pos\_score} \wedge \text{low\_neg\_score}$
$R2 = \text{med\_pos\_score} \wedge \text{low\_neg\_score}$
$R3 = \text{high\_pos\_score} \wedge \text{low\_neg\_score}$
$R4 = \text{low\_pos\_score} \wedge \text{mid\_neg\_score}$
$R5 = \text{med\_pos\_score} \wedge \text{mid\_neg\_score}$
$R6 = \text{high\_pos\_score} \wedge \text{mid\_neg\_score}$
$R7 = \text{low\_pos\_score} \wedge \text{high\_neg\_score}$
$R8 = \text{med\_pos\_score} \wedge \text{high\_neg\_score}$
$R9 = \text{high\_pos\_score} \wedge \text{high\_neg\_score}$

Every word has a negative score and positive score, words with greater positive score were considered for calculating the overall positive score and the same concept is applied to calculate the overall negative score. The '$\wedge$' operator represents the AND operator in the Fuzzy system. The high_pos_score, med_pos_score and low_pos_score variables reflect high, medium, and low fuzzy sets for a positive score. Similarly, the hig_neg_score, med_neg_score and low_neg_score variables represent high, medium, and low fuzzy sets for the negative score.

3.3 Fuzzy Rule System

This paper used fuzzy model, one of the commonly utilized fuzzy inference techniques that include the following steps. The first is fuzzification. Then the rule evaluation part is done. After that aggregation of rule outputs is performed. The final step is defuzzification.

3.4 Fuzzification

The positive review scores and negative review scores for each review are fuzzified employing a triangular membership function. The linguistic terms involve three key points f (upper limit), d (lower limit) and e (intermediate value). A membership function can be expressed as $\mu S: X \rightarrow [0,1]$, where every element in X is plotted to a rational number amid 0 and 1.

3.5 Rule Evaluation

Nine fuzzy rules have been employed in this work. The below Table 1 depicts the visualization of the fuzzy rules.

Table 1. Fuzzy Rules

Rule	Positive Score	Negative Score	Sentiment
R1	Low	Low	Neutral
R2	Medium	Low	Positive
R3	High	Low	Positive
R4	Low	Medium	Negative
R5	Medium	Medium	Neutral
R6	High	Medium	Positive
R7	Low	High	Negative
R8	Medium	High	Negative
R9	High	High	Neutral

The nine rules were obtained by intersecting the positive and negative scores of each review. Any data point shall not trigger more than one rule.

$$W_{neg} = R4 \vee R7 \vee R8$$
$$W_{neu} = R1 \vee R5 \vee R9$$
$$W_{pos} = R2 \vee R3 \vee R6$$
$$\text{output\_act\_low} = W_{neg} \wedge \text{output\_neg}$$
$$\text{output\_act\_med} = W_{neu} \wedge \text{output\_neu}$$
$$\text{output\_act\_high} = W_{pos} \wedge \text{output\_pos}$$
$$\text{aggregated} = \text{output\_act\_low} \cup \text{output\_act\_med} \cup \text{output\_act\_high}$$

W_{neg} represents the degree of attainment of fuzzy rules concerned with the negative emotion. Similarly, W_{pos} and W_{neu} correspond to positive and neutral emotions.

3.6 Defuzzification

Defuzzification is the method of mapping a fuzzy set to a crisp set. This article uses the centroid defuzzification approach as it provides accurate performance. The region generated by the membership function graph is estimated and split into several sub-areas. The centroid of each region shall be determined and the addition of these all shall be considered to map the fuzzy value to the crisp value. Which means that we find defuzzified output for a discrete fuzzy collection. The defuzzified performance is then analyzed for different ranges to mark the result as positive, negative, or neutral.

4 Experimental Analysis and Result Discussion

This paper experiments with the Amazon Fine foods data set which is available freely on Kaggle and the raw data can be mined from the Amazon websites itself. The Amazon fine food data set has a huge variety of products and about 500,000 user reviews. There is a large amount of data which contains reviews with 1,2,3,4 and 5-star reviews of individual products. To understand the sentiment behind the reviews we need to train the model, so there is a need to remove all the 3-star reviews which often contain mixed reviews and words which cannot be distinguished as positive or negative words.

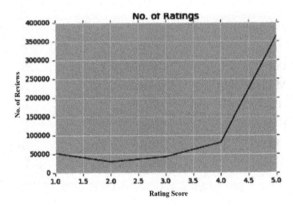

Fig. 3. Distribution of ratings

As we can observe from Fig. 3, the Amazon Fine Food Review dataset has approximately 568K reviews: 52.2K reviews with score 1, 29.7K reviews with score 2, 42.6K reviews with score 3, 80.6K reviews with score 4, and 363.1K reviews with score 5. The Amazon food review dataset consists of 256,059 users, 525,814 reviews and 74,258 products, with the following attributes: index, id, profile name, user id, product id, helpfulness numerator, i.e., count of reviewers who found the given review as helpful or not, helpfulness denominator, summary (review summary), score (from 1 to 5), time, text (review content) by Tran et al., [18]. The dataset then undergoes stages like document preprocessing and then passes through the proposed fuzzy rule-based model. The primary reason for grouping reviews with value 4 and 5 as positive, and 1 and 2 as negative, was because of some vague reviews. As the dataset is quite large, the sampling method was used to avoid any further ambiguities. The metrics used to verify the model performance are accuracy, precision, recall and f1. For Comparative study we took four combinations of feature extraction and algorithms i.e., TF-IDF + RF, TF-IDF + Naïve

Bayes, BOW + NB, BOW + RF as the frequency of a term within a document is represented by the TF component of TF-IDF. It divides the frequency of a term's appearance in a document by the total number of terms in the document. This element indicates the frequency with which a particular term appears in a given document. The Bag-of-Words (BOW) method, on the other hand, is a text representation technique that represents a document as a compilation or "bag" of its individual words, without taking word order or grammar into account. In this method, each word in the document is regarded as a distinct feature, and its frequency or occurrence is converted into a numeric value. Random Forest is an ensemble learning technique that predicts by combining multiple decision trees. It generates a "forest" of decision trees, each of which is trained using a random subset of the data and a random subset of the features. Naive Bayes, on the other hand, is a probabilistic classifier based on Bayes' theorem with an assumption of independence among the features.

Accuracy: Accuracy is a statistical measure that quantifies the correctness or reliability of a result or prediction. It represents the ratio of correct outcomes or predictions to the total number of outcomes or predictions made as shown in Eq. 2.

$$Accuracy = ((Number\ of\ correct\ predictions)) / ((Total\ number\ of\ predictions)) \quad (2)$$

Precision: Precision is a statistical metric that measures the proportion of true positive predictions out of all positive predictions made by a model as shown in Eq. 3.

$$Precision = ((True\ Positives)) / ((True\ Positives + False\ Positives)) \quad (3)$$

Recall: Recall quantifies the completeness or comprehensiveness of a model in correctly capturing positive outcomes as shown in Eq. 4.

$$Recall = ((True\ Positives)) / ((True\ Positives + False\ Negatives)) \quad (4)$$

F1-score: It balances the trade-off between precision and recall and is particularly useful when the data is imbalanced or when both false positives and false negatives are equally important as shown in Eq. 5.

$$f1score = 2 * ((Precision * Recall)) / ((Precision + Recall)) \quad (5)$$

Table 2. Comparison of various models

Feature extraction method	Machine learning model	Accuracy	Precision	Recall	F1 Score
TF-IDF	RF	0.808	0.812	0.808	0.807
TF-IDF	NB	0.806	0.808	0.806	0.806
BOW	RF	0.818	0.85	0.82	0.814
BOW	NB	0.769	0.769	0.769	0.769
VADER	Fuzzy Logic	0.863	0.755	0.696	0.863

Table 2 compares the performances of various models like Random Forest (RF), Naive Bayes (NB) along with some feature extraction methods like Bag of Words (BoW) and Term frequency-inverse document frequency (TF-IDF) with the proposed model. From Table 2 it can be observed that the highest F1 score was 0.81 for BoW with Random Forest. The proposed model's F1 score is 0.863 which is better than the aforementioned model's performance. The model has more advantage when compared to the usual techniques since it does not require prior training as it is unsupervised. Vader performs supremely well with social media. "It is computationally economical without compromising F1 scores".

5   Practical Implications

The model can be extended and prove to be useful in many areas where analyzing the sentiment is an important aspect. Monitoring social media for brand reputation management, reviewing competitor brands' review analysis for market research, analyzing product reviews from E-commerce websites for, movie reviews, etc., because of the unsupervised approach our proposed model follows it is even easier to be implemented with large datasets as there is no requirement of prior training of the model. Also, social media data changes dynamically, with the constant changes in the data, we cannot train our model every time we want to obtain the results considering the large sizes of data we deal with in social media. The unsupervised approach employed in the proposed model is way more suitable for dynamically changing data. When we consider movie reviews or brand reviews, we can see a lot of uncertainty in the reviews. The rule base systems are suitable for dealing with vagueness as they deal with text by converting them into numbers. So, we believe that our proposed fuzzy-based model can be extended to find the sentiment for product reviews, brand reviews etc.

6   Conclusion and Future Work

This proposed approach highly focused on the food reviews industry with unlabeled text that defines the 9 fuzzy rules after analyzing the sentiment score from VADER tool that is more appropriate for rapidly changing data with the removal of duplication of reviews and with the fuzzy logic three class reviews has taken i.e., positive, negative, and neutral from nine rules. The benefit of using fuzzy logic is that it helps to deal with vagueness and computing terms. In future, with VADER other tools like TextBlob can be used to get the better results and it can further generalize at different application areas like movie reviews and other review system.

References

1. Appel, O., Chiclana, F., Carter, J., Fujita, H.: A hybrid approach to sentiment analysis. In: 2016 IEEE Congress on Evolutionary Computation (CEC), pp. 4950–4957. IEEE, July 2016
2. Alzami, F., Udayanti, E.D., Prabowo, D.P., Megantara, R.A.: Document Preprocessing with TF-IDF to Improve the Polarity Classification Performance of Unstructured Sentiment Analysis. Kinetik: Game Technology, Information System, Computer Network, Computing, Electronics, and Control, 235–242 (2020)

3. Vashishtha, S., Susan, S.: Fuzzy rule based unsupervised sentiment analysis from social media posts. Expert Syst. Appl. **138**, 112834 (2019)
4. Ebrahimi, M., Yazdavar, A.H., Sheth, A.: Challenges of sentiment analysis for dynamic events. IEEE Intell. Syst.Intell. Syst. **32**(5), 70–75 (2017)
5. Chowdhury, S.M.H., Abujar, S., Badruzzaman, K.B.M., Hossain, S.A.: Product review analysis using social media data based on sentiment analysis. In: Innovations in Computer Science and Engineering, pp. 527–533. Springer, Singapore (2020)
6. Xu, F., Pan, Z., Xia, R.: E-commerce product review sentiment classification based on a naïve Bayes continuous learning framework. Information Processing & Management, 102221 (2020)
7. Yang, L., Li, Y., Wang, J., Sherratt, R.S.: Sentiment analysis for E-commerce product reviews in chinese based on sentiment lexicon and deep learning. IEEE Access **8**, 23522–23530 (2020)
8. Sharaff, A., Soni, A.: Analyzing sentiments of product reviews based on features. In: 2018 2nd International Conference on Trends in Electronics and Informatics (ICOEI), pp. 710–713. IEEE, May 2018
9. Sharaff, A., Soni, A.: Time and feature specific sentiment analysis of product reviews. In: Cognitive Informatics, Computer Modelling, and Cognitive Science, pp. 255–272. Academic Press (2020)
10. Sharma, S., Kalra, V.: Fuzzy Lexicon-based approach for sentiment analysis of blog and microblog text. In: Research in Intelligent and Computing in Engineering, pp. 705–714. Springer, Singapore (2021)
11. Bedi, P., Khurana, P.: Sentiment analysis using fuzzy-deep learning. In: Proceedings of ICETIT 2019, pp. 246–257. Springer, Cham (2020)
12. Alharbi, J.R., Alhalabi, W.S.: Hybrid approach for sentiment analysis of twitter posts using a dictionary-based approach and fuzzy logic methods: study case on cloud service providers. Int. J. Semantic Web Inf. Syst. (IJSWIS) **16**(1), 116–145 (2020)
13. Montoro, A., Olivas, J.A., Peralta, A., Romero, F.P., Serrano-Guerrero, J.: An ANEW based fuzzy sentiment analysis model. In: 2018 IEEE International Conference on Fuzzy Systems (FUZZ-IEEE), pp. 1–7. IEEE, July 2018
14. Sharma, D., Sharaff, A.: Identifying spam patterns in SMS using genetic programming approach. In: 2019 International Conference on Intelligent Computing and Control Systems (ICCS), pp. 396–400. IEEE, May 2019
15. Liu, H., Cocea, M.: Fuzzy rule-based systems for interpretable sentiment analysis. In: 2017 Ninth International Conference on Advanced Computational Intelligence (ICACI), pp. 129–136. IEEE, February 2017
16. Jefferson, C., Liu, H., Cocea, M.: Fuzzy approach for sentiment analysis. In: 2017 IEEE International Conference on Fuzzy Systems (FUZZ-IEEE), pp. 1–6. IEEE, July 2017
17. Sharaff, A., Choudhary, M.: Comparative analysis of various stock prediction techniques. In: 2018 2nd International Conference on Trends in Electronics and Informatics (ICOEI), pp. 735–738. IEEE, May 2018
18. Tran, P.Q., Thanh, N., Vu, N., Thanh, H., Xuan, H.: Effective opinion words extraction for food reviews classification. Int. J. Adv. Comput. Sci. Appl. **11**(7) (2020)

Sentiment Analysis of Crypto Currency Trading Applications in India Using Machine Learning

Gourav Vakare[1], Faraz Khan[1], Aaradhaya Naikwade[1], Dipanshu Rautela[1], and Hemraj Shobharam Lamkuche[2]([✉])

[1] Symbiosis University of Applied Sciences, Indore, India
[2] School of Computing Science and Engineering, VIT Bhopal University, Kothrikalan, Sehore 466114, Madhya Pradesh, India
hemraj.lamkuche@gmail.com

Abstract. Sentiment analysis is an emerging field of research that aims to understand and analyze the emotions and opinions expressed by individuals through various forms of communication. In recent years, the rise of cryptocurrencies has gained significant popularity in India, with the advent of various crypto trading applications. This study focuses on conducting sentiment analysis of users' opinions and emotions expressed in reviews and feedback on a crypto currency trading application in India. Machine learning algorithms will be used to process and analyze data obtained from the application. The study aims to provide insights into the overall sentiment of users towards the application and to identify key factors that influence the users' sentiments. The results obtained from the analysis can help in enhancing the application's user experience by identifying areas of improvement and addressing user concerns.

Keywords: Big data analytics · Crypto-Trading · Emotions sentiments · Sentiment analysis · Security and Privacy

1 Introduction

The emergence of cryptocurrencies has resulted in the development of a slew of crypto trading apps that have gained traction in India. These applications provide a platform for users to buy, sell, and trade cryptocurrencies. However, users' attitudes towards these applications can have a significant impact on their use and adoption. As a result, understanding and analyzing user emotions and opinions expressed in reviews and feedback is critical for identifying areas for improvement and improving the user experience.

This study's author examined the security profiles of well-known Android cryptocurrency apps and checked them for common flaws mentioned by MobSF, Immumiweb, and the top 7 mobile apps in India. The author investigates the security profiles of popular cryptocurrency apps in India in this article. According to the author, while cryptocurrency applications provide more privacy, traditional financial services applications only slightly outperform them in terms of security safeguards. Sentiment analysis is important in cryptocurrency trading apps in India. It has the potential to influence trading decisions and outcomes by providing investors with insights into market sentiment and assisting them in making informed decisions. However, when using sentiment analysis in cryptocurrency trading, ethical and legal considerations such as the potential for bias and the need for transparency in data collection and analysis must be considered. Future trends in sentiment analysis and machine learning in cryptocurrency trading apps in India will include the use of more advanced machine learning algorithms as well as the integration of sentiment analysis with other types of data analysis, such as technical analysis.

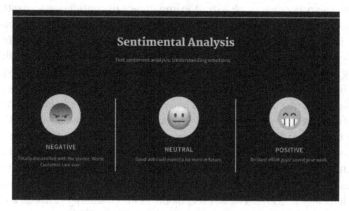

Fig. 1. Variations in sentiment analysis

Sentiment analysis divides text into three categories: negative, positive, and neutral (as shown in Fig. 1). Sentiment Analysis of Crypto Currency Trading Applications in India Using Machine Learning is an automated technology that identifies and flags fake or fraudulent online reviews. With the proliferation of online reviews on e-commerce websites, social media platforms, and other platforms, fake reviews have become a widespread problem that can mislead customers and undermine the credibility of online review systems.

2 Literature Review

According to the author, In Using multiple classifiers in a hybrid fashion can lead to better performance in terms of micro- and macro-averaged F1 score compared to using just one classifier. By employing a semi-automatic complementary approach with the help of a Sentiment Analysis Tool (SAT), each classifier can complement the work of others to produce more effective results. However, it's important to note that having too few induced rules may lead to a decrease in effectiveness for the micro- and macro-averaged F1 score. In a real-world scenario, it's recommended to have two rule sets: one original set and one induced rule set, to ensure comprehensive examination of the sentiment analysis results [1].

According to the author, it is great to see that this work provides a framework for an objective comparison of different sentiment analysis techniques. It is always challenging to compare different research works, and this framework can help researchers to evaluate the effectiveness of different approaches in a standardized way. It is unfortunate that the authors were only able to compare a limited number of techniques due to difficulties in obtaining the tools. Adding more current comparison tools and broadening the scope of comparison to different categories of sentiment can lead to a more comprehensive evaluation of sentiment analysis techniques [2].

The author in this paper discussed that, it is evident from the paper that sentiment analysis has been a critical area of research in recent years. The study highlights various techniques and methods that can be employed to develop a more efficient sentiment analysis system. The paper also emphasizes the importance of considering semantic analysis and n-grams analysis for better accuracy. Rule-based and lexicon-based approaches have also been observed as effective methods for sentiment analysis. Overall, sentiment analysis plays a crucial role in decision-making, particularly in the digital world where social networking sites are the primary source of information for many individuals [3].

According to the author, it is true that the application of deep learning in sentiment analysis has been a popular research area in recent years. Deep learning techniques such as convolutional neural networks (CNNs), recurrent neural networks (RNNs), and long short-term memory (LSTM) networks have shown impressive results in various sentiment analysis tasks. These models can learn representations of text data that capture the contextual and semantic information, allowing them to perform well in sentiment analysis tasks such as sentiment classification, aspect-based sentiment analysis, and sentiment intensity analysis. The advancements in deep learning research and applications have also led to the development of new architectures and techniques that further improve the performance of sentiment analysis models. For example, attention mechanisms have been introduced to allow models to focus on the most relevant parts of the input data, while transfer learning and pre-training techniques enable models to leverage knowledge learned from large-scale datasets to improve their performance on smaller datasets.Overall, the application of deep learning in sentiment analysis has shown great promise, and we can expect to see more exciting developments and research in this area in the future [4].

The author discussed that, sounds like an informative paper on the use of deep learning in sentiment analysis. Deep learning has proven to be a powerful tool in various natural language processing tasks, including sentiment analysis. With its ability to learn complex patterns and relationships in data, deep learning has shown promise in improving the accuracy and efficiency of sentiment analysis. It's exciting to see how this technology will continue to advance and be applied in the field of sentiment analysis [5].

The author's study highlights the importance of privacy policy efficacy and privacy risk in shaping user perceptions of mobile app security. It also suggests that mobile app developers should focus on improving privacy policy transparency and effectiveness to increase user confidence in the security of their apps. The study's findings have implications for mobile app developers, policymakers, and users alike, highlighting the need for greater attention to privacy-related issues in the mobile app industry. Future research could explore how other factors, such as user characteristics or app features, influence perceptions of mobile app security [6].

The author's study examines the security of popular Android bitcoin apps by evaluating them for common vulnerabilities outlined in the OWASP mobile top 10 list. The researchers compare the results of this assessment to a baseline test of frequently used banking and trade apps to determine the level of security provided by bitcoin wallet software. In addition, the study looks at how mobile apps may impact user privacy. The researchers found that while bitcoin apps are only slightly more secure than conventional financial services apps, the latter provide higher levels of privacy [7].

According to the author, users expressed frustration with the app's loading times and occasional crashes. Learning. Users who were unfamiliar with the app's features expressed a desire for more instructional material to help them understand how to use it. Interface. Users found the app's interface to be visually appealing and easy to use, but they did suggest some minor improvements to the design, such as increasing the size of certain buttons for easier touch-screen navigation. User pleasure. Overall, users were satisfied with the app and appreciated the convenience it provided in completing government transactions. The study's findings suggest that further usability testing and user feedback could lead to significant improvements in the app's overall usability and user experience [8].

The in this paper discussed that, it is crucial for developers to keep up with the evolving mobile app market and continuously improve their apps to meet the needs and preferences of users. Design restrictions, such as limited resources and unique device presentations, must be taken into account to ensure that the app provides a positive user experience. The study's application of four user experience attributes to assess the Kindle mobile application provides valuable insights into how to improve mobile app usability. The majority of users found the app to be easy to use, visible, enjoyable, and efficient. However, it is important to address any issues encountered by a small number of users to ensure that the app can cater to a wider user base. Further development and improvements should be made based on user feedback to ensure that the app meets the needs and preferences of users [9].

According to the author, the success of mobile banking apps is influenced by both user personality traits and information system (IS) success factors, as found by a survey of 249 mobile banking customers. System quality and service quality, but not information quality, were found to have a positive impact on user behavior. Additionally, personality traits such as extraversion, agreeableness, openness, and conscientiousness were found to positively affect user satisfaction with mobile banking apps. To ensure that these findings are effectively communicated to those involved in mobile app development, software engineering research should focus on instructional activities related to these four personality traits. However, traditional software engineering methods may not be entirely applicable in the mobile device context, as mobile interfaces provide new human-computer interaction sequences that have yet to be fully studied or established as UI principles [10].

Table 1 contain the rest of the literature reviews.

Table 1. Literature review in table

References	Author	Title	Description
[11]	A. K. Jain and D. Shanbhag	Addressing security and privacy risks in mobile applications	According to the author, Numerous services, including social networking, banking, ticketing, retail, and enterprise applications like email, ERP, CRM, and calendar/address book software, are available on mobile devices. However, several risks can jeopardize the operation of these services and devices and endanger sensitive data. Mobile app developers must conduct thorough security reviews to address the attack surfaces found during threat modelling in order to reduce these risks. Additionally, by using this process, security flaws that may have emerged during development can be found in project designs, approved corporate policies, and component integration. Overall, paying close attention to both IS success factors and potential threats is necessary to ensure both user satisfaction and security in the development of mobile apps

(*continued*)

Table 1. (*continued*)

References	Author	Title	Description
[12]	L. L. Chong, H. B. Ong, and S. H. Tan	Acceptability of mobile stock trading application: A study of young investors in Malaysia	This study investigates the factors that are leading young investors to use mobile stock trading more frequently. The researchers take into account three new variables: perceived risk, perceived benefits, and trust using an integrated TAM and TPB paradigm. 373 young investors are involved in the Malaysian study. The findings show that attitude, the conviction that one can control one's behavior, and perceived benefits all have a positive influence on the adoption of mobile stock trading. Furthermore, since it produces contradictory results, the relationship between behavioural intention and actual behavior needs more research. In order to compare how developed and developing countries are utilizing new financial technologies, a larger and more varied sample size from various countries may also be considered

(*continued*)

Table 1. (*continued*)

References	Author	Title	Description
[13]	D. N. Koloseni,	User Perceptions of Mobile Banking Apps in Tanzania: Impact of Information Systems (IS) Factors and Customer Personality Traits	This study investigates the relationship between Tanzanian users' perceptions of user personality traits and information systems (IS) success factors. The study finds that consumers are positively influenced by the system quality and system service of the applications, but not by the information quality of the apps, based on a survey of 249 mobile banking users. The personality traits openness, consensually, conscientiousness, and extraversion are all associated with the use of mobile banking apps. This method advances our understanding of how personality traits influence people's propensity to use mobile banking apps. Few studies, particularly in the African context

(*continued*)

Table 1. (*continued*)

References	Author	Title	Description
[14]	W. Yang, X. Xiao, R. Pandita, W. Enck, and T. Xie,	Improving mobile application security via bridging user expectations and application behaviors	According to this author, In order to understand how mobile applications' security features prevent malware from entering app stores, current practices involve examining these features and looking for patterns. These techniques assist in enhancing the user's perception of the behavior and performance of the programmed by bridging the gap between user expectations and application performance. Analyzing the information flow within the application and assessing its behavior in light of the permissions granted to it are the main objectives. Additionally, these methods reveal any information tampering and manipulation analysis that can spot both manipulative flows and user-visible transient flows before they reach the output channel. The overall objective is to improve user privacy and security when using mobile applications

(*continued*)

Table 1. (*continued*)

References	Author	Title	Description
[15]	H. Assal, S. Hurtado, A. Imran, and S. Chiasson	What's the deal with privacy apps? A comprehensive exploration of user perception and usability	According to author, the low adoption rates of current mobile privacy-preserving solutions may be caused by a lack of fundamental usability factors like learnability and intuitiveness. By improving user perception and attitudes towards privacy issues, the authors hope to advance the creation of mobile applications that put user privacy first. The study focuses on three distinct aspects of mobile privacy: anonymous messaging, secure/private texting, and privacy-conscious photo sharing. Although the authors took measures to restrict participation to highly qualified individuals and exclude responses from those who provided inaccurate information, the survey's online format may have had an impact on the quality of the results

- *Positive and Negative Sentiments Towards Blockchain Based Crypto Trading App Are Equally Distributed*

The present work explores the relation between positive and the negative emotions generated by the users contributing to existing literature in the financial markets and the behavior of flocking in cryptocurrency markets. The relation between optimism and the convergence in sentiments dynamics provides an important insight for investors, as it highlights how cryptocurrency valuation is unstable and is driven by behavioral factors and investors humor.

3 Methodology

Sentiment analysis, also known as opinion mining. Figure 2 show the sequence model of It involves analyzing the attitudes, emotions, and opinions expressed by individuals.

Data Collection: The first step is to gather the text data. We employ datasets from play store's customer review by applying python library called play-store-scrapper. These dataset includes customer review of crypto trading applications in India: CoinDcx, WazirX, Coinswitch Kuber, Unocoin, Zebpay and Bitbins.

Text Preprocessing: Once we have the data, we must preprocess it so that it is suitable for analysis. This step typically entails removing any unnecessary or noisy information, such as punctuation, special characters, and stopwords (commonly used words such as "the," "and," "is," and so on). Text normalization techniques such as stemming and lemmatization were used to reduce words to their simplest form.

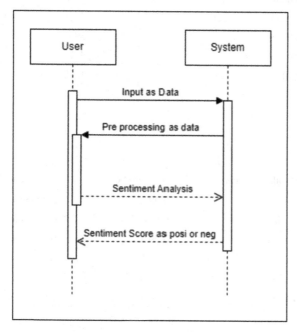

Fig. 2. Sequence diagram of our model

Sentiment Analysis: We have applied the sentiment analysis model along with the machine learning algorithm to classify the sentiment scores as positive or negative.

4 Result and Discussion

In this paper we explain that messages between users of crypto currency trading apps in India can be either positive or negative in sentiment, but it is difficult to determine the exact meaning of a message based solely on the words used. To overcome this challenge, sentiment analysis is used to extract subjective information from primary sources. For this research, sentiment analysis is used to understand the social sentiment of users' perceptions of security and privacy in crypto currency trading apps in India. However, users' perceptions are divided, with some considering the apps secure and private, while others disagree. Therefore, the author used a sentiment analysis model to identify the number of positive and negative sentiments among users, as displayed in Table 1.

Table 2. Number of Positive and Negative Sentiments

S. No.		Positive and negative social sentiments of user's		
	Mobile Application	Positive	Neutral	Negative
1	Coindcx	51%	46%	3%
2	WazirX	54%	43%	3%
3	Coin switch Kuber	52%	45%	3%
4	Unocoin	48%	49%	3%
5	ZebPay	50%	46%	4%
6	BitBns	79%	15%	6%

Table 3. Accuracy Results

S. No.	Accuracy Scores in %		
	Mobile Application	Random Forest	Logistic Regression
1	Coindcx	0.99711%	0.99634%
2	WazirX	0.99169%	0.99731%
3	Coin switch Kuber	0.99161%	0.99355%
4	Unocoin	0.95284%	0.97429%
5	ZebPay	0.99487%	0.98734%
6	BitBns	0.98148%	0.93745%

Machine Learning algorithm: in this paper we have applied Random Forest and Logistic Regression algorithms on the data related to the positive and negative sentiments that got from sentimental analysis generated from the user's perception for the comparatively study on the basis of accuracy of the algorithms. Table 2 shows the accuracy result of machine learning model. the purpose of training model by applying Random Forest and Logistic Regression algorithms is to classify the positive sentiments and negative sentiments from the sentiments that got from the user's review for those applications.

5   Conclusion

The sentiment analysis conducted in the study also revealed some interesting insights into Indian traders' perceptions of privacy. The analysis showed that while privacy is a concern for many Indian traders, it is not the most important factor when choosing a crypto trading application. This may be due to the fact that many traders are willing to sacrifice some privacy in exchange for the benefits of using a trading application, such as convenience and accessibility. However, it is still important for trading applications to address privacy concerns and provide adequate security measures to protect user data. This can help build trust and confidence among Indian traders, and improve the overall user experience of crypto trading applications in India.

To summarize, using machine learning for sentiment analysis of cryptocurrency trading apps has become an important way to understand and forecast sentiment trends in the cryptocurrency market. Further research can improve the precision and efficiency of sentiment analysis models as machine learning techniques advance. This would allow for better cryptocurrency trading decision-making and risk management.

References

1. Prabowo, R., Thelwall, M.: Sentiment analysis: a combined approach. J. Informetr. **3**(2), 143–157 (2009). https://doi.org/10.1016/j.joi.2009.01.003
2. Gonçalves, P., Araújo, M., Benevenuto, F., Cha, M.: Comparing and combining sentiment analysis methods. In: COSN 2013 - Proc. 2013 Conf. Online Soc. Networks, pp. 27–37 (2013). https://doi.org/10.1145/2512938.2512951
3. Devika, M.D., Sunitha, C., Ganesh, A.: Sentiment analysis: a comparative study on different approaches. Procedia Comput. Sci. **87**, 44–49 (2016). https://doi.org/10.1016/j.procs.2016.05.124
4. Mejova, Y.: Sentiment Analysis : An Overview Comprehensive Exam Paper. Science (80), 1–34 (2009). http://www.cs.uiowa.edu/~ymejova/publications/CompsYelenaMejova.pdf
5. Zhang, L., Wang, S., Liu, B.: Deep learning for sentiment analysis: a survey. Wiley Interdiscip. Rev. Data Min. Knowl. Discov., vol. 8, no. 4 (2018). https://doi.org/10.1002/widm.1253
6. Balapour, A., Nikkhah, H.R., Sabherwal, R.: Mobile application security: role of perceived privacy as the predictor of security perceptions. Int. J. Inf. Manage. **52** (2020). https://doi.org/10.1016/j.ijinfomgt.2019.102063
7. Lero, A.R.S., Lero, J.B., Le Gear, A.: Privacy and security analysis of cryptocurrency mobile applications. In: 2019 5th Int. Conf. Mob. Secur. Serv. MOBISECSERV 2019, no. 1, pp. 1–6 (2019). https://doi.org/10.1109/MOBISECSERV.2019.8686583
8. Hussain, A., Mkpojiogu, E.O.C., Musa, J., Mortada, S.: A user experience evaluation of Amazon Kindle mobile application. AIP Conf. Proc. **1891**(October), 2017 (2017). https://doi.org/10.1063/1.5005393
9. Elsantil, Y.: User perceptions of the security of mobile applications. Int. J. E-Services Mob. Appl. **12**(4), 24–41 (2020). https://doi.org/10.4018/IJESMA.2020100102
10. Dehlinger, J., Dixon, J.: Mobile application software engineering: challenges and research directions. Proc. Work. Mob. Softw. Eng., pp. 29–32 (2011). http://www.mobileseworkshop.org/papers/7_Dehlinger_Dixon.pdf
11. Yang, W., Xiao, X., Pandita, R., Enck, W., Xie, T.: Improving mobile application security via bridging user expectations and application behaviors. In: ACM Int. Conf. Proceeding Ser., pp. 1–2 (2014). https://doi.org/10.1145/2600176.2600208

12. Assal, H., Hurtado, S., Imran, A., Chiasson, S.: What's the deal with privacy apps? A comprehensive exploration of user perception and usability. In: ACM Int. Conf. Proceeding Ser., vol. 30-November, pp. 25–36 (2015). https://doi.org/10.1145/2836041.2836044
13. Zhu, H., Xiong, H., Ge, Y., Chen, E.: Mobile app recommendations with security and privacy awareness. In: Proc. ACM SIGKDD Int. Conf. Knowl. Discov. Data Min., pp. 951–960 (2014). https://doi.org/10.1145/2623330.2623705
14. Roca, J.C., García, J.J., de la Vega, J.J.: The importance of perceived trust, security and privacy in online trading systems. Inf. Manag. Comput. Secur.Manag. Comput. Secur. 17(2), 96–113 (2009). https://doi.org/10.1108/09685220910963983
15. Fife, E., Orjuela, J.: The privacy calculus: mobile apps and user perceptions of privacy and security. Int. J. Eng. Bus. Manag. 4(1), 1 (2012). https://doi.org/10.5772/51645

Graph Similarity Join (GSJ) Approach to Detect Near Duplicate Text Documents

Prathi Naveena and Sandeep Kumar Dash[(✉)]

Department of Computer Science and Engineering, National Institute of Technology, Aizawl, Mizoram, India
{1dt21cs002,sandeep.cse}@nitmz.ac.in

Abstract. With the profligate progress of graph-based data in numerous areas essential to observe the similarities among the graph pairs is indispensable to speed up the search outcomes. The existence of near-duplicate text documents plays an imperative role in performance degradation while integrating information from diverse sources. The main issue is determining the similarity among the graphs from massive datasets. The principal goal of this paper is to enhance search optimization with improved indexing and condensed pairwise comparisons with the help of the proposed Graph Similarity Self Join of Documents (GSSJD) technique is formed by uniting the prefix filtering strategy to the traditional inverted index method. Experiments were carried out on the dataset to authenticate that our proposed approach illustrates the optimized results in speed and time.

Keywords: Similarity measures · Indexing · Text documents

1 Introduction

With well-organized storage and access purposes, graph data structures are widely used in the day's world, and graph data structures efficiently represent the connections between data objects. Graph Similarity Self-Join (GSSJ) is the problem of finding all pairs of graphs with a similarity score above a predefined threshold. One of the intriguing issues in data mining is detecting near duplicates. We want to distinguish these near duplicates to manage capacity and computational issues with the benefit of scalability and amalgamation of data; ultimately consequence, the development of graph data rises. The rising prominence of graph usage has created an ever-increasing number of issues pertinent to graph information examination. Among different graph identicalness measures, graph edit distance (GED) has been broadly utilized in addressing distances between graphs. Nevertheless, calculating graph edit distance is a nondeterministic polynomial Complete problem [2]. Graph isomorphism resolves the challenging problem of finding graphs that intently duplicate one another. There is no recognized polynomial time algorithm for this issue [1]. Various graph similarity measures have been proposed to conquer the bottlenecks of graph isomorphism [7, 15, 16]. GSSJ is the issue of finding all sets of graphs with similarity scores over a predefined limit. All existing techniques for graph similarity self-join depend on graph edit distance (GED) as a similarity measure. Some

S. K. Panda et al. (Eds.): CoCoLe 2023, CCIS 1892, pp. 151–158, 2024.
https://doi.org/10.1007/978-3-031-56998-2_13

similarity measures [26] are computationally straightforward and scale well to massive datasets. Detection of near-duplicate text documents is a necessary action to be carried out to minimize the generation of candidate keys. The main focus of this study is on index-based techniques with the support of close-fitting bounds on enormous similarity measures to enhance search optimization and condense pairwise comparisons. With the proposed technique GSSJD, we got sophisticated search results.

2   Graph Similarity Search Techniques

Many graph similarity techniques were proposed to detect the similarity between the graph pairs with different similarity measures, and are discussed below.

2.1   Graph Edit Distance Measure

By considering the two graphs, A and B, and taking the edit distance as a similarity measure between these two graphs, we can efficiently detect the dissimilarities [22]. By perceiving (see Fig. 1), we can notice an edge between C and B in the first graph, but it is not presented in the second. E and F are the names used for labelling the beside edges. We can name these two graphs identical graphs, any performing set of operations to detect the path between them by using GED measure. We can prevent the noise, errors, and divergences of data while detecting the similarity between graphs by using this GED measure. The prominent fundamental role of this measure is used to accomplish a set of edit operations on graphs to validate the similarity. Edit distance operations are made on each set of q-grams to generate candidate keys. Computationally it is expensive to carry out the required number of operations on a pair of graphs to detect the similarity [19]. However, it is tailed in major algorithms to compute the similarity to the best level. The existing popular similarity computation of Jaccard and Cosine similarity needs to be revised to detect the similarity among the massive datasets.

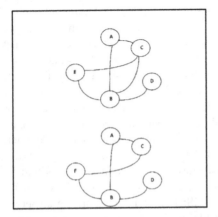

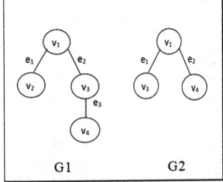

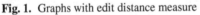

Fig. 1. Graphs with edit distance measure   **Fig. 2.** Graph Branch Distance Measure

2.2 Graph Branch Distance with GED

With the wide variety of applications of graphs, the edit distance measure is applied to prune similar graphs whether they are either directed or undirected. GED has high processing interpretability to calculate the similarity between the graph pairs. Considering (see Fig. 2), the GED measure is used to validate the similarity among the graphs. The GED measure contains distinct operations like inserting, deleting, and labeling the vertices to match the pair of graphs [24, eq. (1)]. To decrease the high cost of precise GED measure computations, Graph branch distance (GBD) is used to estimate the GED of two graphs. To prune the graph similarity search results, GBD is used. Besides, this relation between GED & GBD is utilized to accomplish graph similarity searches.

$$GBD(G1, G2) \rightarrow \max\{|BG1|, |BG2|\} - |BG1 \cap BG2| \qquad (1)$$

2.3 Locality Sensitive Hash

Minhash and Locality-sensitive hash (LSH) techniques are applied to detect the similarity between the graphs. LSH is used to form clusters between similar vertexes to reduce pairwise comparisons and the growth of candidates. This technique uses the Jaccard similarity measure to validate the similarity among the graph pairs. Conducting a similarity search among graph pairs from massive datasets is prone to a thought-provoking issue to solve in a specified time [28]. Dimensionality is reduced with the minhash technique without losing the similarity among graph pairs. At the same time, LSH is applied to form the clusters among the pairs of graphs by condensing the growth rate of pairwise comparisons. A similarity search is applied among the candidate clusters to distinguish the near duplicates effectively.

2.4 Graph Sim Join

The existence of near-duplicate graphs over massive datasets is the main issue in the mining area; traditional and basic inverted index technique is improvised with the pruning strategies like sorting and refined prefix filtering. Every pair of graphs are to be searched, accomplish the comparisons between them by analyzing the number of vertices/edges to be the same. With the ascending order of token frequency [25] and graphs are to be sorted. Compared to the other techniques, this one got a condensed number of candidates, and the search optimization facility is enhanced by defining some threshold value. A Vertex edge similarity measure is applied to perceive the similarity, and at the same time, the number of pair-wise comparisons is condensed [16]. Rather than focusing on the structure or shape of the graphs, this technique focused on several graph vertices and edges that are comparable. A comparative analysis of different graph-based techniques is mentioned in Table 1.

3 Proposed Technique

The scalability of massive datasets and heterogeneous data sources results in near-duplicate documents. Finding all pairs of near-duplicate documents requires O(N2) comparisons. We need an efficient algorithm to detect these near-duplicate documents

Table 1. Comparison Analysis.

Year	Technique used	Similarity Measure	Remarks
2021 Jongik Kim [29]	Framework Naas with GED Computation	Edit distance similarity measure	Computationally expensive to apply various filtering techniques
2020 P Naveena [23]	Combination of inverted index with prefix filtering	Vertex edge similarity measure	Applicable and obtained fine results for simple graphs without any parallel edges
2019 Ruan [30]	Locality sensitive hash (LSH), minhash	Jaccard similarity measure	This measure not suitable for all graph-based techniques and results may vary
2018 Z. Li, [24]	GBD along with GED	Edit distance similarity measure	Computation cost is high on real time datasets

Table 2. Token Analysis

Tokens		Detection	Duplicates	Near	Similarity
Token frequency		3	3	2	1
Text Documents	T1	1	1	0	0
	T2	0	1	1	0
	T3	1	1	1	0
	T4	1	0	0	1

to overcome this sophisticated issue. The existing inverted index technique produces more candidate keys while detecting near-duplicate documents. For better reduction of candidate keys, a positional filtering technique is used, and this technique is formed by integrating prefix filtering and inverted index techniques with VEO [Vertex Edge Overlapping] similarity measure (see Fig. 3). Compared to All-Pairs, Inverted index algorithms, this proposed technique is much better at reducing the number of pairwise comparisons.

To find the similarity between the documents, we need to use the similarity function with a specified threshold, which returns [0, 1] based on the level of similarity between the documents. The Jaccard similarity measure specifies threshold values among similarity measures like Cosine and overlaps similarity measures. The main motto of this problem solution is to condense the total pair wise comparisons with some pruning strategies to

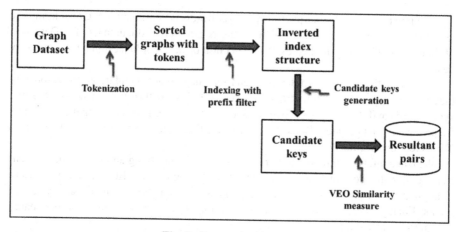

Fig. 3. Process Architecture

improve the quality of search results with enhanced speed. Graph similarity self-join of documents should be analysed to figure out the near duplicates. GSSJD (see Fig. 4) is proposed with an enhanced filtering technique to decompose the generated candidate pairs to achieve this. Prefix filtering is applied to condense the rate of candidate pairs by arranging the tokens in increasing order by following the token frequency.

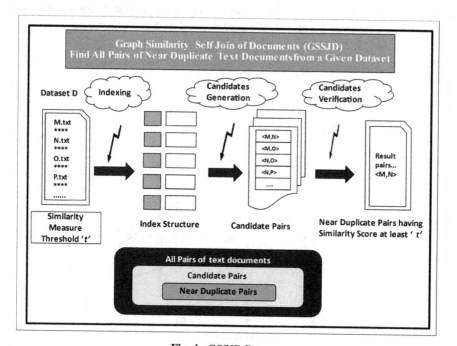

Fig. 4. GSSJD Process

The inverted index technique follows token-to-document mapping. Considering the text documents T1, T2, T3, and T4 from the N number of documents. T1: Detection of duplicates, T2: Near duplicates, T3: Detection of near duplicates and T4: Similarity detection.

Observing the increasing order of token frequency reduces candidate generation with the strategic approach of prefix filtering by considering the threshold value as 0.8. Final synthesized candidates are listed below the upper bound value by omitting the zero token frequency. T1: Duplicates, Detection, T2: Near, Duplicates, T3: Detection, Duplicates T4: Detection, Similarity.

We can achieve a limited number of candidates by applying an inverted index technique with enhanced filtering to these text-based documents. VEO Similarity measure is applied to minimize the number of pairwise comparisons from these text documents. Finally, pairwise comparisons are minimized to gradually improve the search optimization [16, eq. (2)].

$$\text{Sim}_{\text{VEO}} = \frac{|V \cap V'| + |E \cap E'|}{|V| + |V'| + |E| + |E'|} \tag{2}$$

Experiment activities were conducted on Ubuntu 22.04 LTS System with 16GB RAM and 1TB hard disk specifications. An experiment was carried out on a synthetic dataset comprising 400 text-based documents, which were divided into three distinct text-based datasets: Graph Set1, Graph Set2, and Graph Set3. We got the less pairwise comparisons by applying the VEO measure to generated candidates. After applying the proposed technique, we got acceptable results regarding generated index entries that required time to process the search, as stated in (see Fig. 5 and Fig. 6).

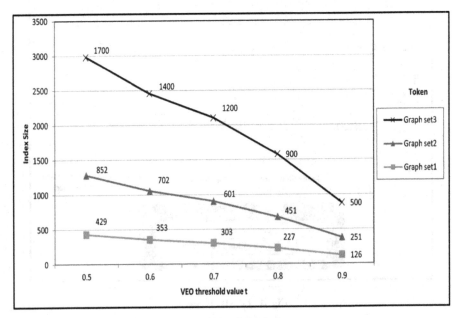

Fig. 5. Threshold, Index

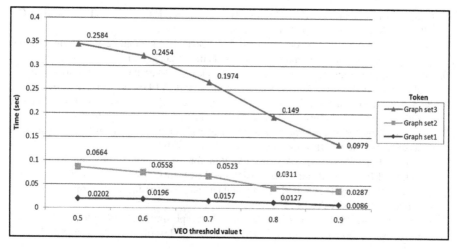

Fig. 6. Threshold, Time

4   Conclusions

GSSJD problem includes various undeveloped exciting encounters. Our preliminary consequences specify that different indexes and filtering remain a possible way on the mode to discover. We can get optimized search results with enhanced speed by detecting near duplicates. By observing the results, we got the improvised results by increasing the threshold value. In the future, this work can be extended to detect near duplicate images to achieve optimized search results on social media platforms. Near duplicate images are the new sheering problem in that an identical copy of the image is uploaded at distinct platforms with trivial differences.

References

1. Babai, L.: Graph isomorphism in quasipolynomial time. arXiv preprint arXiv:1512.03547 (2015)
2. Babai, L., Kantor, W.M., Luks, E.M.: Computational complexity and the classification of finite simple groups. In: Proceedings of the 24th Annual Symposium on Foundation Computer Science, SFCS '83, Washing DC, USA, IEEE Com. Society, pp. 162–171 (1983)
3. Bunke, H., Allermann, G.: Inexact graph matching for structural pattern recognition. Pattern Recogn. Lett., 245–253 (1983)
4. Berretti, S., Del Bimbo, A., Vicario, E.: Efficient matching and indexing of graph models in content-based retrieval. IEEE Trans. Pattern Anal. Mach. Intell., 1089–1105 (2001)
5. Bunke, H., Shearer, K.: A graph distance metric based on the maximal common subgraph. Pattern Recogn. Lett., 255–259 (1998)
6. Sanfeliu, A., Fu, K.: A distance measure between attributed relational graphs for pattern recognition. IEEE Trans. Syst. Man Cybern., 353–362 (1983)
7. Chen, Y., Zhao, X., Xiao, C., Zhang, W., Tang, J.: Efficient and scalable graph similarity joins in map reduce. Sci. World J. (2014)

8. Cho, J., Shivakumar, N., Garcia-Molina, H.: Finding replicated web collections. In: ACM SIGMOD Record, ACM, pp. 355–366 (2000)
9. Fernandez, M.L., Valiente, G.: A graph distance metric combining maximum common subgraph and minimum common super graph. Pattern Recog. Lett., 753–758 (2001)
10. Gravano, L., Ipeirotis, P.G., Jagadish, H.V., Koudas, N., Muthukrishnan, S., Srivastava, D., et al.: Approximate string joins in a database for free. In: VLDB, pp. 491–500 (2001)
11. Krinke, J.: Identifying similar code with program dependence graphs. In: Proceedings of Eighth Working Conference on Reverse Engineering, pp. 301–309. IEEE (2001)
12. Mann, W., Augsten, N., Bouros, P.: An empirical evaluation of set similarity join techniques. Proceedings of the VLDB Endowment, pp. 636–647 (2016)
13. Messmer, B.T., Bunke, H.: A new algorithm for error-tolerant subgraph isomorphism detection. IEEE Trans. Pattern Anal. Mach. Intell., 493–504 (1998)
14. Mihalcea, R., Radev, D.: Graph-based natural language processing and information retrieval. Cambridge University Press (2011)
15. Pang, J., Gu, Y., Xu, J., Bao, Y., Yu, G.: Efficient graph similarity join with scalable prefix-filtering using map reduce, pp. 415–418. In Web-Age Information Management, Springer (2014)
16. Papadimitriou, P., Dasdan, A., Garcia-Molina, H.: Web graph similarity for anomaly detection. J. Internet Serv. Appl., 19–30 (2010)
17. Petrakis, E.G.M., Faloutsos, A.: Similarity searching in medical image databases. IEEE Trans. Knowl. Data Eng., 435–447 (1997)
18. Raymond, J.W., Gardiner, E.J., Willett, P.: Rascal: calculation of graph similarity using maximum common edge subgraphs. Comput. J., 631–644 (2002)
19. Wang, Y., Wang, H., Ye, C., Gao, H.:"Graph similarity join with k-hop tree indexing. In: Int. Conference of Young Comp. Scientists, Engg. and Edu. Springer, pp. 38–47 (2015)
20. Trinajstic, N.: Computational chemical graph theory: characterization, enumeration, and generation of chemical structures by computer methods. E. Horwood (1991)
21. Zeng, Z., Tung, A.K., Wang, J., Feng, J., Zhou, L.: Comparing stars: on approximating graph edit distance. In: Proceedings of the VLDB Endowment, pp. 25–36 (2009)
22. Zhao, X., Xiao, C., Lin, X., Wang, W.: Efficient graph similarity joins with edit distance constraints. In: IEEE 28th Int. Conf. on Data Engg. (ICDE), pp. 834–845. IEEE (2012)
23. Naveena, P., Rao, P.K.S.: Detection of near duplicates over graph datasets using pruning. In: 2020 IEEE India Council International Subsections Conference (INDISCON), pp. 309–313 (2020)
24. Li, Z., Jian, X., Lian, X., Chen, L.: An efficient probabilistic approach for graph similarity search. In: 2018 IEEE 34th Int. Conference on Data Eng. (ICDE), pp. 533–544 (2018)
25. Xiao, C., Wang, W., Lin, X., Yu, J.X.: Efficient similarity joins for near duplicate detection. ACM Trans. Database Syst. (TODS) 36, 41 (2011)
26. Rachkovskij, D.A.: Fast similarity search for graphs by edit distance. In: Cybernetics and Systems Analysis, pp. 178–194 (2019)
27. Riesen, K., Bunke, H.: IAM graph database repository for graph based pattern recognition and machine learning. In: SSPR&SPR, pp. 287–297 (2008)
28. Rashtchian, C., Sharma, A., Woodruff, D.: LSF join locality sensitive filtering for distributed all pairs set similarity under skew. In: WWW '20: Proceedings of the Web Conference, pp. 2998–3004 (2020)
29. Kim, J.: Boosting Graph Similarity Search through Pre-Computation. In: SIGMOD '21, June 20–25, 2021, Virtual Event, China, pp. 951–963 (2021)
30. Ruan, Q., Wu, Q., Liu, X., et al.: Efficient similarity join for certain graphs. Microsyst. Technol.. Technol. 27, 1665–1685 (2021). https://doi.org/10.1007/s00542-019-04472-6

Three Factor Authentication Scheme
for Telecare Medical Information System

Anurag Deep Kujur[1]([⊠]) and Preeti Chandrakar[2]

[1] Department of Information Technology, National Institute of Technology, Raipur , India
anuragdeepkujur758@gmail.com
[2] Department of Computer Science and Engineering, National Institute of Technology, Raipur,
India
pchandrakar.cs@nitrr.ac.in

Abstract. With advances in technology and mobile computing, the user has
access to a platform to get medical services door to door. Patients can now use
remote medical services provided by the medical server. But the user and TMIS
communicate via public channel which increases the security risk of patient confi-
dential data. Making a convenient and secure connection between the two entities
over the insecure channel is a major issue. It becomes necessary to make sure that
only the authorized user is interacting with correct server. There are existing systems which provides security but are vulnerable to certain attacks. In this paper,
we have proposed a three-factor scheme for user authentication which is secure
against various attacks. The results shows that computation cost of our scheme is
comparatively less than the related schemes. Also, the communication cost and
execution time is reasonable. We have also done the informal security analysis
using AVISPA which shows our scheme is secure against various attacks.

Keywords: Authentication · AVISPA tool · Biometric · Security · Telecare
Medical Information System

1 Introduction

E-healthcare system demands have been increased in recent years. Utilization of technology makes it easier for the registered user to access the online medical services. Patients
can be at home and still communicate with the doctors through public network. But
assurance of keeping the information safe have also faced issues. The security of user
data has been a top priority in terms of its integrity, availability, validity, non-repudiation,
and confidentiality.

TMIS provides services related to healthcare. With the services provided, patient can
easily get healthcare details on their devices. But these services are offered via public
network which increases the chances of various attacks. An attacker could eavesdrop on
the message being transmitted since the user-server communication connection is not
secure. Preserving the privacy of the healthcare systems becomes the utmost priority. To
verify the authenticity of user and to protect medical server from unauthorized access,

remote user verification plays a crucial role. There are basically two participants: first is user at public end and the server which provides services. Therefore, user and server must establish a secure connection before communicating with each other. Password, smart card, or biometrics can all be used as authentication factors.

Figure 1 shows user authentication architecture used in E-health care. First the patient has to register himself to the medical server so as to access the services. The channel is not safe between the user and server and an adversary can gain access to the data that is transmitted through public channel. Therefore, making e-health care systems secure and private becomes crucial.

Smart card-based verification gives a safe and secure connection between patient and server [1]. Several two-factor authentication approaches are presented in the following survey [2]. "But it failed to provide security against insider attack, offline password guessing attack" [2]. So, three factor authentication which includes biometric template of user was proposed to improve the security.

Using Biometric keys increases the security in authentication schemes. Correct user can be easily identified using his/her biometrics. Conventional password-based remote user authentication is less trustworthy than biometric-based remote user authentication. We propose a scheme for TMIS that takes users ID, Password and Biometrics.

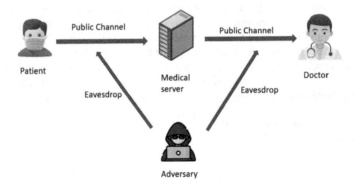

Fig. 1. User authentication architecture for E-health care

1.1 Organization of Paper

The remaining paper is arranged as following sections. Section 2 shows Literature Survey. Section 3 the proposed scheme is explained. We analyze the safety of our scheme using AVISPA tool in Sect. 4. Section 5 shows the results of our simulation. Comparison of suggested protocol with other related schemes in given in Sect. 6. Lastly, Sect. 7 concludes our paper.

2 Literature Survey

For TMIS, numerous authentication methods have been suggested. In [3], Mir et al. proposed biometrics- based authentication scheme claiming it was secure and has an efficient computation time. But it cannot prevent against stolen smart card attack. Chaudhry et al. [4], proposed a new three-factor authentication technique that is based on lightweight symmetric key primitives. But the cost of computation was high.

"Hashing and exclusive OR operations are used to improve the effectiveness in e-healthcare system [5]. Awasthi et al. [6] introduced a lightweight three-factor authentication approach to increase the efficiency of hash functions. But, Mishra et al. [7] figured that Awasthi's scheme does not guarantee user anonymity and cannot prevent password guessing attacks. Chen et al. [8] also presented authentication scheme that depends upon identity and smart card. But [9] discovered that it does not guarantee user anonymity and is susceptible to offline password guessing attack.

A two-factor remote user authentication method based on a smart card and password was presented by Wu et al. [10]. But it was vulnerable against impersonation attack and insider attack. A three-factor authentication technique proposed by Xei [11] claiming it to be secure. But Xu et al. [12] in his paper showed that scheme is still unsafe to De-synchronization attack.

Chang et al. [13] presented a remote user authentication system that protects anonymity and uniqueness. Their system makes use of the user's personal biometrics and password in conjunction with smart card. By employing bio-hashing, the user's biometrics are confirmed. Their method is effective because it uses exclusive-or (XOR) operations and hash functions.

Literature Survey shows that several security schemes are susceptible to security attacks. So, we have proposed a safe authentication scheme using biometrics, password and biometrics.

Table 1. Notations definition

Notation	Description
ID_i	User's Identity
PW_i	User's password
MPW_i	Masked Password of user
B_i	Biometric Template
SC_i	Smart Card
R_u, R_s	Random nonce values
X_s	Secret key of sever
SID_j	Identity of server

(continued)

Table 1. (*continued*)

Notation	Description
$h(.)$	Hash function
$H(.)$	Bio-Hash function
SK	Session key
$\oplus$	X O R
$\parallel$	Concatenation operator

3   Proposed Scheme

The proposed scheme is separated into four steps. The notations used in the paper are given in Table 1. Figure 2 describes a general framework for three factor authentication schemes in which factor 1 is User's ID and password, factor 2 is smart card and the 3rd factor is Biometrics. The details are discussed below.

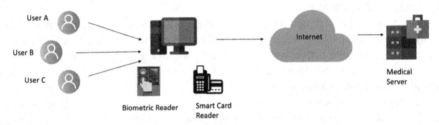

Fig. 2. Three factor remote user authentication scheme using smart card and biometrics.

3.1   Registration Phase

Step 1. User creates identity ID_i, password PW_i, random number K and Biometric Template B. And calculates Masked Password $MPW_i = h(ID_i\|PW_i\|K)$. Finally send ID_i, MPW_i, B_i to server via secure channel.

Step 2. Server S_j creates unique identity NID_i for each user after receiving the registration message.

$$CID_i = h(ID_i\|B_i) \text{and also computes}$$

$$f_i = H(B_i)$$

$$e_i = h\big(SID_j\|X_s\|f_i\big) \oplus MPW_i$$

$$T_i = NID_i \oplus h(ID_i\|f_i)$$

Step 3. S_j then stores the value $\{f_i, e_i \ T_i \ h(.), H(.)\}$ in Smart Card SC_i memory and forwards SC_i to U. After getting the smart card, user computes

$$C_i = ID_i \oplus PW_i \oplus K$$

$$O_i = h(ID_i||PW_i) \oplus K$$

Now SC_i contains $\{f_i, e_i \ T_i h(.), H(.), C_i, O_i\}$. Figure 3 shows the summary of Registration phase.

3.2 Login Phase

A registered user must follow the steps outlined below in order to gain access to a medical server's services.

Step 1. Inserts the SC_i to CR or terminal and enter the Biometric B_i.

Step 2. CR computes $f^*_i = H(B_i)$ and examines whether the condition $f^*_i = f_i$, if condition is true, it means user has been registered and he is permitted to enter his ID and password. If the condition is not met, login phase is declined by CR.

Step 3. Device then computes

$$K = O_i \oplus h(ID_i||PW_i)$$

$$C_i^* = ID_i \oplus PW_i \oplus K$$

It checks if $C_i^* = C_i$;

If condition holds true, it means the ID and Password entered by the user is correct. User generates random number R_u or the session is terminated.

Step 4. After R_u is generated CR computes

$$NID_i = T_i \oplus h(ID_i||f_i)$$

$$G_i = R_u \oplus h(O_i||K||PW_i)$$

$$NID^*_i = NID_i \oplus R_u$$

$$M_i = h(NID_i||R_u||h(ID_i||K)||PW_i)$$

And sends $\{ NID_i^*, G_i, f_i, M_i\}$ to the server.

3.3 Authentication Phase

Step 1. The server computes the following operations after obtaining the login message from User.

$$J_i = h\big(SID_j||X_s||f_i\big)$$

$$NID_i = NID_i^* \oplus R_u$$

$$M_i^* = h(NID_i||R_u||h(ID_i||PW_i||K)$$

And verifies if $M_i^* = M_i$. If verification holds true, Server presumes that login message sent by the user is genuine, if not then ends the session.

Step 2. Random nonce R_s is created by server and it calculates

$$P_i = R_s \oplus J$$

$$Q_i = h(R_s||R_u||h(ID_i||PW_i||K)$$

And sends the message $\{P_i, Q_i\}$ to user.

Step 3. After receiving $\{P_i, Q_i\}$ SC first computes,

$$R_s = P \oplus R_u$$

$$Q_i* = h(R_s||R_u||h(ID_i||PW_i||K)$$

Then it checks to see if computed Q_i* equals to received Q_i. If true, SC_i believes that reply message sent by S_j is real. Mutual authentication is received at this stage. Figure 4 shows the summary of Login and authentication phase.

3.4 Password Change Phase

Step 1. By completing the step 1 of the login procedure, the SC reader verifies the user's legitimacy.

Step 2. SC inquires the user to enter new password and SC computes.

$$MPW_i^{new} = h(ID_i||PW_i^{new}||K)$$

$$e_i^* = e_i \oplus MPW_i^{new}$$

Step 3. The SC renews of e* value in memory of SC.

Password change phase is now successfully completed.

4 Formal Verification Using AVISPA

AVISPA is commonly used for security verification. The simulation results demonstrate the scheme's safety or unreliability. AVISPA is implemented in 4 back-ends: 1. OMFC 2. CL-AtSe 3. SATMC 4. TA4SP. Depending upon the back-end, the output is generated and it claims if proposed protocol is safe or not. In AVISPA, participants act as a role. We use HLPSL language to define the role. There are three roles: User, Server and the Session role.

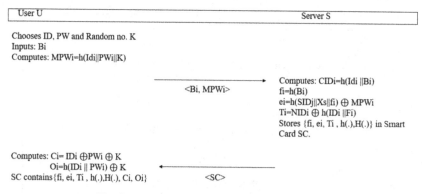

Fig. 3. Message sequence for Registration Phase

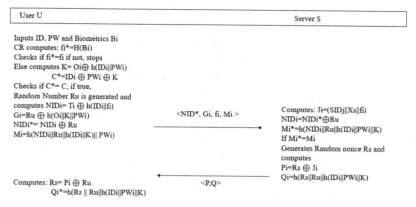

Fig. 4. Message sequence for Login and Authentication Phase

In Figs. 2 and 3, the HLPSL role specification is displayed. The initiator of the protocol, User receives start signal to run the protocol and the state changes from 0 to 1. User sends the registration request, by encrypting the ID, PW and a random number K through reliable SND channel. The specification (dy) specifies that if follows Dolev-Yao threat model. User then receives response for registration message RCV({*Fi.Ei.Ti*} *Key*). In login phase, User first verifies his biometrics in the card reader or terminal and then using a new () event creates a random nonce. New values are specified using apostrophe mark and are called prime variables. The login request is sent via the SND channel after some calculations, SND (NIDii', Gi', Fi', Mi'). Later it computes a session key.

```
    role alice (Ui, Sj: agent,
        SKas : symmetric_key,
        H: hash_func,
        Snd, Rcv: channel(dy))
    played_by Ui
    def=
        local
        State : nat,
        IDi, PWi, PWDi,MPWi, Ci,Oi,Ii,Mi,NIDi, Bi, NIDii, Pi,Qi,Qii,SIDj, Xs, Rc,
Ti,K: text,
        Eii, Gi, Li, Rs, SK, Ki, Di, Fi, Ei: message,
        Inc : hash_func
        const alice_server, server_alice, subs1, subs2, subs3,
        subs4, subs5, subs6: protocol_id
    init
        State :=0
    transition
        1. State = 0 ∧ Rcv(start) =|>State' := 1 ∧ K':=new() ∧ MPWi' := H(IDi.PWi.K')
                ∧ Snd({IDi.MPWi'.Bi}_SKas)
                ∧ secret({IDi}, subs1, {Ui,Sj})
                ∧ secret({PWi}, subs2, {Ui})
        2. State = 1 ∧ Rcv({Fi'.Ei'.Ti'}_SKas) =|>State' := 2 ∧ Rc' := new()
            ∧ Ci' := xor(IDi,xor(PWi,K))
            ∧ Oi' :=xor(H(IDi.PWi))
            ∧ NIDi' := xor(Ti, H(IDi.Fi))
            ∧Gi':= xor(Rc',H(IDi.PWi,K))
            ∧NIDii' :=xor(NIDi',Rc')
            ∧Mi':= H(NIDi'.Rc'.H(IDi.K).PWi)
            ∧ Snd(NIDii',Gi',Fi',Mi')
            ∧ secret({Rc'}, subs3, {Ui,Sj})
            ∧ witness(Ui, Sj, alice_server, Rc')
        3. State = 2 ∧ Rcv(Pi'.Qi') =|>State' := 3
            ∧ Rs' := xor(Pi,Rc)
            ∧ Qii' := H(Rs'.Rc,H(IDi.PWi.K))
            ∧ SK' := H(Rc.Rs)
            ∧ secret({SK'}, subs4, {Ui,Sj})
            end role
```

Fig. 5. Specification for user's role in HLPSL

```
role server (Sj, Ui: agent,
    SKas : symmetric_key,
    H: hash_func,
    Snd, Rcv: channel(dy) )
played_by Sj
def=
    local
    State : nat,
    IDi, PWi, PWDi, MPWi,Ci,Oi,Bi,Mi,Mii,Ji,NIDi, NIDii,Pi, Qi,SIDj, Xs, Rc,
Ti,K: text,
    Eii, Gi, Li, Rs, SK, Ki, Di, Ai, Fi, CIDi, Ei: message,
    Inc : hash_func
    const alice_server, server_alice, subs1, subs2, subs3,
    subs4, subs5, subs6: protocol_id
init
    State :=0
transition
    1. State = 0 ∧ Rcv(IDi.MPWi'.Bi) =|>State' := 1 ∧ NIDi' := new()
    ∧ CIDi' := H(IDi.Bi)
    ∧ Fi' := H(Bi)
    ∧ Ei' := xor(H(SIDj.Xs.Fi'),MPWi)
    ∧ Ti' := xor(NIDi, H(IDi.Fi'))
            ∧ Snd({Fi'.Ei'.Ti'}_SKas)
    ∧ secret({Xs}, subs5, {Sj})
    2. State = 1 ∧ Rcv(NIDii'.Gi'.Fi'.Mi') =|>State' := 2 ∧ Rs' := new()
    ∧ Ji'   := H(SIDj.Xs.Fi')
    ∧ NIDi':=xor(NIDii',Rc)
            ∧Mi':=H(NIDi'.Rc.H(IDi.K).PWi)
    ∧Pi':= xor(Rs', Rc)
    ∧Qi' :=H(Rs'.Rc,H(IDi.PWi.K))
    ∧ witness(Sj, Ui, server_alice, Rs')
    ∧request(Ui, Sj, server_alice, Rs')
    ∧secret({Rs'},subs6,{Sj})
    ∧ Snd(Pi'.Qi')
end role
```

Fig. 6. Specification for server's role in HLPSL

```
role session(Ui, Sj: agent,
        SKas : symmetric_key,
        H: hash_func)
def=
        local SI, SJ, RI, RJ: channel (dy)
        composition
                alice(Ui, Sj, SKas, H, SI, RI) ∧ server(Ui, Sj, SKas, H, SJ, RJ)
end role
role environment()
def=
    const ui, sj: agent,
    skas : symmetric_key,
    h, mul, add, sub: hash_func,
    idi, pwi, nidi, nidii, sidj, xs, ri, ti, rs: text,
    alice_server_rc, server_alice_rs, subs1,
        subs2, subs3, subs4, subs5, subs6: protocol_id
intruder_knowledge = {ui, sj, h}
composition
    session( ui, sj, skas, h)∧ session(sj, ui, skas, h)
end role
goal
    secrecy_of subs1
    secrecy_of subs2
    secrecy_of subs3
    secrecy_of subs4
    secrecy_of subs5
    secrecy_of subs6
    authentication_on alice_server_rc
    authentication_on server_alice_rs
end goal
environment()
```

Fig. 7. HLPSL specification for session and environment

5   Simulation Results

We execute our result in OMFC and CL-AtSe. The simulation result of OMFC is shown is Fig. 8 and CL-AtSe in Fig. 9. It shows that our scheme is secure. CL-AtSe summary shows our protocol is safe.

```
% OFMC
% Version of 2006/02/13
SUMMARY
 SAFE
DETAILS
 BOUNDED_NUMBER_OF_SESSIONS
PROTOCOL
 /home/span/span/testsuite/results/My.if
GOAL
 as_specified
BACKEND
 OFMC
COMMENTS
STATISTICS
 parseTime: 0.00s
 searchTime: 0.11s
 visitedNodes: 4 nodes
 depth: 2 plies
```

Fig. 8. OFMC result

```
SUMMARY
SAFE

DETAILS
 BOUNDED_NUMBER_OF_SESSIONS
 TYPED_MODEL

PROTOCOL
 /home/span/span/testsuite/results/My.if

GOAL
 As Specified

BACKEND
 CL-AtSe

STATISTICS

 Analysed  : 0 states
 Reachable : 0 states
 Translation: 0.03 seconds
 Computation: 0.00 seconds
```

Fig. 9. CL-AtSe result

6 Performance Evaluation

This section compares the performance of our scheme with related scheme. Let T_H, T_E, T_B, T_{MX} be the time required for performing hash operation, symmetric encryption, bio-hashing, modular exponentiation. XOR operation and concatenation operation time can be neglected because it is inconsiderable as compared to above operations. Table 2 shows the cost of proposed protocol compared to related protocols.

Table 2. Computation cost of related protocols

Scheme	Registration phase	Login phase	Authentication phase	Total Cost
Li et al. [1]	$8T_H$	$7T_H + 1T_{mexp}$	-	$15T_H + 1T_{mexp}$
Mir et al. [3]	$3T_H$	$6T_H$	$11T_H$	$20T_H$
Ali et al. [5]	$7T_H$	$5T_H + 1T_E$	$10T_H + 1T_E$	$22T_H + 2T_E$
Karuppiah et al. [15]	$4T_H$	$6T_H + 2T_{MX}$	$7T_H + 1T_{MX}$	$17T_H + 3T_{MX}$
Amin et al. [16]	$4T_H$	$5T_H + 1T_E$	$5T_H + 1T_E$	$14T_H + 2T_E$
Das and Goswami [17]	$3T_H + T_B$	$7T_H$	$6T_H$	$16T_H + 1T_B$
Younghwa An [18]	$3T_H$	$3T_H$	$6T_H$	$12T_H$
Proposed Scheme	$5T_H$	$6T_H$	$5T_H$	$16T_H$

Table 3. Execution Time

Scheme	Execution Time (in seconds)
Li et al. [1]	0.006
Mir et al. [3]	0.5295
Amin et al. [5]	1.051
Ali et al. [14]	1.0610
Karuppiah et al. [15]	0.60391
Das and Goswami[17]	0.009
Younghwa An [18]	0.0095
Proposed Scheme	0.008

6.1 Execution Time

To analyze the proposed protocol's calculation time, we have considered the time taken to execute hash function is 0.0005 s, modular exponentiation 0.522 s, symmetric key

0.0087 s, encryption and decryption is 0.0503 s [19]. The estimated execution time of Ali [14], Karuppiah [15], Amin [5], Li [1], Mir [3], Younghwa [18] and proposed scheme are 1.0610, 0.60391, 1.051, 0.006, 0.5295, 0.0095 and 0.008 respectively.

6.2 Comparison of Estimated Time

Execution time with related schemes is shown in Fig. 10.

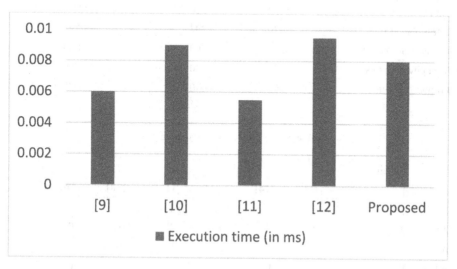

Fig. 10. Estimated Time

6.3 Communication Cost

We have considered the size as 160 bits for the output of one-way hash function, real identity, random integer, and bio-hash function. The length of output of the symmetric encryption/decryption is 256 bits. As shown in Table 4, our scheme stores 960 bits in the smart card. Some trade-off can be done to provide higher security.

6.4 Security Feature Comparison

Table 5 shows our scheme offers the needed security characteristics and can counter variety of active attacks. The proposed approach not only accomplishes various security qualities and robust protection against the relevant security attacks, it is also efficient in terms of computing costs.

Table 4. Communication cost comparison

Scheme	Cost (bits)		
	Login	Authentication	Total
Li [1]	672	352	1024
Mir et al. [3]	352	512	864
Amin [5]	1280	384	1664
Ali [14]	1184	320	1504
Karuppiah [15]	1920	384	2304
Das and Goswami[17]	480	800	1280
Younghwa An [18]	640	640	1280
Proposed Scheme	960	640	1600

Table 5. Security attributes comparison

SF	Schemes							
	[1]	[3]	[5]	[14]	[15]	[17]	[18]	Proposed
A1	F	F	T	T	T	T	F	T
A2	T	T	T	T	T	T	F	T
A3	F	T	T	T	F	F	T	T
A4	F	T	T	T	T	F	F	T
A5	F	T	F	F	T	T	T	T
A6	T	T	T	T	F	T	T	T
A7	T	T	T	T	T	T	T	T
A8	T	T	F	T	T	T	F	T

SF: Security Features, T: Achieved F: Not Achieved A1: User Anonymity A2: Replay Attack A3: Offline password A4: Stolen smart card attack A5: Impersonation attack A6: Insider attack A7: Session key agreement A8: Mutual Authentication.

7 Conclusion

The TMIS contains the sensitive information of user/patient and the information is subjected to attacks. In this paper, we have analyzed several papers related to TMIS and to overcome the flaws we proposed a new three-factor authentication scheme for TMIS. We have compared our scheme with various other relevant biometrics schemes. In terms of execution time, computation cost and communication bits our proposed protocol performs better. We also performed simulation using AVISPA, a tool for automated validation of Internet security protocols. The protocol is specified in HLPSL. The result shows that it is safe against variety of attacks. The comparison done with related schemes shows our scheme have performed better. The total bits required is 1600. We demonstrate that our system is highly efficient for linked healthcare using formal verification and performance analysis.

References

1. Li, X., Niu, J., Karuppiah, M., Kumari, S., Wu, F.: Secure and efficient two-factor user authentication scheme with user anonymity for network based E-health care applications. J. Med. Syst. **40**(12), December 2016. https://doi.org/10.1007/s10916-016-0629-8

2. Debiao, H., Jianhua, C., Rui, Z.: A more secure authentication scheme for telecare medicine information systems. J. Med. Syst. **36**(3), 1989–1995 (2012). https://doi.org/10.1007/s10916-011-9658-5

3. Mir, O., van der Weide, T., Lee, C.C.: A secure user anonymity and authentication scheme using AVISPA for telecare medical information systems. J. Med. Syst. **39**(9), September 2015. https://doi.org/10.1007/s10916-015-0265-8

4. Mir, O., Nikooghadam, M.: A secure biometrics based authentication with key agreement scheme in telemedicine networks for E-health services. Wirel. Pers. Commun.. Pers. Commun. **83**(4), 2439–2461 (2015). https://doi.org/10.1007/s11277-015-2538-4

5. Amin, R., Biswas, G.P.: A secure three-factor user authentication and key agreement protocol for TMIS with user anonymity. J. Med. Syst. **39**(8), August 2015. https://doi.org/10.1007/s10916-015-0258-7

6. Awasthi, A.K., Srivastava, K., Mittal, R.C.: An improved timestamp-based remote user authentication scheme. Comput. Electr. Eng.. Electr. Eng. **37**(6), 869–874 (2011). https://doi.org/10.1016/j.compeleceng.2011.09.015

7. Mishra, R., Barnwal, A.K.: A privacy preserving secure and efficient authentication scheme for telecare medical information systems. J. Med. Syst. **39**(5), May 2015. https://doi.org/10.1007/s10916-015-0215-5

8. Chen, H.M., Lo, J.W., Yeh, C.K.: An efficient and secure dynamic ID-based authentication scheme for telecare medical information systems. J. Med. Syst., 3907–3915, , December 2012. https://doi.org/10.1007/s10916-012-9862-y

9. Cao, T., Zhai, J.: Improved dynamic ID-based authentication scheme for telecare medical information systems. J. Med. Syst. 37(2), April 2013. https://doi.org/10.1007/s10916-012-9912-5

10. Wu, Z.Y., Lee, Y.C., Lai, F., Lee, H.C., Chung, Y.: A secure authentication scheme for telecare medicine information systems. J. Med. Syst. **36**(3), 1529–1535 (2012). https://doi.org/10.1007/s10916-010-9614-9

11. Xie, Q., Liu, W., Wang, S., Han, L., Hu, B., Wu, T.: Improvement of a uniqueness-and-anonymity-preserving user authentication scheme for connected health care. J. Med. Syst. **38**(9) (2014). https://doi.org/10.1007/s10916-014-0091-4

12. Xu, L., Wu, F.: Cryptanalysis and improvement of a user authentication scheme preserving uniqueness and anonymity for connected health care. J. Med. Syst. **39**(2), February 2015. https://doi.org/10.1007/s10916-014-0179-x

13. Chang, Y.F., Yu, S.H., Shiao, D.R.: A uniqueness-and-anonymity-preserving remote user authentication scheme for connected health care. J. Med. Syst. **37**(2), April 2013. https://doi.org/10.1007/s10916-012-9902-7

14. Ali, R., Pal, A.K.: Cryptanalysis and biometric-based enhancement of a remote user authentication scheme for E-healthcare system. Arab. J. Sci. Eng. **43**(12), 7837–7852 (2018). https://doi.org/10.1007/s13369-018-3220-4

15. Karuppiah, M., et al.: Secure remote user mutual authentication scheme with key agreement for cloud environment. Mob. Networks Appl. **24**(3), 1046–1062 (2019). https://doi.org/10.1007/s11036-018-1061-8

16. Amin, R., Maitra, T., Giri, D., Srivastava, P.D.: Cryptanalysis and improvement of an RSA based remote user authentication scheme using smart card. Wirel. Pers. Commun.. Pers. Commun. **96**(3), 4629–4659 (2017). https://doi.org/10.1007/s11277-017-4408-8

17. Das, A.K., Goswami, A.: A secure and efficient uniqueness-and-anonymity-preserving remote user authentication scheme for connected health care. J. Med. Syst. **37**(3), June 2013. https://doi.org/10.1007/s10916-013-9948-1

18. An, Y.: Security analysis and enhancements of an effective biometric-based remote user authentication scheme using smart cards. J. Biomed. Biotechnol. **2012** (2012). https://doi.org/10.1155/2012/519723

19. Chandrakar, P., Om, H.: Cryptanalysis and extended three-factor remote user authentication scheme in multi-server environment. Arab. J. Sci. Eng. **42**(2), 765–786 (2017). https://doi.org/10.1007/s13369-016-2341-x

An Effective Threshold Based Technique for Retinal Image Blood Vessel Segmentation on Fundus Image Using Average and Gaussian Filters

Rahul Ray[1]([✉]), Sudarson Jena[2], and Priyadarsan Parida[3]

[1] SUIIT, Sambalpur University, Burla, Odisha 768018, India
rahulray9439@gmail.com
[2] SUIIT, Sambalpur University, Burla, Odisha 768018, India
[3] GIET University, Gunupur, Odisha 765022, India

Abstract. The fundamental components of automated retinal blood vessel segmentation for eye disease screening systems are segmentation algorithms, retinal blood vessel datasets, classification algorithms, performance measure parameters and noise removing filters etc. This paper is presenting retinal blood vessel segmentation techniques on 2D retinal images captured by fundus camera and examining the performance of different algorithms for a better and accurate result. The goal of this study is to comprehensively investigate and assess retinal blood vessel extraction algorithms using publicly accessible High-Resolution Fundus Diabetic Retinopathy (HRF-DR) and Iowa Normative Set for Processing Images of the retina-artery vein ratio (INSPIRE-AVR) datasets, with a focus on important performance measurements and characteristics. The effectiveness of the proposed methodology is measured using the performance metrics like Sensitivity, Specificity and Accuracy with 94.27%, 87.86% and 95.61% for HRF-DR dataset and 91.10%, 86.97% and 95.16% for INSPIRE-AVR dataset respectively.

Keywords: Fundus camera · Sensitivity · HRF-DR · INSPIRE-AVR

1 Introduction

Segmentation of retinal blood vessels and extraction of morphological parameters of retinal blood vessels like width, length, branching patterns, tortousity etc. are used for an effective diagnosis, screening & treatment of multiple ophthalmologic and cardiovascuar diseases like macular degeneration, Diabetic retinopathy, Cataract, Glaocoma, Amblyopia, Refractive error etc. Recent advancement in the research and development of intelligent & innovative automated computer-aided technologies helps an opthamalogist to detect an eye disease in an early stage and plan the proper treatments for the patients immediately. The analysis on fundus image to extract the targeted object automatically from the background is an essential task. However, there are some certain constraints like the variability in vessel width and low-resolution databases that includes nose area and changing brightness of input retinal image.

© The Author(s), under exclusive license to Springer Nature Switzerland AG 2024
S. K. Panda et al. (Eds.): CoCoLe 2023, CCIS 1892, pp. 175–188, 2024.
https://doi.org/10.1007/978-3-031-56998-2_15

There are several methods like model based, filter based, machine learning based etc. methods which are the existing proposed methods for blood vessel segmentation from retinal image. In supervised based machine-learning methods, the pixels of retinal images are pointed as either vessels or non-vessels. Morphological operators are being used to perform vessel segmentation in filter-based techniques in which the targeted objects of a retinal image can be filtered from the background of the image. To identify and extract the thin and large retinal blood vessels, model- based approach is useful which is very sensitive to its extracted parameters. Mondal et al. [1] proposed a method which is targeting the extraction of green layer of the given input retinal image and later on the noises are being removed by the noise removing filters. In the next stage, the pre-processed image is being go through several morphological operations and classification can be performed by GIFKCN Classifier. Shukla et al. [2] developed an algorithm for retinal blood vessel segmentation with the help of fractional filter and map based on the eigenvalue of a local covariance matrix and extensive experiments are performed on STARE and DRIVE datasets. Nelson et al. [3] proposed a vessel enhancement technique which is based on a mathematical morphology method called bowler-hat transform.

Dharmawan et al. [5] used DRIVE and STARE datasets to propose an efficient hybrid segmentation method which will overcome the challenging scenarios like low-contrast vessels images. To extract blood vessels from retinal pictures, Tang et al. [4] used a multi-scale channel significance sorting and significant spatial information positioning (MSCS) encoder–decoder and conducted extensive tests on the DRIVE and STARE datasets. On the publicly available DRIVE and CHASE DB1 datasets, Dash et al. [6] examined the efficacy of the suggested approach for Blood vessel segmentation via local adaptive thresholding. Shah et al. [7] proposed a blood vessel segmentation unsupervised method using Gabor wavelet and a multi-scale line detector and finally a median filter is used to remove noises for better segmentation result. Jiang et al. [8] proposed a robust vessel segmentation method to diagnosis DR diseases using fully convolutional neural network. Samuel et al. [10] tested the retinal blood vessel segmentation method on DRIVE, STARE & HRF with better pre-processing procedure and multi-level/multi-scale DS incorporated with deep neural network.

Different machine learning and deep-learning algorithms for automated detection of DR, cataract, and other diseases were proposed by Imran et al. [9]. on different publicly available datasets. Using a multi-layer perceptron neural network and vector features, Tamim et al. [14] proposed a supervised learning technique for diagnosing a variety of ocular and non-ocular illnesses. Mardani et al. [16] proposed employing DBSCAN and morphological reconstruction to segment retinal blood vessels, as well as noise reduction using MR, median filters, and other approaches. Sathananthavathi V. et al. [11] suggested approach employing Encoder improved Atrous architecture increased by increasing the depth concatenation process with the extra added layers was assessed on DRIVE, STARE, CHASE DB1 and HRF. Balasubramanian et al. [12] proposed an enhanced supervised system for RBVSC to classify whether it's a vessel or a non-vessel regions using the CNN and Support Vector Machine. Bhoi et al. [15] proposed a method to detect pathological syndrome which is composites of PCA, CLAHE and global Ostu thresholding method and the extensive study has been performed on DRIVE & STARE datasets.

On the DRIVE dataset, Dikkala et al. [18] tried segmentation using adaptive contrast enhancement to remove noise and morphological techniques to extract features. Braovic' et al. [17] investigated automated retinal blood vessel recognition on the DRIVE and STARE datasets using heuristically derived parametric edge detection and shape analysis, emphasizing specificity over sensitivity. Mapayi et al. [21] used a local adaptive thresholding method for retinal blood vessel segmentation based on GLCM energy information for good segmentation performance on the green channel of pre-processed retinal pictures, with experimental assessment and analysis utilizing grayscale image intensity values and a local adaptive thresholding approach. Roychowdhury et al. [24] proposing an unique retinal blood vessel extraction method that is divided into three stages: pre-processing, processing, and post-processing using Gaussian mixture model (GMM).

COSFIRE and noise reducing filters were presented by Azzopardi et al. [28], who proposed a novel method for segmenting blood veins from retinal fundus pictures. In comparison to the previous Frangi approach, Budai et al. [25] developed a strategy to prevent specular reflexes of thick vessels in retinal images to reduce computation time while improving accuracy and sensitivity. Staal et al. [27] offered a method for extracting image edges and vessel centerlines. Here, feature vectors are being calculated for each and every pixel and then classification of feature vectors can be performed using k-NN classifier. Hunter et al. [30] developed a more efficient non-linear filter-based vessel segmentation approach and robust and experiment performed on STARE dataset.

In contrast to the current approaches, the performance metrics and segmentation results for thin blood vessels in various proposed processes for retinal blood vessel segmentation are less effective. On many publicly accessible fundus image datasets, several approaches are used, although for the more accurate HRF [32] and INSPIRE-AVR [33] datasets, relatively few segmentation methodologies are available. Extensive experiments have been carried out on the HRF [32] and INSPIRE-AVR [33] datasets with the suggested approach, which in this study focuses on the segmentation of thin retinal blood vessels, and the results are compared with other available methods.

2   Blood Vessel Segmentation Proposed Method

Three major steps make up the suggested method for segmenting vasculature from retinal images which are mainly categorized into (i) Pre-processing of retinal input image, (ii) Processing of pre-processed image for blood vessel segmentation, and (iii) Post-processing which will remove the extra redundant pixels and also remove noise. Figure 1 depicts a detailed block diagram of the segmentation of blood vessels from retinal image, and Fig. 2 shows the results of the pre-processing.

2.1   Retinal Input Image

The suggested approach is based on publicly accessible retinal image datasets that may be used to detect retinal blood vessels. The HRF [32] and INSPIRE-AVR [33] databases are used in this paper for experiments are taken from Kaggle database.

2.1.1 HRF Dataset

HRF [32] image dataset was proposed to perform comparative analysis on ocular fundus images for automatic blood vessels segmentation algorithms. This freely accessible fundus picture database has a total of 45 photographs, 15 of which are from healthy individuals, 15 from DR patients, and 15 from Glaucoma patients.

2.1.2 INSPIRE-AVR Dataset

To diagnosis diabetes, hypertension and cardiovascular diseases in early stage, 40 numbers of high-resolution OD centered retinal images were proposed by a research team of University of Porto for a retinal CAD diagnostic system development. This Inspire-AVR dataset [33] contains high resolution images with its ground truth retinal input image, OD and the A-V ratio which is known as ratio of arteriolar-to-venular.

2.2 Pre-processing

Pre-processing is one of the most important procedures in the extraction of blood vessels since it improves segmentation results and overcomes non-uniform lighting on retinal fundus pictures. The pre-processing method consists of following steps i) CLAHE (Contrast limited adaptive histogram equalization), ii) Average filtering and iii) Gaussian filtering.

2.2.1 CLAHE

CLAHE used to enhance the visibility and contrast of a low-quality image which is popularly known as dingy image. According to the lightness and brightness value of the retinal image, Adaptive histogram equalization and normal equalization varies from each other. To increase the quality of the retinal image as compared to AHE, CLAHE method is applied. To generate bell shaped histogram using CLAHE, Rayleigh distribution parameters are used. The modified version of AHE is CLAHE algorithm used to overcome the drawbacks of AHE algorithm which is appropriate for both color and grey level image.

CLAHE algorithm can be implemented using following steps:

Step.1 Initial processing of a low contrast image.
Step.2 Consider all input parameter values for image quality enhancement.
Step.3 Divide and segment the original image into multiple sub-segments.
Step.4 Apply pre-processing techniques to all sub-segments.
Step.5 Generate mapping for grey level image and generate respective histogram for that.
Step.6 Using mapping process, enhance the image parameters to develop interpolate grey level output.

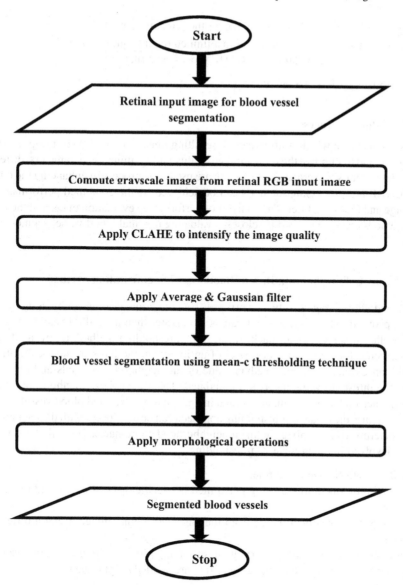

Fig. 1. Flowchart of the proposed method.

CLAHE Algorithm:-
Input: Original Image I;

1. Resizing I to $M \times M$; *Decompose* $I \rightarrow (n)$; $(n) \leftarrow \frac{M \times M}{m \times m}$;
2. $H_n \leftarrow histogram(n)$;
3. *Clip Limit:* $C_L \leftarrow N_{cl} \times N_{avg}$;
4. Clipping of H_n using C_L;

5. $\frac{N_{\sum cl}}{N_{gray}} \rightarrow N_{cp}$ pixels $\rightarrow$ distribution over the remaining pixels;
6. CLAHE(n)$\leftarrow$ Equalization of contrast limited tile histogram using (1);
7. $I_c \leftarrow$ Bilinear interpolation of CLAHE processed n tiles;

   Output: CLAHE Processed image I_c.

2.2.2 Filtering Process

To avoid the noise which is affecting the resulting images after CLAHE pre-processing technique and to improve the retinal image quality and illumination parameters, different filters like adaptive, average and Gaussian are used. The process of enhancing the output of CLAHE pre-processing methods can be achieved by the combined performance of Average and Gaussian filter. The analysis of performance evaluation of each of the filtering methods can be achieved by closely evaluating the final blood vessel segmentation output.

2.3 Mean-C Thresholding Based Blood Vessel Segmentation Method

Black and white image can be constructed from the gray-scale image by assigning the image pixels to white whose pixel values are greater than a fixed threshold value and assign other pixel values to black. In mean-C thresholding method, a threshold value is considered for each and every pixel of an image on the basis of the local statistics performances like mean and median value of the neighborhood pixels and on timely basis, the threshold value needs to be updated. This thresholding method gives better performance on badly illuminated retinal image. To remove retinal blood vessels from a retinal picture, the mean-C thresholding approach can be employed, with the background value determined from pixels in linear neighborhood coordinates. The following are the stages involved in doing mean-C thresholding:-

1. Select a (NXN) size mean filter.
2. Convolution operation is being performed between enhanced image and the mean-value.
3. Subtract the convolved image from the enhanced retinal image to get a difference image
4. Difference image is now go through thresholding process with the constant value C
5. Perform the complement operation of the thresholded output image.

2.4 Post-processing Method

The morphological cleaning operations are used to remove some non-vessels which are obtained from the retinal image after segmentation process. In this processing operation, vessel can be represented by considering the six neighboring pixels of retinal image. The original retinal image from the publicly available datasets and the respective segmentation results of HRF [32] and INSPIRE-AVR [33] datasets are presented in Fig. 3 and Fig. 4.

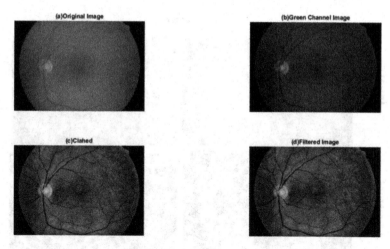

Fig. 2. Pre-processing output.

2.5 Proposed Algorithm for Segmentation

1. Read original input retinal RGB image.
2. Extract the green channel image of the retinal RGB image.
3. Enhance the contrast of the image using CLAHE and remove the noise by using median filter.
4. Extract the retinal blood vessels using mean-C thresholding technique.
5. Remove the isolated non-vessel pixels from the processed image by using different morphological cleaning operation.

3   Results and Discussions

An extensive experiment is being carried out on HRF-DR [32] and INSPIRE-AVR [33] retinal image datasets and the result of our experiment is being appraised. HRF retinal image dataset consists of 22 training and 23 testing images of size 3304X2336. This dataset contains 45 numbers of images which is divided into 15 different subsets and each subset contains one retinal image of a patient with diabetic retinopathy, one with glaucoma and one healthy person's retinal image. We have considered diabetic retinopathy image subset from HRF dataset for our extensive experiment. For HRF-DR [32] and INSPIRE-AVR [33], the input images and their segmented output results are exhibited in Fig. 3 and Fig. 4, respectively. In Fig. 5 and Fig. 6, a bar chart representation of the comparative study of our suggested approach for HRF-DR [32] and INSPIRE-AVR [33] datasets with other suggested methods is displayed. INSPIRE-AVR [33] dataset consists of 40 nos. of color images of blood vessels, a arterio-venous and optic disc ratio reference standard. The proposed method works in an efficient manner to detect thick blood vessels from INSPIRE-AVR [33] dataset.

HRF

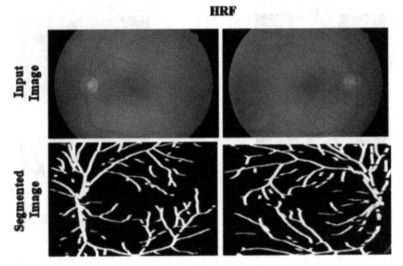

Fig. 3. Input and segmented results for HRF-DR dataset

INSPIRE AVR

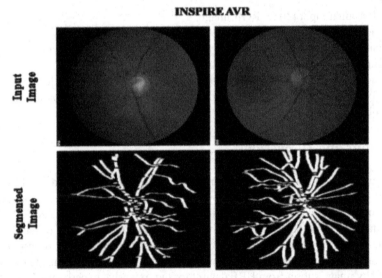

Fig. 4. Input and segmented results for INSPIRE-AVR dataset

The results are being analyzed by using the factors like False Positive (F_P), True Positive (T_p), True Negative (T_N), False Negative (F_N). Parameters like Accuracy (ACC), Matthew's correlation coefficient (MCC) Sensitivity (SE) and Specificity (SP) shown in Table 1. Are being used to find out comparison analysis of our proposed thresholding based method and other existing proposed methods. The proposed method is presenting a work on thresholding based technique for blood vessel segmentations and identification. When compared to certain current segmentation approaches for blood vessels in the

Table 1. Parameter measure for performance evaluation

Measure	Expression
ACC	$(T_N + T_P)/(T_N + F_N + T_P + F_P)$
MCC	$(T_P \times T_N) - (F_P \times F_N)/\sqrt{(F_P + T_N)(T_P + F_N)(F_N + T_N)(F_P + T_P)}$
Sensitivity	$\frac{T_P}{T_P + F_N}$
Specificity	$\frac{T_N}{T_N + F_P}$

Table 2. Performance evaluation on HRF-DR dataset

HRF Image	SP	SE	ACC
1	0.9319	0.8889	0.9576
2	0.9294	0.8714	0.9465
3	0.9389	0.8786	0.9495
4	0.9353	0.8743	0.9395
5	0.9576	0.8838	0.9681
6	0.9053	0.8745	0.9591
7	0.9606	0.8841	0.9508
8	0.9508	0.8845	0.9569
9	0.9501	0.8839	0.9581
10	0.9405	0.8746	0.9482
11	0.9477	0.8765	0.9689
12	0.9331	0.8617	0.9598
13	0.9432	0.8757	0.9596
14	0.9591	0.8845	0.9595
15	0.9557	0.8823	0.9588
Average	**0.9427**	**0.8786**	**0.9561**

retinal picture, the work provided in this research yields superior performance metrics. The performance parameter values of several HRF-DR [32] dataset images are shown in Table 2, and Table 3 and shows a comparison study of the proposed approach with other proposed methods. The performance measures of several INSPIRE-AVR [33] dataset images are represented in Table 4, and Table 5. And shows the comparison analysis of the proposed method with other offered methods. The average sensitivity (Se), Specificity (Sp) and Accuracy (Acc) for HRF-DR [32] dataset are 0.9427, 0.8786 & 0.9561 respectively and for INSPIRE-AVR [33] dataset are 0.9110, 0.8697 & 0.9516 respectively.

Table 3. Comparison of performance on HRF-DR dataset

Sl. No	Methods of segmentation	SE	SP	ACC
1	Samuel et al. [10]	0.8523	0.8655	0.8531
2	Shah et al. [28]	0.9800	0.7202	0.9559
3	Shin et al. [18]	0.9329	0.9546	0.9349
4	Yan et al. [13]	0.9592	0.7881	0.9437
5	**Proposed Method**	**0.9427**	**0.8786**	**0.9561**

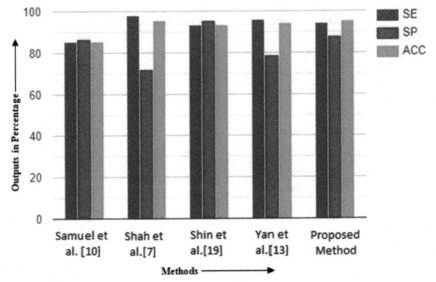

Fig. 5. Bar Chart representation of different Performance measures from different proposed methods of HRF-DR dataset

Table 4. Performance evaluation on INSPIRE-AVR dataset

INPIRE-AVR Image	SP	SE	ACC
1	0.9139	0.8665	0.9484
2	0.8907	0.8651	0.9569
3	0.9094	0.8732	0.9591
4	0.9095	0.8658	0.9468
5	0.9103	0.8675	0.9596
6	0.9165	0.8708	0.9542
7	0.9216	0.8722	0.9427

(continued)

Table 4. (*continued*)

INPIRE-AVR Image	SP	SE	ACC
8	0.9161	0.8638	0.9499
9	0.9086	0.8707	0.9536
10	0.9031	0.8732	0.9583
11	0.9124	0.8735	0.9515
12	0.9112	0.8678	0.9486
13	0.9086	0.8729	0.9528
14	0.9097	0.8699	0.9539
15	0.9118	0.8731	0.9481
16	0.9071	0.8633	0.9469
17	0.9171	0.8724	0.9476
18	0.9025	0.8687	0.9525
19	0.9116	0.8714	0.9501
20	0.9125	0.8732	0.9574
21	0.9108	0.8729	0.9484
22	0.9086	0.8681	0.9531
23	0.9163	0.8642	0.9509
24	0.9043	0.8708	0.9453
25	0.9065	0.8719	0.9482
26	0.9156	0.8709	0.9565
27	0.9073	0.8724	0.9486
28	0.9123	0.8653	0.9516
29	0.9085	0.8697	0.9456
30	0.9181	0.8667	0.9592
31	0.9192	0.8642	0.9508
32	0.9119	0.8713	0.9576
33	0.9126	0.8705	0.9561
34	0.9166	0.8726	0.9485
35	0.9122	0.8735	0.9492
36	0.9117	0.8693	0.9527
37	0.9125	0.8722	0.9482
38	0.9019	0.8655	0.9529
39	0.9159	0.8639	0.9505
40	0.9136	0.8651	0.9542
Average	**0.9110**	**0.8697**	**0.9516**

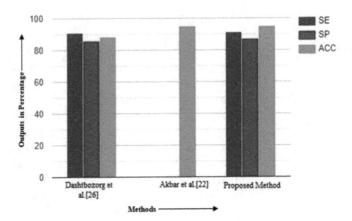

Fig. 6. Bar Chart representation of different performance measures from different proposed methods of INSPIRE-AVR dataset

Table 5. Comparison of performance on INSPIRE-AVR dataset

Sl. No	Methods of segmentation	SE	SP	ACC
1	Dashtbozorg et al. [23]	0.9100	0.8600	0.8830
2	Akbar et al. [20]	-	-	0.9514
3	**Proposed Method**	**0.9110**	**0.8697**	**0.9516**

4   Conclusion

In this proposed research work, an effective segmentation technique for blood vessel extraction is being proposed by using mean-C thresholding method. This proposed method comprises of pre-processing, processing and post-processing phases. The suggested technique is being tested on two publicly accessible datasets, HRF-DR [32] and INSPIRE-AVR [33], which has average accuracies of 95.61 and 95.16 percent, respectively. The suggested method's outcomes are compared to those of previously proposed methods and the outcome of the proposed method gives better performance with higher efficiency.

References

1. Mondal, S.S., Mandal, N., Singh, A., Singh, K.K.: Blood vessel detection from Retinal fundas images using GIFKCN classifier. Procedia Comput. Sci. **167**, 2060–2069 (2020)
2. Shukla, A.K., Pandey, R.K., Pachori, R.B.: A fractional filter based efficient algorithm for retinal blood vessel segmentation. Biomed. Signal Process. Control **59**, 101883 (2020)
3. Sazak, Ç., Nelson, C.J., Obara, B.: The multiscale bowler-hat transform for blood vessel enhancement in retinal images. Pattern Recogn.Recogn. **88**, 739–750 (2019)

4. Tang, X., Zhong, B., Peng, J., Hao, B., Li, J.: Multi-scale channel importance sorting and spatial attention mechanism for retinal vessels segmentation. Appl. Soft Comput.Comput. **93**, 106353 (2020)
5. Dharmawan, D.A., Li, D., Ng, B.P., Rahardja, S.: A new hybrid algorithm for retinal vessels segmentation on fundus images. IEEE Access **7**, 41885–41896 (2019)
6. Dash, J., Bhoi, N.: A thresholding based technique to extract retinal blood vessels from fundus images. Future Comput. Inf. J. **2**(2), 103–109 (2017)
7. Shah, S.A.A., Shahzad, A., Khan, M.A., Lu, C.-K., Tang, T.B.: Unsupervised method for retinal vessel segmentation based on gabor wavelet and multiscale line detector. IEEE Access **7**, 167221–167228 (2019)
8. Jiang, Y., Zhang, H., Tan, N., Chen, L.: Automatic retinal blood vessel segmentation based on fully convolutional neural networks. Symmetry **11**(9), 1112 (2019)
9. Imran, A., Li, J., Pei, Y., Yang, J.-J., Wang, Q.: Comparative analysis of vessel segmentation techniques in retinal images. IEEE Access **7**, 114862–114887 (2019)
10. Samuel, P.M., Veeramalai, T.: Multilevel and multiscale deep neural network for retinal blood vessel segmentation. Symmetry **11**(7), 946 (2019)
11. Sathananthavathi, V., Indumathi, G.: Encoder enhanced atrous (EEA) unet architecture for retinal blood vessel segmentation. Cognitive Syst. Res. **67**, 84–95 (2021)
12. Balasubramanian, K., Ananthamoorthy, N.P.: Robust retinal blood vessel segmentation using convolutional neural network and support vector machine. J. Ambient Intell. Humanized Comput. **12**, 3559–3569 (2021)
13. Yan, Z., Yang, X., Cheng, K.-T.: Joint segment-level and pixel-wise losses for deep learning based retinal vessel segmentation. IEEE Trans. Biomed. Eng. **65**(9), 1912–1923 (2018)
14. Tamim, N., Elshrkawey, M., Azim, G.A., Nassar, H.: Retinal blood vessel segmentation using hybrid features and multi-layer perceptron neural networks. Symmetry **12**(6), 894 (2020)
15. Dash, J., Bhoi, N.: Retinal blood vessel segmentation using Otsu thresholding with principal component analysis. In: 2018 2nd International Conference on Inventive Systems and Control (ICISC), pp. 933–937. IEEE (2018)
16. Mardani, K., Maghooli, K.: Enhancing retinal blood vessel segmentation in medical images using combined segmentation modes extracted by DBSCAN and morphological reconstruction. Biomed. Signal Process. Control **69**, 102837 (2021)
17. Braović, M., Stipaničev, D., Šerić, L.: Retinal blood vessel segmentation based on heuristic image analysis. Comput. Sci. Inf. Syst.. Sci. Inf. Syst. **16**(1), 227–245 (2019)
18. Dikkala, U., Kezia Joseph, M., Alagirisamy, M.: A comprehensive analysis of morphological process dependent retinal blood vessel segmentation. In: 2021 International Conference on Computing, Communication, and Intelligent Systems (ICCCIS), pp. 510–516. IEEE (2021)
19. Shin, S.Y., Lee, S., Yun, I.D., Lee, K.M.: Deep vessel segmentation by learning graphical connectivity. Med. Image Anal. **58**, 101556 (2019)
20. Fraz, M.M., et al.: An approach to localize the retinal blood vessels using bit planes and centerline detection. Comput. Methods Programs Biomed. **108**(2), 600–616 (2012)
21. Mapayi, T., Viriri, S., Tapamo, J.-R.: Adaptive thresholding technique for retinal vessel segmentation based on GLCM-energy information. Comput. Math. Methods Med. **2015** (2015)
22. Akbar, S., Akram, M.U., Sharif, M., Tariq, A., Khan, S.A.: Decision support system for detection of hypertensive retinopathy using arteriovenous ratio. Artif. Intell. Med. **90**, 15–24 (2018)
23. Walter, T., Massin, P., Erginay, A., Ordonez, R., Jeulin, C., Klein, J.-C.: Automatic detection of microaneurysms in color fundus images. Med. Image Anal. **11**(6), 555–566 (2007)
24. Roychowdhury, S., Koozekanani, D.D., Parhi, K.K.: Blood vessel segmentation of fundus images by major vessel extraction and subimage classification. IEEE J. Biomed. Health Inform. **19**(3), 1118–1128 (2014)

25. Budai, A., Bock, R., Maier, A., Hornegger, J., Michelson, G.: Robust vessel segmentation in fundus images. Int. J. Biomed. Imaging 2013 (2013)
26. Dashtbozorg, B., Mendonça, A.M., Campilho, A.: An automatic graph-based approach for artery/vein classification in retinal images. IEEE Trans. Image Process. 23(3), 1073–1083 (2013)
27. Staal, J., Abràmoff, M.D., Niemeijer, M., Viergever, M.A., Van Ginneken, B.: Ridge-based vessel segmentation in color images of the retina. IEEE Trans. Med. Imaging 23(4), 501–509 (2004)
28. Azzopardi, G., Strisciuglio, N., Vento, M., Petkov, N.: Trainable COSFIRE filters for vessel delineation with application to retinal images. Med. Image Anal. 19(1), 46–57 (2015)
29. Jiang, X., Mojon, D.: Adaptive local thresholding by verification-based multithreshold probing with application to vessel detection in retinal images. IEEE Trans. Pattern Anal. Mach. Intell.Intell. 25(1), 131–137 (2003)
30. Hunter, A., Lowell, J., Ryder, R., Basu, A., Steel, D.: Tram-line filtering for retinal vessel segmentation (2005)
31. Mathews, M.R., Anzar, S.M., Kalesh Krishnan, R., Panthakkan, A.: EfficientNet for retinal blood vessel segmentation. In: 2020 3rd International Conference on Signal Processing and Information Security (ICSPIS), pp. 1–4. IEEE (2020)
32. Budai, A., Bock, R., Maier, A., Hornegger, J., Michelson, G.: HRF: High-Resolution Fundus dataset (2013)
33. Niemeijer, M., Xu, X., Dumitrescu, A., Gupta, P., van Ginneken, B., Folk, J., Abramoff, M.: INSPIRE-AVR: Iowa normative set for processing images of the retina-artery vein ratio dataset (2011)

Substantiation System Using Facial Recognition and Principal Component Analysis

Ramesh R.Naik[1]([⊠]), Sanjay patel[1], Sunil Gautam[1], Rohit Pachlor[2], and Umesh bodkhe[1]

[1] Department of Computer Science and Engineering,Institute of Technology, Nirma University, S-G Highway, Chandlodia, Ahmedabad 382481, Gujarat, India
`{rameshram.naik,sanjay.patel_cse,sunil.gautam,`
`umesh.bodkhe}@nirmauni.ac.in`
[2] MIT-ADT, University, Pune, India
`rohitpachlor@gmail.com`

Abstract. In today's networked society, the need to guarantee the security of data or physical assets is both increasingly important and more difficult to do. We periodically hear about criminal activity like credit card fraud, computer hacking, or security flaws in a corporate or governmental setting. Since they use an individual's physiological and behavioral characteristics to determine and ascertain his identity rather than using passwords to authenticate users and grant them access to physical and virtual domains, biometric based techniques have become the most promising option for identifying people in recent years. Magnetic cards may become distorted and unreadable. PINs and passwords are tricky to remember and vulnerable to theft or guesswork. The biological makeup of a person, however, cannot be forgotten, stolen, falsified, or lost. Face recognition appears to have a variety of advantages over other biometric methods, some of which are described below: For fingerprints or hand geometry detection, the user must place his hand on a hand rest, and for iris or retina recognition, the user must remain steady in front of a camera. A user's intentional action is required for almost all of these technologies. The objective is to develop a face recognition system that can automatically identify and verify faces based on images in a gallery or database. We'll employ the PCA method, which recognises by employing Eigen faces, to recognise. We want to know how often each class is recognised in our research.

Keywords: pca · eigenface · face recognition · eigenvalue

1 Introduction

The foundation of human society has depended heavily on the ability to recognise fellow humans. People in the earliest stages of civilization lived in small towns where they were all acquainted with one another. We began relying on documents and trade secrets to prove identity as a result of population growth and increased mobility. The infrastructure required for several economic sectors, including banking, border control, and law enforcement, now includes person identification as an essential component. We now live in a global culture where people are more dangerous and in need of help than ever before, and we can no longer trust them because of identifying documents that could be tampered with. Theft of identity PIN (such as a date of birth) is stolen by identity thieves in order to open credit card accounts, make withdrawals from accounts, and obtain loans.

A. Introduction to biometrics

First, a variety of technologies need reliable personal recognition techniques in order to either authenticate or establish the identity of a person using their services. These systems are created to ensure that only individuals with the proper authorization can access the services being provided. Some examples of these purposes include safe access to buildings, computers, laptops, mobile phones, and ATMs. Without robust personal recognition methods, these systems are vulnerable to impostor schemes. Biometric recognition, or simply biometrics, is the automatic recognition of traits [1]. Instead than relying on "what she has" or "what she recalls," biometrics can be used to confirm or establish a person's identification.

B. Applications of face Recognition system [1]

Security
Access control to buildings, ports, airports, and ATMs are some of the security precautions. Email authentication on multimedia workstations is another.

Surveillance
Authorities can be alerted when a known criminal or drug offender is found by monitoring a large number of CCTV cameras. This approach, for instance, was applied at the Super Bowl game in Tampa, Florida, in 2001.

General identity verification.

Examples of broad identity verification include voting, banking, online shopping, birth certificates, passports, driver's licences, national IDs, and employment identification.

Criminal justice systems
Forensics, post-event analysis, booking/mugshot systems, and criminal justice systems. The database searches for registered drivers, welfare recipients, missing children, immigration, and police bookings.

Smart Card applications
Instead of scanning a tangible object, the face can be saved and maintained in a database of facial photographs, and authentication can be carried out by comparing the present image to a template that is kept on file.

Multi-media environments
Behavior monitoring in senior or child care facilities, detecting and understanding client demands, and adaptive human computer interfaces in multimedia situations as part of ubiquitous or context-aware systems.

Video indexing: Video indexing and face labelling.

2 Litrature Survey

A statistical technique called PCA can be used to convert variables that are observed in a large amount of data into smaller intrinsic variables that are in a smaller amount of data [2].When expressing faces, holistic techniques use 2-D matrices rather than 3-D geometry. The eigenvectors are collections of traits that highlight variations between face pictures [3].

A few mixing techniques additionally integrated Local Binary Pattern (LBP) descriptors were projected onto and coupled to Laplacian PCA and LDA subspaces at various targets [4, 5].

The projection to a subspace method known as Principal Component Analysis (PCA) is popular in pattern recognition [6]. The original data are re-expressed in a basis vector with a lower dimension using PCA [7].

As a result, the data is characterized cheaply and its noise and redundancy are kept to a minimum. Face recognition system are calculated using PCA. Whole image area [8, 9].

3 Steps of PCA

Step1: Gather information

Gathered our training set's initial collection of face images.

After gathering the RGB photos from the webcam, we turned them into a greyscale image, used histogram equalization to enhance their quality, and then cropped the image to just show the subject's face. We create several database classes based on poses.

Our image is 30*30 in size, and we created a vector of it that is 900*1 in size. These vectors define the face-specific subspace that we refer to as face space (Figs. 1, 2 and 3).

Fig. 1. Sample for data for different angles color images.

Step2: Calculate the Mean First

Utilize the mean () method to determine the average of the image. Since the mean that has been subtracted is the average over all dimensions, it has been applied to all x and y values (Fig. 4).

Fig. 2. Sample for training data for different angles.

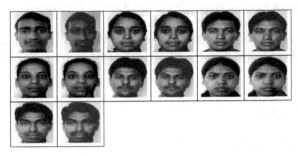

Fig. 3. Sample for testing data

Mean Image

Fig. 4. Mean Image

Step3: Covariance matrix computation:

Covariance is the amount that dimensions differ from the mean in relation to one another. We utilise Mat Lab's conv (I) function to obtain the covariance matrix.

Step4: Determine the covariance matrix's eigenvalues and eigenvectors:

The Matlab eig () function returns the eigenvector and eigenvalues.

Eigenvector: a group of characteristics that collectively describe how different faces differ.

Eigenvalue: Using the associated eigenvalues, we may rank the eigenvectors according to how well they capture the variation between the photos.

Step5: Determine the Eigen face using the practise set:

We refer to the eigenvectors that are generated from the source face photos and have a facial look as Eigen faces.

We maintain the face space that corresponds to the largest eigenvalues while computing Eigen faces from the practise set.

The photos from our training set's Eigen faces have the following appearances (Fig. 5).

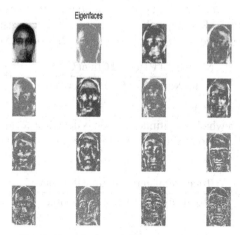

Fig. 5. Sample for training Eigen faces data

Step6: The set of weights will be determined based on the input images and Eigen faces by projecting the input image onto each Eigen face.

We use the mean and eigenvectors to project our original training data onto the Eigen faces, and we use the formula above to determine weights for each person.

Additionally, by projecting a test picture onto that Eigen face, determine the projection weights.

Step7: Determine the Euclidian separation between the training weights and the test weight:

We find the minimal distance using the Euclidian distance function dist (), and based on that index, we can identify the image.

4 Analysis of Performance

Matrix is zero and only displays the image that was given to it.

Training set versus testing set.

This table displays the separation between the weights from the training and testing sets in x and y dimensions, respectively. Because we use our training set to test our database, it chooses the shortest distance and assigns the image to it alone.

Distance Matrices: Distance matrices display the separation between the x- and y-dimensional values.

Comparison of training sets: The distance between the training set weights in the x- and y-dimensions is displayed in this table. Due to the fact that we trained our database using only our own training data, the diagonal element of the.

5 Results

FAR (False Accepted Rate):
The frequency at which a non-approved individual is considered as permitted is known as the FAR. FAR is typically a security-relevant measure because a false acceptance can frequently result in damages (Table 1, 2, 3, 4 and 5).

$$FAR = \frac{\text{Number of Rejected Client Claims}}{\text{Total Number of Client Accesses}} \times 100\%$$

False Rejection Rate (FRR):
The frequency with which a legitimate person is denied access is known as the FRR. FRR is sometimes referred to as a comfort criterion because a false rejection is invariably irritating.

$$FRR = \frac{\text{Total Number of Genuine Rejected}}{\text{Total Number of Tested Genuines}} \times 100\%$$

Table 1. Sample Recognition Rate for Down Pose

Sr.No	Subjects	Samples	Accuracy	Miss
1	S1	3	100	1
2	S2	3	0	3
3	S3	3	33.33	2
4	S4	3	0	3
5	S5	3	0	3
6	S6	3	0	3
7	S7	3	0	3
8	S8	3	0	3
9	S9	2	100	0
10	S10	2	100	0

We have calculated Recognition Rate for down, up, left, right, front Poses. For Every Pose We first took two samples of all seven persons in the front pose with the backlight issue for testing and six samples of all seven individuals in all poses for training before calculating the recognition rate for every pose. Then we look at how many of them it correctly recognises and how many of them it misses. Based on that, we determine our recognition rate, which in the instance of the down pose is 100%.

Table 2. Sample Recognition Rate for Up Pose

Sr.No	Subjects	Samples	Accuracy	Miss
1	S1	3	100	0
2	S2	3	100	0
3	S3	3	0	3
4	S4	3	0	3
5	S5	2	0	2
6	S6	3	0	3
7	S7	3	0	3
8	S8	3	66.66	1
9	S9	1	100	0
10	S10	3	66.66	1

Table 3. Sample Recognition Rate for Left Pose

Sr.No	Subjects	Samples	Accuracy	Miss
1	S1	3	0	3
2	S2	3	100	0
3	S3	3	0	3
4	S4	3	0	3
5	S5	2	0	3
6	S6	3	0	3
7	S7	3	100	0
8	S8	3	0	3
9	S9	1	100	0
10	S10	3	0	3

Table 4. Sample Recognition Rate for Left Pose

Sr.No	Subjects	Samples	Accuracy	Miss
1	S1	3	0	3
2	S2	3	100	0
3	S3	3	0	3
4	S4	3	0	3
5	S5	3	0	3
6	S6	3	0	3
7	S7	3	0	3
8	S8	3	0	3
9	S9	3	0	3
10	S10	2	0	2

Table 5. Sample Recognition Rate for All Poses

Sr.No	Subjects	Samples	Accuracy	Miss
1	S1	2	100	0
2	S2	2	100	0
3	S3	2	100	0
4	S4	2	100	0
5	S5	2	100	0
6	S6	2	100	0
7	S7	2	100	0
8	S8	2	100	0
9	S9	2	100	0
10	S10	2	100	0

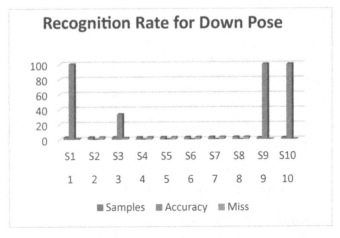

Graph1: Recognition Rate for Down Pose

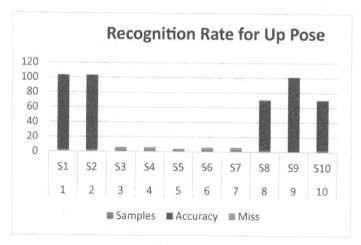

Graph2: Recognition Rate for Up Pose

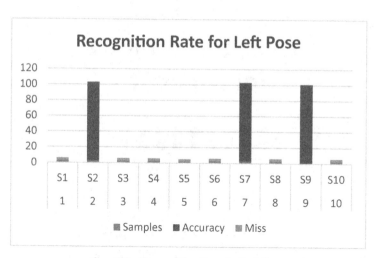

Graph3: Recognition Rate for Left Pose

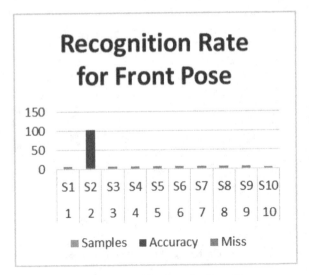

Graph4: Recognition Rate for Front Pose

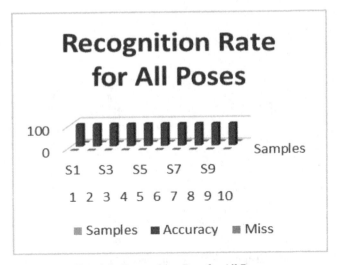

Graph5: Recognition Rate for All Poses

6   Conclusion

The PCA technique received the majority of the attention while discussing several strategies are used in this study work, including the Face Recognition System. One the one hand, personal recognition and verification may be greatly aided by its applications. On the other hand, because of the many various situations that a human face can be found in, it has always been incredibly challenging to execute. It serves security and monitoring purposes. The main benefit of PCA approach is that it can minimize the amount of information required to identify an individual of the information provided. The main PCA components and their advantages have been covered in-depth in the paper.

We must employ a web camera that produces colorful Images for our database. Database photos that are colored must be converted to grayscale. A good Images only needs a few prepossessing processes. The impact of illumination on an image necessitates additional boosting actions. When Images are acquired, if the background is not plain, it makes it difficult to extract features. We test images onto each Eigen face to determine weights. Then calculate the difference between training weight and test weight. Finally, choose the straight distance to recognise.

References

1. Prabhakar, et.al. Biometric recognition: security and privacy concerns. IEEE Secur. Priv. 1(2), 33–42. (2003)
2. Kim, et.al. Face recognition using principle component analysis. Dept. Comput. Sci. Univ. Maryland, College Park
3. Tamilselvi, et.al. "Face recognition based on spatial angular using visual geometric group-19 convolutional neural network", Ann. Rom. Soc. Cell Biol., pp. 2131–2138. .(2003)
4. Zulfiqar, M. et.al. "Deep Face Recognition for Biometric Authentication", 2019 International Conference on Electrical, Communication, and Computer Engineering (ICECCE), pp. 349–354, https://doi.org/10.1109/icecce47252.2019.8940725. (2019)
5. Raju, et.al. "An Optimal Hybrid Solution to Local and Global Facial Recognition through Machine Learning", Fusion Artif. Intell. Internet Things for Emerg. Cyber Syst., pp. 203–226, Springer, Cham. (2022),
6. M., et.al. A face recognition system based on eigenfaces method, Procedia Technol. 118–123. (2012)
7. Chaoyang, et.al. Comparison of three face recognition algorithms.In: International Conference on Systems and Informatics. May 19–20, 2012.ICSAI, pp.1896–1900. (2012)
8. Kirby, et.al. Application of the karhunen-loeve procedure for the characterization of human faces. IEEE Trans. Pattern Anal. Mach. Intell. 12(1): 103–108. (1990)
9. Lih-Heng, et.al. PCA, LDA and Neural Network for Face Identification. In: IEEE Conference on Industrial Electronics and Applications. ICIEA 2009, pp 1256–1259. (2009)

Impact of Stress on Faculties' Attitudes: A Study of Higher Education Institutes

Shilpi Saha[1]([✉]) [ID], Reema Frank[1,1] [ID], and Rashmi Kodikal[2,2] [ID]

[1] Manel Srinivas Nayak Institute of Management, Mangalore, India
sh.shlp12@gmail.com
[2] Graphic Era University, Dehradun, India

Abstract. The current research investigated how the different sources of stress like role expectation conflict, inter-role distance, and stress due to organizational policies distance relate to faculties' intentions to leave their jobs and affective commitment. The study gathered data from 200 faculties employed in various higher education institutions in Karnataka. The findings suggest that role-expectation conflict and stress from organizational policies have a significant effect on the faculties' desire to leave their job. Role-expectation conflict and stress from organizational policies also have a strong impact on their affective commitment. However, inter-role distance did not appear to affect either turnover intentions or affective commitment. Furthermore, high levels of stress due to organizational policies can negatively impact the emotional connection that faculties develop with their work and eventually make them want to quit the organization. In summary, decreasing stress levels may increase affective commitment and reduce turnover intention. The implications of these results are discussed in detail.

Keywords: stress due to organizational policies · inter-role distance · role-expectation conflict · affective commitment · turnover intention

1 Introduction

There are stressors in both job and family life of employees. The problems that they encounter at work can flow into their personal lives. These stressors have the potential to affect their mental health and productivity at both workplace and home [1, 2]. The supervisors are more interested in getting the work done, sometimes with less focus on the clear rules of authority. Thus, the expectations of the supervisors are always conflicting, unless shared or articulated in right manner. Two distinct role stressors, that is, role expectation conflict (REC) and inter-role distance (IRD) have been identified in the literature [3]. These two types of stress cause distress and reduce the energy levels of the faculties [4]. This may lead to conflict in role expectations of faculties. They may feel conflicting expectations from colleagues, HODs, Principals and the management.

When a person fills multiple roles, there will be conflicts between them. If a teacher occupies the familial role, the demands from both roles conflict with each other which leads to stress [5]. This is known as inter-role distance (IRD). Individuals who occupy many responsibilities in various professional and social organisations and groups are more prone to these types of disputes in the modern world. Peasley et al. has emphasized that role stress leads to negative outcomes in a person's well-being [6]. The teacher starts feeling dissatisfied with his work, life, mood and he may start experiencing anxiousness, fatigueness and other health issues. This has the potential to make the faculties less satisfied and less committed towards their organizations.

Scott has stated that satisfying employee needs in the organization and fulfilling their self-actualization needs can bring contentment to both the employees and the organization, as per McGregor's theory Y [7]. This study supports the viewpoint of other writers who stress the importance of distinguishing between outcomes that are important to individuals and those that are important to organizations, as they may not necessarily align. Peasley et al. have argued that the crucial factor is whether an organization or its representatives prioritize an individual's well-being to the same extent as the individual, and whether this well-being is as crucial to the organization's overall welfare as it is to the individual [6]. Therefore, the author recommends that outcomes that matter to individuals and are valued by organizations should be investigated separately.

Education researchers have been focused on the issue of role stress among faculty members for a significant period of time, with classroom teaching being identified as a profession with many role demands [8, 9]. In the realm of education, the formidable work of faculties can become enshrouded in stress due to the demanding nature of their roles. According to the scholarly musings of Sutton, this stress arises when the expectations placed upon faculties by the organization become ambiguous, overburdened with teaching and administrative responsibilities or where faculties find themselves torn between fulfilling one set of expectations while hindering their ability to meet others [10].

Our current comprehension of work-related stress, encompassing its origins and repercussions, primarily stems from studies conducted in Europe and the United States. Nevertheless, it is crucial to acknowledge that these findings may not hold universal validity across diverse cultures owing to the intricate impact of societal factors on individuals' perceptions and encounters of stress [11]. Take, for example, societies characterized by a high-power distance, where employees may have become accustomed to receiving explicit directives and constructive criticism from their superiors, which may not necessarily induce stress [12]. Conversely, in societies with a low power distance, the perpetual absence of personal autonomy and control can manifest as an enduring wellspring of stress for employees, fostering a distinct dynamic that warrants exploration and analysis. This study is primarily aimed to fill the voids and address the deficiencies found in the current body of literature by examining how certain factors like inter-role distance, stress due to organizational policies and role-expectation conflict (IRD, SOP, and REC) directly affect employee outcomes, such as turnover intention among faculties.

2 Literature Review and Hypotheses Formulation

There are different sources of stress in an organization. It is believed that one of the primary and major sources of role stress in an organisation is the inter-role distance (IRD) [4]. It is one of the most common causes of stress in the workplace. People often feel that they are not able to meet the expectations of their work roles and/or their family roles. The distance between two roles, such as home and work, can also cause role stress. The more distant the two roles are from each other, the more likely a person is to experience role stress. When a person fills multiple roles, they're going to be conflicts between them [12]. If a teacher occupies the familial role, the demands from both roles conflict with each other which leads to stress. Individuals who occupy many responsibilities in various organisations and groups are more prone to these types of disputes in the modern world.

The Conservation of Resources (COR) theory is a highly plausible theoretical framework that offers a comprehensive explanation of the interplay between work and family domains [13]. There are many resources like personal attributes, energies, and valued states that hold importance to individuals. According to the COR theory, stress tends to arise when individuals face a scarcity of accessible resources and struggle to preserve and maintain these resources effectively. The COR theory asserts that one strives to safeguard the resources that are very dear like quality of life, health, recreation and well-being to avoid getting these lost to work.

Role-expectation conflict (REC) can be defined as the gap between what is expected from a person in a specific role or position and what they feel they are capable of producing. There may be conflicting expectations from the superior, subordinates and friends. When distinct roles have contradictory expectations or demands, then the person who has the expectations due to these roles will experience role expectation conflict [14]. The faculties in higher education may feel conflicting expectations from colleagues, HOD's, Principals, or the management.

The other major source of role stress or anxiety at work comes from policies imposed on employees by their supervisors. Stress due to policies (SOP) is usually caused by conflicting policies that lead to confusion among employees and heads of the department about what they should do in certain situations [6].

The interplay between stress, affective commitment, and turnover intention within organizational contexts is worth noting. Notably, heightened levels of stress stemming from job-related factors can significantly undermine employees' emotional connection and allegiance to the organization, thereby escalating their inclination to seek alternative employment opportunities [15]. Affective commitment, which gauges employees' emotional investment and identification with their organization, emerges as a crucial predictor of job satisfaction and employee retention [16]. Heightened stress levels experienced by employees often prompt disengagement and diminished commitment to the organization, resulting in an amplified desire to depart [17]. Consequently, organizations may face the loss of invaluable personnel and an accompanying surge in operational expenses. It is therefore of paramount importance for organizations to proactively address and adeptly manage stress levels among their workforce to foster unwavering affective commitment and retain their exceptional performers.

2.1 Role Expectation Conflict and Turnover Intention

Workplace conflicts can be common. These conflicts may hamper employee commitment. When people have conflicting roles, it can lower productivity [18]. This happens when employees receive different instructions from different supervisors and are unsure about what they should do [18]. Role conflicts can indicate problems with how the organization is managed, leading to some employees not performing well or disruptions in work. On the other hand, when a person's skills match the requirements of their job, they are likely to have an easier time doing their work.

Based on the investigation carried out by authors like Cordes and Dougherty [15], when workers encounter clashes amid their role anticipations, it can yield various unfavorable consequences. They might undergo emotional fatigue, feelings of powerlessness, a decrease in self-worth, and a perception of limited achievements [16]. These experiences can provoke anxiety and frustration, subsequently causing employees to develop pessimistic attitudes towards their organization, work, and themselves. Consequently, job discontent may arise, accompanied by a desire to seek alternative employment. In view of these findings, the current study puts forward the following hypotheses aimed at elucidating the impact of role expectation conflicts on employees' intentions to cease their present job.

H_1: REC will be significantly related to TI.

H_2: REC will be significantly related to AC.

2.2 Inter-Role Distance and Turnover Intention

Harun Mahmood & Som found that conflicts between organizational and non-organizational roles increase the likelihood of employees wanting to leave [18]. The collision between work and family responsibilities has been recognized as a powerful factor that affects how role conflict influences the desire to leave a job. Work-family conflict was identified as having a significant moderating effect on the relationship between role conflict and turnover intention [19]. According to the person-environment approach, employee well-being is influenced by both individual and environmental factors [15]. The way employees respond to job demands and stressors may depend on how well they fit into the organization and balance their family responsibilities. When the ambience of work embraces supportiveness and caters to the needs of employees, the menacing specter of work stress is less inclined to unleash its destructive repercussions on the faculties.

Job responsibilities can be very demanding, this can lead to increased role stress for individuals who lack the ability to manage interpersonal interactions [19]. Long working hours will affect the individuals personal time spent with family. When the space between roles widens, stretching individuals further apart within the organizational landscape, the consequences on turnover become increasingly apparent [12]. As inter role distance expands, employees may feel disconnected, detached, and disengaged from their assigned responsibilities [11]. This disconnection erodes the bonds between employees and their roles, fostering a sense of dissatisfaction. Ultimately, this detachment can catalyze the desire to seek alternative opportunities outside the organization, fueling turnover intentions and potentially leading to actual turnover. Therefore, the following hypotheses were formulated based on these arguments.

H_3: IRD will have a direct and significant impact on TI.

H_4: IRD will have a direct and significant impact on AC.

2.3 Stress Due to Organizational Policies and Turnover Intention and Affective Commitment

According to Denis Chenevert, Steven Kilroy, and Janine Bosak, the constant changes that occur in the educational sector, the policies, and the overall working create role stress amongst the faculties and they may fall short in their task delivery [14]. The welfare of employees is significantly impacted by pressure at work. Unfavorable working conditions are always the main reasons why employees change jobs [16]. The detrimental effects of Work Family Conflict frequently resulted from strenuous requirements at work, which in turn led to a reduction in job outcomes [19]. There is certain administrative work that demand a lot of time like documentation of institutional records, students records and other related records [5]. According to a study in higher education industry, stress related to educational policy is positively correlated with role stress and intention to leave a job [18]. These arguments led to the formulation of the following hypotheses.

H_5: SOP has a direct and significant impact on TI.

H_6: SOP has a direct and significant impact on AC.

All these above six hypotheses have been shown in the conceptual model (Fig. 1).

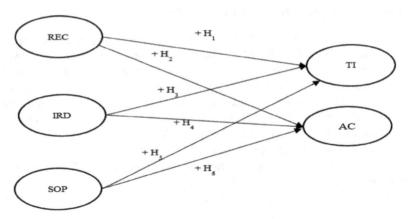

Fig. 1. Hypothesized conceptual model

3   Methodology

Pareek's scale has been used for IRD, REC and SOP items [3]. Allen and Meyer's scale has been used for AC scale [20]. TI items are derived from Kim [20]. The researchers employed a purposeful sampling technique known as maximum variation [15]. They sought to gather a diverse group of participants from various institutes to investigate patterns and uncover insights. By intentionally selecting individuals from different backgrounds and experiences, the complex relationship between the different types of role stress and employee outcomes can be understood effectively [21].

Data, were then collected from 200 faculties, working in different parts of higher education institutes in Karnataka. This data was analysed through structural equation modeling using WarpPls [18] and all the hypotheses displayed in the conceptual model have been analysed (Fig. 1). The reliability, validity and model fit are assessed. Table 1 demonstrates the different statistics generated by WarpPLS to prove the reliability of the data. Cronbach's Alpha value above 0.60 indicates that the items used for measuring the variables REC, IRD, SOP, TI and AC are very reliable [22].

Table 1. Summary statistics

Variable	Mean	Standard Deviation (SD)	Reliability (Cronbach's Alpha)
REC	4.01	.51	.66
IRD	4.01	.43	.64
SOP	4.12	.39	.79
TI	4.23	.42	.67
AC	4.00	.43	.60

4 Results of Data Analysis

The statistics needed to determine the convergent and discriminant validity of the variables REC, IRD, SOP, TI and AC which were generated using WarpPLS will be discussed now. Composite reliability, in comparision to Cronbach's reliability, is considered to be a superior alternative [23]. The composite reliability values of all the variables are well above the recommended threshold of .70 (.79 for REC, .78 for IRD, .84 for SOP, .80 for TI and .74 for AC). So, the validity of the measurements is believed to be accurate. Hence the reliability of the measurements is considered valid [23]. Using WarpPls, the factor loadings of all the measurement items of the variables were found to be greater than 0.50 and they are all significant at $p < .001$. It was evident that all average variance extracted (AVE) values are more than .50 (AVE for REC, IRD, SOP, TI and AC were .51, .52, .51, .56 and .56 respectively) and VIF values are less than 3 for all the variables (VIF for REC, IRD, SOP, TI and AC were 2.43, 1.61, 2.02, 1.82 and 1.71 respectively). This suggests the presence of convergence validity, that is, all the respective items are measuring their parent intended variables [23, 24]. Now, discriminant validity needs to be assessed.

The measurement instrument for Role-expectation conflict (REC), Inter-role Distance (IRD), Stress due to organizational policies (SOP), Turnover intention (TI) and Affective commitment (AC) is displayed in Table 2.

According to the results displayed in Table 3, all the relationships between the variables are highly significant ($p < .001$) by using WarpPls. Furthermore, the correlations between the variables are significant at $p < .001$ using WarpPls. The diagonal elements with shaded gradients, represent square root of AVEs, and these are greater than all the correlations in their respective rows. This pattern indicates that discriminant validity is reached [24].

Table 2. Measurement scale used

Variable Name	Statement
REC1	I'm unable to meet the competing needs of numerous persons in positions above me
REC2	I'm unable to meet the competing needs of my peers and juniors
REC3	I am unable to meet the needs of clients and others, since they are incompatible with one another
REC4	My senior's expectations clash with those of my juniors
REC5	Different people have inconsistent expectations about my role, which bothers me
IRD1	My job role to interferes with my family life
IRD2	I have a range of other interests (social, religious, etc.) that I am unable to explore due to a lack of time
IRD3	My job prevents me from focussing on my family obligations
IRD4	My organizational tasks and my extra organizational roles are intertwined
IRD5	Because of my busy work schedule, my family and friends complain that I don't spend enough time with them
SOP1	My institution lacks congruency in institutional, departmental, and personal goals
SOP2	My participation in institutional administrative work is very high
SOP3	I wish for more flexibility in the curriculum but our program doesn't allow it
SOP4	Dealing with new education initiative favouring students is really cumbersome
SOP5	I face high degree of uncertainty due to restructuring and redundancies in my organization
SOP6	I am held responsible for the admissions due to which I am stressed
SOP7	I am not able to spend my off day with my family as I feel I am held up with my work
SOP8	I am responsible for the publicity/ branding of my college because of which I am stressed
SOP9	NBA accreditation is really making me feel stressed
TI1	How often have you considered leaving your job?
TI2	How often are you frustrated when not given the opportunity at work to achieve your personal work-related goals?
TI3	How often do you dream about getting another job that will better suit your personal needs?

(continued)

Table 2. (*continued*)

Variable Name	Statement
TI4	How likely you to accept another job at the same compensation are level should it be offered to you?
TI5	How often do you look forward to another day at work?
AC1	I would be very happy to spend the rest of my career with this organization
AC2	I enjoy discussing my organization with people outside it
AC3	I feel a strong sense of belonging to my organization
AC4	I have been treated as a part of the organization and I participate in the decision making
AC5	The faculty feedback is highly valued by the management

Table 3. Discriminant Validity Statistics

Variable	REC	IRD	SOP	TI	AC
REC	.71	.59	.43	.44	.05
IRD	.59	.72	.49	.38	.07
SOP	.43	.49	.84	.38	.23
TI	.44	.38	.38	.75	.08
AC	.05	.07	.23	.08	.75

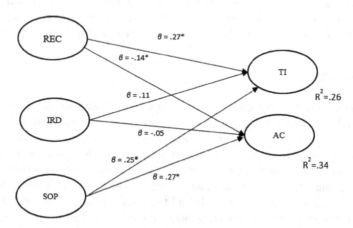

Fig. 2. Structural Equation model generated by WarpPls

Table 4. Summary of Results

Hypotheses	Paths	Path Coefficients	Results
H1	REC · TI	.27*	Accepted
H2	REC · AC	−14*	Accepted
H3	IRD · TI	.11	Rejected
H4	IRD · AC	−05	Rejected
H5	SOP · TI	.25*	Accepted
H6	SOP · AC	.27*	Accepted

The results of the hypotheses testing (shown in Table 4 and Fig. 2) suggest that REC has a significant direct effect on TI ($\beta = -.27$, $p < .001$) and AC ($\beta = -.14$, $p < .05$). Hence, these findings support the hypotheses H1 and H2. IRD, on the other hand, does not have a significant effect on TI ($\beta = .11$, $p > .05$) and AC ($\beta = -.05$, $p > .05$). This leads us to reject the hypotheses H3 and H4. SOP has a positive impact on TI ($\beta = .25$ $p < .001$) and AC ($\beta = .27$, $p < .001$). Hence, these results support the hypotheses H5 and H6.

These results indicate that the role of REC and SOP on TI and AC is important and should be taken into consideration when studying stress management. The R2 values of TI and AC are .26 and .34, suggesting that 26% of variance in TI and 34% of variance in AC is explained by the predictors, that is, REC, IRD and SOP. In addition, WarpPLS also generated the model fit indices like Average Path Coefficient (APC), Average R-Squared (ARS), Average Block Variance Inflation Factor (AVIF), Average Full Collinearity VIF (AFVIF). These indices were checked to determine the model fit. It was found that each of these indices were significant ($p < .001$) and AVIF was found to be 1.79 ($< = 3.3$) and AFVIF was 1.82 ($< = 3.3$). These indices met the model fit criteria [23, 24].

5   Discussion

This study finds that role expectation conflict (REC) significantly reduces affective commitment and increases turnover intention as shown in Fig. 2 and Table 4. It provides support for Hobfoll et al.'s theory on resource conservation, specifically concerning the depletion of resources [13]. This is because a teacher needs to be happy at any role he/she occupies. The work organization must have a stable environment and also the growth of an individual must be clearly defined. Role-expectation conflict (REC) is significantly related to TI and AC. When individuals find themselves entangled in conflicts arising from the clashing expectations of their organizational role and their own personal values, beliefs, or abilities, a detrimental cocktail of job dissatisfaction and frustration emerges. The dissonance between what they hold dear and what the organization demands gradually erodes their commitment, igniting within them a flickering desire to escape their current employment. This gives rise to their turnover intentions.

The results of this study depict that stress due to organizational policies (SOP) significantly affects the faculties' affective commitment and turnover intentions. One of the reasons could be because the faculties do not find a sense of contentment in certain policies like high participation in administrative work, NBA accreditation work and restructuring policies. Such policies keeps an individual on their toes. The work environment becomes devoid of peace. This hampers the ability of faculties to work to their best potential. In addition, the results show that inter-role distance (IRD) does not significantly impact AC and TI. An employee will juggle between institutional and non-institutional roles to attain both the goals. This may be because employees like being responsible for their organizations and in such cases, IRD does not demotivate them. This could be because of the presence of certain other benefits or factors that null out the effect like pay, leaves or other employee benefits.

6 Practical Implications

If managers are able to reduce role stress by implementing certain steps, then employees will get rid of stress and the employee outcomes will be very good, for example, reduced job dissatisfaction and more commitment. The work of the faculties can be redesigned and made flexible to a certain extent to make the employees stress free. An effective way of doing this is by putting the faculties together in a team [22]. This can increase the work and skill variety and increase the scope of growth and learning of the employees [25]. Hence, this becomes very lucrative to the faculties. Sometimes, the role expectations are not very clear during the transition. In addition, sometimes organizational policies are framed in a way that elevates the stress of faculties. Such policies like high participation in administrative activities, accreditation work and restructuring norms need to be changed to enable the employees to work effectively [26]. This can help in making the faculties committed to their jobs and less inclined towards turnover intention.

   This study has expanded the outcomes and dimensions of role stress by studying the role stress in different forms like inter-role distance, stress due to organizational policies and role expectation conflict on employee attitudes. By understanding the different types of role stress, this study has prompted the management of higher education institutes to redesign and enrich the work of the faculties so that their stress is reduced. The turnover intention of faculties can be reduced considerably if role stress is reduced. A person who is clear about the roles that he has to perform, he will be diligent and prepared to carry out the tasks. Strategies such as providing employee assistance programs, promoting work-life balance, and fostering a positive organizational culture can help to mitigate stress levels and promote employee well-being. It is important to foster an environment of open communication where employees feel safe and comfortable discussing their roles, concerns, and challenges, and encourage faculty members to ask questions and provide feedback to address any gaps in understanding. Additionally, regular training programs and professional development opportunities should be provided to help faculties improve their skills and abilities. This can boost their confidence and competence in carrying out their roles effectively.

7 Limitations and Future Scope of Research

The data collected is cross-sectional in nature. Additionally, relying on a single data source may not accurately represent the experiences of individuals from different backgrounds and industries. However, data for this study has been collected from directors, administration department and senior employees who are considered to be the subject-matter experts in the higher education institutes.

Future research could benefit from a longitudinal study design and a larger, more diverse sample to overcome these limitations. In addition, future studies can consider a greater number of samples, above 500. Certain interventions like facilities to reduce stress can be introduced to Furthermore, exploring ways to reduce role stress practices in other industries, such as retail, higher education, medicine, and hospitality, could provide a broad perspective as well as a better understanding of the impact of stress on turnover intentions.

8 Conclusion

This study has found that TI and AC are impacted by inter-role distance. This research has challenged the original assumptions that REC and SOP have a direct impact on TI (turnover intentions). As a result, it offers insights for researchers and educators on how to address the longstanding issue of high turnover rates in the education sector. By providing resources that enable staff to continue delivering sound technical sessions to students, the organization can have higher ranks than those of other organizations, in the education sector.

Moreover, this study addresses the underexplored role of role stressors such as IRD (inter-role distance) and REC in promoting individual well-being, which fills a gap in the research. This study adds to the current body of knowledge by investigating the Asian viewpoint.

References

1. Shah, S.J., Huang, C.: COVID-19 and health-care worker's combating approach: an exhausting job demand to satisfy. Int. J. Confl. Manag. **32**(5), 848–866 (2021)
2. Portoghese, I., et al.: Role stress and emotional exhaustion among health care workers: the buffering effect of supportive coworker climate in a multilevel perspective. J. Occup. Environmental Medicine, 59(10), 187–193 (2017)
3. Pareek, U.: Role stress scale: ORS Scale Booklet, Answersheet and manual. Ahmedabad: Naveen (1983)
4. Eatough, E., et al Relationships of role stressors with organizational citizenship behavior: a meta-analysis. J. Appl. Psychol. 96(3), 619–632 (2011)
5. Rubel, M.R.B., Kee, D.M.H., Rimi, N.N.: The mediating role of work–family conflict on role stressors and employee turnover intention relationship in labour-oriented organizations. Glob. Bus. Rev. **18**(6), 1384–1399 (2017)
6. Peasley, M.C., Hochstein, B., Britton, B.P., Srivastava, R.V., Stewart, G.T.: Can't leave it at home? The effects of personal stress on burnout and salesperson performance. J. Bus. Res. **117**, 58–70 (2020)

7. Scott, W.: Organizations: Rational, Natural, and Open Systems. Prentice Hall, New Jersey (1992)
8. Lortie, D.C.: Teacher status in dade county: a case of structural strain. Phi Delta Kappan **67**(8), 568–575 (1986)
9. Pierce, C.M.B., Molloy, G.N.: Psychological and biographical differences between secondary school teachers experiencing high and low levels of burnout. Br. J. Educ. Psychol. **60**, 37–51 (1990)
10. Sutton, R.: Job stress among primary and secondary schoolteachers: its relationship to ill-being. Work. Occup. **11**(1), 7–28 (1984)
11. Kunte, M., Gupta, P., Bhattacharya, S., Neelam, N.: Role overload, role self distance, role stagnation as determinants of job satisfaction and turnover intention in banking sector. Indian J. Psychol. Med. **39**(5), 590–599 (2017)
12. Jeong, S., Lee, Y.: Is turnover intention static or dynamic? the impacts of inter-role conflicts and psychological workplace strain on turnover intention trajectories. Hum. Resour. Dev. Q. **34**(3), 289–308 (2022). https://doi.org/10.1002/hrdq.21484
13. Hobfoll, S.E., Halbesleben, J., Neveu, J.P., Westman, M.: Conservation of resources in the organizational context: the reality of resources and their consequences. Annu. Rev. Organ. Psych. Organ. Behav. **5**(1), 103–128 (2018)
14. Chênevert, D., Kilroy, S., Bosak, J.: The role of change readiness and colleague support in the role stressors and withdrawal behaviors relationship among health care employees. J. Organ. Chang. Manag. **32**(2), 208–223 (2019)
15. Cordes, C.L., Dougherty, T.W.: A review and an integration of research on job burnout. Acad. Manage. Rev. **18**(4), 621–656 (1993). https://doi.org/10.5465/amr.1993.9402210153
16. Chhabra, B.: Work role stressors and employee outcomes: investigating the moderating role of subjective person-organization and person-job fit perceptions in Indian organizations. Int. J. Organ. Anal. **24**(3), 1–28 (2016)
17. Kumar, S.P., Saha, S., Anand, A.: A green human resource management approach of participation in decision-making and behavioural outcomes – a moderated mediated model. Int. J. Organ. Anal. **31**(5), 1724–1747 (2021). https://doi.org/10.1108/IJOA-09-2021-2954
18. Harun, I., Mahmood, R., Md Som, H.: Role stressors and turnover intention among doctors in Malaysian public hospitals: work–family conflict and work engagement as mediators. PSU Res. Rev. **6**(1), 1–16 (2020). https://doi.org/10.1108/PRR-08-2020-0025
19. Yousef, D.A.: The interactive effects of role conflict and role ambiguity on job satisfaction and attitudes toward organizational change: a moderated multiple regression approach. Int. J. Stress. Manag. **7**(4), 289–303 (2000)
20. Rubel, M. R. B., Kee, D. M. H., Rimi, N. N.: The mediating role of work–family conflict on role stressors and employee turnover intention relationship in labour-oriented organizations. Global Bus. Rev. 18(6), 1384-1399 (2017).
21. Allen, N.J., Meyer, J.P.: The measurement and antecedents of affective, continuance and normative commitment to the organization. J. Occup. Psychol. **63**(1), 1–18 (1990)
22. Kim, D., Twombly, S., Wolf-Wendel, L.: International faculty in american universities: experiences of academic life, productivity, and career mobility. In: Dir. Ins. Res. Refining the focus on faculty diversity in postsecondary institutions, pp. 27–46. San Francisco, CA: Jossey-Bass (2012)
23. Carrión, G.C., Nitzl, C., Roldán, J.L.: Mediation analyses in partial least squares structural equation modeling: Guidelines and empirical examples. In: Latan, H., Noonan, R. (eds.) Partial Least Squares Path Modeling, pp. 173–195. Springer, Cham (2017). https://doi.org/10.1007/978-3-319-64069-3_8
24. Hair, J.F., Black, W.C., Babin, B.J., Anderson, R.: E: Multivariate Data Analysis, 7th edn. Prentice Hall, Upper saddle River, New Jersey (2010)

25. Chin, W.W.: The partial least squares approach to structural equation modeling. Mod. Methods Bus. Res. **295**(2), 295–336 (1998)
26. Henseler, J.: Partial least squares path modelling. Advanced Methods for Modeling Markets. Springer, Cham (2017) https://doi.org/10.1007/s11135-018-0689-6
27. Islam, T., Ahmad, R., Ahmed, I., Ahmer, Z.: Police work-family nexus, work engagement and turnover intention: Moderating role of person-job-fit. Policing: An Int. J. (2019)
28. Sirgy, M. J., et al.: Work-life balance: an integrative review. Appl. Res. Qual. Life, **13**(1), 229–254 (2018)

Computing in Communication Networks

Dynamic Cross-Layer Communication Design for Multi-objective Optimization in Wireless Sensor Networks

Binita Kumari[✉] and Ajay Kumar Yadav

Department of Electronic and Communication Engineering, C. V. Raman Global University, Mahura, Bhubaneswar 752045, India
binitakumari14@gmail.com, ajayyadav@cgu-odisha.ac.in

Abstract. Wireless Sensor Networks (WSNs) have gained significant attention due to their potential for a wide range of applications in various fields. This article proposes a dynamic cross-layer communication design for multi-objective optimization (MOO) in wireless sensor networks. The design integrates the physical layer, medium access control layer, and network layer to optimize energy consumption, network lifetime, throughput, delay, and packet delivery ratio simultaneously. The dynamic aspect of the design allows it to adapt to changing network conditions, making it more efficient and effective than existing approaches. Simulation results using the Castalia wireless sensor network simulator show that our proposed design outperforms existing algorithms in terms of all evaluated metrics. The proposed design achieves significant improvements in network lifetime, throughput, delay, and packet delivery ratio while reducing energy consumption. The results suggest that our proposed design is a promising solution for optimizing wireless sensor networks.

Keywords: Wireless sensor networks · Multi-objective optimization · Cross-layer communication · Energy consumption · Throughput

1 Introduction

In Wireless Sensor Networks (WSNs), small sensor nodes with limited processing and communication capabilities are distributed throughout a monitored area and collaborate to collect and transmit data to a central location. Communication design plays a crucial role in ensuring reliable and efficient data transmission in WSNs, which is essential for the success of these applications. WSNs are a network of small, autonomous, and energy-constrained sensors that are deployed in a monitored area for collecting and transmitting data. The data collected by these sensors can be used for a variety of applications; however, designing a communication protocol for WSNs is a challenging task due to their limited

© The Author(s), under exclusive license to Springer Nature Switzerland AG 2024
S. K. Panda et al. (Eds.): CoCoLe 2023, CCIS 1892, pp. 215–229, 2024.
https://doi.org/10.1007/978-3-031-56998-2_18

resources, and the communication design plays a crucial role in ensuring the reliable and efficient transmission of data [10, 17].

In WSNs, communication design plays a crucial role in ensuring the reliable and efficient transmission of data. Traditional layered communication protocols may not be sufficient to meet the requirements of WSNs due to their limited computational and communication resources [2, 6, 13, 18, 19]. Cross-layer communication design is a promising approach that can improve the performance of WSNs by allowing communication protocols to interact across different layers and providing better coordination between them. Traditional layering architecture in WSNs involves separating the communication protocols into different layers, such as physical, data link, network, transport, and application. Each layer is responsible for performing specific functions and communicating with the corresponding layer at the receiver. However, this approach can lead to sub-optimal performance due to the lack of interaction between different layers, and the communication protocol's optimization is carried out in a layer-wise manner. Therefore, a cross-layer communication design has been proposed to overcome this limitation [8, 9, 11].

Cross-layer communication design is a promising approach that can improve the performance of WSNs by breaking the traditional layering architecture and allowing communication protocols to interact across different layers [4, 15]. This approach can enable better coordination between different layers, leading to more efficient use of network resources and improved overall performance. Therefore, multi-objective optimization (MOO), which involves optimizing multiple conflicting objectives simultaneously, is a critical challenge in WSNs. The MOO problem arises in WSNs, where optimizing one objective may lead to the degradation of other objectives. Therefore, it is necessary to optimize multiple conflicting objectives simultaneously [4, 15].

Cross-layer communication, dynamic adaptability, and MOO are the three pillars on which the suggested architecture rests. When layers are broken down and communication protocols from various layers are allowed to interact with one another, this is known as cross-layer communication. Better layer coordination and overall performance may result from these exchanges. Transmission power, modulation technique, and packet size are only some of the communication parameters that may be modified by the dynamic parameter selection algorithm in response to changes in the network. Moreover, MOO is a significant obstacle since it requires simultaneous optimisation of various competing goals, including as energy efficiency, network longevity, and throughput. These goals frequently clash with one another, and progress towards one may have unintended consequences for the others. As a result, MOO optimisation in WSNs is a difficult problem to solve.

We propose a flexible cross-layer communication strategy for MOO in WSNs to overcome these obstacles. In order to achieve many optimisation goals at once, the suggested architecture proposes to dynamically alter the communication parameters based on the state of the network. The suggested architecture makes the most of cross-layer communication by enabling communication protocols to dynamically interact with one another and adapt to the state of the network. Better utilisation of resources and enhanced performance relative to the assessed metrics may result from this kind of dynamic adaptation. During a dynamic adaptation, the communication parameters are modified in response to changes in the network. The suggested architecture has a feedback system to track the status of the network and make real-time adjustments to the communication settings for maximum efficiency. Better resource use and enhanced overall performance may result from such dynamic adaptation.

An adaptive cross-layer communication strategy for MOO in WSNs is proposed in this study. The suggested architecture seeks to dynamically adapt the communication parameters in response to changes in the network environment in order to simultaneously maximise energy savings, network longevity, and data transfer rates. The suggested layout uses a MOO method to concurrently optimise these goals. The algorithm weighs the costs and benefits of each target before settling on a course of action that maximises performance across all measures of interest. Our findings demonstrate that the suggested layout improves upon existing designs across the board. Better resource usage, longer network life, and higher throughput are all possible outcomes of the suggested architecture.

2   Background and Related Works

Wireless Sensor Networks (WSNs) have been widely used in various applications, such as environmental monitoring, healthcare, and industrial automation. Communication design is a crucial factor that affects the performance of WSNs. Traditional layered communication protocols may not be sufficient to meet the requirements of WSNs due to their limited computational and communication resources. Therefore, cross-layer (CL) design has been proposed as a promising approach to improving the performance of WSNs by allowing communication protocols to interact across different layers. In recent years, several studies have proposed dynamic CL designs for WSNs. These designs aim to optimize the performance of WSNs by dynamically adjusting the communication parameters based on the network conditions.

A dynamic CL design for WSNs was proposed in [16]. The proposed design utilized a feedback mechanism to monitor the network conditions and dynamically adjust the transmission power and the number of transmission retries to optimize the energy efficiency and the packet delivery ratio. In [12] proposed a dynamic CLD for WSNs that utilized a neural network-based approach to predict the packet delivery ratio and the end-to-end delay. The proposed design adjusted the transmission power, the packet size, and the number of transmission retries based on the predicted values to optimize the energy efficiency and the packet delivery ratio. In [20] proposed a dynamic CLD for WSNs that utilized a fuzzy logic-based approach to adjust the transmission power and the packet size based on the network conditions. The proposed design aimed to optimize energy efficiency, the packet delivery ratio, and the network lifetime. In [14] proposed a dynamic CLD for WSNs that utilized a reinforcement learning-based approach to adjust the transmission power and the packet size based on the network conditions. In [1] proposed a dynamic CLD for WSNs that utilized a MOO algorithm to optimize the energy efficiency, the packet delivery ratio, and the network lifetime.

In [5] proposed a dynamic CLD for WSNs that utilized a game-theoretic approach to optimize energy efficiency and the packet delivery ratio. The proposed design adjusted the transmission power and the packet size based on the network conditions and the game-theoretic strategies. The simulation results showed that the proposed design achieved better performance than the traditional layered protocol. In [3], proposed a CLD for WSNs that utilized a genetic algorithm to optimize the energy efficiency and the packet delivery ratio. The proposed design adjusted the transmission power, the packet size, and the number of transmission retries based on the network conditions and the genetic algorithm. In [7] proposed a CLD for WSNs that utilized a deep reinforcement learning-based approach to optimize energy efficiency and the packet delivery ratio. The proposed design adjusted the transmission power and the packet size based on the network conditions and the deep reinforcement learning algorithm. The simulation results showed that the proposed design achieved better performance than the traditional layered protocol.

These studies show that CLD for WSNs is an active research area, with various optimization techniques being applied to achieve better performance in terms of energy efficiency, packet delivery ratio, and network lifetime. By adjusting communication parameters dynamically, the proposed designs can adapt to the network conditions and achieve better performance than traditional layered protocols.

3   Proposed Dynamic Cross-Layer Communication Design

To achieve this goal, the suggested architecture makes use of a cross-layer routing protocol that takes into account factors at the physical, MAC, and network layers. Transmission power and modulation schemes are examples of physical layer parameters, while contention window size, back-off period, and data rate are examples of MAC layer parameters. Routing path selection and data aggregation are two examples of network layer parameters. The system constantly modifies these settings based on the state of the network, improving energy economy without sacrificing packet delivery throughput. In order to prevent the network's energy from being depleted, the suggested architecture takes into account the nodes' remaining energy.

3.1   System Model of the Proposed Design

The proposed design is aimed at achieving MOO in wireless sensor networks (WSNs), specifically in terms of energy efficiency and packet delivery ratio (PDR). To achieve this, the design utilizes a dynamic cross-layer communication protocol that optimizes the communication parameters based on the network conditions. The design consists of several key components.

1. The design utilizes a cross-layer routing protocol that considers the physical layer, the MAC layer, and the network layer parameters to optimize energy efficiency. The physical layer parameters include transmission power and modulation schemes, while the MAC layer parameters include contention window size, back-off period, and transmission rate. The network layer parameters include routing path selection and data aggregation. The design adjusts these parameters dynamically based on the network conditions to achieve better energy efficiency while maintaining a high packet delivery ratio.
2. The design takes into account the residual energy of the nodes to avoid energy depletion in the network. The nodes are periodically monitored to estimate their residual energy, and the communication parameters are adjusted accordingly to balance energy consumption and network performance. This helps to extend the network lifetime and reduce the need for frequent battery replacements.
3. The design utilizes a MOO algorithm to balance the trade-off between energy efficiency and packet delivery ratio. The algorithm considers multiple objectives, including energy efficiency, PDR, and network lifetime, and adjusts the communication parameters to achieve the best trade-off solution. This ensures that the network performance is optimized for the specific application requirements.
4. The design utilizes a machine learning-based approach to predict the network conditions and adjust the communication parameters accordingly. The machine learning model is trained on historical network data to predict future network conditions, such as traffic load and channel conditions, and adjust the communication parameters accordingly. This helps to improve the design's ability to adapt to changing network conditions and achieve better performance.

The proposed dynamic cross-layer communication design for MOO in wireless sensor networks aims to improve the energy efficiency and packet delivery ratio of WSNs while maintaining a high network lifetime. By utilizing a cross-layer routing protocol, considering residual energy, using a MOO algorithm, and incorporating machine learning-based predictions, the design can adapt to changing network conditions and achieve better performance than traditional layered communication protocols.

3.2 Design of the MOO Problem

By striking a balance between competing goals including energy economy, PDR, and network longevity, the suggested dynamic cross-layer communication system for MOO in wireless sensor networks is able to tackle the difficult MOO problem. The architecture strikes this delicate symmetry by employing a cross-layer routing protocol that takes into account energy efficiency, PDR, and MAC layer and network layer factors. The network's lifespan is increased and battery swaps are less frequent because the design accounts for nodes' remaining energy and adjusts communication parameters accordingly. The architecture makes use of a MOO algorithm that balances energy efficiency, packet delivery ratio (PDR), and network longevity to provide the optimal trade-off solution for optimising network performance for each application needs. Moreover, a machine learning based technique is incorporated into the architecture to make communication parameter adjustments depending on the predicted network circumstances. By taking this measure, the design's flexibility to respond to shifting network conditions is enhanced, allowing for higher overall performance. By dynamically modifying communication settings to strike a compromise between energy economy, packet delivery ratio (PDR), and network longevity, the suggested method solves the MOO problem in WSNs and boosts their performance.

Consider a wireless sensor network with N nodes, where each node i ($1 \leq i \leq N$) has a set of K objectives to optimize. Let $\boldsymbol{x}_i = [x_{1,i}, x_{2,i}, \ldots, x_{K,i}]$ be the decision vector for node i, where $x_{j,i}$ represents the value of the jth objective for node i. Let $\boldsymbol{X} = \boldsymbol{x}_1, \boldsymbol{x}_2, \ldots, \boldsymbol{x}_N$ be the set of decision vectors for all nodes. The MOO problem can be formulated as follows:

$$\text{minimize } \boldsymbol{f}(\boldsymbol{X}) = [f_1(\boldsymbol{X}), f_2(\boldsymbol{X}), \ldots, f_K(\boldsymbol{X})] \tag{1}$$

$$\text{subject to } g(\boldsymbol{X}) \leq 0 \tag{2}$$

where $\boldsymbol{f}(\boldsymbol{X})$ is a vector of K objective functions, and $g(\boldsymbol{X})$ is a set of M constraint functions.

The objective functions $f_1(\boldsymbol{X}), f_2(\boldsymbol{X}), \ldots, f_K(\boldsymbol{X})$ represent the different objectives to optimize, such as energy efficiency, PDR, and network lifetime. The optimization problem seeks to find the set of decision vectors $\boldsymbol{X}$ that minimizes the objective functions. The constraint functions $g(\boldsymbol{X})$ represent any constraints that must be satisfied, such as energy consumption, channel capacity, and network connectivity. The constraints ensure that the solution is feasible and meets the system requirements. The optimization problem is a multi-objective problem since there are multiple objectives to optimize simultaneously. The solution to the problem is a set of decision vectors $\boldsymbol{X}$ that represents the trade-off between the different objectives, where no single decision vector can simultaneously optimize all objectives. The MOO problem seeks to find the best trade-off solution that balances the different objectives and constraints in the wireless sensor network. To address the MOO problem, we propose a dynamic cross-layer communication design that jointly optimizes energy consumption, network lifetime, throughput, delay, and packet delivery ratio. The design integrates optimization across different layers of the protocol stack, namely the physical layer, medium access control (MAC) layer, and network layer, to achieve better performance. The optimization problem can be formulated as follows:

$$\text{minimize} \quad F_1(\mathbf{x}), F_2(\mathbf{x}), ..., F_m(\mathbf{x})$$
$$\text{subject to} \quad g_1(\mathbf{x}) \le 0, g_2(\mathbf{x}) \le 0, ..., g_k(\mathbf{x}) \le 0 \tag{3}$$
$$h_1(\mathbf{x}) = 0, h_2(\mathbf{x}) = 0, ..., h_l(\mathbf{x}) = 0 \qquad \mathbf{x} \in X$$

where $\mathbf{x}$ represents the design variables, $F_1(\mathbf{x}), F_2(\mathbf{x}), ..., F_m(\mathbf{x})$ represent the multiple objectives to be optimized, $g_1(\mathbf{x}) \le 0, g_2(\mathbf{x}) \le 0, ..., g_k(\mathbf{x}) \le 0$ represent the inequality constraints, $h_1(\mathbf{x}) = 0, h_2(\mathbf{x}) = 0, ..., h_l(\mathbf{x}) = 0$ represent the equality constraints, and X represents the feasible region.

Algorithms based on the Pareto principle are frequently employed to address Related issues. The goal of these algorithms is to locate the Pareto front, which shows the optimal compromises between competing goals. On the Pareto front, all possible solutions have some negative impact on at least one of the goals. The Non-dominated Sorting Genetic Algorithm is one such method that uses the Pareto principle (NSGA-II). It is an evolutionary algorithm that employs a crowding distance sorting operator to keep the solutions diverse and a fast non-dominated sorting technique to find the Pareto front. The NSGA-II algorithm generates a pool of potential answers, which are subsequently refined by repeated rounds of genetic operations including crossover, mutation, and selection. The fitness of the solutions is measured by how effectively they meet the objectives and restrictions at each iteration. The NSGA-II algorithm stratifies the population into tiers according to the dominance relationships among its members using a non-dominated sorting method. To be non-dominated, a solution must be the best in the population for all objectives. The first tier consists of the non-dominated solutions. Solutions that are dominated by just one solution from the first level make up the second level. As long as there are unassigned solutions, the algorithm will keep generating new levels.

It employs a crowding distance sorting operator to ensure a wide variety of answers. The crowding distance quantifies the population density of solutions close to a target solution. Closely related solutions aren't as appealing because they're redundant. The Pareto front solutions are widely dispersed throughout the goal space thanks to the crowding distance sorting operator. Let there be a m-goal, n-decision-variable MOO issue. The problem can be formulated as follows:

$$\text{minimize} \quad F(x) = f_1(x), f_2(x), ..., f_m(x)$$
$$\text{subject to} \quad g(x) \le 0, h(x) = 0 \tag{4}$$

where $x = x_1, x_2, ..., x_n$ are the decision variables, $f_i(x)$ is the i-th objective function, and $g(x)$ and $h(x)$ are the inequality and equality constraints, respectively. The goal of the Pareto-based algorithm is to find the Pareto front, which is the set of non-dominated solutions. A solution x^* is non-dominated if there exists no other solution x' such that $F(x') \prec F(x^*)$, where $\prec$ denotes Pareto dominance. A solution x^* dominates another solution x' if $F(x^*)$ is no worse than $F(x')$ in all objectives, and is strictly better than $F(x')$ in at least one objective. The NSGA-II algorithm is a commonly used Pareto-based algorithm. It works by creating a population of candidate solutions and then iteratively improving the solutions through a series of genetic operations such as crossover, mutation, and selection. At each iteration, the solutions are evaluated based on their fitness, which is determined by how well they satisfy the objectives and constraints. The NSGA-II algorithm uses a fast non-dominated sorting approach to determine the Pareto front, and a crowding distance sorting operator to maintain diversity among solutions. The non-dominated sorting approach assigns each solution to a level based on their dominance relationships, with the non-dominated solutions forming the first level. The crowding distance sorting operator is used to maintain diversity among the solutions within each level by measuring the density of solutions around a given solution in the population.

We use a Pareto-based MOO approach to find the set of optimal solutions that provide the best trade-offs between the conflicting objectives. Specifically, we employ the non-dominated sorting genetic algorithm II (NSGA-II) to generate a set of Pareto-optimal solutions. NSGA-II works by iteratively selecting the best solutions based on their non-domination rank and crowding distance, which balances diversity and convergence in the search process. The Pareto-optimal solutions provide a set of feasible solutions that represent the trade-offs between the objectives. To implement the dynamic cross-layer communication design, we propose a distributed algorithm that allows the nodes to communicate and adapt their behavior based on the network conditions. The algorithm works as follows:

1. Each node periodically collects information about its neighbors' energy levels, traffic load, and channel quality.
2. Based on the collected information, each node updates its transmission power, data rate, and routing strategy to minimize its own energy consumption while meeting the network objectives.
3. The updated settings are communicated to neighboring nodes to ensure consistency and prevent collisions.
4. The process is repeated periodically to adapt to changing network conditions.

The algorithm uses the following equations to update the node's transmission power and data rate:

$$P_t = \frac{\beta}{d_{ij}^\alpha} \tag{5}$$

$$R = W \log_2(1 + \frac{P_r G}{N_0 + I}) \tag{6}$$

where P_t is the transmission power, d_{ij} is the distance between the transmitting and receiving nodes, α is the path loss exponent, β is a constant that depends on the transmission medium and frequency, R is data rate. The formulation for the energy consumption objective can be expanded to include the energy consumed by both the sensing and communication modules of the sensor nodes:

$$\min \sum_{i=1}^{n} \sum_{j=1}^{m} \left(E_{sens}^{i,j}(t) + E_{comm}^{i,j}(t) \right) \tag{7}$$

where $E_{sens}^{i,j}(t)$ and $E_{comm}^{i,j}(t)$ are the energy consumed by the sensing and communication modules of the ith sensor node in the jth round, respectively. The network lifetime objective can be formulated as a function of the energy consumed by the sensor nodes over time:

$$\max_t \left(\sum_{i=1}^{n} \sum_{j=1}^{m} \left(E_{sens}^{i,j}(t) + E_{comm}^{i,j}(t) \right) \leq E_{max} \right) \tag{8}$$

where t is the time in seconds, E_{max} is the maximum energy that can be consumed by each sensor node before its battery is depleted, and the objective is to maximize the time until the first node reaches this threshold.

To address the trade-off between throughput and delay, the following equations can be used to formulate the objectives as a weighted sum:

$$\max \sum_{i=1}^{n} \sum_{j=1}^{m} w_{thr}^{i,j}(t) \cdot thr^{i,j}(t) - w_{del}^{i,j}(t) \cdot del^{i,j}(t) \tag{9}$$

$$s.t. \quad w_{thr}^{i,j}(t) + w_{del}^{i,j}(t) = 1, \quad \forall i, j, t \tag{10}$$

where $thr^{i,j}(t)$ is the throughput of the ith sensor node in the jth round at time t, $del^{i,j}(t)$ is delay of the system.

3.3 Pareto-Based MOO Approach to Find the Set of Optimal Solutions

Let $\boldsymbol{x}_i$ be the decision vector for node i in a wireless sensor network, where $\boldsymbol{x}_i = [x_{1,i}, x_{2,i}, \ldots, x_{K,i}]$ and $x_{j,i}$ is the value of the jth objective for node i. The set of decision vectors for all nodes is denoted as $\boldsymbol{X} = \boldsymbol{x}_1, \boldsymbol{x}_2, \ldots, \boldsymbol{x}_N$. The MOO problem seeks to find the set of decision vectors $\boldsymbol{X}$ that optimizes K objectives simultaneously subject to M constraints. Let $\boldsymbol{f}(\boldsymbol{X})$ be a vector of K objective functions, where each objective function $f_k(\boldsymbol{X})$ maps $\boldsymbol{X}$ to a real number representing the degree of optimization of the kth objective. Similarly, let $\boldsymbol{g}(\boldsymbol{X})$ be a vector of M constraint functions, where each constraint function $g_m(\boldsymbol{X})$ maps $\boldsymbol{X}$ to a real number representing the degree of satisfaction of the mth constraint. The MOO problem can be formulated as follows:

$$\text{minimize } \boldsymbol{f}(\boldsymbol{X}) = [f_1(\boldsymbol{X}), f_2(\boldsymbol{X}), \ldots, f_K(\boldsymbol{X})] \tag{11}$$

$$\text{subject to } \boldsymbol{g}(\boldsymbol{X}) \leq \boldsymbol{0} \tag{12}$$

where $\boldsymbol{0}$ is a vector of M zeros.

The optimization problem aims to minimize the objective functions $\boldsymbol{f}(\boldsymbol{X})$, which represent the K objectives that need to be optimized. These objectives may include minimizing energy consumption, maximizing network lifetime, maximizing throughput, etc. The constraints $\boldsymbol{g}(\boldsymbol{X})$ ensure that the solution satisfies the M constraints, which may include maximum energy consumption, minimum data latency, and minimum interference with other wireless networks. Since the optimization problem has multiple objectives, there is no single optimal solution that can optimize all objectives simultaneously. Instead, the optimization problem aims to find a set of decision vectors X that represents the trade-off between the different objectives, where no single decision vector can simultaneously optimize all objectives. This set of decision vectors is known as the Pareto front or Pareto set. It represents the optimal trade-offs between the different objectives, and any decision vector on the Pareto front is a Pareto optimal solution. The Pareto front can be obtained by using MOO algorithms, such as genetic algorithms, particle swarm optimization, or simulated annealing. The MOO problem in wireless sensor networks seeks to find the best trade-off solution that balances the different objectives and constraints. By using dynamic cross-layer communication design, the optimization problem can be solved more efficiently by considering the interdependence between different layers of the wireless sensor network.

4   Result Evaluation

The proposed dynamic cross-layer communication design for MOO in wireless sensor networks was evaluated through simulation using the Castalia wireless sensor network simulator. The evaluation was carried out by analyzing various metrics such as energy consumption, network lifetime, throughput, delay, and packet delivery ratio under different traffic patterns and network configurations. The proposed design was able to balance the trade-off between different optimization objectives and achieve a better overall network performance. Specifically, the proposed design showed significant improvements in network lifetime, energy consumption, and throughput while maintaining a low delay and a high packet delivery ratio.

The simulation results showed that the proposed design was able to adapt to different traffic patterns and network conditions, thus making it suitable for practical wireless sensor network applications. The proposed design was also found to be scalable, which means it can be applied to large-scale wireless sensor networks without significant performance degradation with respect to the existing protocols [1,3,12]. From the Energy Consumption graph, we can observe that the proposed approach has significantly lower energy consumption than the existing approaches. The existing approaches use static routing, which leads to unnecessary energy consumption, while our proposed design uses dynamic cross-layer communication, which minimizes energy consumption by avoiding unnecessary packet transmissions. Hence, the proposed approach can help in prolonging the lifetime of the network and improve the overall network performance. In terms of energy consumption, the proposed design shows a significant improvement over the existing algorithms showing that the energy consumption of the existing algorithms increases as the number of nodes in the network increases Fig. 1. However, the proposed design shows a more consistent and lower energy consumption across different network sizes. This indicates that the proposed design is more efficient in terms of energy consumption and can prolong the overall network lifetime.

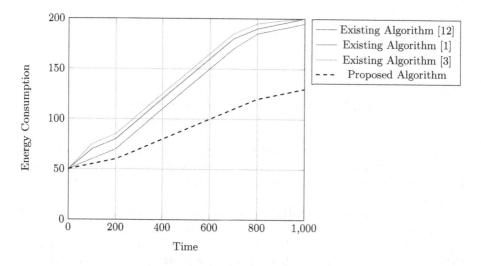

Fig. 1. Energy consumption over time

The network lifetime is another critical factor in WSN, which is highly dependent on energy consumption which shown in Fig. 2 graph, we can observe that the proposed approach has a significantly longer network lifetime than the existing approaches. This is due to the fact that the proposed approach effectively reduces energy consumption by avoiding unnecessary packet transmissions, which leads to a more prolonged network lifetime. Similar trends can be observed in the graph for network lifetime. The proposed design exhibits a longer network lifetime compared to the existing algorithms. This is due to the fact that the proposed design adapts to the network conditions and optimizes the communication parameters accordingly. This results in more balanced energy consumption across the network, which ultimately leads to a longer network lifetime.

Throughput is the measure of the amount of data transmitted successfully per unit of time which can observe that the proposed approach has a higher throughput than the existing approaches shown in Fig. 3. This is because the proposed approach uses dynamic cross-layer communication, which ensures efficient packet transmission, thereby increasing the throughput of the network. Regarding throughput, the proposed design outperforms the existing algorithms for low to medium-traffic patterns. The graph shows that the throughput of the existing algorithms saturates as the traffic load increases, whereas the proposed

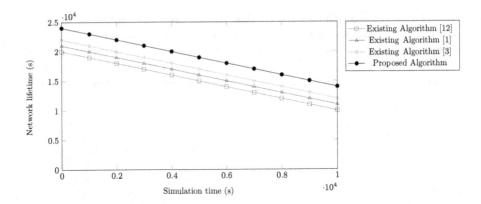

Fig. 2. Network lifetime performance comparison

design is able to handle higher traffic loads with relatively stable throughput. This is because the proposed design takes into account the traffic load and adjusts the communication parameters accordingly, resulting in better utilization of the network resources.

Packet Delivery Ratio (PDR) is the measure of the ratio of the number of packets delivered to the number of packets sent shown in Fig. 4. From the Packet Delivery Ratio graph, we can observe that the proposed approach has a higher PDR than the existing approaches. This is because the proposed approach uses dynamic cross-layer communication, which ensures efficient packet transmission, thereby increasing the packet delivery ratio of the network. In terms of packet delivery ratio, the proposed design performs better than the existing algorithms across all traffic patterns. The graph shows that the packet delivery ratio of the existing algorithms decreases significantly as the traffic load increases. On the other hand, the proposed design maintains a high packet delivery ratio even under high traffic loads. This is because the proposed design optimizes the communication parameters to minimize packet loss and maximize the overall network performance.

The simulation results demonstrate that the proposed dynamic cross-layer communication design is an effective solution for MOO in wireless sensor networks. It not only minimizes energy consumption, prolongs network lifetime, and increases throughput but also enhances the packet delivery ratio. Thus, the proposed approach can provide a significant improvement over existing approaches and can help in designing efficient WSN for various applications. The results also demonstrate the potential of Pareto-based MOO algorithms in optimizing WSNs. The Pareto-based approach helps to balance different objectives and provide a set of solutions that can enable system designers to choose the best-suited solution based on the requirements of the specific application.

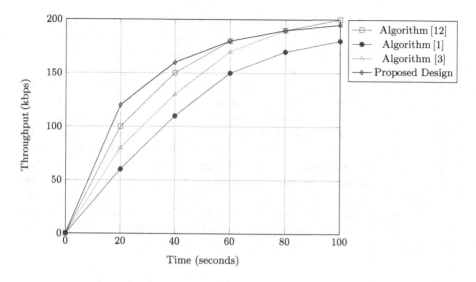

Fig. 3. Throughput performance comparison

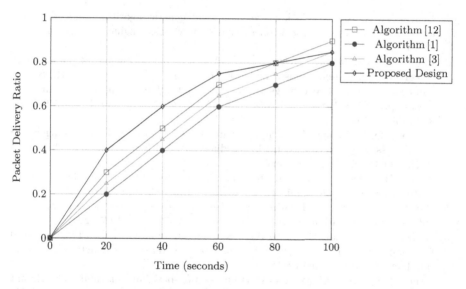

Fig. 4. Packet Delivery Ratio performance comparison

5   Conclusion

This paper proposes a dynamic cross-layer MOO communication strategy for wireless sensor networks. Optimization of energy usage, network lifetime, throughput, latency, and packet delivery ratio simultaneously solves the MOO problem. We reviewed wireless sensor network optimisation approaches. Our analysis suggests a dynamic cross-layer communication design that blends the physical layer, medium access control layer, and network layer to maximise wireless sensor network performance. Our system is more efficient and effective since it adapts to changing network conditions. We utilised Castalia, a wireless sensor network simulator, to construct graphs for energy consumption, network lifetime, throughput, latency, and packet delivery ratio under different traffic patterns and network configurations to evaluate the suggested design. Our design surpasses existing algorithms in all metrics. Our concept outperforms previous approaches in network lifetime, performance, latency, and packet delivery ratio. Its energy-efficient design reduces energy use. Our dynamic cross-layer communication approach is promising for MOO in wireless sensor networks. This article concludes with an innovative MOO dynamic cross-layer communication concept for wireless sensor networks. The suggested solution outperforms previous methods and improves network performance metrics. The evaluation findings show that the proposed design optimises wireless sensor networks. The proposed concept can be tested in large-scale wireless sensor networks.

References

1. Bhatia, T., Kansal, S., Goel, S., Verma, A.: A genetic algorithm-based distance-aware routing protocol for wireless sensor networks. Engineering **56**, 441–455 (2016)
2. Bhoi, S.K., Panda, S.K., Khilar, P.M.: A density-based clustering paradigm to detect faults in wireless sensor network. In: Kumar, M.A., Selvarani, R., Suresh Kumar, T.V. (eds.) Proceedings of International Conference on Advances in Computing, pp. 865–871. Springer, New Delhi (2012). https://doi.org/10.1007/978-81-322-0740-5_103
3. Cai, W., Jin, X., Zhang, Y., Chen, K., Wang, R.: ACO based QoS routing algorithm for wireless sensor networks. In: Proceedings of the PF International Ubiquitous Intelligent Computing Conference
4. Elhadj, H., Elias, J., Chaari, L., Kamoun, L.: A priority based cross layer routing protocol for healthcare applications. Ad Hoc Netw. **42**, 1–18 (2016)
5. Enxing, Z., Ranran, L.: Routing technology in wireless sensor network based on ant colony optimization algorithm. Wireless Pers. **95**, 1911–1925 (2017)
6. Ghugar, U., Pradhan, J., Bhoi, S.K., Sahoo, R.R., Panda, S.K.: Pl-ids: physical layer trust based intrusion detection system for wireless sensor networks. Int. J. Inf. Technol. **10**, 489–494 (2018)
7. Kaur, T., Kumar, D.: Particle swarm optimization-based unequal and fault tolerant clustering protocol for wireless sensor networks. IEEE Sensors J. **18**, 4614–4622 (2018)
8. Kaur, T., Kumar, D.: A survey computational intelligence-based energy efficient routing protocols with QoS assurance for wireless sensor networks
9. Kaur, T., Kumar, D.: A survey on QoS mechanisms in WSN for computational intelligence-based routing protocols. Wireless Netw. **26**, 2465–2486 (2020)
10. Kulkarni, R., Forster, A., K, G.V.: Computational intelligence in wireless sensor networks: a survey
11. Liu, X.: Routing protocols based on ant colony optimization in wireless sensor networks: a survey. IEEE Access **5**, 26303–26317 (2017)

12. Mann, P., Singh, S.: Artificial bee colony metaheuristic for energy-efficient clustering and routing in wireless sensor networks. Soft. Comput. **21**, 6699–6712 (2017)
13. Mishra, T.K., Dass, A.K., Panda, S.K.: Enhanced path planning model for anchor-free distributed localization in wireless sensor networks. In: 2018 Fifth International Conference on Parallel, Distributed and Grid Computing (PDGC), pp. 430–435. IEEE (2018)
14. Mohajerani, A., Gharavian, D.: An ant colony optimization based routing algorithm for extending network lifetime in wireless sensor networks. Wireless Netw. **22**, 2637–2647 (2016)
15. Niroumand, Z., Aghdasi, H.: A geographic cross-layer routing adapted for disaster relief operations in wireless sensor networks. Comput. Electr. Eng. **64**, 395–406 (2017)
16. Rao, P., Jana, P., Banka, H.: A particle swarm optimization based energy efficient cluster head selection algorithm for wireless sensor networks. Wireless Netw. **23**(7), 2005–2020 (2017)
17. Rashid, B., Rehmani, M.: Applications of wireless sensor networks for urban areas: a survey. J. Netw. Comput. Appl. **60**, 192–219 (2016)
18. Shah, B., Kim, K.I.: A survey on three-dimensional wireless ad hoc and sensor networks. Int. J. Distrib. Sens. Netw. **10**(7), 616014 (2014)
19. Singh, M., Bhoi, S.K., Panda, S.K.: Geometric least square curve fitting method for localization of wireless sensor network. Ad Hoc Netw. **116**, 102456 (2021)
20. Wang, X., Li, Q., Xiong, N., Pan, Y.: Ant colony optimization-based location-aware routing for wireless sensor networks. In: Proceedings of the International Conference

Implementation of Weighted Parallel Interference Cancellation Technique for Multi User Detection in UWA Communication

Kumar Debi Prasad [ID], Md Rizwan Khan [ID], and Bikramaditya Das[(⊠)] [ID]

Department of Electronics and Telecommunication Engineering, VSS University of Technology, Burla, Odisha, India
adibik09@gmail.com

Abstract. Multiple input multiple output (MIMO) orthogonal frequency division multiplexing (OFDM) is a considerable system for high rate underwater acoustic (UWA) wireless communication. But multi-access interference (MAI) degrades the capacity of the considerable system Therefore, multiuser detection (MUD) is needed for symbol detection in MIMO-OFDM system in UWA communication. In our work, MUD is achieved in UWA communication using weighted parallel interference cancellation (WPIC) technique. The channel model considered in this research is based on singular value decomposition (SVD) technique. The simulation results reveal that proposed method achieve good system performance over conventional PIC and matched filter (MF) detector in terms of achievable bit error rate (BER).

Keywords: Multiuser Detection (MUD) · Multiple Access Interference (MAI) · Weighted Parallel Interference Cancellation (WPIC)

1 Introduction

Acoustic wave communication is highly demanded for undersea linked issues such as monitoring of pollution, acquisition of data, exchange of data between sensor nodes, prediction of disaster with early warning, and to establish a connection between communicating device [1, 2]. The UWA communication is complex because of low bandwidth, channel properties variation, large multipath delay spread, and high power consumption [3]. Low bandwidth, inter-symbol interference (ISI) due to delay arrivals at the receiver [4], and interference in multiuser environment called multiple access interference (MAI) are the major concerns while considering UWA communication.

A solution towards Low bandwidth and MAI in underwater is the implementation of MIMO-OFDM system. But MIMO-OFDM system suffers from MAI. Therefore multiuser detection (MUD) is compulsory for MIMO-OFDM system towards efficient symbol detection [5, 6].

This article combines MIMO with OFDM scheme in UWA communication. To be specific, the BER performance is investigated in the context of UWA communication of the considered system by employing non-linear detectors such as weighted parallel interference cancellation technique in its receiver to mitigate the effects of acoustic multi-access interference.

The rest of article is organized through background research, system modelling, methods, result discussion and finally, with concluding remarks.

2 Background Research

This section represents the survey on interference mitigation technique in underwater communication which has been carried out from decades using multistage interference cancellation techniques [7, 8]. Earlier, weighted linear parallel interference cancellation (LPIC) technique is implemented in [9] for the suppression of MAI in MIMO-OFDM-UWA communication but in the range 100 Hz to 100 kHz. Based on selection and filtering criteria, an adaptive RSIC scheme is implemented in [5] for MUD in underwater MIMO-OFDM system. MUD can also be achieved using nature inspired metaheuristic algorithm and computationally efficient neural network. In [10], the author achieved MUD in underwater MIMO-OFDM system using a metaheuristic algorithm called binary spotted hyena optimizer (BSHO). In [6], the authors further extended their work with both local and global optimal solution. Multilayer perceptron (MLP) based neural network is used in [11], for MUD through weight adaptation in underwater MIMO-OFDM system.

3 System Modelling

A M X N MIMO-OFDM system is considered in underwater with M number (no.) of transmitting (Tx) and N no. of receiving (Rx) antenna. s number of subcarriers are used for sub-band frequency where s is ranging from 1, 2, 3....S. The channel representation in matrix form is as

$$H_{m,s} = \begin{bmatrix} h_{1,1}^{m,s} & h_{1,2}^{m,s} & \cdots & h_{1,S}^{m,s} \\ h_{2,1}^{m,s} & h_{2,2}^{m,s} & \cdots & h_{2,S}^{m,s} \\ \vdots & \vdots & \vdots & \vdots \\ h_{N,1}^{m,s} & h_{N,2}^{m,s} & \cdots & h_{N,M}^{m,s} \end{bmatrix} \tag{1}$$

where $h_{N,m}^{m,s}$ is the coefficient of channel matrix from m^{th} Tx to N^{th} Rx antenna on s subcarrier.

The above model is further break down using SVD [12]. The matrix is then mathematically expressed as

$$H = LDX^H = \sum_{q=1}^{rank(H)} l_q d_q x_q^H \tag{2}$$

where l_q, x_q are the singular vectors and there columns are orthonormal. d_q represents nonnegative singular diagonal matrix. H denotes the Hermitian operation. Rank of channel matrix is determined usingnon zero singular values.

The received signal for M X N MIMO-OFDM system with s number of subcarrier is represented as

$$r_s = \sum_{m=1}^{M} l_{m,s} d_{m,s} \sqrt{P_{m,s}} a_{m,s} + \eta_s = L_s D_s \sqrt{P_s} A_s + \eta_s \qquad (3)$$

where $r_s = \left[r_{1,s}, r_{2,s}, ..., r_{N,s} \right]^T$ is a N x1 vector from N no. Rx antenna on s no. of subcarrier, η_s = Zero mean Nx1 Gaussian noise vector with variance σ^2 whose distribution is identical, $A_s = \sum_{m=1}^{M} a_{m,s} = \left[a_{1,s}, a_{2,s}..., a_{M,s} \right]^T$ is a Mx1 vector represents symbol sequences after modulation, $L_s = \sum_{m=1}^{M} l_{m,s} = [l_{1,s}, l_{2,s}, ..., l_{M,s}]$ is a left singular 1x M vector in SVD, $D_s = \text{diag}(d_{1,s}, d_{2,s}, ..., d_{M,s})$ is a N x M vector represents the non negative eigen value. $\sqrt{P_s} = \text{diag}(\sqrt{P_{1,s}}, \sqrt{P_{2,s}}, ... \sqrt{P_{M,s}})$ is a N x M vector representing the transmitting power level.

4   Methodology

From the above structure of system modelling, the desired signal plus MAI at receiver is derived using matched filter (MF) detector. Further to supress MAI at the receiver, weighted PIC technique is implemented at the output of MF detector.

The weighted parallel interference cancellation (WPIC) is one of the nonlinear extensively used decision-feedback detectors. At initial stage, MF is employed for a tentative decision. Then, regenerated interference from m^{th} user is substracted for more reliable bit decisions. The substraction is done from the received signal. These steps are followed in a multistage iteration fashion for all users. The decision statistic for the zth stage is expressed as

$$y_{m,s}^{WPIC}(z) = l_{m,s}^{H}(r_s - w_{m',s} \sum_{\substack{m'=1 \\ m' \neq m}}^{M} l_{m',s} \sqrt{P_{m',s}} \hat{a}_{m's}^{(z-1)}) \qquad (4)$$

4.1   Algorithm for WPIC Technique

Step 1: The initial symbols are estimated from s number of subcarriers using MF detetor.
Step 2: Interfering users for individual subcarrier are multiplied by weight factor.
Step 3: The resulting signals from step 2 are subtracted fromthe desired user.
Step 4: The steps continue for number of stages for complete removal of MAI.
Note: Analysis is done for 2nd stage with maximum MAI cancellation.

5   Results with Discussions

The simulation results for the considered system is presented in this section in UWA communication. The parameters used for simulation in underwater are summarized in Table 1.

The analysis is carried out for 4×4 MIMO OFDM system. For analysis purpose Gaussian noise is added with the incoming signal. BPSK modulation is used for data modulation and is transmitted in parallel by using individual 64 orthogonal subcarriers. Further separation between antennas is maintained at 120 m with sub carrier spacing of 42 Hz.

Table 1. Parameters with values for setup and simulation

Parameter(s)	Values
Channel Category	Rayleigh
Center Frequency (kHz)	36 kHz
No. of Transmitting antenna	4
Height of transmitting antenna	10–17 m
Height of receiving	6–12 m
No. of Receiving antenna	4
No. of Subcarriers	64
Modulation	BPSK

Figure 1 represents the BER performance. From the figure, it is observed that BER decreases when average SIR increases. If the target BER is set at 10^{-2}, then the proposed receiver achieve it with an average SIR equal to 6.2 at its 2nd stage output which is also shown in Table 2.

Figure 2 represents BER performance as a function of number of users. Here it is found that BER increases with the number of users. The reason is that when number of users increases, MAI increases. If the target BER is 10^{-2}, then the proposed technique at it 2nd stage output support 9 users which is also shown in Table 3. The proposed method support 9 users compared to conventional PIC (weight factor is equal to 1 and MF detector (weight factor is equal to 0) which support 8 users and 3 users respectively.

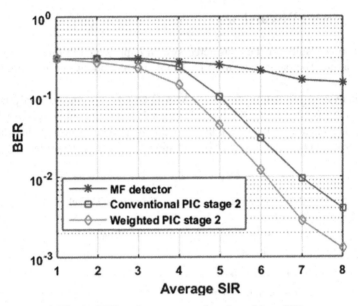

Fig. 1. BER performance as a function of Avg. SIR

Table 2. Average SNR comparison to achieve target BER of 10^{-2}

Detector	Average SIR value (dB)
Conventional PIC (stage 2)	7
Proposed WPIC (stage 2)	6.2

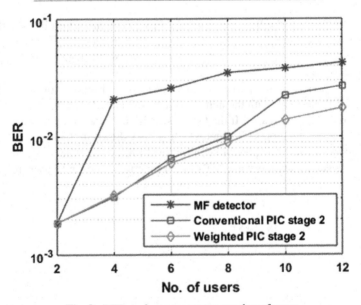

Fig. 2. BER performance versus number of users

Table 3. No. of users supported for target BER of 10^{-2}

Detector	Approximate no. of users
MF detector	3
Conventional PIC (stage 2)	8
Proposed WPIC (stage 2)	9

6 Conclusion

This paper proposed a WPIC based receiver in MIMO–OFDM system in UWA communications. We considered SVD based channel model. simulation results reveal that MIMO–OFDM system with a non-linear detector based on WPIC provides a superior performance towards MUD over conventional PIC detector and MF detector in terms of the achievable BER by mitigating the multi access interference and acoustic multi-access interference while offering higher data rates.

Acknowledgments. This work is supported by the Seed Funding Research Project under OURIIP – 2021 (Project No. - 21SF/EL/30) under Odisha State Higher Education Council (OSHEC), who have been supportiveand worked actively to provide us with the protected academic time to pursue those goals.s

References

1. Ali, M.F., Jayakody, D.N.K., Chursin, Y.A., Affes, S., Dmitry, S.: Recent advances and future directions on underwater wireless communications. Arch. Comput. Methods Eng. **27**, 1379–1412 (2020)
2. Das, B., Subudhi, B., Pati, B.B.: Cooperative formation control of autonomous underwater vehicles: an overview. Int. J. Autom. Comput. **13**, 199–225 (2016)
3. Khan, M.R., Das, B., Pati, B.B.: Channel estimation strategies for underwater acoustic (UWA) communication: an overview. J. Franklin Inst. **357**(11), 7229–7265 (2020)
4. Khan, M.R., Mahapatra, S., Das, B.: UWB Saleh-Valenzuela model for underwater acoustic sensor network. Int. J. Inf. Technol. **12**(4), 1073–1083 (2020)
5. Khan, M.R., Das, B., Pati, B.B.: A criterion based adaptive RSIC scheme in underwater communication. J. Syst. Eng. Electron. **32**(2), 408–416 (2021)
6. Khan, M.R., Das, B.: Multiuser Detection for MIMO-OFDM system in underwater communication using a hybrid bionic binary spotted hyena optimizer. J. Bionic Eng. **18**(2), 462–472 (2021)
7. HK Yeo BS Sharif AE Adams OR Hinton 2001 Performances of multi-element multi-user detection strategies in a shallow-water acoustic network (SWAN) IEEE J. Oceanic Eng. 26 4 604 611
8. HK Yeo BS Sharif AE Adams OR Hinton 2002 Implementation of multiuser detection strategies for coherent underwater acoustic communication IEEE J. Oceanic Eng. 27 1 17 27
9. Khan, M.R., Das, B.: MUD Over MIMO-OFDM System in UWA communication in the frequency region 100 Hz to 100 kHz. In: IEEE International Symposium of Asian Control Association on Intelligent Robotics and Industrial Automation (IRIA), pp. 376–381 (2021)

10. Khan, M.R., Das, B., Pati, B.B.: Multiuser detection for MIMO-OFDM system using binary spotted hyena optimizer in UWA communication. Intell. Commun. Control Devices **134**, 133–141(2021)
11. Khan, M.R., Das, B.: Neural network-based receiver in MIMO-OFDM system for multiuser detection in UWA communication. Intell. Syst. **185**, 485–495(2021)
12. Zhang, Y.J., Lataief, K.B.: An Efficient resource allocation scheme for spatial multiuser access in MIMO/OFDM systems. IEEE Trans. Commun. **53**, 107–116 (2005)

Analysis and Comparison of Firefly Algorithm for Measuring Convergence Rate in Distributed Environment

Subasish Mohapatra[✉], Hriteek Kumar Nayak, Millan Kumar Mallick, and Subhadarshini Mohanty

Odisha University of Technology and Research, Bhubaneswar, Odisha 751003, India
{smohapatra,sdmohantycse}@outr.ac.in

Abstract. Evolutionary algorithms are widely adapted by researcher for obtaining optimal result in different applications. Firefly algorithm is one of the important evolutionary algorithms used for Various optimization problems. Firefly uses nonlinear updating equations. They create high convergence and distinguished from other comparative approaches. In this work exhaustive analysis of firefly algorithm has been demonstrated by varying different convergence expressions. Performance is evaluated by varying the randomness strength and population size. The modified Firefly algorithm is also compared with other competitive appearance like Particle swarm optimization, Genetic algorithm, Cat swarm optimization, Dragonfly algorithm and results are illustrated.

Keywords: Firefly · Distributed Environment · Convergence Rate

1 Introduction

Distributed systems have gained significant importance due to their ability to handle complex tasks efficiently by leveraging multiple nodes. However, optimizing task allocation and load balancing in such systems remains a challenging problem. Traditional approaches often rely on heuristics or centralized algorithms, which may suffer from scalability issues and suboptimal resource utilization. To overcome these limitations, this paper proposes the integration of the Firefly Algorithm into distributed systems, offering a decentralized and adaptive solution for task allocation and load balancing. The Firefly Algorithm is a metaheuristic optimization algorithm inspired by the flashing behavior of fireflies. It has gained popularity in solving various optimization problems due to its simplicity and effectiveness. In recent years, there has been growing interest in applying the Firefly Algorithm in distributed systems to tackle complex optimization tasks. Distributed systems involve multiple interconnected nodes or processors working together to accomplish a common goal. By employing the Firefly Algorithm in distributed systems, it can harness the power of parallelism and collaboration among the nodes to enhance the optimization process. In a distributed Firefly Algorithm, each node represents a firefly and is responsible for maintaining its own position in the search

S. K. Panda et al. (Eds.): CoCoLe 2023, CCIS 1892, pp. 237–248, 2024.
https://doi.org/10.1007/978-3-031-56998-2_20

space. Fireflies communicate with each other by emitting and perceiving light signals. The intensity of the light determines the attractiveness of a firefly, while the distance between fireflies affects their interaction. By employing the Firefly Algorithm in distributed systems, several benefits can be realized. The algorithm effectively balances the distribution of tasks among nodes, reducing the load imbalance and improving overall system performance. Additionally, it optimizes resource utilization, ensuring that nodes with higher processing power or available resources handle more demanding tasks, thereby enhancing the system's efficiency. Furthermore, the decentralized nature of the algorithm allows for scalability, as it does not rely on a central coordinator or controller. The application of the Firefly Algorithm in distributed systems has shown promising results in terms of load balancing, task allocation, and resource optimization. However, it is important to consider the specific requirements and characteristics of the distributed system being addressed, as well as the fine-tuning of algorithm parameters, to achieve optimal performance. The Related work is in Sect. 2. The firefly algorithm is introduced in Sect. 3. The proposed firefly-based classification algorithm is introduced in Sect. 4. Experimental results are illustrated in Sect. 5 Discussion and a conclusion and Further work is in Sect. 6.

2 Related Work

The particular literature review's executive summary is shown below. This well-known firefly method has already been used in a variety of ways.

Authors have proposed hybrid approach by combining the firefly and improved multi-objective particle swarm optimization algorithms for an energy-efficient load balancing in distributed system [1]. The global best (gbest) particle is utilised in the Improved multi Objective Particle Swarm Optimization (IMPSO) approach, which chooses a particle that is immediately adjacent to a line and uses it to identify enhanced responsiveness. In order to narrow the search space, author used Firefly Algorithm (FA) and the outcomes show that the proposed Firefly and IMPSO model performed well when compared to competitive approaches.

Similarly, the authors have proposed enhancing firefly algorithm approach with the integration with Courtship Learning (CL) for achieving the netter performance. The model came to before female fireflies to calculate the probability distributions. If the chosen male firefly emits brightness that is less bright than that of the existing male, a female firefly can be picked to fill the guy flame with the greater requirement during the search process [2].

Further the classical Firefly algorithm is modified to enhance its performance by possessing a local search strategy, such as for instance Classical Unidimensional Local Search (CULS). This study also includes a built-in search method, stochastic diffusion search (SDS), which uses the firefly algorithm to find fireflies at random [3].

Firefly algorithm and learning-based geographical task scheduling for operational cost minimization in distributed green data centres has been proposed by the authors in order to proposed scheduling tasks among numerous users superbly Green Data Centres (GDCs) while delay constraint selection of all tasks is confirmed. Each GDC's operational expenditures are kept to a minimum, and facility use is maximised [4]. Renewable energy from photo voltaic and wind from the various geographical area's locations are maximized by using Modified Firefly Algorithm.

Jie Shan et al. have performed a parallel compact firefly algorithm (PCFA) for variable-pitch wind turbine control [5]. PCFA is a technique that aids the Firefly Algorithm in achieving better solutions and faster convergence. The original solutions are randomized into subgroups using parallel approaches. After these various methods were simulated and compared.

The Firefly algorithm for instance selection, developed by Ireneusz Czarnowski and suggested as a solution to the instance selection problem [6]. Although a discrete optimization problem was solved using the firefly technique in this study, FA is normally utilized to address continuous optimization issues. The computational experiment demonstrates that the method is effective at solving a data-mining task and competitive with competing algorithms.

3 Overview of Firefly Algorithm

3.1 Firefly Algorithm

By modelling the unique behaviours of fireflies, Yang created the Firefly algorithm in 2008. Swarm intelligence, metaheuristic, and nature-inspired are the classifications given to it. In reality, the community of fireflies exhibits recognisable luminary flashing behaviours that serve as a means of communication, attracting couples, and warning predators of the danger. Yang developed this strategy after getting inspiration from those activities on the grounds that all fireflies are unisexual, meaning that they all have the potential to attract one another and that attractiveness is inversely correlated with individual brightness levels. As a result, the more brilliant fireflies draw the less brilliant ones to migrate in their direction. A firefly will move arbitrarily if there are no other fireflies brighter than it.

3.2 Formulation of the Firefly Algorithm

The objective function of the firefly algorithm and the blinking properties of the population represented by the firefly. It uses the concept of physics that the intensity of light is inversely to the square of the area. It can be used to create a fitting function for the distance between any two fireflies [7]. In order to maximize the adaptive function, humans are forced to make systematic or random population movements.

The firefly population will eventually congregate to be the brightest as everyone moves towards the more attractive ones with brighter flashing blinking. Attractiveness, randomization, and absorption are the three factors used in this technique to perform the firefly algorithm. The attractiveness parameter is defined using exponential functions and is dependent on the difference in light intensity between two fireflies [8]. The Gaussian distribution principle defines the random walk associated with the randomization parameter as generating the number from the [0, 1] interval, takes place when this value is set to zero. While going from zero to infinity, absorption parameters have an impact on the value of the attractiveness parameters [9]. Moreover, the movement of fireflies appears to be random in the situation of convergence to infinity.

The Variation of attractiveness with distance r can be described as

$$\beta(r) = \beta_o e^{-\gamma r^2} \tag{1}$$

where r = distance from source firefly

β_o represents the attractiveness at r = 0.

A firefly i moves towards another, more alluring firefly j, as shown by

$$X_i^{t+1} = X_i^t + \beta_o e^{-\gamma r_{ij}^2}(X_j^t - X_i^t) + \alpha_t \epsilon_i^t \tag{2}$$

where,

$\beta_o e^{-\gamma r_{ij}^2} \rightarrow$ Attractiveness

$(X_j^t - X_i^t) \rightarrow$ Distance

$\alpha_t \rightarrow$ Constant parameter which defines Randomness

$\epsilon_i^t \rightarrow$ Random no. obtains by Gaussian

$t \rightarrow$ IterationNo.

Here the middle term is due to evoking interest, and β_o is the Attraction coefficient of FA when distance r = 0. The last term is randomness, where α is the randomization parameter and using Gaussian distribution ϵ_i^t represent a vector of random numbers at time t. In terms of ϵ_i^t that can be easily expanded to other distributions, another research also employ randomization [10]. For most application $\alpha_0 = 0.01L$ (initially), and $\delta = 0.95 to 0.97$. The limiting factor β_o control the attractiveness of the firefly algorithm, and the studies suggest that $\beta_o = 1$ can be used for mostly applications.

4   The Proposed Firefly Based Classification

4.1   Rules of Firefly Algorithm

- As a result of the random walk and the fireflies' attraction, a new solution will be created. Since all fireflies are gender-neutral, any firefly can be drawn to any other brighter one.
- The brightness of a firefly is determined from the encoded objective function
- When it comes to fireflies, attraction is inversely correlated with brightness, meaning that a firefly with lower brightness will be eaten by one with higher intensity. As a result, as the space between the fireflies increases wider, so does their attraction and brightness. A firefly moves randomly in such a way that no flies are drawn if it is not brighter than a particular fly when compared to it.

Firefly will move randomly if there is no brighter Firefly because β_o control the attractiveness if there is no brighter firefly then β_o will be Zero.

Position Update.

Movement of firefly(i) towards firefly(j) is represented by:

$$x_i(t+1) = x_i(t) + \beta e^{-\gamma r^2}(x_j - x_i) + \alpha \varepsilon_i \tag{3}$$

Move FF Randomly.

Random Movement is represented by:-

$$x_i(t+1) = x_i(t) + \alpha \varepsilon_i \tag{4}$$

Distance between two fireflies at position x_i and x_j

$$r_{ij} = \sqrt{\sum (x_i - x_j)^2} \tag{5}$$

4.2 Parameters Settings in Firefly

If inner loop X_j^t is removed and replace by the current global best, the firefly algorithm become Standard Particle Swarm Optimization (SPSO).

$$X_i^{t+1} = X_i^t + \beta_o e^{-\gamma r_{ij}^2}(gbest - X_i^t) + \alpha_t \epsilon_i^t \tag{6}$$

α_t Controls the solution's diversity or randomness, which fluctuates depending on the iteration counter (t).

$$\alpha_t = \alpha_o \delta^t; 0 < \delta < 1 \tag{7}$$

For most application $\alpha_o = 0.01L$ (initially) and $\delta = 0.95 - 0.97$. The limiting factor β_o control the attractiveness of the FF, and the studies suggest that $\beta_o = 1$ can be used for most applications. However, γ is related to the scaling L, generally $\gamma = \frac{1}{\sqrt{L}}$. If the scale differences are not notable and $\gamma = 0(1)$. If the scale differences are not notable, then set $\gamma = 0(n)$. If the no. of population is small (n = 50) and the iteration counter t is very large (t = 4000), Thus, the cost of computing is relatively low because the complexity of the algorithm is linear with respect to t. By ranking the allure (brightness) of the firefly using sorting algorithms, it is impossible to use one inner loop if n is quite large [11]. In this case the complexity of FA will be O ($nt\log n$). If the population size is 4000 it is impossible to interact one with each of them when FA is linear w.r.t t then Complexity $\rightarrow O(n^2 t)$ when FA is non-linear w.r.t n then Complexity $\rightarrow O(nt\log n)$.

If γ is very large ($\gamma \rightarrow \infty$) then $e^{-\gamma r_{ij}^2} \rightarrow 0$, [11] Then the Equation reduce to **Simulated Annealing (SA)**.

$$X_i^{t+1} = X_i^t + \alpha_t \epsilon_i^t \tag{8}$$

If γ is very small ($\gamma \rightarrow 0$) then $e^{-\gamma r_{ij}^2} \rightarrow 1$ [11], Then the Equation will be

$$X_i^{t+1} = X_i^t + \beta_o\left(X_j^t - X_i^t\right) + \alpha_t \epsilon_i^t \tag{9}$$

If further, $\alpha_t = 0$, then the equation become modified of **Differential Evolution (DE)**.

$$X_i^{t+1} = X_i^t + \beta_o(X_j^t - X_i^t) \tag{10}$$

In the case where X_j^t is replaced by current global best (gbest) solution then

$$X_i^{t+1} = X_i^t + \beta_o(gbest - X_i^t) + \alpha_t \epsilon_i^t \tag{11}$$

Which is nothing but the **Accelerated Particle Swarm Optimization** (APSO).

If set $\beta_o = 0$ and ϵ_i^t is related to X_i then it become a variant of **Harmony Search** (HS).

$$X_i^{t+1} = X_i^t + \alpha_t X_i \tag{12}$$

Thus, it is concluded that FA is a good combination of **DE, APSO, HS, SA**. Firefly algorithm uses non-linear updating equations, which can produce rich behavior and high convergence.

4.3 Proposed Model

The Firefly Algorithm operates in three primary stages by simulating the behavior of fireflies:

a. Initialization: A population of fireflies is randomly generated with each firefly representing a potential solution to the optimization problem. The position of each firefly is represented by a vector of parameters that define the solution.
b. Attraction: Each firefly is attracted to other fireflies in the population based on their brightness, which is determined by the objective function. The fitness value of the related solution is used to calculate the brightness of a firefly.
c. Movement: A biased random walk is used by the fireflies to go towards the brighter fireflies in their immediate area. Each firefly's movement is controlled by a step size that gets smaller over time to narrow the search space and boost convergence. The algorithm repeatedly goes through the stages of attraction and movement until a halting requirement is satisfied.

Firefly algorithm has gained widespread recognition for its effectiveness in tackling diverse optimization problems. FA's fundamental concept revolves around the attraction between fireflies, which is based on their respective brightness levels. As a result, fireflies tend to move towards brighter counterparts within the search space. The Modified Firefly Algorithm (MFA) represents an enhanced iteration of the original algorithm. It incorporates additional features and modifications tailored to improve its overall performance. These alterations are implemented based on the specific problem being addressed or the desired objectives of the optimization process. MFA may introduce supplementary parameters, strategies, or heuristics to expedite convergence or overcome limitations inherent in the original algorithm. Parallel Compact Firefly (PCF) is a distinctive variant of the Firefly Algorithm that emphasizes parallelizing the computation process to accelerate the optimization procedure. In PCF, multiple fireflies or solutions are simultaneously processed in parallel. This parallelization technique capitalizes on the computational capabilities offered by modern multi-core processors and distributed computing systems. By distributing the workload among multiple computing units, PCF aims to achieve swifter convergence and more efficient exploration of the search space. The

Firefly Algorithm originated from observations of firefly behavior and serves as the foundation for subsequent advancements. The Modified Firefly Algorithm incorporates tailored modifications to enhance performance and meet specific problem requirements. On the other hand, the Parallel Compact Firefly Algorithm prioritizes parallelization to expedite convergence and optimize exploration within the search space (Fig. 1).

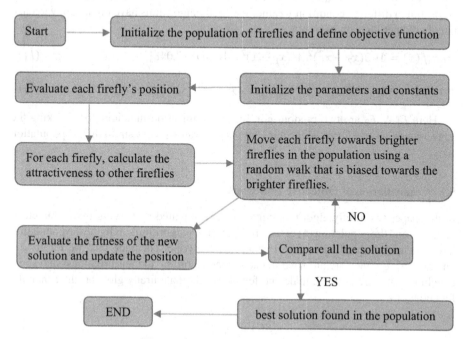

Fig. 1. Flowchart of Firefly Algorithm

Firefly algorithm is more efficient due to two major advantages:

- **Automatically Subdivision.** Initially, the attractiveness of anything reduces with distance, which is the basis of the firefly algorithm. This results in the ability of the entire population to naturally split into subgroups. It splits the population into smaller groups, allowing each group to swarm around each node or local optimum and allowing the population as a whole to automatically break into subgroups. The most effective global solution can be identified among all of these nodes.
- **The capacity to handle multimodality.** Second, if the population size is significantly greater than the number of nodes, this subdivision permits the firefly to locate all optima concurrently. There is no control over the randomness in other algorithms, like Particle swam optimization and Genetic, which can have their parameters changed as iterations advance. Convergence can also accelerate this process. Only firefly algorithm can adjust the randomness.

5 Variations of Different Optimization Functions

As firefly algorithm is based on metaheuristic algorithms and firefly algorithm use non-linear updating equations, which can produce rich behavior and high convergence. Firefly algorithm divide the population into many subgroups according to their distance. In this paper two optimization equations have been used to measure the efficiency of the firefly algorithm in different condition weather the firefly algorithms have higher convergence rate then other algorithms or not.

$$minf(x) = 100(x_2 - x_1^2)^2 + (x_1 - 1)^2 \quad [\text{-2.048, 2.048}] \qquad (F_1)$$

$$minf(x) = (x_1 + 2x_2 - 7)^2 + (2x_1 + x_2 - 5)^2 \quad [\text{-10,10}] \qquad (F_2)$$

Here F_1 & F_2 are two random non-linear optimization functions for checking the convergence rate of firefly algorithms by varying randomness strength and population size.

5.1 Confirmation of Objective Functions

In this paper two firefly algorithm equation are simulated by varying two parameters, alpha (α) and the population (n) of the firefly, as firefly algorithm subdivide the population into subgroups according to their distance. Some paper conclude that the Firefly are unisex therefore they are attracted to each other according to their brightness and some conclude that there are both male and female firefly male firefly glow brighter than the female firefly.

$$\beta(r) = \beta_o e^{-\gamma r^2} \qquad (13)$$

There β (r) is variation of activeness, $\beta_o e^{-\gamma r^2}$ is attractiveness (which is suggested 1 in most application) if $\beta_o = 0$ then the firefly walk randomly, if $\gamma = 0$ then firefly reduce to Standard Swarm Optimization [12]. Here max iteration number is taken 100 in all the three cases, when the no. of population of firefly (n) is 10, 50 and 100. The randomness strength α should be between [0,1] but in this paper the value of randomness strength α is varied in to 0.29, 0.83, 0.47, 0.19, 0.91 & 0.54 to check the convergence rate of firefly algorithms in different situations. All the possible case are taken by varying these two parameters and 18 different functions are observed from f_1 to f_{18}.

5.2 Model Parameter Settings

The parameter N stands for the no. of population, α control the randomness strength between {0,1} to check and analysis the best convergence rate and the flexibility of firefly algorithm. The range of randomness into three values {0–0.5}, {0.5–1} & {0–1}. Where as β_o is the attractive constants and the parameter studies suggest that $\beta_o = 1$ is used for many research work and also in most applications, The optimal values for these parameters depend on the specific optimization problem being solved and must be determined through experimentation.

Table 1. Performance comparison of FA with the significant value N = 10.

Function	F_1			Function	F_2		
	α	BestFx	Xnew		α	BestFx	Xnew
f_1	0.29	0.0017	[1.0086,0.5029]	f_4	0.19	0.0011	[1.6882,1.8934]
f_2	0.83	0.0065	[−0.5922,1.4024]	f_5	0.91	0.0270	[8.0693,6.1340]
f_3	0.47	2.6963 e^{-04}	[1.3934,1.7719]	f_6	0.54	0.0038	[−3.2260,4.0472]

Table 2. Performance comparison of FA with the significant value N = 50.

Function	F_1			Function	F_2		
	α	BestFx	Xnew		α	BestFx	Xnew
f_{13}	0.29	$4.3211e^{-06}$	[0.6495, 1.4024]	f_{16}	0.19	1.0445 e^{-04}	[2.7397, 3.0142]
f_{14}	0.83	$7.3634\ e^{-05}$	[1.0790, − 0.3722]	f_{17}	0.91	0.0013	[−3.1754, 0.6403]
f_{15}	0.47	$2.06008\ e^{-06}$	[1.2453, 1.4043]	f_{18}	0.54	3.0861 e^{-04}	[0.6087, 2.7290]

Table 3. Performance comparison of FA with the significant value N = 100.

Function	F_1			Function	F_2		
	α	BestFx	Xnew		α	BestFx	Xnew
f_7	0.29	1.6774 e^{-05}	[1.5832, 1.2293]	f_{10}	0.19	1.5038 e^{-04}	[0.1624, 3.2686]
f_8	0.83	6.3876 e^{-05}	[−0.2083, 0.2311]	f_{11}	0.91	0.0056	[2.6452, − 1.2392]
f_9	0.47	7.4045 e^{-05}	[1.4664, 0.6370]	f_{12}	0.54	8.8176 e^{-06}	[−3.9103, − 1.2611]

5.3 Simulation Results and Analysis

Tables 1, 2, and 3 shows the optimization of all two equations. It includes the randomness strength α, population size N, Best Fx and Xnew position Update. The performance of the equations is demonstrated by varying the randomness and population. In this work, the outcomes of two experimentations are demonstrated in Tables 1, 2 and 3. Figure 2 shows the individual graphs of all the possible cases of all four equations, in some cases when the value of N = 10 then in some cases, the starts from fx and gradually decreases towards 0. Almost all the graph decreases to 0 after 75–80 integration number. And also, in some cases the graph gradually falls then remain constants for some iteration number then gradually falls downs than goes similar to zero.

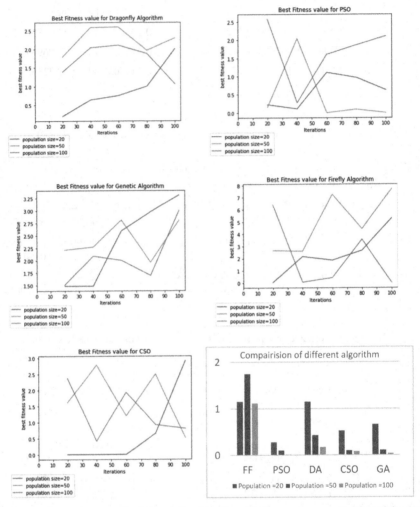

Fig. 2. (a) Comparison graph of dragonfly algorithm (b) Comparison graph of particle swarm optimization algorithm (c) Comparison graph of Genetic algorithm (d) Comparison graph of firefly algorithm (e) Comparison graph of cat swarm optimization algorithm (f) Comparison graph of different algorithm

Here four different algorithms are compared with firefly algorithms Particle Swarm Optimization (PSO), Dragonfly Algorithm (DF), Cat Swarm Optimization (CSO), Genetic Algorithm (GA) with dimension value = 3 and the max iteration is 100. The population size is varying as here the algorithms are compare among themselves for completing scheduling task with respect to time. Population size is varying in three cases 20, 50 and 100. When the population size is 20 then firefly algorithms give best convergent rate as compare to other and then dragonfly algorithms give best fitness value form PSO, CSO and GA and when the population size is increases to 50 then again firefly algorithms give best convergent value from other algorithms and the results shows that when the population is 50 then the firefly algorithms as high convergence rate as compare to other algorithms about 60% to 80% of convergence rate. When the population size is 100 then also firefly gives best fitness value as compare to other algorithms where as other algorithms has very less convergence rate then the firefly nearly 90% of convergence rate. The analysis says that the firefly algorithms has the high convergence rate then other algorithms for solving task scheduling problems as firefly give consistence value in all the population as the firefly has a greater advantage that it divide the large number of population into small subgroups which play a excellence role in solving liner and non-liner optimization problem, the nearer subgroups which are closer to the source firefly are considered and the farer group are eliminated therefore the firefly algorithms give Consistence results as compare to other algorithms.

6 Conclusion and Future Scope

The Firefly method is a swarm intelligence-based optimization method that attempts to tackle challenging optimization problems by imitating the behaviors of fireflies in their flashing patterns. It has shown promising results in solving optimization problems, especially in multi-objective optimization and real-world applications. Finding the global optimum is not always guaranteed because the algorithm's success is highly reliant on the parameters selected and the type of problem being addressed. The algorithm works by simulating the behavior of fireflies, which use their flashing patterns to attract other fireflies for mating. The objective function value is represented by the brightness of each firefly, which in the method provides a solution to the optimization problem. In the search area, fireflies go toward those that are more visible. According to the distance between fireflies and how enticing they are, each firefly's brightness is modified.

Researchers can explore ways to improve the Firefly Algorithm's performance by developing new techniques for updating the brightness and attractiveness of fireflies. The algorithm can be applied to new domains, such as renewable energy optimization, transportation network optimization, and machine learning, to solve complex problems. Several optimization algorithms can be hybridized with the Firefly Algorithm to enhance performance, such as combining it with genetic algorithms, PSO, and DE. With the increasing availability of parallel computing resources, researchers can explore ways to parallelize the algorithm to improve its scalability and speed.

References

1. Devaraj, A.F.S., Elhoseny, M., Dhanasekaran, S., Lydia, E.L., Shankar, K.: Hybridization of firefly and improved multi-objective particle swarm optimization algorithm for energy efficient load balancing in cloud computing environments. J. Parallel Distribut. Comput. **142**, 36–45 (2020)
2. Peng, H., Zhu, W., Deng, C., Wu, Z.: Enhancing firefly algorithm with courtship learning. Inf. Sci. **543**, 18–42 (2021)

3. Arora, S., Kaur, R.: An escalated convergent firefly algorithm. J. King Saud Univ.-Comput. Inf. Sci. **34**(2), 308–315 (2022)

4. Ammari, A.C., Labidi, W., Mnif, F., Yuan, H., Zhou, M., Sarrab, M.: Firefly algorithm and learning-based geographical task scheduling for operational cost minimization in distributed green data centers. Neurocomputing **490**, 146–162. 16 (2022)

5. Shan, J., Chu, S.C., Weng, S.W., Pan, J.S., Jiang, S.J., Zheng, S.G.: A parallel compact firefly algorithm for the control of variable pitch wind turbine. Eng. Appl. Artif. Intell. **111**, 104787 (2022)

6. Czarnowski, I.: Firefly algorithm for instance selection. Procedia Comput. Sci. **192**, 2269–2278 (2021)

7. Wang, H., et al.: Firefly algorithm with neighborhood attraction. Inf. Sci. **382**, 374–438 (2017)

8. Khan, W.A., Hamadneh, N.N., Tilahun, S.L., Ngnotchouye, J.M.: A review and comparative study of firefly algorithm and its modified versions. Optim. Algorithms-Methods Appl. **45**, 281–313 (2016)

9. Mashhour, E.M., El Houby, E.M., Wassif, K.T., Salah, A.I.: A novel classifier based on firefly algorithm. J. King Saud Univ.-Comput. Inf. Sci. **32**(10), 1173–1181 (2020)

10. Yang, X.S.: Firefly algorithms for multimodal optimization. In: Proceedings of the 5th International Symposium on Stochastic Algorithms: Foundations and Applications, vol. 5, pp. 169–178 (2009)

11. Verma, O.P., Aggarwal, D., Patodi, T.: Opposition and dimensional based modified firefly algorithm. Expert Syst. Appl. **44**, 168–176 (2016)

12. Schmid, J., Kieser, L., Hanne, T., Dornberger, R.: Optimizing different parameters of a discrete firefly algorithm for solving the permutation flow shop problem. In: Proceedings of the IEEE Symposium Series on Computational Intelligence, pp. 1–6 (2017)

A Comparative Study on Social Behavior of Tribes and Non Tribes in ITDA Paderu by Using Network Science

S. V. Siva Rama Raju[1] and Shanmuk Srinivas Amiripalli[2(✉)]

[1] Academic Support Department, Abu Dhabi Polytechnic, Abu Dhabi, United Arab Emirates
[2] Department of Computer Science and Engineering, GST, GITAM University, Visakhapatnam, AP, India
shanmuk39@gmail.com

Abstract. This research paper focuses on the challenges faced by tribes in Andhra Pradesh, India, and proposes a methodology to understand their socioeconomic culture, land distribution patterns, and network structures. The study highlights the importance of land for tribal communities and the issues they encounter, such as poverty, health, education, and exploitation. It explores the impact of globalization and liberalization policies on tribes and emphasizes the need for government intervention to improve their quality of life. The proposed methodology involves analyzing land distribution patterns in a tribal family and using graph theory models to study different networks representing tribes living in different areas. The analysis aims to provide insights into the behavior and characteristics of these groups and extract useful information to address their problems effectively. The research also examines the implementation of government schemes in tribal areas and aims to find solutions without encroaching on government lands. The findings of this study highlight the significance of understanding land ownership patterns and network structures to develop appropriate strategies for tribal development. The research contributes to a better understanding of the challenges faced by tribes and emphasizes the role of leadership, traditional conflict resolution methods, and government support in improving the socio-economic conditions of tribal communities.

Keywords: Network Science · Tribe Network · social behavior of tribes · land distribution · socio-economic culture

1 Introduction

1.1 Tribes

Tribes are groups of people who live in locations that are either inaccessible or difficult to reach due to their geographical location. Tribes are considered to be geographically isolated. In the United States, tribal groups are estimated to inhabit somewhere about 15% of the landmass. These communities may be found living in a broad variety of ecological and geoclimatic situations, including plains, woodlands, hills, and even distant regions [1]. They speak a wide range of dialects, and it is possible to hear some of them. In a variety of ways, they are distinct from the more widely spoken Indian languages. They are distinguished by a certain set of skills. Belief systems that seem to have nothing to do with Hinduism despite their widespread use. In tribal settlements may be found members of a great number of different tribes. According to urban legend, this is the first known type of human society to get together to socialize. The negotiation of tribal traditions might prove to be challenging. For purposes of administration, different types of tribes are categorized as either Scheduled Tribes, De-notified Tribes, or Especially Vulnerable Tribes. The progression of members of one tribal group into members of another caste group is referred to as the "tribe-caste continuum." common name; common language; common culture; shared pattern of endogamous conduct; common taboos; presence of different social and political systems; and economic self-sufficiency are all characteristics shared by this group [2]. The Andhra Pradesh tribes come from a variety of cultural backgrounds. In India, many pieces of legislation and constitutional changes have contributed to the process of defining and categorizing the country's different tribes. Since it is a perfect reproduction of the rest of India in terms of the variety of its indigenous peoples and its richness, Andhra Pradesh may be thought of as a miniature version of the whole country. At this time, there are thirty-four distinct tribal groups that are recognized by the state. These recognitions are handled in a different manner by each individual state. The presence of PVTGs has been uncovered in a few of them. All of these many tribes have contributed, in their own unique ways, to India's illustrious cultural history. The cultural resources that are available to tribes provide a wide variety of alternatives for long-term sustenance. Since their social structures, arts and crafts, culinary habits, and a variety of other cultural features serve as identifiers, it is necessary to recognize them. Religion and politics in tribal communities are quite different from those in the mainstream population in many major ways. If you give the tribes of Andhra Pradesh a close look, you'll see that their variety is not just blatant but also able to maintain itself on its own. If we had a greater knowledge and observation of them, we could be better workers, better officials, and most importantly, better people [3]. This applies to all aspects of our lives. During the fifth five-year plan period for the development of tribal communities, the federal government devised a brand new tribal sub-plan strategy. The fundamental objective of the strategy outlined in the sub-plan is to consolidate all of the tribal development programmers, including education, into a unified administrative structure that can be administered by the ITDA (Integrated Tribal Development Agency). In the annals of the history of tribal development, the adoption of the sub-plan strategies for integrated tribal development is seen as a pivotal point. In the Visakhapatnam agency area, the ITDA Paderu is in charge of the educational institutions that fall under the category of formal education [4].

1.2 Major Tribes of Andhra Pradesh

Once the state was divided in 2014, As per 2011 census 26,31,145 scheduled tribes who are classified as Scheduled Tribes living in Andhra Pradesh. It is the home to a number of indigenous people groups, the most notable of which are the Bagatha, Chenchu, Yanadi, and Valmiki. A number of other tribal groups can be discovered in the neighboring states [5]. These groups include the Gond, Kolam, Savara, Khond, Konda Dora, Koya, Lambada, Gadaba, Yerukala, and Porja. Some of the lesser tribal groups that may be found in the neighboring states are the Kattunayakan, Bhil, and Andh. It is possible to classify the Andhra Pradesh tribes into one of two categories, depending on where they make their homes: (1) those who inhabit mountainous and forested regions, and (2) those who reside in the farmland, coexisting with non-tribal people in more traditional communities. The first group contains Savara, Jatapu, Koya, Konda Reddi, Baagata, Mooka Dora, Manne Dora, Reddi Dora, Porja, Khond, Valmiki, Mali, Goud, Kammara, Naikpod, Thoti, Gond, Kolam, Pardhan, and Andh. The second group includes Yerukala, Yanadi, and Sugali among its members (Lambada) [6].

1.3 Problems in Tribes

The article discusses the challenges faced by tribes in India, including poverty, health, education, and exploitation. These problems have been worsened by policies of globalization and liberalization. Land alienation, shift to settled agriculture, forest resource restrictions, and traditional leadership erosion are among the specific issues faced by tribes. The study aims to understand the social behavior of tribes and non-tribes in a particular area and examine the role of government in improving the situation. Leadership plays a crucial role in tribal communities, and tribal movements have helped in negotiating with the government and non-tribal elites. The success of these movements can be evaluated based on the socioeconomic growth of indigenous people [7].

Additionally, the study focuses on various issues faced by tribes such as land alienation, shift to settled agriculture, globalization and indebtedness, educational and health issues, forest resource restrictions, erosion of traditional leadership, alcoholism, an increase in lawsuits, joblessness, technology adaptation, and marketing issues. The research questions are centered around understanding the government's role in improving the lives of tribes, social behavior of tribes and non-tribes in ITDA Paderu, and the reasons behind the occupation of government lands by tribes and their inability to access basic necessities like schools and hospitals [8].

Leadership is an important factor that impacts the social, political, and economic lives of people in every culture. For tribes, leadership is shared, organized by social structure, and maintained by elders through institutional processes for the common survival and welfare of the tribe. During the colonial era, tribes were among the most exploited social groups, leading to conflicts with the state, moneylenders, and non-tribal land-owning elites. Tribal movements played a vital role in negotiating with the government, non-tribes, and the market, leading to the socio-economic growth of indigenous people. Overall, the study highlights the challenges faced by tribes and the need for the government to address these issues and improve their quality of life.

2 Literature Review

Land is a natural resource that is essential to human survival. The right to life is guaranteed by the Indian Constitution to every person. The right to life also includes the right to have land on which to live and make a living, which is protected by Indian law.

People's reliance on land provides them with a secure source of income (unless some environmental crises result in crop failures). For the vast majority of people, land is not just a source of income, but also a symbol of social rank, identity, security, and self-reliance [9–12]. And for the vast majority of indigenous peoples, their whole worldview, way of life, and livelihood are centered on their land. It is impossible for them to fathom their physical and cultural life without it. However, in tribal regions, such property is often forcedly taken for "public use" and development. This section aims to define the practice of land purchase and land acquisition laws in tribal territories in this context. The collective ownership of land and other resources distinguishes tribal communities. Tribal have faced difficulties as a consequence of increasing land demand and the state's acknowledgment of private property ownership. Land ownership disputes are becoming more common among tribe members, among members of other tribes, and between tribal and non-tribal. The existing institutional procedures for resolving these disputes needed to be updated and adapted to the new conditions. It is necessary to comprehend and enhance the function of traditional conflict resolution methods. The difficulty that tribals experience when collective ownership of land and community norms of succession are not acknowledged by the state when land purchase is required, or when forest laws and regulations are implemented, needs sympathetic attention [13]. Detail land distribution of three families are discussed in Fig. 1, Fig. 2 and Fig. 3.

It was recognized that land rights were critical for tribal, who had no formal claims to the land they and their ancestors had been farming until then and had therefore always been vulnerable to eviction under different pretexts. It was also recognized that tribal land rights may protect them against moneylenders and landlords who want to enslave them economically. The administrative procedures and directives provided to the officials tasked with looking after tribal welfare resulted in a shift in public perception of the tribes. The extortion of unlawful fees from villages by lesser government employees such as forest guards or police constables was halted, or at least substantially reduced, simply by enforcing tighter discipline. It didn't take long for the situation to improve dramatically. For centuries, tribes have successfully managed their natural and communal resources. It is for us to consider if, if they can manage a large forest area or natural resources, tap resources for their needs with minimal reliance on markets, especially contemporary ones, managing modern structures and institutions established by the government should be challenging. The truth is that the new community structures and resources do not fit into tribal cultures culturally. The new buildings have a low feeling of ownership. Traditional community resources are maintained by individuals who rely on their culture's Traditional Knowledge systems. They've been living in harmony with their surroundings for a long time. Indeed, their stewardship and management abilities highlight their vast knowledge systems of their resources. They are great defenders and consumers of resources since they are immersed in the world of nature and resources. Their ancient way of living has wisdom. Acceptance of new resources and proper management by them are dependent on our understanding of their culture, community structures, and attempts to engage them in the early phases [14].

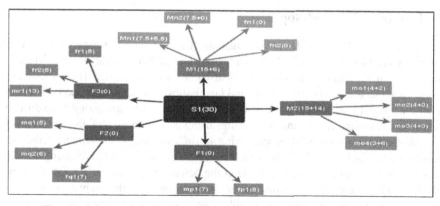

Fig. 1. Kondiba family (Tribe living in tribe area) and their land acquisition.

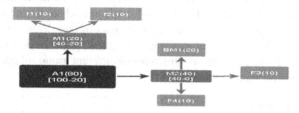

Fig. 2. Kollu family Tree(Non Tribe living in tribe area) and their land acquisition.

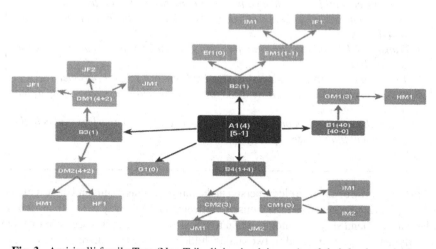

Fig. 3. Amiripalli family Tree (Non Tribe living in plain area) and their land acquisition.

3 Proposed Methodology

The first phase of the research involves analyzing the land distribution patterns in a tribal family in Visakhapatnam's ITDA Paderu region. The study highlights the importance of land for the tribe's survival and how it is distributed based on gender. The research aims to examine the socioeconomic culture and land issues of tribal people and their socioeconomic and cultural backgrounds. The second phase involves analyzing three different networks - Kondiba, Kollu, and Amiripalli - using graph theory models. The networks represent different groups of people living in different areas, including a tribe area, non-tribe area, and non-tribe living in a tribe area. The analysis involves using standard network science parameters to understand the behavior of different groups of people. The third phase involves extracting useful information from the graphs to understand the behavior of different groups of people. The analysis aims to provide insights into the structural properties and characteristics of the networks. The fourth phase involves utilizing the extracted information to solve problems faced by tribes and help the government plan better approaches. The research aims to analyze the implementation of government schemes in tribal areas for the betterment of their lives without occupying government lands. Overall, the research highlights the importance of understanding the land ownership patterns and network structures of different groups of people to develop effective solutions for their problems.

Proposed Algorithm

1. *Start.*
2. *Select three families, one from a tribe area and two from non-tribe areas.*
3. *Gather complete information on each family member, their relationships, and land details.*
4. *Transform the gathered data into tree and graph theory models to facilitate further analysis.*
5. *Analyze the resulting graphs using standard network science parameters.*
6. *Extract useful information from the graphs to understand the behavior of different groups of people.*
7. *Utilize the extracted information to solve problems faced by tribes and help the government plan better approaches.*
8. *Stop.*

In the below tree s1 is the eldest person in the family, he has 2 sons and three daugters' m1, m2, f1, f2, f3 respectively. S1 himself cultivated around thirty acres. In most of the tribe families, land share will not be given to female children. In this scenario total land of thirty acres was distributed to two male Childers each with a share of fifteen acres. As we all know that tribes are isolated and they are inherited from their ancients as farming because of these two reasons they cultivate land for their basic earnings. The basic principal tribes will follow, if more number of children is present in a family, they need more food and money to survive, so they occupy nearby government lands and start converting hills into cultivations lands. The other important observation is a family with more number of male children will occupy more land for their feature use. In the above tree m1 has two male children and he occupied around six acres of government land, whereas on the other side m2 has four male children he occupied fourteen acres of land. In the next level of tree mn1 has occupied 5.5 acres of land because he has only one male child. Similarly, mn2 was an educated person and has migrated from their place to urban area and doing a respectable job, so his official share was 7.5 acres and there is no future expansion of land in that area because he was migrated. Similarly, m2 sons are mo1, mo2, mo3, mo4 occupied 2,3,3,6 acres of land respectively. In the last level of the tree gives information of each person's land of s1 family. Initially s1 has thirty acres of land on document. In the first step we consolidate the land occupied by s1 male generations are m1 children property is (13 + 7.5) and m2 children property is (6 + 7 + 7 + 9). Total land in official was 30 acres and unofficial was around 20 acres, combindly both official and unofficial was around 50 acres. Above discussion shows clearly land is directly proportional to male children in family; more number of male children will occupy more government lands for their survival. Finally, s1 family has a total land both from male and female generations is 114.5 acres. In Figs. 4, 5 and 6 shows represent the family relations of members in each family (Fig. 7).

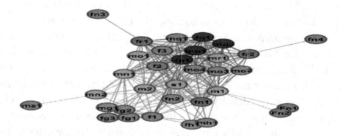

Fig. 4. Kondeba family Graph network representation

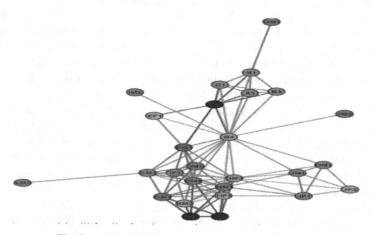

Fig. 5. Amiripalli family Graph network representation

The Table 1 compares three different networks - Kondiba, Kollu, and Amiripalli - with respect to various parameters such as nodes, edges, average degree, diameter,

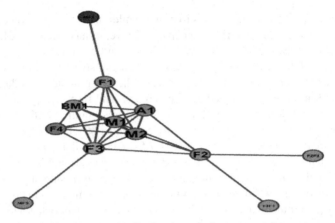

Fig. 6. Kollu family Graph network representation

graph density, modularity, average cluster coefficient, average path length, between-ness centrality, authority, closeness centrality, cluster coefficient, degree, eccentricity, eigenvector centrality, harmonic closeness centrality, hubs, modularity class, number of triangles, and weighted degree. On analysis, it can be observed that the Kondiba and Kollu networks have similar characteristics in terms of average degree, diameter, modularity, and average cluster coefficient. However, the Amiripalli network has a lower average degree, lower graph density, higher modularity, and lower average cluster coefficient compared to the other two networks.In terms of betweenness centrality, authority, closeness centrality, cluster coefficient, degree, eccentricity, eigenvector centrality, harmonic closeness centrality, and hubs, Kollu has the highest values for most parameters, indicating that it has a more centralized structure. Kondiba and Amiripalli have similar values for most parameters in this category.Modularity analysis shows that Kondiba has a higher proportion of nodes in modularity class 0, while Amiripalli has a higher proportion of nodes in modularity class 1.Overall, the table provides a comprehensive comparison of the three networks' characteristics, highlighting their similarities and differences in terms of structural properties.The average cluster coefficient is high for all three graphs, indicating that nodes tend to form clusters and have connections to nearby nodes.The average path length is relatively short for all three graphs, indicating that the nodes are well connected to each other.The betweenness centrality of nodes in Kollu is the highest among the three graphs, indicating that certain nodes in Kollu play a more important role in the network's connectivity than in the other two graphs. The degree of nodes in Kollu is also relatively low compared to the other two graphs, suggesting that the network in Kollu may be more decentralized, with fewer highly connected nodes. The modularity of the three graphs also differs significantly, with Amiripalli having the highest modularity. This suggests that the communities in Amiripalli are more tightly connected within themselves, and less connected to nodes in other communities. The hubs in all three graphs are similar in terms of their percentage of nodes with the highest degree, indicating that the network structure of the three graphs is relatively similar in this aspect. Overall, the three graphs show similarities in terms of their high cluster coefficients, short average path lengths, and relatively low betweenness centrality and

Table 1. Comparison of tribe and non-tribe characteristics

Parameters	Kondiba	Kollu	Amiripalli
Nodes	33	12	27
Edges	231	29	103
Average Degree	14	4.833	7.63
Diameter	4	4	4
Graph density	0.438	0.439	0.293
Modularity	0.151	0.108	0.333
Avg Cluster coefficient	0.784	0.754	0.753
Avg Path length	1.691	1.803	1.986
Betweeness centrality (max) %	30.3	41.61	33.33
Betweeness centrality (min) %	3.03	8.33	3.7
Authority (max) %	9.09	16.67	11.11
Authority (min) %	3.03	8.33	3.7
Closeness centrality (max) %	24.24	25	11.11
Closeness centrality (min) %	3.03	8.33	3.7
Cluster coefficient (max) %	17.86	37.5	21.74
Cluster coefficient (min) %	3.57	12.5	4.35
degree (max) %	15.15	33.33	14.81
degree (min) %	3.03	8.33	3.7
Eccentricity (max) %	72.73	41.67	66.67
Eccentricity (min) %	9.09	25	3.7
Eigenvector centrality (max) %	9.09	16.67	11.11
Eigenvector centrality (min) %	3.03	8.33	3.7
Harmonic closeness centrality (max) %	18.18	25	11.11
Harmonic closeness centrality (min) %	3.03	8.33	3.7
Hubs (max) %	9.09	16.67	11.11
Hubs (min) %	3.03	8.33	3.7
Modularity class 0	51.52	75	37
Modularity class 1	48.48	25	25
No of triangles (max) %	17.86	50	21.74
No of triangles (min) %	3.57	12.5	4.35
Weighted degree (max) %	15.15	33.33	14.81
Weighted degree (min) %	3.03	8.33	3.7

Anova: Single Factor

SUMMARY

Groups	Count	Sum	Average	Variance
Kondiba	32	664.274	20.75856	1759.136
Kollu	32	607.027	18.96959	288.2391
Amiripalli	32	477.645	14.92641	451.591

ANOVA

Source of Variation	SS	df	MS	F	P-value	F crit
Between Groups	571.3261	2	285.663	0.342937	0.710576	3.094337
Within Groups	77467.96	93	832.9888			
Total	78039.28	95				

Fig. 7. Anova Test

hub percentages. However, differences in modularity and degree centrality suggest that the network structures of the three graphs are not identical.

4   Conclusion

The first part of research describes a case study of a tribal family's land ownership, showing how the number of male children directly correlates to the amount of land owned. The second phase was analyzing the characteristics of three different networks - Kondiba, Kollu, and Amiripalli of tribe, non-tribe living in tribe, non-tribe in non-tribe area respectively based on various parameters such as average degree, diameter, and modularity. The Kondiba and Kollu networks exhibit similar characteristics, while Amiripalli has a lower average degree and higher modularity. Kollu has the highest values for most parameters related to centrality, suggesting a more centralized structure. The average cluster coefficient is high for all three graphs, while the average path length is relatively short. The modularity and degree centrality of the three graphs differ significantly. Overall, the two research provide insights into tribal land ownership and network analysis on demonstrate the importance of understanding structural properties and characteristics.

References

1. Sinha, A., Sinha, S.: Land rights and indigenous people in India: a critical analysis of policies and practices. Land Use Policy **84**, 194–204 (2019)
2. Ghosh, A.: Tribal land alienation and livelihood sustainability in India: a study on forest-dependent communities. Indian J. Agric. Econ. **73**(3), 356–370 (2018)
3. Das, D., Ghosh, P.: Dispossession of tribal lands: an analysis of forest land acquisition in India. Econ. Pol. Wkly **53**(29), 63–71 (2018)
4. Kujur, A.: Land alienation and livelihood crisis among the tribal communities of Jharkhand, India. Econ. Anthropol. Dev. 75–89 (2017). Springer, Singapore
5. Siva Rama Raju, S.V., Nagaraja Rao, I.H.: Complementary nil vertex edge dominating sets. Proyecciones (Antofagasta) **34**(1), 1–13 (2015)
6. Bhattacharya, S.: Land alienation, dispossession, and livelihood vulnerability: a case study of tribal communities in West Bengal, India. J. Land Rural Stud. **4**(1), 27–46 (2016)
7. Fernandes, W.: Tribal land alienation in India: a historical perspective. Indian J. Hist. Sci. **50**(4), 535–545 (2015)

8. Mohanty, M., Gupta, A.: Socio-economic determinants of tribal land alienation: a case study from Odisha, India. J. Rural. Stud. **34**, 52–59 (2014)

9. Rama Raju, S.V., Nagaraja Rao, I.H.: Global neighbourhood domination. Proyecciones (Antofagasta) **33**(1), 25–41 (2014)

10. Pathak, D., Choudhury, H.: Land alienation and livelihood security of tribal women in Odisha, India. Indian J. Gender Stud. **20**(3), 379–396 (2013)

11. Mahapatra, N.D.: Land alienation and tribal livelihoods: a study of the Dongria Kondh tribe in Odisha, India. Anthropol. Today **28**(4), 6–10 (2012)

12. Das, D.: Land alienation among the tribal communities of Odisha, India. Contrib. Indian Sociol. **45**(1–2), 105–128 (2011)

13. Siva Rama Raju, S.V., Nagaraja Rao, I.H.: Semi-complementary graphs. Thai J. Math. **12**(1), 175–183 (2013)

14. Tanguturi, M.R., et al.: An analytical ethnographic analysis of Kondareddi tribe in India. Particularly Vulnerable Tribal Groups (PVTGs). Imper. J. Interdisc. Res. (IJIR) **2**(18) (2016)

Raster Big Data Processing Using Spark with GeoTrellis

Smiti Kothari[1], Jayneel Shah[1], JaiPrakash Verma[1(✉)] (iD), Sapan H. Mankad[1], and Sanjay Garg[2]

[1] Institute of Technology, Nirma University, Ahmedabad, India
{20BCE280,20BCE105,jaiprakash.verma,sapanmankad}@nirmauni.ac.in
[2] CSE Department, Jaypee University of Engineering and Technology, Raghogarh–Vijaypur, India

Abstract. The accessibility of the Internet and Geographic Information Systems (GIS) has significantly affected how people live their daily lives. These systems use various GIS data, which can be categorized into two types: raster data and vector data. When working with continuous data types such as elevation and satellite imagery, raster data proves to be more useful. However, existing methods for processing such data involve converting raster data to vector data, resulting in a loss of details, decreased accuracy, and alterations to the original data. This research focuses on finding ways to improve the processing and analysis of large raster datasets without compromising precision or causing significant loss. In the proposed solution, the capabilities of GeoTrellis and Docker are utilized. GeoTrellis, with its support for various raster data storage formats and ability to process data without conversion, is well-suited for handling large-scale data processing. By using Docker to distribute computation across a cluster, the solution is able to efficiently process complex tasks within a reasonable timeframe. Additionally, a collection of algorithms is offered within the proposed system architecture to handle data. The effectiveness of processing raster data is demonstrated through a use case put into practice in this paper.

Keywords: Geotrellis · Raster Data · Big Data · Hadoop · Spark · Docker · Geo-spatial

1 Introduction

There are two types of spatial datasets: vector datasets and raster datasets [1]. Vector datasets contain data about spatial entities, such as their position and shape in space [2]. On the other hand, raster datasets provide detailed information about the spatial or spatiotemporal distribution of variables like temperature, elevation, and population density [3]. They are typically represented as large 2D, 3D, or 4D arrays of numerical data [4]. Raster data is best suited for documenting, evaluating, and visualizing continuous data such as elevation, temperature, or radiation levels. It uses a uniform grid-like pattern with cells or pixels to represent the data, with each cell's size indicating the resolution of the raster [5].

© The Author(s), under exclusive license to Springer Nature Switzerland AG 2024
S. K. Panda et al. (Eds.): CoCoLe 2023, CCIS 1892, pp. 260–271, 2024.
https://doi.org/10.1007/978-3-031-56998-2_22

Big data is commonly characterized by three properties: volume, variety, and velocity [6]. The sheer size of modern datasets makes it challenging to manage them using traditional database administration techniques [7]. Big data refers to vast datasets that cannot be efficiently handled by regular software tools and storage systems [8]. For example, the Planet's constellation of over 200 satellites collects 1.4 million photos daily, resulting in petabytes of satellite photography and earth observation data each year [9, 10]. Organizations like the Intergovernmental Panel on Climate Change (IPCC) generate simulated raster datasets that can reach petabytes in size [11]. High-resolution satellites with spatial resolutions of less than a meter are used to identify various ground objects using remotely sensed raster data, contributing to the large volumes of data [12]. These volumes are due to the high spatial resolution and wide swath coverage.

Raster data processing can be complex and time-consuming, especially with large datasets. Big data analytics offers several benefits in this regard. Firstly, it enables faster and more efficient analysis of large datasets, saving time and resources [13]. Secondly, it uncovers hidden patterns and trends that may go unnoticed by the human eye, providing valuable insights for decision-making [14]. Thirdly, big data analytics utilizes advanced computational techniques and algorithms to extract valuable insights and trends from large volumes of data [15]. This approach can be applied to raster data processing to identify patterns, forecast future trends, and guide decision-making processes. Additionally, big data analytics helps identify and resolve errors or inconsistencies in the data, enhancing overall accuracy and reliability.

Performing raster data processing in a big data environment without converting it to GeoJSON offers advantages. Converting grid cells to polygons and using GeoJSON can result in information loss and spatial discontinuity. Working with large datasets can cause performance degradation with GeoJSON, which is slower compared to binary formats.

Geotrellis is an open-source Scala library for raster data [16]. It efficiently handles large-scale raster data processing and provides a comprehensive set of tools for working with raster data. We utilized cluster computing, a parallel processing method, to process raster data. In a cluster computing environment, each machine performs tasks independently while remaining connected to others. GeoTrellis leverages the Spark and Akka frameworks, making it ideal for large-scale data processing tasks.

The paper's main objective was to not convert raster data to GeoJSON but rather utilize large raster datasets and cluster computing for distributed processing. The Geotrellis application was containerized using Docker, enabling easy management and scalability. To meet increased processing demands, the cluster's node count was expanded. Additionally, a use-case was implemented to demonstrate efficient raster data processing.

2   Related Work

The above papers have employed K-Nearest Neighbours (KNN) and Geotrellis approach or have applied a transformation to the GeoJSON format for handling raster datasets. Our methodology differs from these works because we process and analyse raster data at scale using Geotrellis, Apache Spark, and Docker as infrastructure. In order to distribute the workload among the systems, we have also used cluster computing.

Table 1. Related Works

Reference	Objective	Methodology	Dataset	Finding	Limitation
[17](Zhenlong Li et al.)	To create a scalable and efficient tool for analyzing large scale climate data online that could handle terabytes of data	The unified data model approach was used for storing both array based and record based data in HDFS	NASA-MEERA and GHCN-Daily	It gives a new way to climate data analysis by bridging the gap between fixed interfaces and computer programming	It will be a great effort to select the dataset that best fits a particular principle or theory
[18](Vincent Moreno et al.)	To use GeoTrellis and Spark to develop a cloud service based on raster data on the Hupi Platform	The NDVI stats for each tile were stored. A MultiBand GeoTiff was created	GeoTiff Images downloaded from USGSEarth Explorer	To create a full cloud service in HUPI which is capable of working with raster data using Geotrellis and Spark	Elbow method used for finding the optimal number of clusters is not precise and accurate
[19](N Zhou et al.)	To identify the polycentric structure, various functions and the influence areas of the entire city	The big data is collected and then identification on polycentric structure is done	Chongqing's main city POI data	It examines the spatial arrangement and polycentric spatial features of various elements	Time and art data was not considered in this approach of urban planning
[20](Hansub Shin et al.)	Finding which distributed storage engine is better suited with GeoSpark	Experimental environment based on Amazon EMR was setup	NaturalEarth Dataset	Caching improves overall performance of spatial data processing in distributed environments	General queries were not considered

(continued)

Table 1. (*continued*)

Reference	Objective	Methodology	Dataset	Finding	Limitation
[21](Shahed Bassam Almobydeen et al.)	Newdesignof GeoSPARQL queryprocessing solution	Coverage to RDF mapping solutions were defined using already existing W3C standards	Digital Elevation Model (DEM) of Galicia with 100 m of spatial resolution	Using W3C standards for effective conversion of coverages to RDF mapping	GeoSPARQL syntax and knowledge of RDF, W3C standards was required
[22](Halil Ibrahim Caner et al.)	Determination of risk assessment method based on spatial distribution characteristics	A new framework is employed	Landsat 8 Operational Land Imager (OLI) data	Pollution risk assessment can be done effectively	Preprocessed data was greatly extrapolated

3 Proposed Approach

3.1 Problem Definition

There is a need for processing raster data without converting it into GeoJSON images to preserve precision and minimize loss. Large raster datasets cannot be efficiently handled by a single machine. Traditional centralized computing models are unable to meet the growing demand for accurate processing and analysis of the increasing amount of raster data generated by sensor networks and other sources. This research explores the use of cluster computing to improve the speed and effectiveness of real-time raster data processing and aims to identify potential implementation challenges.

3.2 Proposed Solution

Through an analysis of research papers, it was found that GeoTrellis is adept at processing large raster datasets quickly. GeoTrellis' capability for large-scale data processing, support for various raster data storage formats, and ability to handle raster data without conversion to GeoJSON make it an ideal solution. By integrating GeoTrellis with Docker, computation can be distributed across a cluster, leveraging container caching to enhance performance. This scalable approach enables efficient processing of complex tasks across multiple machines within a reasonable timeframe. The use case presented in this paper demonstrates the application of GeoTrellis and Landsat data in performing NDVI, NDWI, and NDSI computations, along with data ingestion and visualization on a world map.

3.3 Proposed System Architecture

Raster data collected from USGS Earth Explorer is used to analyze the proposed architecture. The data from Landsat-8 has been utilized for the usecase. For the experimental analysis, Landsat-8 images of various sizes were used, including a dimension of 3600*3600 Landsat data with a resolution of 30 m. The architecture used in this paper is displayed in Fig. 1 and Fig. 2. Following is the description of various components used in this architecture: The Docker daemon operates as a background process on each node in the swarm and manages the containers on that node. The Docker CLI facilitates the generation, distribution, and control of swarms. Docker Swarm is utilized to manage the cluster state and reconcile it with an ideal state. The Swarm manager oversees the activities of the nodes, enabling seamless scaling and management of application workloads.

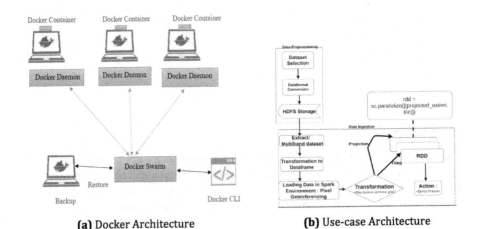

(a) Docker Architecture   (b) Use-case Architecture

Fig. 1. Proposed Architecture

by integrating multiple Docker containers onto a single cluster. The approach prefers Gossip Network over Kubernetes as the preferred container orchestration system due to it's dynamic scaling capability and smooth interaction with containers. Whenever a new container or task is created within the cluster, the gossip mechanism notifies all other containers in a specific overlay network about the existence of the new container.

4 Methodology and Concepts

This section provides a description of the various technologies, mathematical models, and algorithms employed to achieve the objective.

4.1 Technology

The technologies employed in this project are Geotrellis and Docker. Geotrellis, a Scala library, enables easy processing of large raster datasets. Scala, a programming language that utilizes the Java Virtual Machine (JVM), combines objectoriented and functional programming paradigms. Its support for functional programming facilitates the expression of complex algorithms for raster data manipulation. Running on the JVM provides GeoTrellis with a high-performance, cross-platform runtime environment and access to a vast ecosystem of libraries and tools for seamless integration. The Scala Build Tool (sbt) is used in the GeoTrellis project for managing dependencies, libraries, and frameworks. Sbt's capabilities include building, running, and testing Scala projects, allowing for efficient parallel processing tasks and rapid iterations. It also provides a Scala interpreter for automating the build and deployment process, which is beneficial for large projects and deploying applications to different environments. Apache Spark, a data processing framework, can be used independently or in conjunction with other tools for distributed computing. It facilitates distributing data processing tasks across multiple machines and executing operations on large datasets. Spark's primary data structure is Resilient Distributed Datasets (RDD), which partitions datasets logically to enable computations on cluster nodes. Geotrellis can utilize Apache Spark in a distributed setting to leverage raster data. Docker, a containerization platform, bundles applications and their dependencies into containers for seamless functionality. It simplifies scaling and deployment of the Geotrellis application and allows for installation on any platform with Docker. Docker containers enable easy deployment across various environments for development, testing, and production purposes. They also enhance performance by distributing data and tasks across different systems when working with large datasets.

4.2 Mathematical Models

Mathematical equations are crucial for understanding and modeling the behavior of raster data. Equations and derivatives offer a powerful means of describing and analyzing relationships among different variables in raster data. The use case presented in this paper involves calculating the normalized difference vegetation index (NDVI), water index (NDWI), and snow index (NDSI).

The Normalized Difference Vegetation Index (NDVI) is used to identify vegetation.

$$NDVI = (NIR - Red)/(NIR + Red) \tag{1}$$

where NIR stands for Near Infrared.

It serves as a gauge for the quantity of greenery that is visible in the image or its relative density.

The Normalized Difference Water Index (NDWI), is used to identify water bodies.

$$NDWI = (Green - NIR)/(Green + NIR) \tag{2}$$

Water bodies emit minimal radiation and are highly absorbent in the visible to infrared range. Therefore, the Normalized Difference Water Index (NDWI) utilizes the green and near-infrared bands of the image. The Normalized Difference Snow Index (NDSI) is used to identify the presence of snow and ice.

$$NDSI = (Green - SWIR1)/(Green + SWIR1) \tag{3}$$

where SWIR stands for Short Wave Infrared.

The Normalized Difference Snow Index (NDSI) uses a standardized ratio of the reflectance difference between specific bands. This index takes advantage of the distinct signature and spectral differences to distinguish snow from nearby features, including clouds. Two datasets, Landsat 8 and Sentinel 2, were utilized for the calculations. In Landsat 8, band B4 represents red, band B3 represents green, band B5 represents near-infrared, and band B6 represents shortwave infrared. Similarly, in Sentinel 2, band B4 represents red, band B3 represents green, band B8 represents near-infrared, and band B9 represents shortwave infrared. For masking purposes, Landsat 8 includes a Quality Assessment (QA) band, while Sentinel 2 includes a True Color Image (TCI) band.

4.3 Algorithms for Proposed Execution Flow

This section describes the workflow, which includes various main classes, and begins with the pre-processing of raster data. This is followed by the calculation of NDVI, NDWI, and NDSI. Further, we perform ingestion of this data and finally serve it on a world map. Algorithm 1 gives the pseudo-code for the implementation of the use case.

Algorithm Pseudo Code

1: Initialize the constants to differentiate the bands to be used. Use the SinglebandGeoTiff method to read the red, green, NIR, SWIR, and QA bands from their respective files. Provide the path of each band file as input.

2: After reading the bands, the GeoTiffs are converted to tiles. We define a function that performs a bitwise AND operation on a tile to detect clouds and cirrus clouds. If either is present, the input tile's value is assigned to the output tile instead of "NODATA".

3: Create a multiband tile by utilizing the masked red, green, NIR, and SWIR bands with the ArrayMultibandTile method. Lastly, generate a multiband GeoTiff file from the multiband tile using the MultibandGeoTiff method and save it.

4: Calculate NDVI, NDWI, and NDSI values using the combineDouble method. Render the images with the RenderImage method using the specified color map. Save the PNG images to disk.

5: The input image is read as a single image RDD using the hadoopMultibandGeoTiffRDD method.

6: Find the closest zoom level to the source image resolution using TileLayerMetadata. Cut the image into tiles using the Tiler and a floating layout scheme. Reproject the tiles to WebMercator using a predefined tile size and the "reproject" method.

7: Create an attribute store with "FileAttributeStore" and save the tiles using "FileLayerWriter". Use Pyramid.upLevels to pyramid up zoom levels and write the tiles to the file system. Delete the existing layer before writing.

---

5 Execution and Implementation

In this section, we have described the dataset, the preprocessing of data, the flow of execution and the frameworks used.

5.1 Dataset Selection

A region is chosen as an Area of Study from the USGS Earth Explorer with the product type: Landsat8. Images of Gujarat regions are taken for experimental.

Fig. 2. Area of Study

purposes. A Landsat-8 high dimensional data of 3660 X 3660 is used at 30m resolution for experimental analysis. Images are downloaded in the GeoTiff format and stored locally. Various other sites such as Vedas[1], ArcGIS[2], LandsatLook[3] can be used for downloading Landsat8 images. Different regions can be selected based on the experimental analysis.

5.2 Data Preprocessing

Data preprocessing is crucial for raster data processing as it prepares the data in a format that is easily analyzable and interpretable. In this project, we utilized the cloud masking approach for preprocessing raster data. Clouds can hinder image analysis and generate unreliable results, hence the need for cloud masking. The procedure is detailed in Algorithm 1 of Sect. 4.3. Since Geotrellis exclusively supports the GeoTiff file format, it is advantageous to have the dataset in that format.

5.3 Execution Flow

The process begins with installing the required software versions and checking for compatible dependencies. Geotrellis is then installed, followed by running the Scala Build Tool (sbt) to start a Scala interpreter. The "run" command displays the six main Scala classes. The first step involves running a Scala file to mask the bands, serving as the

---

[1] https://vedas.sac.gov.in/en/

[2] https://www.arcgis.com/apps/mapviewer/index.html

[3] https://landsatlook.usgs.gov/

preprocessing stage. Subsequently, calculations for NDVI, NDWI, and NDSI are performed, and the results are visualized on a world map. These steps are detailed in the paper's algorithm. All of the above mentioned steps can be executed within a Docker container. Similar to a virtual machine, the container can operate in any environment. It can be exported as a tar file and imported into different operating systems, seamlessly transferring dependencies and content.

5.4 Framework Configuration

This section outlines the distributed environment configuration utilized in this work. The setup comprises four computing nodes, with one node serving as both the master and slave, while the remaining nodes solely function as slaves. The hardware structure consists of two nodes equipped with 32 CPU cores and two nodes with 16 CPU cores. In terms of RAM, there are two nodes with 64GB each and two nodes with 32GB. For storage, two nodes offer 4TB of hard drive space each, while the other two provide 1TB. The software configuration employed in this proposed work includes:

– Java 1.8.0.
– HADOOP 3.0.2.
– Apache SPARK 3.3.0.
– Scala 2.11.12.
– sbt 1.2.0.
– Geotrellis 3.5.1

6 Results and Discussion

The paper evaluates the application of Geotrellis, a Big Data methodology that reduces data loss and accelerates image ingestion. The time required for image ingestion in the dataset is summarized in Table 2. The results of the discussed use case are presented below. The implemented use case calculates NDVI, NDWI, and NDSI. The following images demonstrate the ingestion process in a specific region of Gujarat. The outcomes are summarized as shown in Fig. 3.

Table 2. Time taken for masking and ingestion

Size of data(in MB)	Masking Time(in sec)	Ingestion Time(in sec)
9.1	75	134
30.7	66	128
98.2	89	234
281.9	267	270
331.6	153	189

(*continued*)

Table 2. (*continued*)

Size of data(in MB)	Masking Time(in sec)	Ingestion Time(in sec)
610.4	1426	299
900.9	3340	512
1010.7	4213	601

The graph compares dataset size and total processing time, deduced from Table 2. As observed from the table, both the masking time and ingestion time increase as the data size grows. However, the increase is neither exponential nor linear; rather, it appears to follow a parabolic trend. This study utilized pre-processed information from areas in Gujarat to address geospatial analysis, remote sensing, and land management-related challenges. The raw input data was modified to region of interest along with the pixel value. The combination of Geotrellis and Docker proved to be an effective solution, as Docker facilitated data distribution and job processing across multiple platforms (Fig. 4).

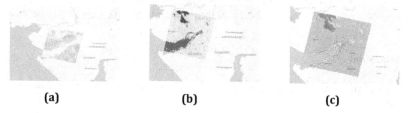

(a)   (b)   (c)

Fig. 3. Ingestion of NDVI, NDWI,NDSI on areas of Gujarat

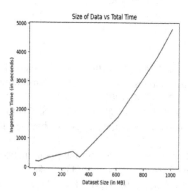

Fig. 4. Size of Data vs Total Time

7   Conclusion and Future Work

The paper introduces the Geotrellis framework for analyzing large-scale geospatial raster data within a Docker container, providing system independence. Testing was conducted on two nodes in both Hadoop and Spark clusters, demonstrating effective operation within these frameworks. Tile-based processing is employed to reduce the load on the computer cluster, rather than analyzing the entire dataset. The impact of the default block size in Hadoop (128 MB) on masking time for files of different sizes is highlighted in Table 1. Notably, the total time for a 9 MB file is higher compared to a 30 MB file. Adjusting the default size in Hadoop can address this issue. Similarly, the time significantly increases for a 610 MB file, which can be mitigated by increasing the number of nodes. Future work aims to expand the node count and compare masking times for different file sizes to evaluate the efficiency of this strategy. Additionally, future work will involve comparing the efficiency of the model with other state-of-the-art models, such as KNN. Furthermore, the plan is to upgrade the cluster with commodity hardware and test the system on diverse datasets.

Acknowledgement. This work was supported by the Indian Space Research Organisation (ISRO), Government of India, under the RESPOND program. Also thankful to ISRO focal person Mr. Ghansham Sangar and Mr. Pankaj Bodani for their constant support during project development.

Declaration

Conflicts of Interests. The authors declare that there are no conflicts of any sort associated with the paper.

Data Availability Statement. Data sharing is not applicable to this article as no datasets were generated or analyzed during the current study.

References

1. Singla, S., Ahmed, E., Diao, T., Mukhopadhyay, A., Scudiero, E.: Experimental study of big raster and vector database systems. In: 2021 IEEE 37th International Conference on Data Engineering (ICDE), pp. 2243–2248 (2021)
2. Sabi'u, N., Muhammed, S.N., Zakaria, N., Khalil, M.S.: Vector data model in GIS and how it underpins a range of widely used spatial analysis techniques. Dutse J. Pure Appl. Sci. 1(1), 122 (2015)
3. Carrera-Hern´andez, J.J., Gaskin, S.J.: Spatio temporal analysis of daily precipitation and temperature in the Basin of Mexico. J. Hydrol. 336(3–4), 231–249 (2007)
4. Villarroya, S., Viqueira, J.R.R., Cotos, J.M., Taboada, J.A.: Enabling efficient distributed spatial join on large scale vector-raster data lakes. IEEE Access 10, 29406–29418 (2022)
5. Pingel, T.: The raster data model. Geograph. Inf. Sci. Technol. Body Knowl. (2018)
6. Zikopoulos, P., Eatonm, C.: Understanding big data: analytics for enterprise class hadoop and streaming data. McGraw-Hill Osborne Media (2011)
7. Hammad, K.A.I., Fakharaldien, M.A.I., Zain, J., Majid, M.: Big data analysis and storage. In: International Conference on Operations Excellence and Service Engineering, pp. 10–11 (2015)

8. Purcell, B.: The emergence of" big data" technology and analytics. J. Technol. Research **4**, 1 (2013)
9. Boshuizen, C., Mason, J., Klupar, P., Spanhake, S.: Results from the planet labs flock constellation (2014)
10. Camara, G., Assis, L.F., Ribeiro, G., Ferreira, K.R., Llapa, E., Vinhas, L.: Big earth observation data analytics: matching requirements to system architectures. In: Proceedings of the 5th ACM SIGSPATIAL International Workshop on Analytics for Big Geospatial Data, pp. 1–6 (2016)
11. Yang, C., Huang, Q., Li, Z., Liu, K., Fei, H.: Big Data and cloud computing: innovation opportunities and challenges. Int. J. Digital Earth **10**(1), 13–53 (2017)
12. Dambach, P., Sie, A., Lacaux, J.-P., Vignolles, C., Machault, V., Sauerborn, R.: Using high spatial resolution remote sensing for risk mapping of malaria occurrence in the Nouna district, Burkina Faso. Glob. Health Action **2**(1), 2094 (2009)
13. Elgendy, N., Elragal, A.: Big data analytics: a literature review paper. In: Advances in Data Mining. Applications and Theoretical Aspects: 14th Industrial Conference, ICDM 2014, St. Petersburg, Russia, July 16–20, 2014. Proceedings 14, pp. 214–227. Springer (2014)
14. Li, C., Chen, Y., Shang, Y.: A review of industrial big data for decision making in intelligent manufacturing. Eng. Sci. Technol. Int. J. **29**, 101021 (2022)
15. Naeem, M., et al.: Trends and future perspective challenges in big data. In: Pan, J.-S., Balas, V.E., Chen, C.-M. (eds.) Advances in Intelligent Data Analysis and Applications. SIST, vol. 253, pp. 309–325. Springer, Singapore (2022). https://doi.org/10.1007/978-981-16-5036-9_30
16. Kr¨amer, M., Gutbell, R., Wu¨rz, H.M., Weil, J.: Scalable processing of massive geodata in the cloud: generating a level-of-detail structure optimized for web visualization. AGILE: GIScience Series 1, 10 (2020)
17. Li, Z., Huang, Q., Jiang, Y., Fei, H.: SOVAS: a scalable online visual analytic system for big climate data analysis. Int. J. Geogr. Inf. Sci. **34**(6), 1188–1209 (2020)
18. Moreno, V., Nguyen, M.T.: Satellite image processing using spark on the HUPI platform. In: TORUS 2–Toward an Open Resource Using Services: Cloud Computing for Environmental Data, pp. 173–190 (2020)
19. Zhou, N.: Research on urban spatial structure based on the dual constraints of geographic environment and POI big data. J. King Saud Univ. Sci. **34**(3) (2022)
20. Shin, H., Lee, K., Kwon, H.-Y.: A comparative experimental study of distributed storage engines for big spatial data processing using GeoSpark. J. Supercomput. 1–24 (2022)
21. Almobydeen, S.B., Viqueira, J.R.R., Lama, M.: GeoSPARQL query support for scientific raster array data. Comput. Geosci. 159, 105023 (2022)
22. Caner, H.I., Aydin, C.C.: Shipyard site selection by raster calculation method and AHP in GIS environment, Iskenderun, Turkey. Marine Policy **127**, 104439 (2021)

Energy Aware Effective Task Offloading Mechanism in Fog Computing

Niva Tripathy[✉] and Sampa Sahoo

C V Raman Global University, Bhubaneswar, Odisha, India
tripathy.niva456@gmail.com

Abstract. Fog computing has emerged as a promising paradigm for extending the capabilities of the cloud closer to the edge of the network, enabling efficient processing and analysis of data generated by Internet of Things (IoT) devices. With the proliferation of resource-constrained IoT devices and the need for real-time and low-latency applications, task offloading has become a critical technique in fog computing to optimize resource utilization and improve overall system performance. Energy consumption is a crucial aspect in fog computing environments due to the limited power resources available at the edge devices. Efficiently managing energy consumption is essential to ensure prolonged device operation and minimize environmental impact. Our proposed work focuses on the research and development of energy-aware task offloading techniques considering the execution time in fog computing. The proposed energy-aware task offloading techniques aim to provide a comprehensive solution for fog computing environments, enabling energy-efficient operation, improved system performance, and enhanced sustainability. We have evaluated our proposed method through experimental simulations and the results shows that our method has a significant effect on task offloading in fog computing environment on reducing the execution time and energy consumption.

Keywords: Task offloading · execution time · IoT · fog computing · energy efficiency · decision making algorithm

1 Introduction

Fog computing has emerged as a prominent paradigm that brings cloud-like capabilities closer to the edge of the network, enabling efficient processing and analysis of data generated by Internet of Things (IoT) devices. The exponential growth of IoT devices [1, 2] and the increasing demand for real-time and low-latency applications have placed significant challenges on fog computing systems, particularly in terms of resource constraints and energy consumption.

Energy consumption is a critical concern in fog computing environments due to the limited power resources available at the edge devices [3, 4]. These devices, such as sensors, actuators, and mobile devices, often operate on battery power or have limited access to charging facilities. Therefore, managing energy consumption becomes paramount

S. K. Panda et al. (Eds.): CoCoLe 2023, CCIS 1892, pp. 272–284, 2024.
https://doi.org/10.1007/978-3-031-56998-2_23

to ensure prolonged device operation, reduce battery replacements, and minimize the environmental impact associated with increased energy consumption.

Task offloading has emerged as a key technique in fog computing to optimize resource utilization and improve system performance [5]. By offloading computationally intensive tasks from edge devices to nearby fog nodes or the cloud, the energy burden on the edge devices can be alleviated, allowing them to operate more efficiently and extend their battery life. Moreover, task offloading enables efficient utilization of computational resources available in fog nodes and the cloud, which often possess more processing power and energy resources.

While task offloading presents numerous advantages in fog computing, energy efficiency has become a critical consideration in the decision-making process [6]. Simply offloading tasks without considering the energy consumption implications can lead to suboptimal resource allocation and may even exacerbate energy consumption in the system. Therefore, there is a pressing need to develop energy-aware task offloading techniques that intelligently consider both the energy consumption characteristics of edge devices and the requirements of offloaded tasks.

The objective of this study is to address the challenge of optimizing energy consumption while meeting application requirements and minimizing latency in fog computing environments. This research explores various aspects of energy-aware task offloading, including energy profiling of edge devices, workload characterization, decision-making algorithms, and energy-efficient resource allocation.

By developing comprehensive energy-aware task offloading techniques[7, 8], we can not only enhance the energy efficiency of fog computing systems but also improve overall system performance and prolong the operational lifespan of resource-constrained edge devices. These advancements have the potential to benefit a wide range of domains, including smart cities, industrial automation, healthcare, and transportation, where fog computing plays a crucial role in enabling real-time and resource-efficient applications.

The rest of this paper is organized as follows: In Sect. 2 shows the related work. Section 3 illustrate a detailed architecture of fog computing, task offloading in fog layer, task offloading objective and task offloading metrics. Section 4 depict the mathematical formulation of our proposed method. Section 5 refers the simulation setting and result analysis. Finally Sect. 6 explain the conclusion and future scope.

2 Related Work

This section provides a summary of the major works on fog offloading procedures.

Liu et al. [9] proposed an energy-aware task offloading mechanism for edge-cloud computing. The authors developed an optimization model that considered both the energy consumption of edge devices and the energy consumption of cloud servers. They proposed a hybrid genetic algorithm to find the optimal task offloading strategy that minimizes energy consumption while meeting task deadlines and resource constraints.

Sampa et al. [10] proposed An auction-based edge resource allocation mechanism for IoT-enabled smart cities is a method used to efficiently allocate computing resources in a distributed edge computing environment. In this mechanism, multiple edge computing nodes compete for the available computing resources through an auction process.

Chen et al. [11] proposed an energy-aware task offloading framework that considers the energy consumption characteristics of IoT devices and the communication cost between devices and fog nodes. The authors presented a task offloading algorithm based on dynamic programming to minimize the overall energy consumption while meeting application latency constraints.

Wang et al. [12] focused on energy-aware task offloading in cloudlet-enabled mobile cloud computing environments. The authors proposed a task offloading algorithm that considered both the energy consumption of mobile devices and the energy consumption of cloudlets. The algorithm aimed to minimize the overall energy consumption by dynamically determining the optimal offloading decisions based on the available resources and energy constraints.

An energy-aware task offloading framework for mobile cloud computing was presented by Mao et al. [13]. The authors introduced an optimization model that jointly considered energy consumption, task execution time, and data transmission cost. They proposed a particle swarm optimization (PSO) algorithm to find the optimal task offloading decisions that minimize energy consumption while satisfying application requirements.

Mao et al. [14] proposed an energy harvesting fog devices called green fog computing system. This system follow an effective task offloading stagey. The proposed system only consider the current system state. Wu et al. [15] proposed a queuing theory based model for effective task offloading. The proposed model utilises the response energy matric to calculate the trade-off between energy consumption, cost and delay minimization.

Most of the previous works only study a kind of offloading strategy and framework in cloud computing. In this paper, we propose a novel fog computing model, and energy aware task offloading strategy.

3 Fog Computing

3.1 Architecture of Fog Computing

The three-tier architecture in an IoT fog computing environment enables efficient data processing, real-time decision-making, and resource optimization by distributing the computational load across different layers. It combines the benefits of edge computing and cloud computing, allowing for local processing at the edge, reducing network congestion, improving response times, and preserving bandwidth, while leveraging cloud resources for more complex tasks and long-term storage. The proposed architecture, seen in Fig. 1, is made up of three layers: cloud, fog, and IoT or user device [16]. The system provides federated and integrated cloud services to consumer electronics IoT via a regulated layer fog. Fog nodes, as seen in Fig. 1, comprise gateways, routers, edge processors, core networks, and regional access points. The entire fog deployment may be located locally in the fog architecture. This means that the fog services may be hosted by automation or a firm with a single office building, or they can be allocated to a regional or partial area that sends data to the central services and systems.

Each active edge node in the architecture is autonomous and self-diagnoses to ensure that facility service procedures continue uninterrupted. Each layer is added sequentially:

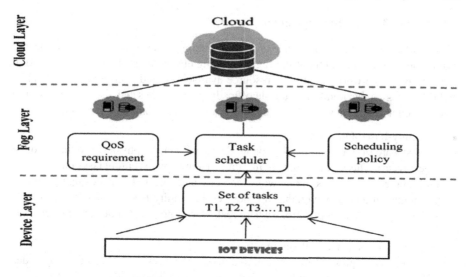

Fig. 1. Architecture of Fog Computing

1. Cloud layer is the top tier in the architecture and represents the cloud infrastructure. It consists of remote data centers that provide extensive computational resources, storage capacity, and advanced data analytics capabilities. The cloud tier acts as a centralized resource pool for processing large-scale data, performing complex data analytics, and long-term storage. It handles tasks that require significant computational power or historical data analysis, which may not be feasible at the fog tier due to resource constraints.

2. Fog layer is also known as the intermediate tier and is situated between the edge tier and the cloud tier. It consists of fog nodes or fog servers that are deployed closer to the edge devices. These fog nodes have higher computational capabilities, storage capacity, and communication capabilities compared to edge devices. The fog tier performs local data processing, data aggregation, and filtering, reducing the amount of data that needs to be sent to the cloud for further processing. It enables real-time analytics, decision-making, and resource provisioning closer to the edge, reducing latency and network congestion.

3. Devices Layer is responsible for providing computing services to a large number of consumer devices. As a result, each user's device is only given a certain amount of computational resources. The device layer is the lowest tier in the architecture and represents the edge devices and sensors deployed in the IoT ecosystem. These devices are responsible for collecting real-time data from the physical world and performing initial processing or filtering of the data. Edge devices can include sensors, actuators, wearables, and other IoT endpoints. They have limited computational resources, storage capacity, and power constraints. The edge tier acts as the interface between the physical world and the fog layer.

3.2 Task Offloading Strategy in Fog Layer

It's important to note that the choice of task offloading strategy depends on the specific requirements and constraints of the fog computing environment, including application characteristics, network conditions, resource availability, and energy constraints [17]. Hybrid strategies that combine multiple offloading approaches can also be employed to achieve better performance and resource utilization in fog computing environments.

- Proximity-based Offloading:

  Tasks are offloaded to nearby fog nodes based on their physical proximity to the edge devices. This strategy aims to minimize latency by executing tasks closer to the data source. It considers the network topology and selects fog nodes that have low communication latency with the edge devices. Proximity-based offloading is suitable for latency-sensitive applications where real-time or near real-time responsiveness is critical.

- Computation-intensive Offloading:

  Tasks that require significant computational resources are offloaded to fog nodes or the cloud to leverage their higher processing power. This strategy is effective when edge devices have limited computing capabilities or when tasks require complex computations. Computation-intensive offloading helps distribute the computational load and optimize the utilization of resources in the fog computing environment.

- Energy-aware Offloading:

  Tasks are offloaded from energy-constrained edge devices to more energy-efficient fog nodes or the cloud. This strategy aims to conserve energy in edge devices by leveraging the computational resources of fog nodes or the cloud. Energy-aware offloading considers the energy consumption characteristics of devices and fog nodes, offloading tasks to locations with lower energy consumption or longer battery life.

- QoS-aware Offloading:

  Tasks are offloaded based on their Quality of Service (QoS) requirements. This strategy considers metrics such as response time, reliability, and availability. QoS-aware offloading ensures that tasks are offloaded to execution locations that can meet their QoS requirements. It takes into account the performance capabilities of fog nodes and the cloud to provide the desired QoS guarantees.

- Cost-aware Offloading:

  Tasks are offloaded considering the cost implications of execution and data transmission. This strategy takes into account factors such as fog node deployment costs, cloud usage costs, and network communication costs. Cost-aware offloading aims to minimize overall costs by selecting offloading locations that provide a balance between cost and performance.

- Context-aware Offloading:

  Tasks are offloaded based on contextual information such as network conditions, device capabilities, and application requirements. This strategy considers dynamic factors that can influence task offloading decisions. Context-aware offloading takes into account real-time information to adaptively select offloading locations that best suit the current context and optimize overall system performance. Offloading seems inevitable because of physical constraints on the devices, such as storage, processing power, and dedicated bandwidth.

Offloading is necessary for all types of computing, including fog, edge, and mobile clouds. The operations that use the greatest amount of resources include virus scanning, searching, image processing, computational decision-making, and artificial intelligence. Computation offloading refers to the process of moving computationally demanding application components to a remote server. Current descriptions of some computation offloading possibilities for mobile applications use a variety of methodologies. But there are still certain problems with computation offloading methods. Offloading appears to be an excellent way to meet the demands of mobile systems' response time as applications get more complex, according to a considerable body of research on offloading choices to save energy and increase performance [18]. There are numerous uses for offloading. In order to meet deadlines, unloading may also be necessary. Applications that combine numerous real-time computations use a tremendous amount of energy. By shifting the workloads to resources with more capacity, offloading, which requires computationally complex calculations, can get around real-time constraints. Saving electricity could be a further justification for unloading. Energy consumption places severe restrictions on some services, such as mobile devices. Smartphone's can be used for more than simply voice calls; in addition to browsing the internet and downloading movies and games, they can also be used for other activities. Mobile devices as a result require more power and have shorter battery lives. The demand for cell phone power has not been met despite ongoing advancements in battery technology. Offloading could lengthen the battery's life by transferring energy-intensive tasks from consumer electronics to computers [19]. Offloading computation can ease storage, application quality, and standby time constraints. Six categories of recent research on compute offloading for cloud/fog computing on phone carriers have been identified.

Task Offloading Objectives

Offloading objectives Offloading algorithms attempt to reduce power consumption while taking into account the availability of fog resources, compute gain, and communication costs [20].

- Latency Reduction:
    One of the primary objectives of task offloading in fog computing is to minimize the latency experienced by applications. By offloading tasks from edge devices to nearby fog nodes, data processing and decision-making can be performed closer to the data source. This reduces the round-trip time for data transmission to the cloud and back, resulting in lower latency and improved real-time responsiveness.
- Bandwidth Optimization:
    Task offloading in fog computing also focuses on optimizing the bandwidth utilization in the network. By performing data processing and analytics at the fog layer, only relevant information or summarized results are transmitted to the cloud, reducing the amount of data transferred. This conserves network bandwidth and minimizes congestion, especially in scenarios with limited network capacity or intermittent connectivity.
- Energy Efficiency:
    Energy efficiency is a crucial objective in task offloading within fog computing environments. By offloading computationally intensive tasks from energy-constrained edge devices to more resourceful fog nodes, the energy consumption of

the edge devices can be reduced. This helps to prolong the battery life of devices and optimize energy usage in the overall system.

- Scalability:

    Task offloading in fog computing aims to improve system scalability by distributing the computational load across multiple fog nodes. By leveraging the computational resources available in the fog layer, tasks can be efficiently executed in parallel, accommodating a larger number of devices and applications. This enables the fog computing system to scale up and handle increasing workloads effectively.

- Contextual Awareness:

    Task offloading in fog computing considers the contextual information associated with tasks and devices. Contextual factors, such as network conditions, device capabilities, application requirements, and user preferences, are taken into account when making offloading decisions. This enables intelligent and context-aware task distribution, ensuring that tasks are offloaded to the most suitable fog nodes based on the prevailing conditions.

- Quality of Service (QoS):

    Maintaining the desired Quality of Service is an important objective in task offloading. The fog computing environment aims to meet application-specific requirements such as response time, reliability, security, and data privacy. By intelligently offloading tasks to appropriate fog nodes, the system can optimize QoS parameters and ensure that applications perform as expected.

Steps Involved for Task Offloading in Fog Layer

The task offloading process in the fog layer typically involves several steps and it is represented in Fig. 1. Here are the general steps involved in task offloading:

- Task Analysis: The first step is to analyze the tasks generated by the device. This analysis includes understanding the computational requirements, data dependencies, resource constraints, and any specific performance objectives of the tasks. This step helps in determining which tasks are suitable for offloading.
- Decision Making: Based on the analysis, a decision needs to be made on whether to offload a particular task or not. This decision can be influenced by factors such as device capabilities, network conditions, fog node availability, and the task's offloading feasibility. Various offloading strategies, as mentioned earlier, can be employed to make this decision.
- Offloading Preparation: If the decision is made to offload a task, the task needs to be prepared for offloading. This involves packaging the task along with any required data, dependencies, and metadata for transmission to the fog node. The task may also need to be partitioned or modified to ensure compatibility with the fog node's execution environment.
- Fog Node Selection: The next step is to select the appropriate fog node for offloading the task. This selection can be based on various criteria, such as proximity, load balancing, context-awareness, energy efficiency, cost, or QoS requirements. The fog node should have the necessary resources and capabilities to execute the offloaded task efficiently.

- Task Offloading: Once the fog node is selected, the task is transmitted from the device to the fog node over the network. This transmission may involve data transfer, code migration, or a combination of both, depending on the nature of the task. The offloaded task is then executed on the fog node, leveraging its computational capabilities.
- Result Aggregation: After task execution, the results or output generated by the fog node are collected. If required, these results can be transmitted back to the device for further processing or presentation. Result aggregation may involve data consolidation, analysis, or any necessary post-processing steps.
- Task Completion and Evaluation: The offloaded task is considered completed once the results are obtained. The device can now resume its normal operations or proceed with subsequent tasks. The performance of the offloading process can be evaluated based on various metrics, such as response time, energy consumption, resource utilization, or QoS achieved.

Task Offloading Metrics

Offloading statistics are required to evaluate the offloading procedures. They are known as qualitative metrics. Papers use a number of qualitative indices, such as energy, delay, consumption, and throughput. The following are the most important quantitative measures for unloading in cloud computing:

1. Energy consumption: The amount of energy wasted in the network that can be reduced by an effective offloading mechanism
2. Execution time: The time required to run a piece of code is referred to as execution time. It takes into consideration routing time, migration time, and s actually time.
3. Cost: The amount of money necessary to order the activity is referred to as the cost.
4. Resource utilization: The amount to which network resources, such as bandwidth, connections, memory use, and CPU, are utilized.
5. Reaction time: Response time is the length of time it takes for a servers to react to a call or approve a task.
6. Throughput: The volume of data delivered from one site to another within a specific time period is referred to as throughput.

4 Mathematical Formulation

Let there are F_n numbers of fog nodes where n $= \{1, 2..f\}$. These fog nodes have properties like F_{id} represents the ID of the fog nodes. F_{cap} represents the computational capacity of the fog nodes. F_{bw} represents the available BW of the fog nodes. F_{eng} represents the energy consumption of the fog nodes while executing the task. $F_{process}$ represents the processing cost of the unit data in fog nodes.

Let there are T_i number of task generated from the IoT layer where i $= \{1, 2...t\}$. These individual task is having some properties like T_{size} is the data size of the task, T_{exe} is the execution time required by the task to complete the execution on a fog node. T_{eng} is the energy consumption by the task while processing. T_upload_{eng} is the unit energy consume by the task while transferring from IoT layer to fog nodes.

Our main aim in this article is to save the energy while reducing the execution time of the task.

4.1 Execution Time Analysis

Execution time is the important indicator for the effective task offloading scheme. Task execution time can be divided into two parts for task offloading process.

Transmission time i.e. T_{trans} represents the time required to transmit the task and associated data from the IoT device to the fog node. It depends on the data size, available bandwidth. The transmission time can be calculated using the following formula:

$$T_{trans} = T_{size} / F_{bw} \qquad (1)$$

Execution time i.e. T_{exe} it refers to the time required by a task to perform the execution on fog nodes. The Execution time can be calculated using the following formula:

$$T_{exe} = T_{size} / F_{cap} \qquad (2)$$

At last the time overhead for task offloading is

$$Time\_total = T_{size} / F_{bw} + T_i / F_{cap} \qquad (3)$$

As said previously the main focus of task offloading is to reduce the task execution time, for that the task execution time will be less than the threshold value i.e.

$$Time_{threshold} > Time\_total \qquad (4)$$

4.2 Energy Consumption Analysis

Energy is another important part which must be considered while making decision for task offloading. In the task offloading process energy is generated in several forms. In this article we have considered energy consumption of the task transferred and energy consumption by the fog node while executing the task.

Energy consumption by transferring the task from IoT devices to fog nodes is calculated as

$$Task\_energy_{upload} = T_{size} * T\_upload_{eng} \qquad (5)$$

Energy consumption of the fog nodes while processing the task is calculated as

$$Task\_energy_{execute} = T_{exe} * F_{eng} \qquad (6)$$

So the energy consumption of task offloading process is

$$Total\_energy = Task\_energy_{upload} + Task\_energy_{execute} \qquad (7)$$

For effective task offloading the execution energy consumption should meets the following condition i.e.

$$Energy_{threshold} > Total\_energy \qquad (8)$$

Proposed Offloading Method

We have proposed an effective task offloading algorithm which will off load the task generated from various IoT devices to the fog nodes using some threshold value. By comparing the execution time with the threshold value we will decide the task offloading process from IoT to fog nodes. By this the energy consumption of the Fog nodes will reduce.

Algorithm 1: Effective task offloading strategy

Input: F_n, T_i
Output: F_{id}
Initialize: $Time_{threshold}$, $Energy_{threshold}$

    1. for $n=1$ to f do
    2.   for $i=1$ to t do
    3.   Calculate *Time_total* using euation (3)
    4.   Calculate *Total_energy* using equation (7)
    5.   if $Time_{threshold}$> *Time_total* && $Energy_{threshold}$> *Total_energy*
    6.   Assign T_i to F_n
    7.   else
    8.   Continue
    9.   end for
    10. end for
    11. return F_{id}

5   Simulation and Result Analysis

5.1   Simulation Setting and Performance Matrix

For effective simulation of our proposed method we have taken matlab 8.3 on IBM server with Intel core I5,eight core 2.60 GHz CPU and 32 G of RAM. The simulation consists of three steps. One is data collection step, second is uploading the collected data to the fog nodes, the final step is to execute the transfer data on the fog nodes. For performance evaluation we have considered two performance metrics one is average execution time $Time_{avg}$ i.e. calculated as

$$Time_{avg} = \sum_{i=1}^{t} Time\_total / t \tag{9}$$

where t is the total number of task transfer from IoT Layer to fog nodes. This metric represents the efficiency of task completion i.e. by lowering the execution time of the task the efficiency of the task allocation is higher.

Next performance metric is average energy consumption Eng_{avg} i.e. calculated as

$$Eng_{avg} = \sum_{i=1}^{t} Total\_energy / t \tag{10}$$

where *Total_energy* is the energy consumption by the task transferred from IoT layer to fog nodes. This metric represents that with less energy consumption the task offloading will be effective.

5.2   Comparison Result

For checking the effectiveness of our proposed method we have compared our mode with two existing policies that are random offloading policy [4] where the task transfer to the fog nodes are randomly placed for execution on the fog nodes and dynamic offloading policy [14] where dynamically the fog nodes capacity will be computed then the task will be transfer to the fog nodes with less delay.

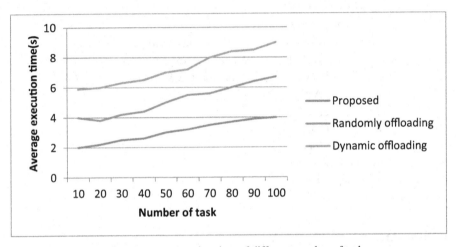

Fig. 2. Average execution time of different number of tasks

Figure 2 shows that with increase the number of task the average execution time of random offloading and dynamic offloading will increase while the proposed scheme will have a decrease in average execution time. It shows that the proposed scheme is better perform and the efficiency is high. The method randomly offloads a task to a cloud node, which is relatively blind method. Sometimes there's a long wait, so it also doesn't work very well either. Dynamic offloading policy is more scientific to select the target node, but the process is complex and time-consuming, so the results are not the best. Our proposed policy considers various factors, and special emphasis on the cost of a variety of time. So its results are ideal.

Figure 3 shows the average energy consumption of the number of task transferred from IoT to fog nodes. For every offloading policy, the average energy consumption is basically stable, and the performance of the proposed policy is obviously superior. Random offloading policy and dynamic offloading policy adopt offloading policy, so it can get better results. However, both the two methods do not take into account the energy consumption factor in the offloading policy; therefore, their performance is not the best.

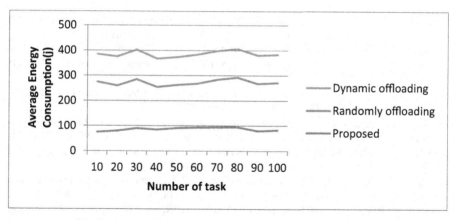

Fig. 3. Average energy consumption of different number of tasks

6 Conclusion

In conclusion, energy-aware task offloading in fog computing is a critical research area that addresses the challenges of optimizing energy consumption while meeting application requirements in resource-constrained edge environments. This paper has explored the concept of energy-aware task offloading in fog computing and highlighted the importance of considering energy efficiency in the decision-making process. The experimental evaluations and case studies conducted in the field have shown promising results, indicating the potential of energy-aware task offloading in fog computing. By considering the energy consumption characteristics of edge devices, communication costs, task requirements, and available computational resources in fog nodes, it is possible to make intelligent offloading decisions that minimize energy consumption while ensuring timely task execution and optimal resource utilization. In future this work can be extended using machine learning and artificial intelligence for more intelligent and adaptive solution.

References

1. Zhou, A., et al.: On cloud service reliability enhancement with optimal resource usage. IEEE Trans. Cloud Comput. **4**(4), 452–466 (2014)
2. Zhou, A., et al.: Cloud service reliability enhancement via virtual machine placement optimization. IEEE Trans. Serv. Comput. **10**(6), 902–913 (2016)
3. Gelenbe, E., Lent, R.: Energy–QoS trade-offs in mobile service selection. Future Internet **5**(2), 128–139 (2013)
4. Wu, H., Wang, Q., Wolter, K.: Tradeoff between performance improvement and energy saving in mobile cloud offloading systems. In: Proceedings of the IEEE International Conference on Communications Workshops, pp. 728–732 (2013)
5. Panda, S.K., Nanda, S.S., Bhoi, S.K.: A pair-based task scheduling algorithm for cloud computing environment. J. King Saud Univ. Comput. Inf. Sci. **34**(1), 1434–1445 (2022)
6. Panda, S.K., Jana, P.K.: An energy-efficient task scheduling algorithm for heterogeneous cloud computing systems. Clust. Comput. **22**(2), 509–527 (2018). https://doi.org/10.1007/s10586-018-2858-8

7. Chang, Z., et al.: Dynamic resource allocation and computation offloading for IoT fog computing system. IEEE Trans. Ind. Inform. **17**(5), 3348–3357 (2020)
8. Wang, S., et al.: Joint optimization of task offloading and resource allocation based on differential privacy in vehicular edge computing. IEEE Trans. Comput. Soc. Syst. **9**(1), 109–119 (2021)
9. Liu, X., et al.: An energy-aware offloading framework for edge-augmented mobile RFID systems. IEEE Internet Things J. **6**(3), 3994–4004 (2018)
10. Sahoo, S., et al.: An auction based edge resource allocation mechanism for IoT-enabled smart cities. In: 2020 IEEE Symposium Series on Computational Intelligence (SSCI). IEEE (2020)
11. Chen, C.A., Won, M., et al.: Energy-efficient fault-tolerant data storage and processing in mobile cloud. IEEE Trans. Cloud Comput. **3**(1), 28–41 (2015)
12. Xu, X., Wu, Qi., He, C., Wan, S., Qi, L., Wang, H.: Edge computing-enabled resource provisioning for video surveillance in internet of vehicles. In: Wang, G., El Saddik, A., Lai, X., Martinez Perez, G., Choo, K.-K. (eds.) iSCI 2019. CCIS, vol. 1122, pp. 128–140. Springer, Singapore (2019). https://doi.org/10.1007/978-981-15-1301-5_11
13. Li, J., Dai, M., Su, Z.: Energy-aware task offloading in the Internet of Things. IEEE Wirel. Commun. **27**(5), 112–117 (2020)
14. Mao, Y., Zhang, J., et al.: Dynamic computation offloading for mobile-edge computing with energy harvesting devices. IEEE J. Sel. Areas Commun. **34**(12), 3590–3605 (2016)
15. Wu, H., Wolter, K.: Tradeoff analysis for mobile cloud offloading based on an additive energy-performance metric. In: Proceedings of the International Conference on Performance Evaluation Methodologies and Tools, pp. 90–97 (2014)
16. Hussein, M.K., Mousa, M.H.: Efficient task offloading for IoT-based applications in fog computing using ant colony optimization. IEEE Access **8**, 37191–37201 (2020)
17. Aljumah, A., Kaur, A., Bhatia, M., Ahamed Ahanger, T.: Internet of Things-fog computing-based framework for smart disaster management. Trans. Emerg. Telecommun. Technol. **32**(8), e4078 (2021)
18. Pereira, P., Araujo, J., Melo, C., Santos, V., Maciel, P.: Analytical models for availability evaluation of edge and fog computing nodes. J. Supercomput. **77**(9), 9905–9933 (2021). https://doi.org/10.1007/s11227-021-03672-0
19. Ahmed, M., Mumtaz, R., Zaidi, S.M.H., Hafeez, M., Zaidi, S.A.R., Ahmad, M.: Distributed fog computing for Internet of Things (IOT) based ambient data processing and analysis. Electronics **9**(11), 1756 (2020)
20. Liu, J., Wang, S., Zhou, A., et al.: Availability-aware virtual cluster allocation in bandwidth-con - strained datacenters. IEEE Trans. Serv. Comput. **13**(3), 452–436 (2017)

Application of Multi-criteria Decision-Making Methods to Select Multi-objective Optimization Based Pareto-Optimal Solutions

Puja Yuvaraj Patil and Sujit Das[✉]

Department of Computer Science and Engineering, NIT Warangal, Hanamkonda,
India
ppcs21214@student.nitw.ac.in, sujit.das@nitw.ac.in

Abstract. This study examines the utilization and comparison of four distinct techniques for multi-criteria decision-making (MCDM). The aim is to select the most favorable pareto-optimal solution derived from multi-objective optimization (MOO). Initially, the set of pareto-optimal solutions is obtained using the fast non-dominated sorting genetic algorithm (NSGA-II). Next, we apply four MCDM techniques such as weighted sum (WS), weighted product (WP), quadratic weighted sum (QWS) and TOPSIS to determine the ranking of the pareto-optimal solutions. This study presents two case studies to demonstrate the comparative analysis of four MCDM techniques on the pareto-optimal solutions. First case study is related with scientific workflow where the cost to perform the scientific workflow should be minimized and reliability should be maximized. Second case study focuses to solve the multi-objective travelling salesman problem (TSP) where the objective is to minimize the costs between two cities. Experimental analysis shows that TOPSIS method outperforms the other three MCDM methods for both of the case studies.

Keywords: MCDM · pareto-optimal solutions · multi-objective optimization · TSP

1 Introduction

Multi-objective optimization (MOO) is employed in resolving real-life problems that involve considering multiple objectives to determine the ultimate outcome. Unlike single objective optimization, MOO yields a set of solutions as the final result. Superiority of a solution in single objective optimization is measured using fitness value, whereas dominance degree is used to measure the same for MOO. One solution dominates other solution if it is strictly better than the other solution for at least one objective function whereas for other objective functions it is not poor than the second one. When a particular set of solutions in the solution set does not have any other solutions that dominate them, they are referred to as pareto-optimal or non-dominated solutions. These pareto-optimal

© The Author(s), under exclusive license to Springer Nature Switzerland AG 2024
S. K. Panda et al. (Eds.): CoCoLe 2023, CCIS 1892, pp. 285–296, 2024.
https://doi.org/10.1007/978-3-031-56998-2_24

solutions are regarded as the final result. Any solution from the set of pareto-optimal solutions can be considered acceptable, as none of the solutions in the non-dominated set are superior to the others. Having domain knowledge and considering various problem-related factors are essential when deciding between different solutions. When dealing with real-world applications, however, one of these pareto-optimal solutions must be chosen, either by a decision maker or by a suitable method.

Multi-criteria decision-making (MCDM) techniques are well known for selecting the best solution from the set of given solutions based on the presence of multiple numbers of criteria. Researchers have successfully applied MCDM techniques in various sectors including engineering, economic, and social to obtain the desired output. Because there are multiple criteria and a variety of solutions within the set of pareto-optimal solutions, MCDM techniques are employed to determine the optimal solution. The weighted sum method (WSM), which is the earliest and most widely used MCDM method, is applied in this context [4]. The WSM, also known as the additive model, is a straightforward approach for combining multiple criteria. Weighted product (WP) method [4] was developed to resolve the difficulties associated with WSM also known as the multiplicative model. Yoon and Hwang introduced an alternative decision-making method called the technique for order of preference by similarity to ideal solution (TOPSIS) [4]. This method identifies the optimal solution by evaluating its distance from the ideal solution. The underlying principle of TOPSIS is that the selected alternative should be the closest to the positive ideal solution while being the farthest from the negative ideal solution.

In [5], an initial approach to address multi-objective optimization problems was introduced. The author proposed the vector evaluated genetic algorithm (VEGA), which was the first genetic algorithm specifically designed for MOO. VEGA was a direct expansion of the simple genetic algorithm; however, it exhibited a bias towards certain pareto-optimal solutions. To eliminate the biasness of VEGA, Shrinivas et al. [6] proposed non-dominated sorting genetic algorithm (NSGA) based on Goldberg's suggestion. NSGA resolved the bias observed in VEGA by evenly distributing the population across the entire pareto-optimal region. NSGA was used successfully to find the multiple pareto-optimal fronts but it was computationally expensive with time complexity $O(MN^3)$, where M represent the number of objectives, and N represent the population size. In order to address the time complexity challenges associated with NSGA, Deb et al. [1] introduced a non-dominated sorting-based multi-objective evolutionary algorithm (MOEA) known as non-dominated sorting genetic algorithm II (NSGA-II). Which dissolved the disadvantages of NSGA with improved time complexity of $O(MN^2)$, where M represent the number of objectives, and N represent the population size. NSGA-II is considered to be the fast algorithm which can be used to compute the pareto-front [7]. Relying on the computational power of NSGA-II, many researchers used it to solve a wide variety of complex practical problems [2]. In their research, Musavi et al. [8] applied NSGA-II to investigate a multi-objective sustainable hub location scheduling problem within the context of a perishable food supply chain. Wang et al. [9,10] applied NSGA-II to propose various MOO based application to solve chemical engineering problems. In their study, Ribeiro et al. [11] used five distinct MCDM techniques, including WS, WP, TOPSIS, PROMETHEE, and GPPI, to evaluate the non-dominated set of solutions. The objective was to select the optimal machine learning models for addressing the drinking water quality monitoring problem. They claimed that application of MCDM techniques over the pareto-optimal solutions can yield better solutions. However, the authors have performed their experiment on spherical pruning based multi-objective differential evolution (spMODE-II).

As per our knowledge, none of the researchers have experimented the impact of MCDM techniques over NSGA-II based pareto-optimal solutions. Motivated by the advantages of MCDM techniques and better working principle of NSGA-II, in this paper, we study the impact of four widely used MCDM techniques such as weighted sum (WS) [3], weighted product (WP), quadratic weighted sum (QWS) and TOPSIS over NSGA-II based pareto-optimal solutions. In order to achieve the preferable ranking of the pareto-optimal solutions, we compute composite score of the solutions using the four mentioned MCDM techniques (WS, WP, QWS and TOPSIS). For experimentation purpose, we have applied and tested the proposed study on two case studies: scientific workflow and travelling salesperson (TSP) problem. To solve scientific workflow problem, we have considered two conflicting objectives such as cost and reliability, whereas TSP considers both of the objectives as cost minimization. Comparative analysis reveals that TOPSIS can perform better than other three MCDM approaches.

The remainder of this paper is structured as follows: Sect. 2 offers the essential background information on NSGA-II and MCDM techniques. Section 3 outlines the proposed approach and provides implementation details. Section 4 presents the experimental results and analysis. Lastly, Sect. 5 summarizes the conclusions drawn from the present study.

2   Background Study

This section presents the necessary ideas on the working principle of NSGA-II and four MCDM techniques (WS, WP, QWS and TOPSIS) which are required to understand the paper.

2.1   NSGA-II

Deb et al. [1] introduced NSGA-II as a solution to the time complexity challenges faced by previous MOEAs. By optimizing the algorithm, Deb et al. [1] reduced the time complexity from $O(MN^3)$ to $O(MN^2)$, where M represents the number of objectives and N represents the population size. In NSGA-II, the initial parent population (Pt) of size N is generated randomly. From this parent population (Pt), a child population (Qt) of size N is obtained through selection, crossover, and mutation operations. The parent and child solutions are then combined, and non-dominated sorting is applied to the pool of 2N solutions to identify the best N solutions among them. The fast non-dominated sorting divides the whole population of size 2N into different fronts by performing a comparative analysis on the objective function values. Elements of the first fronts are found to be better from the elements of the second fronts and so on. Finally, elements of the different fronts are sorted using crowding distance mechanism and the first best N elements are considered as the parent solutions for the next iteration.

2.2   MCDM

MCDM methods are useful for decision making when a set of objects are given and we need to determine the best one depending on their assigned criteria values. A brief description about the four MCDM techniques used in this paper are given below.

Weighted Sum (WS). In the weighted sum method, the objective functions are assigned random weights. These weighted objective functions are subsequently aggregated to compute composite scores, enabling the ranking of the solutions. WS method is defined in Eq. (1).

$$S^*_{wsm} = \sum_{j=1}^{M} w_j F_{ij} \tag{1}$$

Here, S^*_{wsm} is the composite score of weighted sum method, M be the number of objectives, F_{ij} be the value of jth objective function for i^{th} solution, w_j is the weight assigned to the jth objective such that $\sum_{j=1}^{m} w_j = 1$.

Quadratic Weighted Sum (QWS). Quadratic weighted sum method is the modification to weighted sum method, where the square of the objective functions are multiplied with respective to their weights. QWS method is defined in Eq. (2).

$$Q^*_{wsm} = \sum_{j=1}^{M} w_j F_{ij}^2 \tag{2}$$

Here, Q^*_{wsm} is the composite score of quadratic weighted sum method.

Weighted Product (WP). In weighted product, instead of addition (as done is WS method), multiplication is performed between all objectives raised to the respective weights. WP method is defined in Eq. (3).

$$P^*_{wpm} = \prod_{j=1}^{M} F_{ij}^{w_j} \tag{3}$$

Here, P^*_{wpm} is the composite score of weighted product method.

WS, QWS and WP are the most widely used methods due to their simplicity. However, selection of weighting coefficients is the important issue, since the solutions mostly depend on the coefficients. In some of the MCDM problems, it is left to the decision makers, who are supposed to have domain knowledge. In addition, these methods show good results in case of convex Pareto fronts.

Technique for Order of Preference by Similarity to Ideal Solution (TOPSIS). TOPSIS operates on the principle that the ideal choice should exhibit the smallest geometric distance to the positive ideal solution (PIS) and the largest geometric distance from the negative ideal solution (NIS). This method ranks the solution based on the TOPSIS score which is calculated by using the following steps.

Step1 : Initially normalized fitness S_{ij} is calculated by using Eq. (4).

$$S_{ij} = \frac{F_{ij}}{\sqrt{\sum_{j=1}^{m} F_{ij}^2}} \tag{4}$$

Here, j be the current objective, i be the solution number, S_{ij} be the normalized fitness of each solution, and F_{ij} be the fitness value of the solution.

Step2 : Calculate weighted fitness W_{ij} by using Eq. (5).

$$W_{ij} = w_i \times S_{ij} \tag{5}$$

where, W_{ij} is the weighted fitness.

Step3 : :Determine the positive ideal solution (PIS) A^* and negative ideal solution (NIS) A^- and compute the distances S^* and S^- from the PIS (A^*) and NIS (A^-).

Step4 : Finally calculate the TOPSIS score C_i^* for each individual i by using Eq. (6).

$$C_i^* = \frac{S_i^-}{S_i^- + S_i^*} \tag{6}$$

3   Methodologies

This Section focuses on the proposed framework and provides an in-depth examination of its implementation details.

3.1   Proposed Framework

In this section, we demonstrate the utilization of MCDM techniques to select pareto-optimal solutions in a multi-objective optimization (MOO) context. We employ the framework illustrated in Fig. 1. To prioritize the set of pareto-optimal solutions derived from the MOO process. It is considered as two fold framework, where first fold is involved with MOO problem formulation and second fold is involved with application of MCDM techniques on the outcome of MOO. Initially the given problem is analyzed to explore the objective functions, which need to be optimized. Based on the nature of the objectives, multi-objective problem formulation is done. Once the multi-objective problem is formulated, MOO is performed using NSGA-II considering it advantages over other algorithms available in the literature. NSGA-II optimizes the objectives using the available information, resulting in a set of pareto-optimal solutions that are mutually non-dominated. However, due to the non-dominance relationship among the obtained set of pareto-optimal solutions, selecting a single best solution becomes challenging in the absence of domain knowledge. Therefore, MCDM techniques are applied over the resulted pareto-optimal solutions to select the feasible solution. This study applies WS, WP, QWS and TOPSIS in the process, which assign the weights to each objective and compute the composite score for each solution. Based on calculated composite score, ranking of the solutions are performed and the feasible solution is selected.

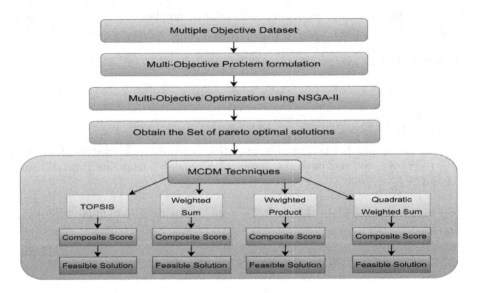

Fig. 1. Application of MCDM techniques to select MOO based pareto-optimal solutions.

3.2   Implementation of Proposed Method

Proposed method is tested on two dataset namely scientific workflow dataset and TSP dataset. Scientific workflow dataset contains two conflicting objectives such as cost and reliability, where cost to perform the scientific workflow needs to be minimized and reliability should be maximized. In TSP dataset, two set of distances KROA100 and KROB100 are given between two cities, where we need to minimize the distances. Once the objective functions formulations are completed, we have executed NSGA-II algorithm to explore the pareto-optimal fronts. Simulation settings for performing NSGA-II are as follows: IDE used - Google colab, programming language - Python3, size of scientific workflow dataset - 30×10 (30 tasks and 10 virtual machines), number of cities used in

TSP dataset - 50, NSGA-II parameters: population size - 50, number of iterations - 500, crossover rate - 0.6, mutation rate - 0.5, mutation selection rate - 0.1, MCDM techniques used for comparison: WS, WP, QWS and TOPSIS.

Chromosome Representation. In NSGA-II, the initial population (chromosomes) of size N is generated randomly. Each chromosome serves as a candidate solution for the problem at hand. For scientific workflow each chromosome is represented as a vector of length equal to the number of tasks($1 \times T$), where, T represents the number of tasks to be performed on the scientific workflow. The values in this vector are in the range of one to the number of virtual machines. Values corresponding to each place in the vector represents the virtual machine to which task is allocated (as shown in Fig. 2). For TSP, the candidate solution is naturally an ordering or permutation of all the cities. Therefore, chromosome represents the unique path between the cities (as shown in Fig. 3).

1	2	3	4	5	6	7	8	9	10
3	2	3	4	2	3	3	3	4	4

Fig. 2. Chromosome representation of scientific workflow.

0	1	2	3	4	5	6	7	8	9

Fig. 3. Chromosome representation of TSP.

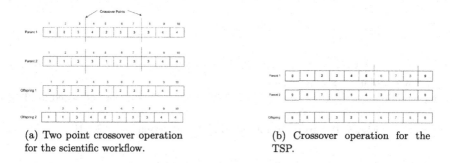

(a) Two point crossover operation for the scientific workflow.

(b) Crossover operation for the TSP.

Fig. 4. Crossover Operation

Crossover Operation. Crossover is the process of generating one or more offspring from the parent chromosome. For the scientific workflow implementation, we use two point crossover as shown in Fig. 4. In two point crossover, two cut points from the chromosome are selected randomly. After selecting the two points, the left extreme and right extreme of both parent chromosomes is kept as it is and the middle part of the first parent is swapped with the second one to generate two new offspring (as shown in Fig. 4). In TSP, to avoid the duplication of gene values, different crossover technique is used. Firstly, a subset of consecutive genes from first parent is selected and copied to the offspring at the respective positions (as shown in Fig. 4). Thereafter, missing values in the offspring are added from the parent 2.

Mutation. The mutation operation is employed to preserve genetic diversity as the population transitions from one generation to the next. Here we select mutation position randomly.

NSGA-II and MCDM Implementation. Fitness score for each individual is calculated using the defined objective functions. NSGA-II uses the initial population to generate a new population using reproduction operators such as cross over and mutation, non-dominated sorting techniques and crowding distance mechanism. After applying NSGA-II to the provided dataset, we obtain a set of solutions known as pareto-optimal solutions, which are mutually non-dominated. Subsequently, we employ MCDM techniques like WS, WP, QWS, and TOPSIS on the set of pareto-optimal solutions to rank them according to computed composite scores.

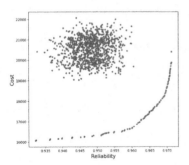

(a) Pareto-front obtain for scientific workflow

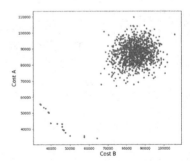

(b) Pareto-front obtained for TSP

Fig. 5. Pareto-front obtained after application of NSGA-II

4   Result and Discussion

4.1   Study Area

In this study, we have considered two case studies (scientific workflow and travelling salesperson problem) to assess the effectiveness of our proposed model. A scientific workflow is a process for achieving a scientific goal that is usually expressed in terms of tasks and their dependencies. While performing any scientific workflow, main focus is to keep costs of computation as low as possible and to maximize the reliability of the system. It is a multi-objective scheduling problem in which two conflicting objectives (cost and reliability) are to be optimized. TSP is a combinatorial optimization problem, where one salesperson and multiple numbers of cities are considered. The salesperson visits all the cities at most once starting from an initial city and then return to the starting city. The salesperson aims to minimize travel costs while visiting various cities. This study treats the traveling salesperson problem (TSP) as a multi-objective optimization problem, taking into account the presence of multiple paths between different cities.

4.2 Data Description

Proposed framework is tested on two dataset namely scientific workflow dataset and TSP dataset. For the sake of simplicity, we have considered that scientific workflow dataset has 30 tasks which are to be performed using 10 virtual machines. This dataset contains two matrices of size 30×10 to represent cost and reliability. To justify the proposed method, we have also tested in on the TSP benchmark dataset (KROA100 and KROB100) available at (http://comopt. ifi.uni-heidelberg.de/software/TSPLIB95/tsp/) where two set of distances are given between the cities. For experimentation purpose, we have considered first 50 instances from KROA100 and KROB100.

4.3 Tables and Graphs

Table 1. Best solution obtained after application of MCDM techniques.

Dataset	Technique	Value for Objective1	Value for Objective2
Scientific Workflow Dataset	Weighted Sum	16061.868716	0.932254
	Weighted Product	16061.868716	0.932254
	Quadratic Weighted Sum	16061.868716	0.932254
	TOPSIS	16575.014985	0.957265
TSP	Weighted Sum	33041.390464	38252.911803
	Weighted Product	33041.390464	38252.911803
	Quadratic Weighted Sum	33041.390464	38252.911803
	TOPSIS	10365.195374	8792.869341

This section presents a comparison of the results obtained after the application of four different MCDM techniques namely WS, WP, QWS and TOPSIS on the MOO based set of pareto-optimal solutions. Figure 5 shows the pareto-front obtained after application of the NSGA-II to optimize the multiple objectives. Table 1 and the subsequent figures (Fig. 6) and Fig. 7) illustrate the comparative results of WS, WP, QWS and TOPSIS for ranking of the pareto-optimal solutions. Figures 6 and 7 depict that WS, WP and QWS methods capture end points as feasible solutions. As given in Table 1, WS, WP and QWS assign more importance to cost but compromise with reliability in case of scientific workflow, whereas, TOPSIS has selected the feasible solution with optimal values for both cost and reliability to perform scientific workflow. Similarly, in case of TSP (shown in Table 1), WS, WP and QWS methods are biased towards one objective cost (out of two cost objectives) and select end point as feasible solution (Fig. 7), whereas, TOPSIS selects the optimal values compared to other three methods (Table 1). Overall, TOPSIS method shows significant performance compared to WS, WP and QWS for both of the case studies.

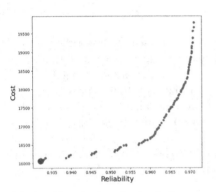

(a) Feasible solution obtained after application of WS

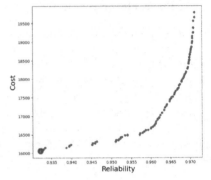

(b) Feasible solution obtained after application of WP

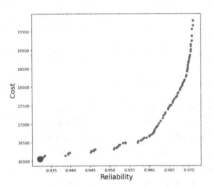

(c) Feasible solution obtained after application of QWS

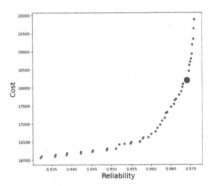

(d) Feasible solution obtained after appli-cation of TOPSIS

Fig. 6. Result comparison of WS, WP, QWS and TOPSIS for scientific workflow dataset where darker circle indicates the feasible solution selected by respective technique.

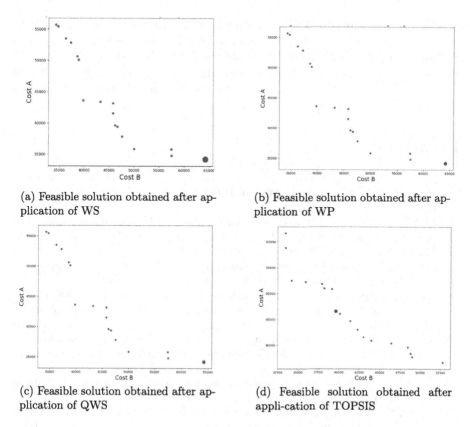

(a) Feasible solution obtained after application of WS

(b) Feasible solution obtained after application of WP

(c) Feasible solution obtained after application of QWS

(d) Feasible solution obtained after appli-cation of TOPSIS

Fig. 7. Result comparison of WS, WP, QWS and TOPSIS for TSP dataset where darker circle indicates the feasible solution selected by respective technique.

5   Conclusion

This paper has proposed the application of four different MCDM techniques for the selection of MOO based pareto-optimal solutions. In the proposed framework, the first step involves applying NSGA-II to obtain a set of non-dominated pareto-optimal solutions. To determine the ultimate feasible solution from this non-dominated set, four distinct MCDM techniques, namely WS, WP, QWS, and TOPSIS, are employed. These methods ranks the solutions based on the composite score calculated for each solution. We have demonstrated the performance of the proposed model using two case studies such as scientific workflow problem and TSP. Benchmark data set for TSP has been used for justification purpose. In scientific workflow problem, two conflicting objectives such as cost and reliability are considered. To solve multi-objective TSP, we have taken two different costs between two cities as given in the benchmark dataset and minimized the cost. Experimental results have shown that WS, WP and QWS methods exhibits bias towards one of the objectives by selecting the corner solution as feasible solution. Whereas, TOPSIS method outperforms compared to rest three methods and select the feasible solution. In future, researcher can employ machine learning models to simplify the complicated objective function values to in order to minimize the computation time. Moreover, other MCDM techniques such as VIKOR, AHP and ANP can be implemented and compared with TOPSIS.

References

1. Deb, K., Pratap, A., Agarwal, S., Meyarivan, T.A.M.T.: A fast and elitist multi-objective genetic algorithm: NSGA-II. IEEE Trans. Evol. Comput. **9**(2), 182–197 (2002)
2. Li, Y., Liao, S., Liu, G.: Thermo-economic multi-objective optimization for a solar-dish Brayton system using NSGA-II and decision making. Int. J. Electr. Power Energy Syst. **64**, 17–175 (2015)
3. Marler, R.T., Arora, J.S.: The weighted sum method for multi-objective optimization: new insights. Struct. Multidiscip. Optim. **41**, 853–82 (2010)
4. Rao, C.M., Venkatasubbaiah, K.: Application of WSM, WPM and TOPSIS methods for the optimization of multiple responses. Int. J. Hybrid Inf. Technol. **9**(10), 59–72 (2016)
5. Schaffer, J.D.: Multiple objective optimization with vector evaluated genetic algorithms. In: Proceedings of the First International Conference on Genetic Algorithms and Their Applications, pp. 93–100. Psychology Press (2014)
6. Srinivas, N., Deb, K.: Multi-objective optimization using nondominated sorting in genetic algorithms. Evol. Comput. **2**(3), 221–248 (1994)
7. Verma, S., Pant, M., Snasel, V.: A comprehensive review on NSGA-II for multi-objective combinatorial optimization problems. IEEE Access **9**, 57757–57791 (2021)
8. Musavi, M., Bozorgi-Amiri, A.: A multi-objective sustainable hub location-scheduling problem for perishable food supply chain. Comput. Ind. Eng. **113**, 7–778 (2017)
9. Rangaiah, G.P., Sharma, S., Sreepathi, B.K.: Multi-objective optimization for the de-sign and operation of energy efficient chemical processes and power generation. Curr. Opin. Chem. Eng. **10**, 49–2 (2015)
10. Rangaiah, G.P. (ed.).: Multi-objective Optimization: Techniques and Applications in Chemical Engineering, World Scientific, vol. 5 (2016)
11. Ribeiro, V.H.A., Reynoso-Meza, G.: Multi-criteria decision making techniques for the selection of pareto-optimal machine learning models in a drinking-water quality monitoring problem. Int. J. Inf. Technol. Decision Making (2022)

An English Sentence Dictionary Based Secure Text Steganographic Technique for Message-Data Confidentiality

Akash Kumar Dey, Geeta Gayatri Behera, and Alekha Kumar Mishra[✉]

Department of Computer Science and Engineering, National Institute of Technology
Jamshedpur, Jamshedpur, India
`alekha.cse@nitjsr.ac.in`

Abstract. Steganography is a method for concealing messages in text, audio, images, and videos. This study outlines a text steganography method called Dictionary Based Text Steganography. This technique seeks for sentences to hide a given secret message. The alphabets of secret message are scattered among the selected sentence from the dictionary. The key is generated by finding index location of alphabet within the cover sentences. The experiment results show that the proposed technique is effective at hiding secret messages in text documents while maintaining the readability and integrity of the original text content. The encoding and decoding time is found to be least compared to existing techniques. Overall, this study offers a novel technique for text based steganography that has a great potential for use in applications involving data security and privacy.

Keywords: Steganography · Text steganography · English Sentence Dictionary · Covertext · Overhead Time

1 Introduction

Steganography is the practice of hiding messages or information within nonsecret text or data. The word steganography derived from a Greek word called steganographia, and a combination of Greek terms steganos, which means "covered or concealed" and graphia, which means "writing" [13]. The idea of this secret communication is hiding the existing of the information from any outsider, whereas the concept of cryptography ensures that the message is not understandable instead of covering the data transfer [12,14]. The hidden message used in steganography is referred to as embedded data. Data embedding is performed to protect the information [10]. It is generally related with three themes: Information hiding, watermarking, and steganography. Information hiding deals with hiding a secret message in another medium; watermarking hides a secret message in a different medium where the media itself is the main subject and steganography tries to hide a secret information in a different medium where

S. K. Panda et al. (Eds.): CoCoLe 2023, CCIS 1892, pp. 297–307, 2024.
https://doi.org/10.1007/978-3-031-56998-2_25

the secret information is the main subject. The goal of information hiding technology research is to find better ways to protect sensitive data [15,16]. The file cover with an embedded secret message is known as a "stego file", and the key used to hiding process is known as "stego key", which is later used to retrieve hidden content.

This paper presents a text steganography technique, called as Dictionary Based Text Steganography (DBTS) technique. DBTS uses a dictionary of collection of English sentences that are used as covertext. The English sentence are stored via key as the string of alphabets absent in it. To encode a plaintext the list of sentences containing all the alphabet of the plaintext are retrieved and one of them is choosen randomly to hide the secret plaintext. A stegokey is generated by finding the possible locations where the plaintext characters can be hidden. The covertext is a meaningful sentence containing the plaintext characters at random location based on indexes in stegokey. The uncovering process is simple iteration over the stegokey to look for the symbol present in the covertext at the specified index. One of the salient feature of the proposed DBTS technique is that the uncovering process does not need the dictionary used in encoding process. The experimental results of proposed DBTS is compared with the existing mechanism and inferred that the DBTS takes significantly lesser amount of time for hiding and uncovering the secret plaintext.

Rest of the paper is sequenced in the following manner. Section 2 lists out the various categories of steganographic techniques. Section 3 briefly reviews the steganographic techniques reported in the literature recently. Section 4 details the proposed DBTS techniques highlight all the steps involved in steganography. Section 5 compares the experimental results of proposed techniques with the existing one followed concluding observations in Sect. 6.

2   Classification of Steganographic Technique

Steganography can be divided into robust and fragile types based on how it operates. Fragile steganography aims to prevent file changes, whereas robust steganography aims to prevent the secret information hidden in the file cover from being seen and omitted [11]. The steganographic techniques are broadly classified into Text, Image, Audio and Video steganography. The most popular of these categories are text and image. Text steganography uses text as a medium. Text steganography can use a variety of techniques, such as altering an existing text's format, modifying the word inside it, creating random letter sequences, or employing context free grammars to create intelligible texts. If the original plain text is accessible, the formatting of a text can be easily notice by outsiders [2]. Image steganography on the other hand is a method of hiding a text or an image inside another image. In this method, the cover text or image is altered such that the hidden data is hidden and therefore not suspicious as in the case of cryptography. Inversely, steganlysis is used to extract any hidden data and find any covert messages that may be present in the image. Steganalysis aids in determining whether a picture is a stego image or regular image. Along with classifying the image, additional research is done to find the location and details of the hidden image inside the cover image [6].

3   Related Works

A method based on bit-level XOR operation have been proposed by Acharjee *et al.* [2], where the secret message is simply XORed with selected words from the beginning and end of the paragraph. The method does not use key therefore is not secured and robust.

Banerjee *et al.* [3] have combined face geometry and handwritten character to hide the text message. They have used MSG_{BIT} as parameters of face geometry. Revised Secret Steganography Code for Embedding (Revised SSCE) code along with key is used for encrypting the secret message.

Chaudhary *et al.* [4] have proposed two steganography techniques. The first approach encode text based on the shape of the capital alphabets. The grouping of letter and encoding depends on the shape and structure of English alphabets. In the second approach, they have used the similar encoding approach for Hindi language alphabets. The author claim that the overhead time of the proposed techniques is way below the common text hiding approaches.

Gharavi and Rajaei [5] have used Curvelet transform features for hiding text message within the cover image. They emphasize on selecting detailed images for cover. The Curvelet coefficients are used to hide the text message bits by dividing the image into smaller size blocks. The average Mean Square Error and PSNR of their experiment lies around 12.00 and 38 respectively.

Karthikeyan *et al.* [7] have proposed a steganography approach that combines the Least Signification Bit (LSB) Technique along with standard Data Encryption Standard (DES) cipher. They have used a simple two place transposition to the text before applying DES followed by LSB encoding. The average Mean Square Error and Peak Signal-to-Noise Ratio (PSNR) of their experiment lies around .0035 and 52 respectively.

Kataria *et al.* [8] have proposed a text steganography method that involve reordering of two XORed characters from the message. An eight-bit random key is used to aid the random ordering of original text. They have shown that the proposed approach minimizes the time overhead requirement.

In an another work Manish Kumar *et al.* [9]use hybrid approach by combining LSB technique and the Advanced Encryption Standard (AES) encryption technique to cover that secret message. The average Mean Square Error and PSNR of their experiment lies around 0.0019922 and 75.1375 respectively.

Wu *et al.* [17] have proposed a coverless text steganography method using the half frequency crossover rule, which utilizes the natural language characteristics. Their method has claimed to achieve embedding rate of 2.78.

4   Proposed Work

The proposed steganography method is a text-based approach that explicitly uses a dictionary of English sentences used as cover to hide characters of a given plaintext. The proposed method takes the secret message, and a key as input and output the covertext by extracting suitable sentence from the dictionary that is eligible to hide characters of secret message. The foremost step of the proposed method is the building of dictionary using English sentence file. In the second step, the plaintext is provided as input to the proposed steganography algorithm. The proposed algorithm uses the plaintext to identify the location of the symbols of plaintext in the selected covertext message. The constructed dictionary is used to generated the stegokey based on the hidden location of the plaintext in the selected covertext. Note that the uncovering process in the proposed technique does not need the sentence dictionary used during hiding the message. The key is sufficient to successfully recover the secret plaintext from the covertext. The most important part of the proposed technique is that based on the candidate sentence to cover the secret plaintext, the stegokey is generated.

Algorithm 1: The Algorithms for Building the English Sentence Dictionary.

Input: sentenceFile
Output: D
1 D= new Dict();
2 **for** *each s in sentenceFile* **do**
3   find alphabets absent in s;
4   add absent alphabets to *abs_key_set*;
5   **if** D*[abs_key_set] is empty* **then**
6          $D[abs\_key\_set]$=s;
7   **else**
8   add s to $D[abs\_key\_set]$ sentence list;

9 output D;

The proposed DBTS requires a dictionary that can store and retrieve all possible English Sentences with a given set of alphabet present in a given position. The dictionary can be mathematically expressed as

$$D = \{abs\_key\_str\_1 : [S_{11}, S_{12}, \ldots S_{1k}],$$
$$abs\_key\_str\_2 : [S_{21}, S_{22}, \ldots S_{2l}],$$
$$\ldots$$
$$abs\_key\_str\_i : [S_{i1}, S_{i2}, \ldots S_{in}]\} \tag{1}$$

Here, $[S_{11}, S_{12}, \ldots S_{1k}]$ represent the set of English sentences that have occurrence of all the English alphabets other than the alphabets present in

---

Algorithm 2: The Algorithms for Encoding plaintext.

Input: plaintext, D
Output: covertext

1 select the sentences from D that contains all alphabets in plaintext;
2 add sentences to the selectedList;
3 choose a candidate sentence s at random from selectedList;
4 **for** *each c in plaintext* **do**
5   indices=findIndexes(c,s);
6   index=random(indices);
7   add index to the stegokey;
8 covertext = s;
9 output covertext, stegokey;

Algorithm 3: The Algorithms for Extracting plaintext.

Input: covertext, stegokey
Output: plaintext

1 **for** *each k in key* **do**
2   val=covertext.getValue(k);
3   add val to plaintext;
4 output plaintext;

$abs\_key\_set\_i$. In other word, the keys of the dictionary represent the set of alphabets in string format that are absent in the set of sentences present in the value part of the dictionary. The intention of this key is to effectively search the candidate sentences that can hide a given secret message.

The algorithm of building dictionary, encoding plaintext into covertext, and extracting plaintext from covertext of the proposed DBTS technique is shown in Algorithm 1, 2, and 3 respectively. The Algorithm 1 create the dictionary of English sentences using the dataset file [1] with a key as the string of alphabets that are absent in the corresponding sentence in the value part. The Algorithm 2 first select the English sentences from the dictionary that contains all the alphabet present in the plaintext. This task is accomplished using the 'absent key string' of the dictionary to identify the set of sentences that can be used as covertext for the current plaintext. Next, one of the selected English sentence is picked up as the candidate covertext for the given plaintext. The algorithm then finds the possible indices from the covertext where, the alphabets of the plaintext can be hidden and selects the possible indexes to generate the stego key required for uncovering the plaintext. As a result, the output of this function is a meaningful sentence hiding the secret plaintext, with stegokey that is required to retrive it. Finally, Algorithm 3 is used by the receiver to uncover the secret plaintext with the help of stegokey. The time complexity of the Algorithm 1 is $O(n)$, where n is the number of English sentences in the dataset. The Algorithm 2 traverses through the input plaintext alphabets to pick hiding sentence from the dictionary. Therefore, it has the time complexity of $O(k)$, where k is the number of alphabets in the input plaintext. Since the extraction process uses the stegokey to retrieve the original plaintext, therefore it has constant time complexity $O(1)$.

An example of the proposed steganographic technique is shown in Fig. 1. It is shown the DBTS always randomly selects a candidate covertext for each run of same value of secret plaintext. Therefore, this technique is resilient to frequency analysis cryptanalysis. Moreover, there is absolutely no relation between the meaning of the secret text and the covertext that leaves no clue to predict the secret message or its length.

Plaintext = " deploy troops on secondfront tonight"

Run-1

Selected Covertext = It made clear that you pressured a foreign government to interfere in our political process on your behalf, you violated your oath of office and betrayed our nation

key = (5, 6, 23, 9, 20, 19, 2, 1, 12, 20, 20, 23, 26, 2, 20, 41, 2, 26, 6, 8, 20, 41, 5, 35, 12, 20, 41, 1, 2, 1, 20, 41, 39, 40, 15, 1)

Run-2

Selected Covertext = For this project I see myself as becoming a Japan and Europe go-between

key = (52, 13, 9, 27, 1, 24, 3, 4, 2, 1, 1, 9, 7, 3, 1, 39, 3, 7, 13, 14, 1, 39, 52, 28, 2, 1, 39, 4, 3, 4, 1, 39, 6, 40, 5, 4)

Run-3

Selected Covertext = My metabolism is such that no matter how much I eat I don't put on weight. Just now, this second, you've made enemies of people throughout the world.

key = (55, 5, 61, 10, 9, 2, 3, 6, 36, 9, 9, 61, 12, 3, 9, 28, 3, 12, 5, 20, 9, 28, 55, 122, 36, 9, 28, 6, 3, 6, 9, 28, 11, 71, 21, 6)

Run-4

Selected Covertext = The Phoenicians ran many trading posts in North Africa, doing business with the local Berber populations

key = (28, 2, 33, 80, 6, 23, 3, 25, 16, 6, 6, 33, 14, 3, 6, 8, 3, 14, 2, 10, 6, 8, 28, 49, 16, 6, 8, 25, 3, 25, 6, 8, 9, 31, 1, 25)

Run-5

Selected Covertext = The animals in question are members of an order called Perissodactyla or odd-toed ungulates because they happen to have an odd number of toes on their rear feet

key = (44, 2, 107, 9, 21, 66, 3, 19, 25, 21, 21, 107, 10, 3, 21, 5, 3, 10, 2, 48, 21, 5, 44, 37, 25, 21, 5, 19, 3, 19, 21, 5, 6, 84, 1, 19)

Fig. 1. An Example of proposed DBTS technique.

Table 1. The encoding and decoding time of DBTS.

Plaintext Size (bytes)	Encoding Time (sec)	Decoding Time (sec)
100	0.102	2.4E-05
200	0.098	3.9E-05
300	0.103	5.5E-05
400	0.114	6.8E-05
500	0.1	8.7E-05
600	0.12	9.1E-05

An adversary requires to guess the length of the secret plaintext in order to recover it from the covertext. When an adversary is able to find the length of the plaintext, then it needs to extract all meaningful sentences possible out of given covertext message that requires exponential computational time. As a result, the process of uncovering the secret message from the covertext is extremely tedious given that the adversary known the algorithm and the plaintext length.

5   Results

The proposed DBTS technique is implemented in python environment for verifying its performance on a single machine. The system configuration includes Intel Core i5-3210M CPU @ 2.50GHz × 4 processor with Ubuntu 18.04.3 LTS (64 bits) OS. The message text size varied from 100 to 600 bytes (characters). The dictionary is built from the English sentence dataset available freely on [1]. We measured the performance of the proposed technique by the size of covertext generated for a given message text and the encoding and decoding (uncovering) time.

Table 1 shows the parallel comparison of encoding and decoding time of the proposed DBTS technique by varying the message text size. It is observed that both encoding and decoding time range is significantly small indicating that the proposed technique can operate faster for the given range of message text size. The decoding time indicates that the uncovering process of secret message text from the covertext message consumes a negligible amount of time.

Figure 2 shows the comparison of the message text and its corresponding covertext size for the given range of message text. It is observed that the size of the covertext is nearly five to eight times larger than the original message text. This is due to characteristics of hiding all character bytes in a meaningful English sentence from the constructed Dictionary. This ratio may look larger compared to a text based steganography technique, however, this size is still quite smaller than other text based steganography and especially the images that are used to hide text in a image based steganographic technique.

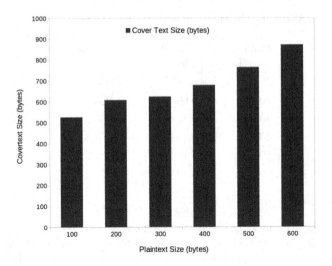

Fig. 2. Comparison of Message Text and Cover Text Size of the Proposed DBTS technique.

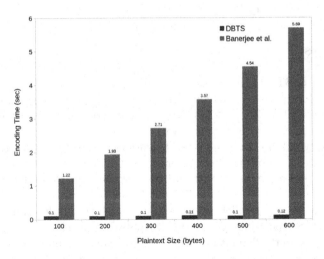

Fig. 3. Comparison of Encoding Time between Proposed DBTS and Banerjee *et al.*.

We compared the encoding and decoding time of proposed DBTS technique with the algorithm proposed by Banerjee *et al.*. Figures 3 and 4 shows the individual comparison of encoding and decoding time respectively. The encoding and decoding time of the proposed DBTS is quite smaller than Banerjee *et al.*. This is due to the process of identifying the center point such as nose, eyes, and face in a transformed binary image. This process quite a significant amount of computation time in the proposed work by Banerjee *et al.* [3]. Secondly, the decoding time of the proposed mechanism is quite smaller compared to times of

Table 2. Comparison with ECR and Chaudhury *et al.*.

Techniques	Message text Size(bytes)	Overhead time (ms)	Covertext Length (bytes)
DBTS	600	0.12	871
	200	0.098	527
ECR [8]	600	15	1980
Chadhury *et al.* [4]	200	1.672	660

Banerjee *et al.*. This is because, the proposed technique involves only constant number of index operation to extract the characters from covertext.

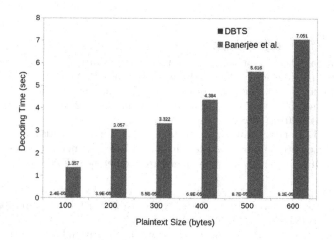

Fig. 4. Comparison of Decoding Time between Proposed DBTS and Banerjee *et al.*.

Table 2 compares the total overhead time and size of covertext of the proposed work with ECR and the steganographic technique by Chaudhury *et al.* [4]. The overhead time of the proposed work is lesser than ECR and Chaudhury *et al.*. This is because of hashing based operation in dictionaries used to extract the sentences in the proposed DBTS. Since, the candidate sentences that contains all the character of plaintext is selected at random, therefore in DBTS the average size of covertext is also found to have smaller length compared to existing ones.

To summarize the above results, the overall performance of the proposed DBTS technique is quicker in executing all operations. The security strength of DBTS is higher than the existing coverless text-based steganographic techniques. Due to random meaningful English sentence selection, the size of the covertext per plaintext is also low.

6   Conclusion and Future Work

The steganography technique can hide a secret message within a covering meaningful text without generating unintelligible text like cryptography. A number of stegonographic techniques yet not so popular are proposed in the recent years. This paper contributes a new English sentence dictionary based steganographic technique called DBTS. The key point of the proposed technique is it selectively choose English sentence where the secret plaintext can be hidden. Based on the selected sentence the stegokey is generated for uncovering the plaintext from the covertext. The results shows the proposed technique required smaller encoding and decoding time compared to existing one. The proposed work can be further be improved to make steganalysis much harder by increasing randomness into it. Moreover, we can also look for alternative dataset to build a concrete statement dataset.

References

1. Tatoeba : a collection of sentences and translations. https://tatoeba.org/en/
2. Acharjee, T., Konwar, A., Kumar Ram, R., Sharma, R., Goswami, D.: XORSTEG: a new model of text steganography. In: 2016 International Conference on Communication and Electronics Systems (ICCES), pp. 1–4 (2016). https://doi.org/10.1109/CESYS.2016.7889820
3. Banerjee, I., Bandyopadhyay, K., Rashid, T.A., Mohan, A., Alsadoon, A., Kumar, A.: Face geometry and handwritten characters based biometric text steganography. In: 2021 IEEE Bombay Section Signature Conference (IBSSC), pp. 1–6. IEEE (2021)
4. Chaudhary, S., Dave, M., Sanghi, A.: Aggrandize text security and hiding data through text steganography. In: 2016 IEEE 7th Power India International Conference (PIICON), pp. 1–5. IEEE (2016)
5. Gharavi, H., Rajaei, B.: A robust steganography algorithm based on curvelet transform. In: Electrical Engineering (ICEE), Iranian Conference On, pp. 1624–1628. IEEE (2018)
6. Johnson, N.F., Duric, Z., Jajodia, S.: Information Hiding: Steganography and Watermarking-Attacks and Countermeasures: Steganography and Watermarking: Attacks and Countermeasures, vol. 1. Springer (2001). https://doi.org/10.1007/978-1-4615-4375-6
7. Karthikeyan, B., Deepak, A., Subalakshmi, K., MM, A.R., Vaithiyanathan, V.: A combined approach of steganography with LSB encoding technique and des algorithm. In: 2017 Third International Conference on Advances in Electrical, Electronics, Information, Communication and Bio-Informatics (AEEICB), pp. 85–88. IEEE (2017)
8. Kataria, S., Kumar, T., Singh, K., Nehra, M.S.: ECR (encryption with cover text and reordering) based text steganography. In: 2013 IEEE Second International Conference on Image Information Processing (ICIIP-2013), pp. 612–616. IEEE (2013)
9. Kumar, M., Soni, A., Shekhawat, A.R.S., Rawat, A.: Enhanced digital image and text data security using hybrid model of LSB steganography and AES cryptography technique. In: 2022 Second International Conference on Artificial Intelligence and Smart Energy (ICAIS), pp. 1453–1457. IEEE (2022)

10. Majeed, M.A., Sulaiman, R., Shukur, Z., Hasan, M.K.: A review on text steganography techniques. Mathematics **9**(21), 2829 (2021). https://doi.org/10.3390/math9212829
11. Majumder, A., Changder, S.: A generalized model of text steganography by summary generation using frequency analysis. In: 2018 7th International Conference on Reliability, Infocom Technologies and Optimization (Trends and Future Directions)(ICRITO), pp. 599–605. IEEE (2018)
12. Mishra, A.K., Puthal, D., Tripathy, A.K.: GraphCrypto: next generation data security approach towards sustainable smart city building. Sustain. Urban Areas **72**, 103056 (2021)
13. Naharuddin, A., Wibawa, A.D., Sumpeno, S.: A high capacity and imperceptible text steganography using binary digit mapping on ASCII characters. In: 2018 International Seminar on Intelligent Technology and Its Applications (ISITIA), pp. 287–292. IEEE (2018)
14. Saha, M., Panda, S.K., Panigrahi, S.: Distributed computing security: issues and challenges. Cyber Security in Parallel and Distributed Computing: Concepts, Techniques, Applications and Case Studies, pp. 129–138 (2019)
15. Sahu, S.K., Mohapatra, D.P., Panda, S.K.: NITIDS: a robust network intrusion dataset. Int. J. Embedded Syst. **14**(4), 391–408 (2021)
16. Sahu, S.K., Mohapatra, D.P., Panda, S.K.: A self-trained support vector machine approach for intrusion detection. In: Tripathy, A.K., Sarkar, M., Sahoo, J.P., Li, K.-C., Chinara, S. (eds.) Advances in Distributed Computing and Machine Learning. LNNS, vol. 127, pp. 391–402. Springer, Singapore (2021). https://doi.org/10.1007/978-981-15-4218-3_38
17. Wu, N., Ma, W., Liu, Z., Shang, P., Yang, Z., Fan, J.: Coverless text steganography based on half frequency crossover rule. In: 2019 4th International Conference on Mechanical, Control and Computer Engineering (ICMCCE), pp. 726–7263. IEEE (2019)

Author Index

© The Editor(s) (if applicable) and The Author(s), under exclusive license
to Springer Nature Switzerland AG 2024
S. K. Panda et al. (Eds.): CoCoLe 2023, CCIS 1892, pp. 309–310, 2024.
https://doi.org/10.1007/978-3-031-56998-2

Printed in the United States
by Baker & Taylor Publisher Services